BIRTH OF THE BORDER

Cormac Moore is a Dublin-based historian and is currently working with Dublin City Council on its Decade of Commemorations programme. He has published widely on Irish history including *The GAA v Douglas Hyde: The Removal of Ireland's First President as GAA Patron* (2012) and *The Irish Soccer Split* (2015).

BIRTH OF THE BORDER
THE IMPACT OF PARTITION IN IRELAND

CORMAC MOORE

MERRION
PRESS

First published in 2019 by
Merrion Press
An imprint of Irish Academic Press
10 George's Street
Newbridge
Co. Kildare
Ireland
www.merrionpress.ie

9781785372933 (Paper)
9781785372940 (Kindle)
9781785372957 (Epub)
9781785372964 (PDF)

British Library Cataloguing in Publication Data
An entry can be found on request

Library of Congress Cataloging in Publication Data
An entry can be found on request

Typeset in Minion Pro 11.5/15pt

Cover front: Still from British Pathé newsreel, 'The Seat of All the Trouble', 1924. (courtesy of British Pathé).

CONTENTS

In memory of my mother, Anne Moore.

Acknowledgements

The idea of this book came about through conversations with Professor Mike Cronin, Academic Director of Boston College whilst researching for my PhD. As a PhD supervisor, Mike was always available and willing to help. He constantly offered new avenues and ideas that aided me immeasurably in looking at the partition of Ireland in very different ways. Professor Martin Polley, Director of the International Centre for Sports History and Culture at De Montfort University in Leicester, also offered great assistance and advice throughout my research for my PhD and this book.

I would like to thank Gráinne Daly, Loughlin Deegan and Tara Doyle for taking the time to meticulously read through the original draft and suggesting many much-needed changes. I bear full responsibility and culpability for any mistakes in the final version. I would also like to thank Hilary Delahunty, Claire Egan, Paul Flanagan, Tom Hunt, Bernard Kelly, Donald McDonald, Frank Mulcahy, Mary Muldowney and Brian Murphy for reading the first draft and making many suggestions which I have incorporated into the book. I would like to thank Oliver P. Rafferty, S.J. for sharing his research with me on the Catholic Church and Dónal McAnallen for sharing his research on the GAA.

I am indebted to the staff members of the Public Record Office of Northern Ireland, the National Library of Ireland, the University College Dublin Archives, the Dublin City Library and Archive, the National Archives of Ireland and the UK National Archives for all of their help on the many visits I made whilst researching this book.

I wish to thank Berni Metcalfe from the National Library of Ireland, Breeda Brennan from the RTÉ Stills Library, Enda Leaney from the Dublin City Library and Archive, Patricia Marsh from the Public Records Office of Northern Ireland, Luci Gosling from the Mary Evans Picture Library,

Samantha McCombe from the Linen Hall Library, Hugh Forrester from the Police Museum of the Police Service of Northern Ireland, Lisa Olrichs from the National Portrait Gallery and Louis Jeffries from British Pathé for their help in sourcing images for the book.

I am very grateful for the help I have received from all of the staff of Merrion Press throughout the publishing process, particularly of the support and assistance from Conor Graham and Fiona Dunne.

I would like to thank all of my family and friends for their encouragement and help throughout the process. To Brigid, my wife, I am thankful for your love and support and for putting up with me for all of the time I spent obsessing over this book. Finally, this book is dedicated to my late mother, Anne Moore, who sadly passed away last year and who I miss deeply.

The Uncertainty and Confusion of Partition

The funeral of Dan Doonan came treacle-slow from the church ... They approached the new Border Customs Post. From a hut, a-buttoning his coat came Barrington.

'Good morning,' he said in that uneasy Civil Servant tone; not so much a greeting to the day as a farewell to personal liberty.

'A few formalities, sir,' he continued, thrusting the Customs card at the priest. 'Read that, will you?'

'We have nothing to declare, sir, this is a funeral.'

'What have you got in the coffin?'

'You must be joking,' said the priest, his face going purple with anger, and his anger going white with rage.

'I'm *not* joking sir, I am merely doing my duty.'

'Very well. Inside the coffin is the body of 98-year-old Dan Doonan. Now let us pass!'

'Not quite finished yet, sir. You intend to bury an Irish citizen in what is now *British* territory?'

'That is true ...'

'I presume the deceased will be staying this side permanently?'

'Unless someone invents a remarkable drug – yes,' answered the priest. 'Then,' went on Barrington, 'he will require the following: an Irish passport stamped with a visa, to be renewed annually for the rest of his –' Barrington almost said 'life' – 'stay,' he concluded.

Spike Milligan, *Puckoon*[1]

Puckoon is a comic novel written in 1963 by Spike Milligan. It is set in 1924, as the Boundary Commission was deciding on the border between Northern Ireland and the Irish Free State. In the novel, the small town of Puckoon ends up having the border running straight through the middle of it, and 'through incompetence, dereliction of duty and sheer perversity ... Houses are divided from outhouses, husbands separated from wives, bars cut off from their patrons, churches sundered from graveyards.'[2] Although a comic novel, such was the confusion and uncertainty surrounding the birth of the border in Ireland that there is more than a hint of real life permeating the novel. In real life, towns, farms and homes were divided by the border. The novel captures the absurdity of drawing lines on a map that divided communities into different political entities.

The creation of Northern Ireland was not a clean-cut operation, and Ireland took a long meandering road on its path towards partition. For a start, there was minimal initial support for two parliaments in Ireland among the Ulster unionists, who wished to remain governed from Westminster, and from nationalists. The vast majority of the people on the island rejected the Government of Ireland Act 1920, including at least one-third of the population of the new northern jurisdiction. There was also significant opposition from politicians in Britain and from the British civil service in Ireland. The process towards and realisation of partition was coloured by bewilderment, rejection, obstruction and constant change. It was also somewhat haphazard in its implementation, with some services remaining in Westminster on the off-chance that an all-Ireland jurisdiction would prevail. The signing of the Anglo-Irish Treaty of 1921 led to increased uncertainty and confusion, superseding the Government of Ireland Act for the south. Both Irish jurisdictions were born at roughly the same time. However, one was granted significantly more powers than the other. There was doubt as to the viability of Northern Ireland for a number of years following its birth, particularly in relation to the size of the area that would remain within its territory. A permanency of sorts was reached in 1925 with the agreement of the British, Free State and Northern Ireland governments to abandon the Boundary Commission report and retain the status quo. Regardless of the maintenance of the status quo, the northern jurisdiction remained a contested entity.

This book does not merely focus on the consequences of partition in terms of politics and security. It also looks at many of the day-to-day implications of it, with chapters exploring areas such as law, business and trade, religion, education, the labour movement, infrastructure and services, and sport. The book follows a rough timeline from 1912 to the tripartite agreement by the British, Irish Free State and northern governments to retain the status-quo in late 1925. In some instances, the timeline extends beyond 1925 to demonstrate the initial impact of partition on different bodies. The first five chapters look at the evolution of partition, from the third Home Rule Crisis of 1912 through to the Anglo-Irish Treaty of 1921. In 1912, partition was seriously considered, for the first time, as a solution to the impasse between Irish nationalists and unionists. Many options were considered thereafter that related to the type of partition, the area to be partitioned and for how long. Up to and during the First World War, a number of attempts were made to solve the Irish question, but all fell short. The concept of creating two Irish parliaments was first introduced in 1919 by the decisive Government of Ireland Bill. It was opposed by almost all, including the Ulster unionists, who had never asked for a devolved government. Eventually, many supporters of Ulster unionism realised the benefits of having their own government and voted in favour of the bill. As the bill was making its way through the houses of parliament, the British government was fighting a war with Sinn Féin and its military wing, the Irish Republican Army (IRA). The Government of Ireland Act was completely rejected by Sinn Féin and almost all citizens in the south and west of Ireland and by one-third of the population designated to belong to the territory of Northern Ireland.

The creation of the machinery and administration of a new jurisdiction is the focus of Chapter Three. With very few templates to work with, Sir Ernest Clark, Assistant Under-Secretary for Ireland and located in Belfast, was primarily responsible for ensuring that a functioning government and administration existed once Northern Ireland came into being in May 1921. Since the Acts of Union of 1800, Ireland had been administered as a separate entity, with almost all government and non-government bodies headquartered in Dublin. The breaking-up of bodies into two was a gargantuan task, often met with resistance. Northern Ireland's future was still uncertain after it was created. It had very few powers, mainly due to the withholding of the transfer of services by the British until negotiations were completed with Sinn Féin.

Sinn Féin and the nationalist minority in the north boycotted the new entity of Northern Ireland and its institutions. From its rise in popularity after the Easter Rising until the truce of July 1921, Sinn Féin had no clear policy on how to deal with the unionist minority in the north-east of Ireland. The negotiations with the British in late 1921 forced Sinn Féin to realistically address the issue of partition for the first time. The resulting Anglo-Irish Treaty included the establishment of the Boundary Commission to determine the size of Northern Ireland. Sinn Féin naively believed the commission would transfer much of the northern territory to the Irish Free State.

Chapter Six looks at the political make-up of Northern Ireland, the political decisions it made to protect its borders and the relationship between both Irish jurisdictions, culminating with the Boundary Commission decision to retain the status quo in late 1925. The majority of decisions were made by the northern government with security in mind, which is the focus of Chapter Seven. Sectarian violence engulfed the north from 1920 to 1922, particularly in Belfast, where some of the most brutal disturbances in Ireland occurred. Heavily armed loyalists, aided by the British, were pitted against the IRA, who were aided by Michael Collins's provisional government during the first half of 1922 in a conflict that amounted to a civil war in all but name. The start of the Irish civil war in the south in June 1922, intervened to ease the pressure on the beleaguered north.

Two new justice systems for Ireland were created under the Government of Ireland Act, perfectly illustrating the complexity and confusion surrounding partition. Whilst the Irish Free State inherited justice systems of the past (i.e. the British justice system and the home-grown Dáil Courts) the northern judiciary had to start from scratch, with no courthouses, staff and no books. The one area where there was cooperation – the education of barristers from all parts of Ireland at King's Inns in Dublin – only lasted for a short period, with both jurisdictions eventually diverging in all aspects of law, as in politics.

It can be argued that the cementing of partition came with the imposition of customs barriers on the border in 1923, a decision made by the Free State government. This decision, following on from the Belfast Boycott of 1920 to 1922, resulted in numerous psychological and physical divisions, including some which had never existed before. Despite the upheavals that led to partition, many organisations and groups continued as before. With no obligation to divide based on the political division, the majority of organisations, trade groups and charities that were all-Ireland bodies prior to 1921 remained so afterwards. Most religious organisations remained all-Ireland entities, regardless of the central role that religion played in the Irish question. They did so, however, under significantly changed circumstances, as they had to operate within two extremely different jurisdictions. This was most clearly demonstrated through the issue of education within both states. Divisions in education that had existed before were worsened by partition. The two jurisdictions adopted very different approaches to education, with the north looking to democratise it whilst the south looked to Gaelicise it. A striking example of Irish nationalism's non-recognition of the northern jurisdiction was the payment of Catholic teachers based in the north by the provisional government in the south.

The labour movement consisted of a divergent group of people – Protestants and Catholics, nationalists and unionists, and internationalists. The political division of the island led to great pressures on the movement. Many trade unions as well as the Labour Party looked to retain a sense of unity by focusing on areas of common interest and offering degrees of autonomy to northern members. The labour movement was deeply affected by partition, and its influence was diluted by the sectarian divide that engulfed the north.

The disruption caused by partition was clearly seen in the necessary changes made to aspects of Ireland's infrastructure and services. The creation of the border impacted greatly on railways, roads, fisheries and postal services, as well as many other areas. The necessary changes to Irish infrastructure and services in order to accommodate the creation of two jurisdictions affected people more on a day-to-day basis than almost anything else.

All sports were affected by partition, with some affected more than others. As with trade, charity, labour and religious organisations, many sports remained or became all-Ireland bodies after partition. Soccer and athletics stand out, however, as they were partitioned along political lines. Those that were governed on an all-Ireland basis navigated the difficult political terrain by accommodating diverse interests and compromising on certain areas of symbolic importance, such as flags, anthems and emblems.

This book demonstrates the vast upheaval of partition, which affected everyone on the island in a political, economic, social and cultural sense. It examines the effects that the creation of a border had on many aspects of people's lives, including how they were affected on a day-to-day basis. It shows the great uncertainty that surrounded Northern Ireland's status for many years after its birth, with this uncertainty feeding into decisions made by numerous bodies, both political and non-political. A unique feature of the partition of Ireland, compared with other jurisdictions, was the number of organisations across most spheres of Irish life that were allowed to, and chose to, ignore the new international frontier and continue as they had before, as all-Ireland entities.

CHAPTER ONE

Towards Partition

The Irish question dominated British party politics for over three decades, beginning when William Ewart Gladstone converted to the cause of Home Rule for Ireland in the 1880s. His decision tied the Liberal Party to the Irish Parliamentary Party while the Conservative Party became aligned to the Ulster unionists. The Irish question did not become the Ulster question during the Home Rule Bills of 1886 and 1893. Both bills were defeated by normal parliamentary procedures, with the 1886 bill defeated by the House of Commons and the 1893 bill defeated by the House of Lords. Joseph Chamberlain, a liberal who became a liberal unionist in opposition to Irish Home Rule, was the first major figure to suggest the partition of Ulster during the first Home Rule Crisis in 1886.[1] He said that 'Ireland is not a homogenous community [...] it is a nation that comprises two nations and two religions'.[2] He floated the concept of 'a federal Britain with a parliament in Belfast,' similar to Quebec's relationship with Canada.[3] There was little support for Chamberlain's proposal at the time, and although Ulster featured more prominently during debates on the second Home Rule Bill in 1893, the Irish question did not become Ulster-centric until the twentieth century. The British electoral rejection of Home Rule in 1886 heralded almost twenty years of conservative and unionist rule, where the policy on Ireland comprised 'killing Home Rule with kindness'.[4] This included the introduction of tax reforms; local government, which established democratically-elected county and urban councils throughout Ireland; and significant land-purchase legislation.[5] Many of the Tory initiatives for Ireland were supported by both nationalists and unionists.

With most unionists based in Ulster, the 'Ulsterisation' of Irish unionism came to the forefront with the formation of the Ulster Unionist

Council in 1905.[6] The exclusion of Ulster from any Home Rule settlement became the overriding issue of the third Home Rule Bill, introduced in 1912. In the House of Commons, the two general elections of 1910 saw the Irish Parliamentary Party hold the balance of power once again, for the first time since the 1890s. John Redmond, the Irish Parliamentary Party leader, promised to support a Liberal government and its Parliament Act, which greatly curbed the powers of the House of Lords on the condition that a Home Rule Bill would be introduced.[7] The real prospect of Home Rule saw a violent reaction from unionists, most vociferously so in Ulster. Edward Carson, the new leader of the Irish Unionist Alliance since 21 February 1910, 'hoped to use Ulster Unionist resistance to prevent Home Rule coming into effect in any part of Ireland'.[8] From an early juncture, Ulster unionists realised that a huge effort was necessary to secure public sympathy in Britain. The effort involved the production and distribution of literary propaganda, demonstrations, canvassing and tours of Ireland and Britain. The most symbolic gesture of opposition to Home Rule was the signing of the Solemn League and Covenant by just under 500,000 men and women on 'Ulster Day' (i.e. 28 September 1912).[9] Ulster unionists also armed themselves and threatened to establish a provisional government in Ulster if Home Rule was brought into Ireland.[10] Their open flouting of the law was supported by 'the British Conservative Party, now re-named the Unionist Party and led from 1912 to 1923 by Andrew Bonar Law'.[11] In July 1913 at Blenheim Palace, Bonar Law warned that there were 'things stronger than parliamentary majorities' and that if Home Rule was imposed on Ulster, he could 'imagine no length of resistance' that Ulster would go to, 'in which I should not be prepared to support them'.[12]

Compounding the strong and blatantly dangerous opposition from the Ulster unionists and the Conservative Party was the lukewarm support for Home Rule within the Liberal Party. The Liberal leader and Prime Minister, Herbert Asquith, brought none of the moral crusade that informed Gladstone's campaign for Home Rule. In the words of Ronan Fanning, 'Asquith was always an unwilling ally, a resentful partner in a loveless marriage' with Redmond and the Irish Parliamentary Party.[13] Senior Liberal Party figures such as David Lloyd George and Winston Churchill were early advocates of some form of Ulster exclusion from Home Rule. At a cabinet meeting in February 1912, they both proposed that each county in Ulster have the right to vote themselves in or out of Home Rule.[14]

Asquith introduced the third Home Rule Bill to the House of Commons on 11 April 1912. No special provision was made for Ulster, as Asquith believed Ireland was 'a nation, not two nations, but one nation'.[15] Although it appeared that Home Rule for the whole island was close at hand, the House of Lords still had the power to delay the bill by two years, meaning that Home Rule could not be enacted until 1914 at the earliest. This gave unionists ample time to spoil the bill, and knowing the Liberal Party's dilemma over Ulster, it soon became apparent that special treatment was needed for Ulster. In June 1912, a Liberal backbencher named T.G. Agar-Robartes tabled an amendment to exclude the four north-eastern counties of Antrim, Armagh, Derry and Down from Home Rule.[16] Although his amendment was greeted with outrage by all political parties and was defeated, he 'was merely expressing a growing frustration at the seemingly intractable impasse between Irish nationalism and Irish (specifically Ulster) unionists as to what should be the future constitutional status of Ireland'.[17] However, it was soon supported by unionists as a tactic to stop the implementation of Home Rule for all of Ireland. Carson introduced his own amendment to exclude the nine counties of Ulster, still as a 'strategic thrust'.[18] The amendment nevertheless alarmed southern unionists, who realised that a drift towards partition was occurring within Ulster unionist and Conservative ranks. Carson, himself a southern unionist from Dublin, was moving away from 'partition as tactic' to 'partition as compromise' and confided in Bonar Law in September 1913 that 'matters were now moving towards a settlement on the basis of six-county exclusion'.[19]

Senior leaders within the Liberal Party were convinced that Home Rule could not be enacted without addressing the Ulster question. They just had to convince their allies, the Irish Parliamentary Party. Redmond had stated around this time that:

This idea of two nations in Ireland is to us revolting and hateful. The idea of our agreeing to the partition of our nation is unthinkable. We want the union in Ireland of all creeds, of all classes, of all races, and we would resist most violently as far as it is within our power to do so … the setting up or [sic] permanent dividing lines between one creed and another and one race and another.[20]

Asquith knew the Irish Parliamentary Party was as reliant on the Liberal Party as the Liberal Party was reliant on the Irish Party. By late 1913, as civil war in Ireland was threatened with unionists and nationalists forming military groups, great pressure was put on Redmond and his deputy leader, John Dillon, to compromise on Ulster. The Irish Parliamentary Party declared itself open to the concept of the Home Rule of Ulster within the Home Rule of Ireland. This was considered totally unacceptable by Carson. Asquith then pressured Redmond to agree to a temporary exclusion, but 'the permanent exclusion of Ulster he [Redmond] would not however consider for a moment'.[21] 'In early March [1914] the proposals were formulated: individual Ulster counties might opt for exclusion for a period of three years, after which they would automatically come under the jurisdiction of the Irish Parliament'.[22] Within days, Redmond was informed by Augustine Birrell, Chief Secretary of Ireland, that the exclusion period needed to be doubled from three to six years.[23] Birrell, realising from 1912 that the Ulster Unionists' 'yells are genuine', delayed dealing with the Ulster conundrum until 1914.[24] Cardinal Michael Logue, the Roman Catholic Primate of Ireland, had little optimism for the future and perceptively wrote:

> I fear the concessions on the Home Rule Bill will be a bad business for us in this part of the North. It will leave us more than ever under the heel of the Orangemen. Worst of all it will leave them free to tamper with our education. I don't think we have seen the last of the concessions.[25]

With the concessions agreed by the Irish Parliamentary Party, partition in some form was almost a certainty, and 'What was now alone at issue was how much of Ulster and for how long'.[26] Birrell and members of the British administration in Dublin Castle looked at a number of different options for partition based on divisions of counties, rural districts or poor law unions. These options could have seen the exclusion of roughly five counties of Ulster.[27] Redmond was adamant that exclusion would be temporary; Carson threatened forceful resistance unless exclusion was permanent and insisted that unionists did not want 'a stay of execution for six years'.[28] The unionist reaction angered the British government, who were further perturbed by the Curragh Mutiny in March 1914. Aware of the anti-Home Rule sentiments of Arthur Paget, Commander-in-Chief of the British army in Ireland, around sixty officers in the Curragh military camp, under the leadership of Brigadier General Hubert Gough, threatened to resign if they were asked to use force on Ulster to enforce Home Rule. Gough claimed that 'if it came to civil war … I would fight for Ulster rather than against her'.[29] Soon after this, the gunrunner Fred Crawford, under orders from the Ulster Unionist Council, landed 25,000 rifles and three million rounds of ammunition in Larne, Donaghdee and Bangor on the night of 24–25 April. Fanning contends that 'the Larne gun running made it almost impossible for the Unionist leaders to agree to any settlement short of the permanent exclusion of at least the six north-eastern counties of Ulster'.[30] Both incidents also made the British government more nervous and eager to reach a solution. As the country spiralled towards civil war, King George V, a keen supporter of Ulster's exclusion from Home Rule, intervened and called a conference of the main parties in Buckingham Palace in July 1914. The conference saw no solution, with Redmond seeking temporary exclusion for counties looking to opt out of Home Rule and Carson seeking permanent exclusion of all of Ulster.[31] Carson originally wanted a 'clean cut' for all of Ulster, arguing 'that the exclusion of the whole province, with its large Catholic minority, was the best guarantee of eventual Irish unity'.[32] According to Eamon Phoenix, at the Buckingham Palace conference:

> Carson revealed his 'irreducible minimum': the proposition that a six-county *bloc*, the area which was later to comprise Northern Ireland, should be precluded permanently from the operation of the Home Rule Act. Though firmly repudiated by the Nationalist leaders, this was a portentous development in the evolution of the partition debate. Among Ulster Unionists, it marked the beginning of a rethink which, in subordinating principle to pragmatism, sought to salvage the maximum possible area from the operation of

Home Rule, whilst projecting an image of 'reasonableness' in the eyes of the British public.[33]

Civil war in Ireland was averted by another war – namely, the First World War, which was, according to Asquith, a case of 'cutting off one's head to get rid of a headache'.[34] Once the war started, the Irish question no longer retained the dominance it once held in British politics. Most politicians in Britain wanted to be rid of the issue. Home Rule was put on the statute book with two important provisos: 'On the one hand, a Suspensory Bill stipulated that the Home Rule Act would not come into operation until the end of the war; secondly, parliament had the Prime Minister's assurance that special provision must be made for Protestant Ulster.'[35] The Irish question was ignored but not completely forgotten about during the war. Fanning states:

> Forty years after its foundation as a separate party [the Irish Parliamentary Party], its members appeared to have achieved their goal and yet they had nothing to show for it: no parliament to set up in Dublin, no offices to fill, no patronage to dispense, no trappings of power to cover their importance in the vortex of a war that sucked up all political energy for four long years.[36]

Redmond and the Irish Party supported the war effort, but when an opportunity presented itself for Redmond to serve in a national government cabinet created in 1915, he declined. 'Bonar Law and Carson accepted ... Unionists, as a result, found themselves at the centre of government; Irish party influence, meanwhile, soon began to dip'.[37] From then until 1921–22, British government policy on Ireland was decided by a coalition government, with strong unionist representation.

The crisis caused by the Easter Rising in 1916 saw Irish Home Rule become an issue once again. Just months after the rising was quashed, Asquith tasked Lloyd George with initiating negotiations to implement the Home Rule Act 'at the earliest practicable moment'.[38] Lloyd George negotiated separately with Redmond and Carson, telling the former the exclusion of six counties of Ulster would be temporary, telling the latter their exclusion would be permanent. Carson secured the support of the

Ulster Unionist Council for the proposals.[39] Despite fierce opposition from nationalists, particularly from clergy members of the Catholic Church and nationalists from what would become the border counties in west and south Ulster, Redmond and the leading Irish Parliamentary Party member from Belfast, Joseph Devlin, secured the backing of Ulster nationalists for the proposals at a conference on 23 June 1916 by 475 to 265 votes.[40] The vote revealed 'a broad dichotomy in the body politic, between a pragmatic east Ulster wing, strongly identified with Joe Devlin, and a stridently anti-partitionist west Ulster alignment'.[41] Once Lloyd George's duplicity was revealed and Redmond was informed that the exclusion of six counties of Ulster would be permanent, he, outmanoeuvred once again, rejected the proposals.[42] Lloyd George's proposals were also vehemently opposed by southern unionists, championed by a member of the war cabinet, Walter Long, on the grounds that 'it would divert the attention of the government and Parliament from the war to complicated and extremely controversial proposals relating to Ireland'.[43] The attempts in 1916 were telling in demonstrating the British government's firm commitment to the permanent exclusion of much of Ulster from Home Rule, particularly with Lloyd George steering government policy on Ireland, as he would continue to do, once he became prime minister in December 1916. The attempts of 1916 comprised yet another blow for Redmond and the Irish Parliamentary Party, whose popularity was in terminal decline due to its continued support of the war and its perceived humiliating concession after concession in accepting some form of partition. John Dillon conceded in December 1918 that the 1916 negotiations 'struck a deadly blow at the Irish Party and, since then, [it] has been going downhill at an ever-accelerated pace'.[44]

The next time an attempt was made to solve the Irish question was in 1917, with the formation of the Irish Convention in July 1917, an effort by Lloyd George to allow Irishmen to 'work out their own salvation'.[45] The Irish Convention was an assembly that met from July 1917 until April 1918 with the aim of finding a resolution to the Irish question. Diarmaid Ferriter states that Carson had in March 1917

prepared a plan to tempt Ulster into devolved Irish government, whereby Ulster would be left out of home rule but an all-Ireland council with representatives of a home rule Parliament and Ulster MPs at Westminster would consider legislative proposals for the whole of Ireland and 'frame a procedure by which if agreement was reached they could be enacted simultaneously in Dublin and the excluded counties'. The British government was open to this and Carson was willing to try to sell it to his party, but it was shelved in favour of the Irish Convention.[46]

With the ever-growing Sinn Féin boycotting the conference and Ulster unionists present in body but not in spirit, the convention was doomed from the start, 'a gigantic irrelevancy' in the words of F.S.L. Lyons.[47] The conference saw the cooperation of the Irish Parliamentary Party with southern unionists, who felt they were abandoned by their northern counterparts. According to Lyons, the Irish Convention 'finally disposed the myth that any settlement was possible ... on the basis of an Ireland which would be at once united and self-governing'.[48] R.B. McDowell, in his study of the convention, considered it 'one of the most striking failures in Irish history ... the gaps were too wide, or, to put it another way, the main groups clung too tightly to their prepared positions. Moreover, the majority of the convention's members were constitutional nationalists who were rapidly losing the confidence of the sections they were supposed to represent'.[49] The convention limped on until April 1918. By this time, Redmond was dead, and the Irish Parliamentary Party was months away from a humiliating defeat in the 1918 general election. By the time the First World War ended in November 1918, the Irish question had been fundamentally transformed. The psychological partition between unionists and nationalists had widened significantly, with entrenched Ulster unionists pitted against a brand of nationalism that espoused a severance from all British ties.[50]

The December 1918 general election, the first since December 1910, was one of the most decisive in Irish history. Sinn Féin obliterated the Irish Parliamentary Party by winning seventy-three of the 105 seats available in Ireland. The Irish Parliamentary Party won just six seats. However, Sinn Féin decided to abstain from taking seats in Westminster, meaning that there would be just a handful of Irish nationalist voices heard in the House of Commons as the future of Ireland was decided.[51]

Sinn Féin had campaigned on an abstentionist policy, claiming that the British could not be trusted to deliver a solution to the Irish question. It repudiated Westminster and Home Rule, seeking a complete severance of ties with Britain instead, through an Irish republic. The election was also a spectacular success for Ulster unionists. Of the thirty-seven seats available in the province of Ulster, unionists won twenty-two. In the six counties that would form Northern Ireland, the unionists won twenty-two of the twenty-nine seats available, with Sinn Féin winning just three seats.[52] 'In the whole of Ulster the Unionists won 265,111 votes to a combined Nationalist total of 177,557; while in the six counties of Antrim, Armagh, Derry, Down, Fermanagh and Tyrone they had a majority of slightly over two to one: 255,819 votes to 116,888.'[53] Whilst three Irish provinces had shown their support for full separation from Britain, it was clear that Ulster was the polar opposite. Remarkably, the nationalists had held more seats in Ulster than the unionists as recently as 1913, with seventeen seats in comparison to the unionists' sixteen.[54] By 1918, the electorate of Ulster had moved decisively in favour of remaining within the union. Unionists were also bolstered by the success of their allies in Britain, the Conservative Party. Lloyd George's national coalition was easily re-elected. Most of the seats in the coalition were won by the Conservatives, winning 339 seats, with Lloyd George's Coalition Liberals winning 136 seats.[55] Afterwards, Lloyd George 'was sensitive to his own vulnerability in the House and felt himself on occasion to be a prisoner of the Coalition'.[56] This greatly influenced his subsequent decisions regarding Ireland. The Irish question barely featured in the election in Britain. The Conservative Party manifesto ruled out two options in relation to Ireland: 'the one leading to a complete severance of Ireland from the British Empire, and the other the forcible submission of the six counties of Ulster to a Home Rule parliament against their will'.[57] With the Conservatives and the unionists winning the vast majority of seats and with no strong nationalist voice remaining in Westminster, the 'Tory stranglehold on Irish policy tightened immeasurably'.[58] According to Michael Laffan, the 1918 general election saw 'a shift in the Irish balance of power from southern nationalists to northern unionists'.[59] This shift became even more apparent when the decisive Government of Ireland Act was introduced in 1920.

CHAPTER TWO

The Government of Ireland Act 1920

The genesis of the Government of Ireland Act 1920 came in the latter half of 1919, once Lloyd George was no longer constrained with the Paris Peace Conference, which lasted for most of the first six months of 1919. Home Rule was still on the statute book and had been since 1914; it could no longer be postponed.[1] It was 'scheduled to come into operation automatically when hostilities were formally concluded with the signature of the last of the peace treaties'.[2] To stop the third Home Rule Bill from coming into effect by default, Lloyd George set up a committee chaired by Walter Long to draft the fourth Home Rule Bill, known as the Government of Ireland Bill.

Walter Long had a relationship with Ireland spanning his entire life. Born in Bath in 1854, his mother, Charlotte Anna, was the fourth daughter of Wentworth Fitzwilliam Dick of Humewood, County Wicklow, who had served as MP from 1852 to 1880.[3] Long was a regular visitor to Ireland for fox hunting and other social events.[4] He was appointed Chief Secretary of Ireland in 1905 and subsequently became very popular amongst Irish unionists due to his trenchant unionist outlook. After losing his parliamentary seat in 1906, he became leader of the Irish Unionist Alliance and chairman of the Ulster Unionist Council in 1907.[5] By 1918, as liaison officer between the war cabinet and the Irish administration, Long was the 'most influential member of the government on Irish affairs'.[6] He then favoured a settlement of the Irish question based on a federal solution for the entire United Kingdom. The federalism approach of the entire United Kingdom was seen by some within British political circles as a way of retaining the unity of the British Empire whilst recognising the differences within its boundaries. After the 1918 general election, Lloyd George appointed him first Lord of the Admiralty. Suffering from ill-health for prolonged periods of his life due to spinal arthritis, he was forced to delegate much of his work to his parliamentary secretary, James Craig, the leading Ulster unionist.[7] Long wanted to resign from the Ulster Unionist Council but was convinced to stay on, and 'thus remained an important linchpin between the cabinet and both the northern Unionists and the executive in Dublin'.[8]

Long was a staunch unionist and rabidly anti-Sinn Féin. As republican violence escalated in Ireland throughout 1919, it was Long who proposed the hiring of ex-servicemen to assist the Royal Irish Constabulary (RIC), a measure that would be adopted in 1920 with the recruitment of the Black and Tans and Auxiliaries to serve in Ireland. 'Ruthless men, he contended, could be countered only by ruthless policies, and by September [1919] he was prepared to recommend that Ireland be governed as a crown colony until such time as home rule became feasible.'[9] Unsurprisingly, the make-up of Long's committee was unionist in outlook. There was no nationalist representation whatsoever, nor were nationalists even consulted about the Government of Ireland Bill. James Craig and his associates were the only Irishmen consulted during the drafting of the bill.[10] The first meeting of Long's committee 'was held on 15 October when a decision was made to create distinct legislatures for Ulster and the southern provinces linked by a common council, comprising representatives from both'.[11] According to Nicholas Mansergh, 'the starting point for a settlement was no longer unity, but division. This was to be the new departure.'[12] This was the first time that a separate parliament was proposed for Ulster, as unionists to date had shown nothing but unyielding advocacy for remaining within Westminster. The reason given by Long's committee for abandoning Ulster to remain fully integrated with the rest of the United Kingdom was that 'Exclusion, whether of the entire province of Ulster or of the six north-eastern counties, would leave large nationalist majorities under British rule, which would clearly infringe the principle of self determination ... British rule in the domestic affairs of Ireland has been the root of the Home Rule movement from start to finish.'[13] The committee believed that the creation of two parliaments in Ireland

would meet 'the fundamental demand of the overwhelming majority of Irishmen ever since the days of [Daniel] O'Connell'; it was 'entirely consistent' with majority resistance in Ulster to rule from Dublin and nationalist resistance in the rest of Ireland to British rule; it was also consistent with the government pledges to Ulster; it would 'enormously minimise' the partition issue, the division of Ireland being a far less serious matter if Home Rule were established in both parts of it and 'all Irishmen' therefore self-governing with 'far the most convenient dividing line' between the two parts being the historic frontiers of Ulster, which, with its comparatively even balance, would minimise the division of Ireland on purely religious lines. To complete the catalogue of merit, there would be a Council of Ireland with members from North and South to keep open the road to unity.[14]

Before the end of the war, the exclusion of Ulster, or at least some of Ulster, was the only option being considered in terms of the province's special treatment. It is difficult to ascertain when exactly the option of providing a Home Rule parliament for Ulster was contemplated. The peace treaties after the war would certainly have been a factor. The treaties of 'Versailles, Trianon and Saint Germain set new borders throughout central and southern Europe in the wake of the defeat of Germany, the collapse of Czarist Russia, and the Austro-Hungarian and Ottoman empires'.[15] The creation of a border in Ireland was unusual, as it involved the division of one of the victorious countries of the war. It was, however, an early 'example of imperial fragmentation and nation-state building' that occurred in the twentieth century.[16] The partition of Ireland was 'the first major partition in which a British cabinet participated in territory which it had formerly controlled, but it provided a precedent for later partitions', including of India and Palestine.[17] According to John Kendle, Long was approached by John Atkinson on 6 June 1919:

who argued that neither the 1914 Home Rule Act nor home rule all round would work. He favoured a scheme that would place Ulster on a par with other provinces within a federal system that 'would be government [sic] by her own Provincial Government plus the Imperial Parliament and Executive, not plus an Irish Central Parliament and an Irish Executive dependent upon it'. 'It is this

Central Irish Government', Atkinson reminded Long, 'that Irish Protestants fear'.[18]

Atkinson was a unionist politician, lawyer and judge from Drogheda in County Louth.[19] On 24 July, *The Times* publicly advocated the two-parliament option for Ireland for the first time. It proposed two provincial or state legislatures, one for the three southern provinces and one for the nine counties of Ulster, with the ultimate aim of the 'establishment of an All-Ireland Parliament'.[20] Whilst acknowledging *The Times*'s proposal as 'a whiff of freshness to the stale atmosphere of our ancient controversy', the *Irish Times* feared 'the scheme would end in that very calamity of permanent Partition which *The Times* properly denounces as the worst of all possible solutions'.[21] At a meeting days later in Trowbridge in Wiltshire, Long claimed that *The Times*'s 'carefully-thought-out scheme' was worthy of close examination.[22] Throughout the summer of 1919, Long made a number of visits to Ireland to consult on the Irish question with Lord Lieutenant John French and Chief Secretary Ian MacPherson. Long tended not to disembark from his yacht, the *Enchantress*, which was docked in Kingstown (present-day Dún Laoghaire) harbour. Instead, both French and MacPherson joined him on the boat to discuss Irish affairs. Based on those meetings, Long sent a memorandum to Lloyd George on 24 September recommending two parliaments for Ireland.[23] This memorandum formed the basis of the subsequent Government of Ireland Bill.

The leading nationalist MP left in Westminster, Joseph Devlin, believed the creation of a parliament for Ulster would result in the 'worst form of partition and, of course, permanent partition. Once they have their own parliament with all the machinery of government and administration, I am afraid anything like subsequent union will be impossible.'[24] Carson, who ideally wished for no Home Rule anywhere in Ireland, saw some attractions of an Ulster parliament, stating 'Once it is granted ... [it] cannot be interfered with. You cannot knock Parliaments up and down as you do a ball, and once you have planted them there, you cannot get rid of them.'[25]

The common council proposed in the Government of Ireland Bill was a Council of Ireland, which would be composed 'of twenty members from each Parliament. In the first year it would look after transport, health, agriculture and similar matters, afterwards working towards [the] unity of the country.[26] It was envisaged that the council would lead to 'the peaceful evolution of a single parliament for all Ireland'.[27] A degree of unity within the central Irish administration headquartered in Dublin would be maintained through a common supreme court, railway policy and other all-Ireland functions.[28] Postal services were also reserved, to be administered by Westminster 'until they could be transferred to an all-Ireland assembly' if Irish unity was realised.[29] It was hoped that further common services could also be handed over to the council.[30] Eamon Phoenix contends that the stated aim of the Council of Ireland to unify Ireland was disingenuous, 'since the details of the Bill were drawn up by a largely Conservative Cabinet in close collaboration with Craig and the Ulster Unionists'.[31] It was an attempt to settle the Ulster question, not the Irish question.

Long's committee also advocated that all nine counties of Ulster be included in the northern parliament. Long knew the proposals would not placate Sinn Féin, 'But nothing short of the setting up of a Republic would satisfy Sinn Fein. Therefore, why not recognise the fact and say so frankly?'[32] It was never the intention of the Government of Ireland Bill to do so. Another committee member, Lord Birkenhead, admitted something similar when he said, 'I assent to this proposed Bill as affording an ingenious strengthening of our tactical position before the world. I am absolutely satisfied that the Sinn Féiners will refuse it. Otherwise in the present state of Ireland I could not even be a party to making the offer.'[33] The British government was only interested in securing the support of Ulster unionists, but initially, there were numerous objections from Ulster. The main objections were the admission of Home Rule, something they had never sought before; the reduction of Ulster representation in Westminster to just twelve seats; and the abandonment of many Protestants and unionists to the southern jurisdiction.[34] There also was a problem with the area to be included in the Ulster parliament. Ulster unionists sought the six counties of Antrim, Armagh, Derry, Down, Fermanagh and Tyrone, not the nine counties of Ulster, as this was the maximum area they felt they could dominate without being 'outbred' by Catholics.[35]

This decision of the Ulster Unionist Council was deeply unpopular amongst the 70,000 Protestants of Donegal, Cavan and Monaghan, who were sacrificed to the southern administration.[36] At a meeting of the Ulster Unionist Council on 10 March 1920:

> Lord Farnham of Cavan moved, and Michael E. Knight of Monaghan seconded, a resolution that the UUC would not accept anything other than the exclusion of the 'whole geographical province of Ulster'. The resolution was rejected. Monaghan unionists condemned the 'selfish policy' of the UUC, worse still, in their eyes the Covenant had been shown to have been nothing more than 'a mere scrap of paper', brushed aside by the UUC so as 'not to endanger their precious six-county safety'.[37]

Others believed there would be no threat to the unionist majority with nine counties, believing six counties would present a 'ridiculous boundary … Donegal would be cut off from its harbours and rivers and there would be no access to it except through the six counties'.[38] Thomas Moles, Westminster MP, explained that the three counties had to be abandoned in order to save the six counties: 'In a sinking ship, with life-boats sufficient for only two-thirds of the ship's company, were all to condemn themselves to death because all could not be saved?'[39] Another meeting of the Ulster Unionist Council on 27 May decided by a margin of 310 to 80 to support a six-county Northern Ireland parliament instead of a nine-county one.[40] Ulster unionists from outside of the six counties resigned from the Ulster Unionist Council.[41] Many members of the Ulster Women's Unionist Council from Cavan, Donegal and Monaghan also resigned.[42] Outside of Ulster, southern unionists left the Irish Unionist Alliance and formed the Unionist Anti-Partition League, in opposition to the impending partition of Ireland.[43] Led by William St John Fremantle Brodrick, Earl of Midleton, amongst its membership were people from the 'largest commercial interests in Dublin, including Lord Iveagh, Sir John Arnott, Andrew Jameson, and Marcus Goodbody'.[44]

The British government only agreed to accede to the Ulster unionists' wishes to confine the northern parliament to six counties in the spring of 1920, just as the bill was being brought before the House of Commons.[45] The Long committee's original argument, that the nine-county proposal 'will enormously minimise the partition issue … it minimises the division of Ireland on purely religious lines. The two religions would be not unevenly balanced in the Parliament of Northern Ireland', was exactly the reason why Ulster unionist leaders preferred six counties.[46] They had no intention of minimising partition. To avoid a nine-county parliament, Craig had even

> suggested the establishment of a Boundary Commission to examine the distribution of population along the borders of the whole of the six Counties, and to take a vote in those districts on either side of and immediately adjoining that boundary in which there was a doubt as to whether they would prefer to be included in the Northern or the Southern Parliamentary area.[47]

By conceding to the demands of the unionists, the British government showed that its commitment to Irish unity was somewhat flexible.

Even though the Ulster Unionist Council reluctantly endorsed the Government of Ireland Bill, many Ulster unionists eventually 'concluded that the scheme proposed in the Government of Ireland Act would cause the least diminution of their Britishness'.[48] Some, such as James Craig's brother Charles, began to see the benefits Ulster unionists would garner from having their own parliament:

> The Bill practically gives us everything that we fought for, everything we armed ourselves for, and to attain which we raised our Volunteers in 1913 and 1914 … We would much prefer to remain part and parcel of the United Kingdom … but we have many enemies in this country, and we feel that an Ulster without a Parliament of its own would not be in nearly as strong a position as one in which a Parliament had been set up, where the Executive had been appointed and where, above all, the paraphernalia of Government was already in existence … We should fear no one and … would then be in a position of absolute security.[49]

He also claimed that 'I would not be fair to the House … if I lent the slightest hope of that union [of Ireland] arising within the lifetime of any man in this House'.[50] Once it was realised that partition was being attempted through the creation of two parliaments, many commentated on the practical implications of such a massive undertaking.

A great deal of confusion surrounded the Government of Ireland Bill. The *Freeman's Journal* described it as a complex problem, especially when one considered that 'The whole scheme of Irish administration is based on recognition of Ireland as a national entity with its centre in Dublin'. There would be a need to have the 'Local Government Board, the Department of Agriculture, the Insurance Commission, the Department of Education, the Estates Commissioners and Congested Districts Board and the Board of Works' to be divided between 'Ulster' and the rest of Ireland.[51] The newspaper deridingly named the bill 'The Dismemberment of Ireland Bill'.[52] The *Irish News* proposed some names for the new jurisdiction, including Carsonia and Craigdom, after the two most prominent unionists, Edward Carson and James Craig.[53] The unionist-leaning Dublin Chamber of Commerce also condemned the bill, saying partition would negatively affect banking by restricting the free flow of business and making it more difficult and expensive to collect debt; dual government would mean increased taxation; political differences would be accentuated; the development of the country would be impeded whilst the creation of a second judiciary would be utterly unfavourable. It concluded by claiming that 'one of the most regrettable effects of partition would be that it would deprive the Southern Parliament of the steadying influence and business training of the men of Ulster'.[54] The Church of Ireland Archbishop of Dublin and Provost of Trinity College Dublin, Dr John Henry Bernard, speaking in his capacity as provost, insisted that Trinity College Dublin was 'an Irish institution, that they stood for the whole of Ireland, that their men came from all parts of Ireland, and that, so far as they were concerned, they would resist by all lawful means any partition of Ireland'.[55] One lawyer believed the withdrawal of legal business from the majority of Ulster counties would greatly diminish the standing of the Four Courts in Dublin.[56] Staff members in the Four Courts agreed, with over a dozen based in Dublin applying for better-paid jobs in the future Northern Ireland.[57]

It has often been cited that the Government of Ireland Bill was allowed to pass relatively unchallenged due to the lack of nationalist representation in Westminster. Instead of eighty Irish nationalist MPs, there were just seven remaining in Westminster (six from Ireland and T.P. O'Connor from

Liverpool) after the 1918 general election.[58] It could be argued that even eighty nationalist MPs would have made little difference when one considers the make-up of the House of Commons after the election. The Conservative Party, Lloyd George's Coalition Liberals and Irish unionists won over 500 seats, an overwhelming majority. The British Labour Party, with fifty-seven seats, opposed the Government of Ireland Bill with little effect.[59] Former Prime Minister Herbert Asquith and his vastly reduced Liberal Party (of just thirty-six seats), also opposed the 'cumbrous, costly, unworkable scheme'.[60] His opposition also failed to make an imprint on the final act. It is doubtful that Sinn Féin's presence would have made a difference either. What little voice the seven nationalist MPs remaining in Westminster had was further diminished by the Catholic Church's belief that they should not participate in the committee stages of the Government of Ireland Bill or suggest amendments to the bill.[61] The Catholic Church was virulently opposed to partition and believed that participating in the framing of the 'Partition Bill' would be seen as a sign of its acceptance. The leading nationalist MP in Westminster, Joseph Devlin, condemned the bill as 'conceived in Bedlam', 'ridiculous' and 'fantastic'. He voted against it but did not in any way contribute to its final form.[62]

Sinn Féin, the leading nationalist movement after the 1918 general election, abstained from Westminster. It formed its own constituent assembly, Dáil Éireann, in the Mansion House in Dublin in January 1919. All Irish MPs, including unionists and members of the Irish Parliamentary Party, were invited to attend the opening session of the Dáil. Unsurprisingly, no one apart from the Sinn Féin MPs accepted.[63] Sinn Féin's policy on partition was almost non-existent from the outset, and it essentially chose to ignore it. Soon after the formation of Dáil Éireann, Louis J. Walsh, a Ballycastle solicitor and one of the leading northern Sinn Féiners, proposed in April 1919 that 'attention should be given to Ulster, for he thought the organisation had not sufficiently grappled with that question'.[64] According to Charles Townshend:

There were some signs in 1919 that the seriousness of this problem was recognised. A pushy Ulster Protestant, adoptive Canadian and Sinn Féin convert, William Forbes Patterson, was asked by Sinn Féin in June to investigate the northern situation. His verdict on republicanism there was bleak: it was effectively stillborn. But he believed that unionism was vulnerable to the (slowly) growing labour movement, and Sinn Féin could do worse than support labour. There were signs of cross-communal industrial action – notably the general strike in Belfast early in 1919 – although, as he saw, the British Labour party was unlikely to escape from its 'English outlook' ... The prospects for military confrontation were grim, Forbes Patterson thought. If faced with a 'pogrom', republicans could not cope.[65]

Sinn Féin, of course, was not in the House of Commons to debate the Government of Ireland Bill. As the bill was making its way through parliament, the British government was waging a war with Sinn Féin and its military wing, the Irish Volunteers (later renamed the IRA). Sinn Féin leaders stuck steadfastly and naively to the view that Ulster would readily join an all-Ireland parliament once Britain was removed from the island. As well as having its own parliament, Sinn Féin also set up a counter-state with its own legal system, police force and local government. That the Government of Ireland Act came into law as Britain was at open war with Sinn Féin, who was supported by a considerable majority on the island, shows the total air of unreality that surrounded the act.[66]

Sinn Féin built on its 1918 general election mandate by taking control of the majority of local authorities in Ireland after the local elections of January and June 1920. The local elections of 1920 were a major disappointment for Ulster unionists, and this may explain part of their reasoning for insisting on Northern Ireland consisting of six instead of nine counties. It was the first time that the proportional representation (PR) system of voting was used in Ireland.[67] PR involves a single transferable vote to be cast in multi-seat constituencies. The introduction of PR 'was intended to protect the unionist minority in the south, but it had the added effect of putting unionist domination of Derry and other parts of the north under threat'.[68] It was also hoped that PR would end systematic discrimination in local government. Jeremiah MacVeagh, nationalist MP for South Down, claimed that in Dungannon there 'were only two Catholic employees under the Unionist council. Out of a total salary and wages list of £575, only £36 goes to Catholics, and that goes to two street scavengers.'[69]

In the six-county area, nationalists won control of 'Derry City, Fermanagh and Tyrone County Councils, ten urban councils, including Armagh, Omagh, Enniskillen, Newry and Strabane, and thirteen rural councils'.[70] Unexpected nationalist and Labour Party victories in places such as Lurgan, Dungannon, Carrickfergus, Larne, Limavady, Cookstown and Lisburn were seen by nationalists as 'a rebuff to plans for partition'.[71] In Belfast Corporation, the local government for Belfast, unionists went from having fifty-two to thirty-seven members; Labour won thirteen seats; Sinn Féin and the Nationalist Party won five seats each.[72] Many unionists had a great 'fear of socialism' and were 'concerned at the success of Labour candidates in 1920' who, on top of winning thirteen seats in Belfast, 'won control of Lurgan' and received representation for the first time in Lisburn and Bangor.[73] According to Michael Farrell, it was the 'first serious challenge to Unionist hegemony in the area'.[74]

The result in Derry City was particularly galling for unionists. Of the forty seats, unionists won nineteen, Sinn Féin and the Nationalist Party won ten seats each, and Hugh C. O'Doherty, an independent nationalist, won the final seat. Margaret Morris was elected for Sinn Féin as the first female member of the Derry Corporation. O'Doherty became 'the first nationalist mayor of the city, and the first Catholic to hold the position since Cormac O'Neill was appointed by James II in 1688'.[75] O'Doherty, a Derry solicitor, 'who, along with removing the name of Lord French from the list of Derry Freemen, also refused to attend any functions where an oath of allegiance was made to the Crown'.[76]

Tensions in the city soon boiled over. In April and May, street riots began, with skirmishes taking place between the IRA and the revived Ulster Volunteer Force (UVF).[77] The violence escalated in June, leading to the deaths of twenty people and many more wounded. Two children were amongst the dead – George Caldwell, a ten-year-old orphan, and Joseph McGlinchey, aged fifteen. Adrian Grant claims that 'there is evidence of deliberate sectarian targeting by both unionists and nationalists, despite efforts of the IRA leaders to contain such action by the latter'.[78] The violence in the city only abated once 1,500 British troops were deployed to Derry on 23 June.[79] Within days, the violence moved further east.

Edward Carson used his 12 July 1920 speech to 25,000 Orangemen at a field in Finaghy to deliver an incendiary message: 'We must proclaim today clearly that come what will and be the consequences what they may, we in Ulster will tolerate no Sinn Féin – no Sinn Féin organisation, no Sinn Féin methods ... And these are not mere words. I hate words without action.'[80] According to Alan F. Parkinson:

> the sheer force of external influences in the summer of 1920 – the spread of death and destruction throughout the south and west of Ireland, including many attacks on Protestants, the ongoing passage of the Better Government of Ireland Bill and the increasing proximity of violence to Belfast, as witnessed by events in Derry – combined to create a most threatening situation in Belfast.[81]

By 1920, the war in the south and west of Ireland had reached Ulster. Before then, 'difficulties experienced by even the most militant IRA units in acquiring weapons and the resolute opposition presented by large sections of both the unionist and nationalist communities meant that the first phase of the War of Independence had virtually no impact in the north-east'.[82] As well as the violence in Derry, there were many IRA attacks on RIC barracks in Monaghan, Cavan, Armagh, Tyrone and Down.[83] Ambushes on railways in Ulster were becoming almost daily occurrences. At Easter 1920, the IRA Belfast Brigade 'took part in a countrywide campaign of arson attacks on tax offices ordered by GHQ [General Headquarters] to mark the anniversary of the 1916 Rising'.[84] The increased activity in Ulster led to Carson's claims of a Sinn Féin 'invasion of Ulster'.[85] Days after his 12 July speech, the RIC divisional commissioner of Munster, Gerard Smyth, a native of Banbridge in County Down, was killed by the IRA in Cork.[86] Loyalists were 'further outraged when the southern rail crew assigned to transport the police chief's body back to his home town of Banbridge refused to do so'.[87] His death and funeral were the catalysts for the violence that spread to Belfast in late July 1920. After his burial in Banbridge, local Catholics and their property were viciously attacked there, as well as in nearby Dromore and Lisburn, with many Catholics driven from their jobs and their homes burned.[88]

The violence then spread to Belfast. Returning from the 12 July holiday on 21 July, shipyard workers were greeted with notices calling for a meeting of 'all Unionist and Protestant workers' during their lunch hour outside

Workman Clark's yard.[89] The meeting called for the expulsion of all 'non-loyal' workers from the shipyards. Straight after this, a mob 'armed with hammers, iron bars, wooden staves and, reportedly, revolvers' went on the rampage, looking for potential victims. Some workers, fearing the worst, left before lunchtime. Others escaped, suffering only verbal abuse. Some of the unluckier ones were stripped to their undergarments in the search for Catholic emblems, such as rosary beads. Many were severely beaten. Others, whilst swimming to safety across the Musgrave Channel, 'were pelted by a fusillade of "shipyard confetti", consisting of iron nuts, bolts, ship rivets and pieces of sharp steel'.[90] Catholics were soon expelled from their jobs by numerous employers, such as the Barbours, Musgraves, Mackies, Gallahers, the Sirrocco Works, McLaughlins and Harveys.[91] Most 'Protestant employers looked on with tacit approval'.[92] According to the Catholic Protection Committee – a welfare agency established by Dr MacRory, the Catholic Bishop of Down and Connor – a total of 10,000 male and 1,000 female workers were expelled (about 10 per cent of the nationalist population of Belfast).[93] Protestant socialists ('rotten prods') were also expelled from their jobs.[94] During the two years of intense sectarian violence in Belfast, from 1920 to 1922, over 1,000 Protestants were forced out of their homes.[95]

The unrest travelled from the workplace to the streets of Belfast, resulting in nineteen dead and many more wounded or homeless within just five days.[96] 'Retaliation from the Catholic community was not long in coming, provoking yet more retribution from the loyalists.'[97] As the city was besieged by sectarian violence, the Government of Ireland Bill was still manoeuvring its way through the House of Commons. Devlin summed up the incredulity felt by many nationalists in relation to the British government's insistence on proceeding with the bill whilst Ireland was in a state of unrest, with the vast majority of its citizens totally opposed to the proposed settlement. He accused the government of not inserting

a single Clause … to safeguard the interests of our people. This is not a scattered minority. Will the House believe we are a hundred thousand Catholics in a population of four hundred thousand? It is a story of weeping women, hungry children, hunted men, homeless in England, houseless in Ireland. If this is what we get when they have not their Parliament, what may we expect when they have that weapon, with wealth and power strongly entrenched? What will we get when they are armed with Britain's rifles, when they are clothed with the authority of government, when they have cast round them the Imperial garb, what mercy, what pity, much less justice or liberty, will be conceded to us then? That is what I have to say about the Ulster Parliament.[98]

Rather than listening to Devlin or those whom he represented, the British government took two steps in late 1920, on the advice of James Craig, that showed the inevitability of partition and highlighted that the only voices being listened to in Ireland were those of the Ulster unionists. Before the Government of Ireland Bill even became law in December 1920, Craig's proposals to commission an official policing force – the Specials – for the area that would become Northern Ireland and create the post of assistant under-secretary for the same area were granted.[99] The machinery of the new northern jurisdiction was being put in place. The partition of Ireland was taking a tangible form.

CHAPTER THREE

'Armed only with a table, a chair and an Act of Parliament'

During the summer of violence in Ulster in 1920, unionists looked to take responsibility for the enforcement of public order in the province. Although the UVF had not been active between 1914 and 1919, its members had retained their weapons.[1] As the unrest spread to Ulster, many started to organise into vigilante groups. One, 'Fermanagh Vigilance', was organised by Sir Basil Brooke, future Prime Minister of Northern Ireland, who 'felt that the hotheads on the Ulstermen's side might take the matter into their own hands, if not organised'.[2] He urged Dublin Castle to form an official special constabulary in June.[3] Another vigilante group, 'Protective Patrol', formed by John Webster in Armagh city, sought and received 174 UVF rifles from the Ulster Unionist Council.[4] 'Worried lest Loyalists at the local level should pass beyond the Unionist Party's own control, Sir James Craig assigned Colonel W.B. Spender the task of resurrecting the Ulster Volunteer Force (UVF) in order to harness Loyalists' militant energies'.[5] Unionists looked to police themselves as they did not trust the RIC. As an all-Ireland body, its membership was mainly Catholic, and with the IRA campaign, 'the authorities had begun to transfer the most zealous and strongly loyalist RIC men to the South and West and send old, inefficient, unenthusiastic or even suspect men to the North'.[6]

The violence that accompanied the expulsion of workers dissipated in late July. However, another wave began after the death of RIC district inspector Oswald Swanzy in Lisburn in August. Swanzy was believed to have been involved in the killing of the Lord Mayor of Cork, Thomas MacCurtain, in March 1920, thus making him a prime target of the IRA.[7]

He was shot dead on 22 August as he left a church service in Lisburn. The loyalist reaction led to the expulsion of almost the entire Catholic population of Lisburn from their homes. 300 homes were destroyed.[8] Catholic families fleeing Lisburn took trains to Belfast or Newry, and many had to walk to Belfast, crossing the Divis Mountain en route. The rioting spread to Belfast, where twenty-two people were killed in just five days.[9] On 30 August, 'the military authorities brought in a curfew from 10:30pm to 5:00am for the Belfast area. It was to last, with variations in the times, until 1924.'[10]

Even though most of the violence was perpetrated against Catholics, Craig warned 'that the loyalists were losing faith in the government's determination to protect them, and were threatening an immediate recourse to arms which would precipitate a civil war.'[11] He attended a ministerial conference in London on 2 September where he used the pretext of attempting to keep the extreme loyalist elements in harness to demand a special Ulster constabulary to serve only the area that would become Northern Ireland. Ultimately, Craig wanted the nucleus of the UVF to form an armed constabulary for the six counties. The Conservative Party leader, Bonar Law, was unsure and pointed out that 'if we armed Ulster, public opinions in this country would say the Government was taking sides and ceasing to govern impartially.'[12] The military Commander-in-Chief in Ireland, Nevil Macready, and the leading civil servant in Dublin Castle, Under-Secretary John Anderson, were also opposed. Macready wrote to Bonar Law, stating that a remobilised and rearmed UVF 'would undoubtedly consist entirely of Protestants, and no amounts [sic] of so-called loyalty is likely to restrain them if the religious question becomes acute ... the arming of the Protestant population of Ulster will mean the outbreak of civil war in this country, as distinct from the attempted suppression of rebellion with which we are engaged at present.'[13]

He threatened to resign if the UVF was recognised. It wasn't. However, helped by the backing of Arthur Balfour and Bonar Law, Craig was granted his special constabulary. Balfour felt that 'in view of the terms of the Bill the government would be justified in thus hiving off the Ulster administration forthwith from that of the rest of Ireland.'[14] The British government, fearing the public would think they were taking sides, wanted it to appear as if they had had the idea. Otherwise, as Bonar Law told Lloyd

George, it would seem 'as if we were acting on their dictation'.[15] The special constabulary was meant to be for all of Ireland, but 'the relevant Cabinet minutes betray the government's actual motivation: they refer to the creation of the special constabulary in "Ireland", with "Ireland" written in pen over the crossed out "Ulster" in typescript'.[16]

The Ulster Special Constabulary came into public existence in October 1920, with enrolment starting on 1 November and an initial strength of 3,000 planned. Its members were organised into three classes: The 'A' class consisted of full-time uniformed police auxiliaries; the 'B' class were employed on a part-time basis and allowed to keep their weapons at home, whilst the 'C' class, the largest group, were only to be called out for emergencies, such as invasions.[17] Enrolment was slow at first, with many suspicious that they would be asked to serve in the south or west of Ireland. They had to be reassured that they would only have to serve in the six counties.[18] According to Robert Lynch, while northern Catholics were officially allowed to join the force, few did nor were they actively encouraged to do so. From the very beginning, northern nationalists saw the Specials as being 'nothing more and nothing less that the dregs of the Orange lodges, armed and equipped to overawe Nationalists and Catholics, and with ... an inclination to invent "crimes" against Nationalists and Catholics'.[19]

The new special constabulary was placed under the command of Lieutenant-Colonel Charles Wickham, the divisional commissioner of the RIC for Ulster, partly answering to another new appointee, the Assistant Under-Secretary for Ireland to be based in Belfast, Sir Ernest Clark.[20] Craig also won the support of the British government in securing the appointment of the Assistant Under-Secretary (Clark) with responsibility for the area that would make up Northern Ireland before the Government of Ireland Bill was enacted in December 1920. Clark claimed that his appointment was not a preliminary step to partition.[21] In reality, however, it was, and signified yet another concession to Ulster unionists.

Born in Kent in 1864, Ernest Clark joined the British civil service in 1881, where he built up a reputation as a leading taxation expert. This brought him to the Cape Colony government in 1904–5 where he witnessed for the first time the establishment of a Home Rule territory – the South African federation.[22] Clark's 'bluster about "setting up" the South

African government' caused some annoyance later on with personnel in Dublin Castle.[23] He served as Assistant Under-Secretary to Ireland from September 1920 until November 1921. Following this, with the formal transfer of services, he became Permanent Secretary of the Ministry of Finance and head of the civil service of Northern Ireland, a position he held until 1925. He subsequently served as governor of Tasmania from 1933 to 1945.[24] His work as Assistant Under-Secretary was crucial in creating the structures of a functioning government for Northern Ireland when it came into being in the summer of 1921. Basil Brooke described him as the 'midwife to the new Province of Ulster'.[25]

John Anderson, who himself favoured a different settlement to the Government of Ireland Bill, recommended Clark for the post in Belfast. Years later, Clark described a letter he received from Anderson in September 1920:

> asking me whether I still was in a mind to come to Ireland and if so, whether I would take the position at Belfast of Assistant Under Secretary for Ireland … His letter ended with a sentence which at the time I did not understand; 'I suppose you are not by any chance a Roman Catholic?' … he realised as I subsequently did, that had I been a Roman Catholic I could never have been accepted by the Northern Government or been able to carry out my duties, even had I survived to undertake them.[26]

Once he expressed interest, he was interviewed in London by Hamar Greenwood, who had recently replaced MacPherson as Chief Secretary for Ireland. Greenwood then brought Clark to James Craig's office in the Admiralty, where he was 'vetted' by Craig and two other prominent Ulster unionists, Wilfrid Spender and Richard Dawson-Bates. Clark later revealed, 'I afterwards found … that really I was on show to Craig (and possibly also to Spender and Bates)'.[27] At the meeting, Clark recalled that the Ulster unionists 'were full of grievances' and painted 'a picture of the deathly peril which threatened all loyalists'. He later 'discovered by experience how necessary it has always been to emphasise, even to exaggerate, the conditions in Ireland in order to arrest the attention of the ordinary Englishman'.[28] As the meeting was ending,

Sir James Craig walked across to me and towering above this little man said 'Now you are coming to Ulster you must write one word across your heart', and he tapped out with his finger on my chest "ULSTER". I fear that I only saw the humour of this and not understanding its importance at the time said, 'Sir James, I can hardly do that, for the space is already occupied by two names ... "The British Empire" and "England". I am afraid "Ulster" can only be written after these'.[29]

Clark experienced a degree of distrust, even hostility, from some loyalists. Unionists were also unhappy with Clark's 'subordination to Dublin Castle: he would not, as had been construed from initial reports, enjoy the full authority of an under-secretary for Ulster'.[30] At a meeting in Belfast on 13 October between Greenwood, Anderson, Clark and leading Ulster unionists, the latter declared they had 'not the smallest confidence in the officials in Dublin Castle'.[31] They believed many in Dublin Castle were nationalists, even Sinn Féin sympathisers. They wanted 'an assurance that Sir Ernest Clark would have direct communication with the Chief Secretary. They did not want any possibility of leakage'.[32] Greenwood responded that Clark 'can send me information he can withhold from the King, the Pope and James MacMahon'.[33] MacMahon, a Catholic born in Belfast who grew up in Armagh, was, like Anderson, an under-secretary in Dublin Castle. He was believed to be 'sympathetic to nationalist aspirations for self-rule'.[34] He came in for particular ire from unionists. At the 13 October meeting, responding to criticism of MacMahon, Greenwood said he had total faith in MacMahon, 'an Ulsterman himself'. Thomas Moles replied, 'Not necessarily a horse because born in a stable,' which Greenwood said was 'a most unhappy metaphor. The Saviour of the world was born in a stable.' MacMahon 'cannot help his birth or his religion'.[35] Clark remained answerable to Dublin Castle, but as time went on, he became more and more independent of Dublin. He 'knew what was expected of him and he soon dispelled Unionist apprehension. From the start he worked consistently and uncompromisingly for the interests of the future Northern Ireland government'.[36]

Northern Ireland was presented with a workable administration from the very moment it came into being, thanks largely to the efforts of Ernest

Clark. He, supported by a small team of no more than twenty, worked tirelessly following his appointment in September 1920 to set up the machinery of a new jurisdiction with very little to work with. He later testified, 'I found myself ... setting out to form a new "administration" armed only with a table, a chair and an Act of Parliament.'[37] He also claimed, 'I will do my best to fulfil my role as "John the Baptist", and as far as can be done with the small staff at my disposal, get together information and "prepare the way".'[38] He established a framework for seven new government departments, organised buildings for those departments as well as their furniture and office equipment, attempted to source accommodation for the new civil service and secured instructions, guidelines and templates from different departments in London and Dublin in relation to how to run a department.[39] Since most of the equipment was obtained from Dublin, as Belfast merchants could not supply the office furniture in a standard form and in the quantity the new administration required, some Dublin businesses were 'able to benefit commercially from the creation of the new civil service in Northern Ireland'.[40] Clark's efforts were somewhat 'handicapped in that the existing all-Ireland system was bureaucratic, cumbersome, and quite unsuited to modern means'.[41] Also, under 'the Union the powers of government in Ireland had been distributed among some thirty different departments, and the problem was how these powers could be most efficiently grouped in Northern Ireland without producing too many office-holders in parliament'.[42]

Clark was in constant communication with Craig in the lead-up to the formation of Northern Ireland, ensuring a functioning state would be operational from day one.[43] He consulted Craig on many 'mundane essentials of laying down the North's administrative foundations. Craig, for example, was directly involved in the problem of determining the appropriate number and functions of the future Northern departments.'[44] Clark sent a memo to Craig regarding the recruitment recommendations for the Northern Ireland civil service, including the instructions that 'no preference [is] to be given to anyone based on religious belief' and 'competition for places should be open to women'.[45] He warned 'against adopting an official policy that would disadvantage Catholics in securing government employment,' as religious discrimination was illegal under the

Government of Ireland Act 1920.[46] At this stage, though, Craig had no official role: he was the presumptive Prime Minister of Northern Ireland. Carson resigned as Ulster Unionist leader in February 1921, handing the leadership to Craig.[47] Greenwood, the Chief Secretary of Ireland, was also guilty of 'displaying a telling disregard for British civil service tradition of neutrality in party politics, directed existing departments to prepare for partition by communicating with the Ulster Unionists'.[48]

When Clark moved to Belfast, he was initially tasked with establishing the Ulster Special Constabulary and dealing with the 'expelled workers' from the Belfast shipyards.[49] The expulsions of workers and the sectarian violence in the north in 1920 saw Sinn Féin make one of its first decisions directly relating to the north. It started a boycott. The boycott in many ways increased the likelihood of partition. Once the violence in the north began, Dáil Éireann felt it could not stand idly by. It imposed a boycott 'of goods from Belfast and a withdrawal of funds from Belfast-based banks'.[50] In reality, the boycott soon extended to other businesses and farms, and beyond Belfast too. Many saw it as an anti-partitionist move, a way to show that Northern Ireland could not survive without the rest of Ireland.[51] The *Westmeath Independent* had suggested in January 1920 'a clean commercial cut with "Ulster"' as a protest against those in favour of partition ("the dirty birds that soil the mother nest") … 'Ireland could manage very well if Belfast fell into the Lagan.'[52] Traders in Tuam in County Galway voted to boycott businesses from any part of Ireland that 'permits itself to be separated from the common life of the country'.[53] According to Michael Laffan, the boycott 'met with some disapproval in the south, and particularly in 1920 its impact was uneven and its direction sometimes faulty; southern protestants and northern catholics suffered as well as Ulster unionists'.[54] When Seán MacEntee, TD for Monaghan South, proposed in Dáil Éireann in August 1920 'a commercial boycott of Belfast' in response to the 'pogrom' perpetrated against Catholics in Belfast, another TD from Monaghan, Ernest Blythe, was 'entirely opposed to a blockade against Belfast … If it were taken it would destroy for ever the possibility of any union'. Countess Constance Markievicz, the first woman elected to parliament for Britain or Ireland in 1918, agreed with Blythe that 'a blockade would be playing into the hands of the enemy and giving them a good excuse for partition'.[55] Despite the opposition, the Dáil and its cabinet approved the instigation of the boycott. It was also supported by county councils under Sinn Féin control, trade unions and members of the Catholic clergy.[56] Nationalist firms in Belfast were also affected by the boycott. Ironically, Denis McCullough, one of the organisers of the Irish Republican Brotherhood (IRB) in Belfast and originally a supporter of the boycott, was forced to close his bagpipe factory as 'the Irish public because of the Boycott, buy British-made pipes rather than support this purely republican firm'.[57]

It was in an atmosphere of war, sectarian hatred and boycotts that the Government of Ireland Bill became an act on 23 December 1920, and elections to the new parliaments were set for the following May, which was selected due to the 'confidence of the British military that martial law could bring the IRA to heel within five months'.[58] Many pondered on what the new political realities would bring. Bryan Follis in *A State Under Siege* remarked:

> at the stage when the Act became law, Northern Ireland existed not as an entity but only in name and on paper. Not only had Northern Ireland no parliament and no government: it had no civil service to support and serve it, no police or defence force to enforce whatever laws it might make, protect its people, or defend its territory from possible (and indeed likely) attack, nor had it a judiciary to uphold its laws and administer justice.[59]

The main concern came from those who lived close to what would become the new border between northern and southern Ireland. In January 1921, the Lord Mayor of Derry, Hugh O'Doherty, claimed that partition 'drew a barbed wire entanglement around six counties'.[60] O'Doherty, as well as five of the nine county council chairmen of Ulster, sent a letter to the British government protesting against partition in late 1920.[61] The Derry No. 2 Rural District was informed by the Local Government Board that it would be annexed to the relevant body in Letterkenny by 1 April, as it was located in County Donegal, which would form part of Southern Ireland, with Derry forming part of Northern Ireland. This was much to the chagrin of unionist Derry Council members.[62] The Local Government Board 'also intimated that … the portion of County Armagh that is situated in the Castleblayney [Co. Monaghan] Union will be transferred to the Newry

[Co. Armagh] Union, and, similarly, Belleek district of Fermanagh will be transferred from the Ballyshannon [Co. Donegal] Union to the Enniskillen [Co. Fermanagh] Union'.[63] This suggestion was rejected by Sinn Féin in Fermanagh, which advised that the letter from the Local Government Board be 'thrown in the waste paper basket' and that 'Northern Sinn Feiners would never enter the Ulster Parliament'.[64] One observer, Godfrey Fetherstonhaugh from Dublin, claimed that 'by way of *reductio ad absurdum* that Donegal, the most northern county of Ireland, is to form part of "Southern" Ireland' with 'a narrow strip only a couple of miles wide, near Bundoran, being the connection' between Donegal and the rest of 'Southern' Ireland.[65]

The *Irish Times*, in an article written in February 1921, revealed the level of confusion surrounding partition at the time. Partition, it contended, would 'have old-established bodies to be broken up and destroyed, but, in most cases two new ones put in place of each old one. The heads of departments are called upon to decide what portion of their duties is concerned with Southern Ireland, and what with Northern they have to allocate their various staffs in the same way'.[66]

Many in the civil service, which was administered in Dublin, were reluctant to move to Belfast and uproot their families and homes, even in instances where their work solely related to the area that would become Northern Ireland.[67] George Chester Duggan, a civil servant who did move to Belfast, claimed that everyone in the civil service in Dublin 'seemed to believe that the Government of Ireland Act in its present form would never become law, that something would happen to prevent the partition of Ireland'.[68] Martin Maguire also asserts:

> For the civil service itself 'the nightmare of transfer to Belfast' as it was described in *Red Tape*, the civil service journal, seemed remote. Such was the conviction within the civil service associations that partition would not happen or, if it did, would not work, that they several times repeated their determination that they would remain as all-Ireland associations.[69]

Members of the old RIC from throughout Ireland did move to Northern Ireland in large numbers to join the Royal Ulster Constabulary (RUC) when it was formed in 1922, perhaps not surprising considering their unpopularity in most parts of Ireland at the time.[70] The leadership of the civil service trade unions worked to prevent the forced movement of civil servants to Belfast. They also secretly maintained contact with the revolutionary forces in Dáil Éireann, just in case Sinn Féin would be in power one day.[71]

The breaking up of the Department of Agriculture was particularly bemoaned, as it was seen as a great success since its formation twenty-one years earlier. However, two of its functions – namely, fisheries and the administration of the Diseases of Animals Acts, were reserved for the Council of Ireland.[72] There was a sense of nostalgia at the last all-Ireland Council of Agriculture meeting on 15 March 1921. At the meeting, T.P. Gill, council secretary, made the following resolution:

> That this Board, representative of all parts of Ireland, desire to place on record the fact that for twenty-one years they have worked together in unbroken harmony, in discharging the responsible duties entrusted to them, and they venture to express the hope that under some arrangement or other, this useful and gratifying co-operation will not be wholly dispensed with in the future.[73]

The Council of Agriculture had seen close cooperation between unionists and nationalists throughout its existence, as had other all-Ireland bodies, such as the Association of Municipal Authorities, where 'Southern *Sinn Feiners* and Northern Unionists' were known to work comfortably with each other.[74] The Royal College of Science, the Albert Model Farm in Glasnevin, the Royal Veterinary College at Ballsbridge, the National Museum and the Metropolitan School of Art were all administered by the Department of Agriculture, all based in Dublin. It was unclear how those institutions could be split in two, it not being an option to move half of them, in situ, to Belfast.[75] There was also confusion surrounding art treasures. Would the National Gallery in Dublin also be expected to be split in two, with half of its valuable contents shipped to Belfast and the other half remaining in Dublin?[76]

The *Freeman's Journal* posed the question, 'Will anyone even adduce a single fact to show that such breaking up is not ruinous from every point of view?'[77] Teachers met in Belfast in March 1921 to prepare for the impending six-counties education bill, where it was advised that 'individual representatives of the various organisations whose ramifications extend throughout all Ireland to keep in sympathy and close touch with the general ideals of those associations' until a proper Department of Education for Northern Ireland was formed.[78] As the body that controlled primary education in Ireland, the National Board, was not established through an act of parliament (the advisory committee members were nominated by the Lord Lieutenant of Ireland instead) there were doubts about whether the Government of Ireland Act was capable of breaking it up and establishing two education departments.[79] Insurance companies envisaged that they would be disastrously affected by partition. To illustrate the complications that 'the sea of confusion' of partition would bring, the *Freeman's Journal* provided a breakdown of health insurance holders in Ireland in April 1921:

> There are approximately 750,000 insured persons in Ireland who are members of Approved Societies. Of these about 474,000 reside in Southern Ireland and 276,000 in Northern Ireland. Of the 474,000 who reside in Southern Ireland it is estimated that 357,000 belong to societies with headquarters in Southern Ireland, 13,000 to societies with headquarters in Northern Ireland, and 94,000 to societies in Great Britain. Of the 276,000 who reside in Northern Ireland it is estimated that 119,000 belong to societies with headquarters in Northern Ireland, 50,000 to societies with headquarters in Southern Ireland, and 107,000 to societies with headquarters in Great Britain.[80]

The transfer of the National Health Insurance to the governments of Northern and Southern Ireland, it was believed, would seriously affect the ability of insurance companies to operate, considering the geographical composition of their membership.

Despite the substantial opposition to the Government of Ireland Act, the British government continued with its implementation. Elections for the two new parliaments were set for May 1921. The *Manchester Guardian* summed up what it saw as the seriously flawed nature of the government's actions:

To-day is the 'appointed day' under the Government of Ireland Act
... The date of the elections must be fixed, the machinery for
election under the novel system of proportional representation
must be provided, and many other arrangements for the division of
the administration and judicial machinery at present common to
the whole of Ireland into separate parts must be begun. It is an
extensive and a critical process, and will take place under conditions
the most adverse imaginable. The grant of self-government to
Ireland should have been an occasion full of rejoicing and hope,
and so with a consenting Ireland it would have been. But Ireland
has not consented; four-fifths of it has refused. The proffered gift is
not welcomed; it is rejected, and rejected with anger and with
scorn. An act which should have been an act of conciliation and
friendship has taken on the guise simply of another exercise of
power. It postulates calm and peace; it takes place in presence of
the extremes of violence and in an atmosphere of hate. It forebodes
not the cessation but the continuance of strife. Such are the fruits of
a policy which has substituted force for statesmanship, which
plants thorns and bids us gather grapes. It has brought us nothing
but suffering, failure, and disgrace. Is there not yet some remnant
of sense and courage among our governing men which shall suffice
to put an end now, at long last, to this travesty of justice, this
mockery of the very elements of wise statesmanship?[81]

The Government of Ireland Act came into effect on 3 May 1921. Three
weeks later, elections were held for the two parliaments. Known as the
'Partition Election', it determined the make-up of the first parliament of
the new entity that was Northern Ireland.

CHAPTER FOUR

Northern Ireland is Born

Although nationalists vehemently opposed the Government of Ireland Act, the nationalist parties still contested the election for Northern Ireland. Áine Ceannt, widow of executed Easter Rising leader Éamonn, disagreed with this decision, claiming that as Dáil Éireann was the only government she recognised, 'no one else would order a general election', and certainly not the British government whip.[1] Some commentators have contended that 'by participating in the Home Rule elections, Sinn Fein recognised partition and assisted in the establishment of a separate government for the six counties'.[2] Sinn Féin leader Éamon de Valera

> recognised the danger of contesting if Republicans and Nationalists couldn't be sure of winning at least ten seats. If they couldn't manage that, the British would claim that partition was justified, and it would be better to boycott the elections. But if they could realistically hope to win a quarter or so of the seats, 'the arguments are altogether in favour of vigorously contesting ... the representatives elected will become members of Dáil Éireann'. Failing to contest would also be taken as an acceptance of partition and would, according to de Valera, drive supporters into the Nationalist Party camp – 'a result which might later have a dangerous reactionary effect, by contagion, on the South'.[3]

Sinn Féin sought cooperation with the United Irish League (UIL), led by Joseph Devlin. Sinn Féin and the UIL signed an agreement on 17 March on the basis of 'accepting the principle of self-determination for Ireland, and abstaining from the Northern Parliament'. Both parties agreed to form an anti-partition ticket. They also agreed 'that each party would advise its supporters to give their lower preference to the candidates of the other party'.[4] All nationalists fought the election in Northern Ireland from an anti-partitionist stance, claiming partition would mean 'national suicide'.[5] According to Donal Hall:

> considerable effort, funded in a large part by Sinn Féin in Dublin, was put into [the] advertising and circulation of anti-partition pamphlets. The economic difficulties which Northern Ireland would face were emphasised, particularly the danger of the destruction of its commercial and industrial industries by the loss of their market in the south and west of Ireland. Farmers were warned that their prosperity was in danger because the urban industrial vote exceeded their political strength in the region.[6]

Sinn Féin's 'campaign, while vast in scale, was also marked by its crudity and lack of reference to Unionist sensibilities'.[7] Sinn Féin formed an internal sub-committee to run the propaganda campaign for the election in the north, with Sinn Féin and the Dáil contributing £1,000 each towards it. Membership of the sub-committee consisted of de Valera, Hanna Sheehy-Skeffington, Jenny Wyse-Power, Erskine Childers and Seán MacEntee. The sub-committee published a newspaper they called the *Unionist* and distributed it to unionist strongholds.[8] Unionists were warned by legitimate unionist newspapers, such as the *Belfast Newsletter*, that 'the periodical is on the side of the enemy, and that the title has been adopted with the intention of deceiving Unionist electors'.[9] The same newspaper also claimed Sinn Féin had signed a treaty with the Bolsheviks, 'binding for ten years', where the Bolsheviks would 'provide the rebels with arms and to give their leaders permission to study military and naval problems in Russia'.[10] Éamonn Donnelly, Sinn Féin organiser for Ulster, claimed the only effect their literature and leaflets would have on the unionist community would be 'to bring them out to vote against us in great numbers'.[11] Despite Sinn Féin's wholehearted election campaign, it had to overcome considerable intimidation. It was an illegal organisation and of the nineteen candidates, eight were either in jail or interned, and seven were on the run. Its 'candidates, organisers, and supporters were attacked; raids on the houses of Sinn Féin election organisers were carried out; and speakers and election agents were arrested'.[12] Éamonn Donnelly accused opponents of 'wholesale terrorism' on the day of the election, 24 May 1921.[13]

Chastened by the results of local elections in 1920, unionists were determined to maximise their vote for the 1921 general election. Like the local elections, the PR system of voting was used for the general election – the first time it was used in a general election in Britain or Ireland. All unionist candidates were greatly assisted by the Ulster Women's Unionist Council, which coordinated canvassing events with the men's association, provided funding, held classes and showed films explaining the novel PR voting system.[14] On the issue of women being selected as candidates, the president of the Ulster Women's Unionist Council, the Duchess of Abercorn, 'expressed the opinion that the time was not ripe for this, and the essential thing in the first Parliament was to preserve the safety of the Unionist cause, that much organisation and construction work would be necessary for which perhaps women had not the necessary experience, and except in the case of outstanding qualifications, men candidates were preferable'.[15]

Many members disagreed with her, believing women candidates were necessary to address issues such as 'Poor Law reform, which will necessitate re-organisation of the system of Medical Relief, some form of provision for necessitous widows with children, and drastic reform of the laws affecting the unmarried mother and her child'.[16] Two female unionist candidates did run – Dehra Chichester (she became Dehra Parker after 1928) and Julia McMordie – and both were elected.[17] In fact, all forty unionist candidates were elected to the northern parliament.

Held on Empire Day, 24 May, the general election, with a turnout of 89 per cent, was an astounding victory for Ulster unionists, who won all but twelve of the fifty-two seats. Sinn Féin won just six seats, with the UIL winning the other six. It was a bitter blow for Sinn Féin; de Valera had predicted that at least seventeen, if not half the seats, would be won by nationalists.[18] Indicative of the lack of penetration of Sinn Féin in the north were the profiles of the six people elected under its banner: de Valera, Michael Collins, Arthur Griffith, Eoin MacNeill, Seán Milroy and Seán O'Mahony. Most of them were high-profile figures in the south, with O'Mahony the only one not also elected to a Southern Ireland constituency.

The UIL result showed its dependence on Devlin, who won two of its six seats, in Antrim and West Belfast. The unionist victory prompted Carson to say to Bonar Law, the Conservative Party leader, that 'It would take a very brave man … to take away Ulster's parliament'.[19] Winston Churchill similarly claimed, 'From that moment the position of Ulster became unassailable'.[20] The breakdown of the results showed the truly sectarian nature of the electorate. Ernest Clark sent John Anderson, the Under Secretary of Ireland in Dublin Castle, a letter with a table (see Table 1) showing 'that the percentage of votes cast for the Unionists and the other party respectively was almost identical with the percentage of Protestants and Roman Catholics in the various constituencies'.[21]

The elected nationalists decided to abstain from taking their seats in the new Northern Ireland parliament, thus granting unionists a monopoly on proceedings.[22] For the Southern Ireland parliament, not one seat was contested. Sinn Féin secured 124 seats – every seat except for the four seats in Dublin University.[23] Sinn Féin used the occasion to elect a second Dáil.[24] Outside of Northern Ireland, the Government of Ireland Act was effectively ignored. Commenting on its one and only meeting, the *Irish Times* remarked, 'The formal opening of the Southern Parliament in Dublin on June 28 was a subdued spectacle. Fifteen senators and four Commoners – the members for Trinity College – attended'.[25]

The northern parliament held its first official sitting on 7 June in Belfast's City Hall, where the state opening was also held later in the month. Such was the makeshift nature of the new entity that a temporary home had to be found at the Presbyterian church in Ireland's Assembly College from September 1921, with a permanent parliament in Stormont not opened until 1932.[26] In October, the northern government decided not to install electric lighting in the temporary parliament, as it was not an 'absolutely necessary' expense.[27] At the first meeting, Hugh O'Neill, was elected the speaker of the house.[28] Four days later, twenty-four people were elected to the upper house, the senate. The senate consisted of twenty-six members, the other two were 'the Lord Mayor of Belfast and Mayor of Londonderry – sitting *ex officio*'.[29] Whilst the senators in the north were elected from the northern House of Commons, the southern senate had to include different minority groups. Patrick Buckland claims that 'Ulster unionists justified this difference … by arguing that the circumstances of

Table 1. 1921 Northern Ireland general election vote breakdown per constituency, based on religion and political party

	Votes Polled (Excluding Spoiled Votes) 1st Preference						Percentage of Votes Polled					% of Population Census 1911	
	Total	Unionist	Independent & Socialist	Nationalist	Sinn Féin	Nationalist & Sinn Féin	Unionist	Independent & Socialist	Nationalist	Sinn Féin	Nationalist & Sinn Féin	Protestant	Roman Catholic
Antrim	79949	64269	–	9448	6232	15680	80.39	–	11.82	7.79	19.611	79.5	20.5
Armagh	46532	25718	–	6857	13957	20814	55.27	–	14.74	29.99	44.73	54.67	45.33
Down	81180	55930	1188	7644	16418	24062	68.90	1.46	9.42	20.22	29.64	68.44	31.56
Fermanagh & Tyrone	83701	37935	–	12591	33175	45766	45.32	–	15.43	39.25	54.68	43.40	56.60
Derry	53988	30330	–	7772	15886	23658	56.18	–	14.40	29.42	43.82	54.20	45.80
Belfast not Queen's University Belfast	165514	127448	2813	16502	18751	35253	77.00	1.70	9.97	11.33	21.30	75.90	24.10
Total	510864	341630	4001	60814	104419	165233	66.87	.79	11.90	20.44	32.34	65.60	34.40

Source: PRONI – D1022/2/17 – Files of Correspondence, mainly between Clark and Sir James Craig, Dealing with Various Aspects of the Setting Up of the Northern Ireland Ministries and Departments – 1921–1922, 28 May 1921.

the minorities differed: the southern minority would be virtually unrepresented in the southern House of Commons, whereas northern nationalists and Catholics would have considerable representation in the northern House of Commons'.[30] Joseph Devlin claimed this arrangement was 'the most dishonest' transaction he had heard in his life.[31] James Craig, the Prime Minister, and his cabinet also took up office in early June. The cabinet consisted of Hugh Pollock as Minister of Finance, Richard Dawson-Bates as Minister of Home Affairs, Lord Londonderry as Minister of Education, John Andrews as Minister of Labour and Edward Archdale as Minister of Agriculture and Minister of Commerce.[32] At the cabinet's first meeting on 15 June, Northern Ireland's twenty representatives for the Council of Ireland were selected – thirteen from the House of Commons and seven from the senate.[33] That meeting was primarily concerned with arranging the state opening of the northern parliament by King George V a week later.

22 June 1921 was a day of pomp and ceremony as it ushered in a new era in Ireland's history. Despite 'dire warnings', the king and queen came to Belfast to officially open the new parliament. Belfast was draped with flags and bunting; pavements and lamp posts were painted red, white and blue. On the city streets, many banners reading 'We will not have Home Rule' were visible.[34] The irony seemed lost on the banner holders that this was a Home Rule jurisdiction, up and running before one in the south was. The event was boycotted by almost the entire Catholic community, with Cardinal Logue turning down his invitation to the opening ceremony due to 'a prior engagement'.[35] For the opening ceremony, Craig drafted a speech that 'greatly distressed' the king. 'He feels he is being made a mouthpiece of Ulster in the speech rather than that of the Empire.'[36] The king felt that Lloyd George, the British Prime Minister, and not Craig, should be responsible for the king's speech; it was not up to Ulster to dictate the king's utterances. The king's speech was subsequently changed, partly written by Lloyd George and partly on the advice of Jan Smuts, South African Prime Minister. Smuts convinced King George V to use his speech as an olive branch to Sinn Féin, as the 'establishment of the Northern Parliament definitely eliminates the coercion of Ulster' and cleared the road 'to deal on the most statesmanlike lines with the rest of Ireland'.[37] In his pacifying speech, the king appealed 'to all Irishmen to pause, to stretch out the hand

of forbearance and conciliation, to forgive and to forget, and to join in making for the land which they love a new era of peace, contentment, and goodwill', paving the way for the truce between Sinn Féin and British forces weeks later.[38]

Notwithstanding the fanfare surrounding the occasion and the conciliatory speech delivered by the king, violence and the threat of it permeated the new jurisdiction. On the day of the ceremony itself, 'there was enormous security, with armed policemen placed in commandeered houses along the route'.[39] To mark the occasion, the IRA attacked 'a troop train returning from the official opening of the Belfast Parliament', derailing it 'at Adavoyle on the Louth/Armagh border. Four men and eighty horses were killed'.[40] The majority of the first cabinet meetings of the northern government were dominated with security issues. On 23 June, Nevil Macready and John Anderson were present to highlight measures being planned to curb Sinn Féin and the IRA, including 'the establishment of Posts along the Border of Ulster, and the invention of a very strict Passport system', which, it was hoped, would 'curtail Passenger Service to less than one-fourth of its present dimensions' into Ireland.[41] Before the truce of 11 July 1921, the British military had proposed that in southern Ireland, 'all males between the ages of 16 and 50 will be required to provide themselves with Identification Cards. The Identification Card will include a Photograph of the Bearer'.[42] The authorities believed the identification system would be 'ineffective unless the Government of Northern Ireland will consent to establish a similar system along a belt on the frontier line, running from the Coast of County Down to the Sea Coast on the Southern Border of Donegal'.[43] The northern government promised to assist the British authorities by

> introducing a Passport system similar to that in the South, but so arranged that the facilities for obtaining Passports by all loyal persons in the North should be as easy as possible. It was agreed that Passport Offices would be necessary in Londonderry as well as Belfast, but that Newry might reasonably be restricted owing to its being really in the 'disturbed' area.[44]

Wickham, commissioner of the Specials, doubted the system would be effective given that there were '110 roads across the Southern frontier of

Northern Ireland' and that 'Sinn Fein gangs' would be able to 'congregate North of the Belt and commit their atrocities'.[45] With the truce of 11 July, the identification system was abandoned. Whilst hostilities ceased in the south, the birth of Northern Ireland in the summer of 1921 had witnessed another wave of intense sectarian violence engulfing Belfast, resulting in 'the highest number of casualties since the shipyard expulsions of the previous summer'.[46]

.   After a RIC constable was killed in Belfast on 10 June, three Catholics were dragged from their homes the following night and shot dead as a reprisal. Two more Catholics were killed similarly after a 'B' Special was shot on 12 June. There was intense rioting in York Street, where 150 Catholic families were driven from their homes. Catholic families were forced to live in schools, halls and other makeshift accommodation. A bomb was thrown into the Catholic Dock Lane, killing one man and injuring twenty. Fourteen people were killed in Belfast in June 1921 – ten Catholics and four Protestants.[47] On the eve of the truce, 10 July 1921, fourteen people were killed and over 150 Catholic homes burnt down. It became known as Belfast's 'Bloody Sunday'.[48] The timing of the truce, 11 July, a day before the most testing day in Ulster, further inflamed the sectarian violence. As a result of the truce, the Specials were demobilised, and the IRA was officially recognised, a move vehemently opposed by the northern government:

> the withdrawal of the protection hitherto afforded, by which peace was secured in this area, cannot be justified, in view of the occurrences during the past week, beginning with the murderous attack by Sinn Fein Gunmen on the Police in Belfast on Sunday last, and culminating in last night's riots, when many persons were shot, including a young girl killed, and Mr. Grant, M.P. [Labour Member for Duncairn], and District-Inspector of Police wounded.[49]

There were many Specials to demobilise. According to Michael Farrell, by July 1921, there were 3,515 'A' Specials, just under 16,000 'B' Specials and 1,310 'C' Specials.[50] The truce, which by and large held in the south, was 'not observed by either side in the north,' according to IRA member Tom Fitzpatrick. Another IRA member, Roger McCorley, claimed that in

Belfast, 'the Truce itself lasted six hours only'.[51] The truce saw the IRA gain new respect from the Catholic community and many new recruits, mockingly dubbed 'Trucileers' by IRA veterans.[52] With the demobilisation of the Specials, loyalists joined the revived UVF and new vigilante groups such as the 'Imperial Guards' and 'Cromwell Clubs'. They filled the void left by the Specials until full responsibility of policing was handed over to the northern government in November 1921.[53] This move, on top of transferring other services at the same time, further increased the legitimacy of the northern jurisdiction, which beforehand was seen merely as a 'glorified county council'.[54] Patrick Buckland maintains that even with services transferred, the northern government was 'given responsibility without real power'.[55]

When Northern Ireland came into being in the summer of 1921, the jurisdiction had very limited powers. In its first year of existence, Westminster controlled about 88 per cent of Northern Ireland's revenue and 60 per cent of its expenditure.[56] Its fiscal functions were extremely restricted, with Westminster reserving the power to levy income tax and customs and excise.[57] On the same day that the northern government came into existence, 7 June, the *Belfast Gazette* was issued for the first time to publish government notices, announcing the specific functions of each government department 'without prejudice to the powers and duties of existing departments and authorities pending the transfer of services'.[58] The northern domain had come into existence, but it needed to be equipped with government services. The transfer of services was stalled due to only one of the Irish jurisdictions being operational under the Government of Ireland Act. The British government insisted that both Irish governments needed to be in place in order for this to happen, something that was acutely embarrassing for the northern government. It had no control over its policing or its laws.

With the creation of a border, there were numerous teething problems, many of a legal nature. Soon after Northern Ireland came into being, the Manorhamilton Board of Guardians in County Leitrim heard a case of a man in distress seeking relief. The man had recently received four shillings of relief money from Enniskillen, now part of a new jurisdiction.[59] A Donegal man who was summoned to the Derry Petty Sessions Court for selling adulterated buttermilk claimed the Derry magistrates had no jurisdiction over Donegal. The case was adjourned.[60] Two judges, one who was County Court judge for counties Armagh and Louth and the other who was County Court judge for counties Monaghan and Fermanagh, solved the problem caused by partition, with one taking on responsibility for the two counties in Northern Ireland and the other for counties Monaghan and Louth.[61] The Law Society claimed that solicitors in Ireland now had to contend themselves with three legal systems instead of one, which had been the case for centuries.[62]

Samuel Watt, Permanent Secretary to the northern Ministry of Home Affairs, contended that by delaying the transfer of services, 'the whole of the northern government will prove to be a farce, and that the northern parliament will be nothing more than a debating society, as it will not have the power to legislate on or discuss any matter arising out of the services to be transferred'.[63] The northern House of Commons was adjourned for a lengthy period, from 24 June until 20 September 1921. A cabinet meeting beforehand believed 'the Government would be in a very unsatisfactory position when Parliament met on September 20th, without any Financial powers, and with no Departments for the Ministers which had been set up'.[64] On resuming in September, Craig and his government were inundated with questions regarding the delay in the transfer of services, particularly in relation to policing. At one session on 27 September, the Minister of Home Affairs, Dawson-Bates, was unable to satisfactorily answer questions relating to issues such as non-compliant county councils (Tyrone and Fermanagh), state grants, road maintenance and motor licenses due to the northern government still waiting to have control over the local government for the area.[65] Craig stated:

> my chief reason for asking for so prolonged an interval was that I hoped we would have been in a position to secure the transfer of various services under the Government of Ireland Act, that my Ministers would have their departments in thorough-going order, and that we could report, at all events, to the House, not necessarily the possibility of immediate legislation but at all events that the full machinery of Government was now in your hands, and that you would be able to proceed, as we have all been looking forward to, with the carrying out of the Act passed by the Imperial Parliament.[66]

One of the main reasons for the delay in the transfer of services was the changed situation in Ireland due to the truce with Sinn Féin. This led to a change in the prioritising of the Irish question for the British government. According to John McColgan, 'in the summer of 1921 a new phase emerged in which the task of transferring full powers to the government of Northern Ireland was subordinated to the requirements of the larger Irish policy – the need to reach agreement with the South'.[67] This was reflected in Dublin Castle's tardiness in assisting Ernest Clark in establishing a civil service for Northern Ireland. Craig complained to Hamar Greenwood about the delay in the transfer of services and staff from Dublin Castle. There was also bad blood between Dublin Castle and Belfast, where 'stories were circulating Dublin departments to the effect that the better posts in the prospective Northern administration were being reserved for certain officials in London and Dublin departments with influence in the North'. Clark countered by stating 'that the various departments in Dublin are selecting their "duds" for submission to the civil service committee as suitable for transfer'.[68] The northern government also expressed dissatisfaction with the civil service examinations being only held in Dublin and wanted a centre established in Belfast for the 'forthcoming Typists' Examination in September'.[69]

The role for Catholics in the northern civil service was uncertain from the start. At a cabinet meeting, the Ulster Ex-Service Association objected to the appointment of J.V. Coyle to the Department of Agriculture. Archdale, the Minister of Agriculture and Commerce, stated that 'Mr. Coyle was a Roman Catholic, a loyalist he had known for 20 years and he proposed to appoint him as his Head of one of his branches.' At the same meeting, the government committed to 'enrol members of all creeds in their Staff provided their loyalty was unquestioned'.[70] However, when the British Treasury recommended H.P. Boland for appointment to a senior post in the new Northern Ireland civil service as an official with 'a wide and varied experience of civil service administration … intimately concerned with the reorganisation of several large departments', and who had 'an exceptionable knowledge of the various problems of civil service organisation', Boland, a Catholic, was turned down. The northern government responded with "Thank you very much, but no. I believe you know the reason why".[71] It was clear that very few Catholics would find a place in the new civil service.

By June 1921, Craig and his colleagues had achieved a number of key milestones that safeguarded their future by not being subservient to a Dublin parliament. The Government of Ireland Act was passed into law, elections were held in the six counties and a parliament had been convened. The machinery of government was taking shape without the transfer of services required to give it further structure. Despite these victories, the future of Northern Ireland as an entity in its original form was still uncertain. This became clear once the British government began its negotiations with Sinn Féin following the truce in July 1921.

CHAPTER FIVE

The Treaty

Sinn Féin secured a clear mandate from three provinces of Ireland at the 1918 and 1921 general elections. In Ulster, it did not achieve such a mandate and battled with the Irish Parliamentary Party/United Irish League for hegemony within the nationalist community, with both of them significantly below the level of political support for Ulster unionism in the province. With the electoral destruction of the Irish Parliamentary Party in 1918, Sinn Féin became the effective voice of Irish nationalism. At this juncture, the partition of Ireland was being enforced, yet Sinn Féin had no coherent policy on the issue. Other than the counter-productive Belfast Boycott, the party was devoid of any clear strategy to end partition or deal with it. With the birth of the northern jurisdiction and the truce of July 1921, it had to finally confront the issue head-on.

In the preceding years, Sinn Féin leaders tended to over emphasise the blame attributed to Britain for causing partition and to downplay the real hostility of Ulster unionists to being governed by a Dublin parliament. There seemed a genuine, albeit wholly naïve belief that if Britain withdrew from Ireland, Ulster unionists would be open to a united Ireland. De Valera felt that the troubles in Ulster were 'due to British guile and nothing else'.[1] Sinn Féin founder Arthur Griffith claimed the division of Ireland was 'unnatural', maintaining that if the Ulster unionists did not have the backing of the British government, 'we could settle the Ulster question'.[2] Likewise, another Sinn Féin leader, Michael Collins, maintained that 'the tendency of sentiment in the North East, when not interfered with ... was national, and in favour of freedom and unity'.[3] Whilst not holding a monopoly on threatening rhetoric, some of the comments made by Sinn Féin representatives were not conducive to creating a favourable impression amongst the unionist community. De Valera often described Ulster

unionists as a 'foreign garrison' and 'not Irish people'. If they rejected Sinn
Féin solutions, 'they would have to go under', and if they stood 'in our way
to freedom we will clear you out of it'.[4] Griffith stated that Ulster unionists
'must make up their minds either to throw in their lot with the Irish nation
or stand out as the English garrison. If they did the latter the Irish nation
must deal with them.'[5] Cahir Healy, writing as Sinn Féin MP for Fermanagh
and Tyrone in 1925, attacked the party's policy towards the north in the
years since 1916:

> The truth is that none of the Irish leaders understood the northern
> situation or the northern mind. Griffith, the sanest and best
> informed of them all, nursed a delusion for years – that the
> (solution) of the problem lay in London. Not even de Valera's non-
> recognition of it nor the rather jumpy efforts which, with Collins,
> passed for statecraft, could possibly bring us one day nearer peace.[6]

De Valera modified his views, becoming open to accommodating unionists
in a federal Ireland externally associated within the British Commonwealth.[7]
He moved from a stance of 'Ulster must be coerced if she stood in the way'
to one of ruling out the use of force against Ulster by 1921.[8]

This more conciliatory approach was evident in his willingness to meet
Craig in May 1921. Alfred Cope from Dublin Castle 'arranged a "theatrically
clandestine" but essentially pointless meeting on 5 May between de Valera
and James Craig'.[9] Craig courageously agreed to 'be conducted by a number
of IRA men to meet de Valera. The party changed cars before arriving at a
house on Howth Road protected by a number of guards disguised as
workmen.'[10] Craig wanted an agreement on the border; de Valera wanted
an agreement on Irish unity. Both were as unrealistic as the other. Craig
claimed that de Valera spent the time 'harping on the grievances of ... the
last 700 years ... After half an hour he had reached the era of Brian Boru.
After another half hour he had advanced to the period of some king a
century or two later. By this time I was getting tired.'[11] Although no
agreement was reached, they both expressed an openness to meet again,
but this never happened. The meeting also showed that Craig was open to
negotiating with Sinn Féin. The meeting was supported by his party, the
hierarchy of the Catholic Church, Ulster farmers and 'the trading

community is also pleased as there looks to be a hope that by some understanding the boycott can be lifted'.[12]

Just days after King George V's speech at the state opening of the northern parliament, Lloyd George invited de Valera, 'the chosen leader of the great majority in Southern Ireland', and Craig, 'Premier of Northern Ireland', to negotiations, without preconditions – another step towards a truce. Equally, it could be construed as recognition of partition by de Valera if he accepted.[13] De Valera turned down the invitation, as it denied 'Ireland's essential unity' and instead sought a conference in Dublin with 'certain representatives of the political minority in this country', including Craig, the Earl of Midleton (William St John Fremantle Brodrick), Sir Maurice E. Dockrell, Sir Robert H. Woods and Andrew Jameson. He also believed if he went to a conference in London with Craig, 'they would be like two bad boys and would start fighting themselves at once and the Government would exploit their differences'.[14] In his letter to invitees, de Valera stated:

> The reply which I, as spokesman for the Irish Nation, shall make to Mr. Lloyd George will affect the lives and fortunes of the political minority in this island, no less than those of the majority.
>
> Before sending the reply, therefore, I would like to confer with you and to learn from you at first hand the views of a certain section of our people of whom you are representative.[15]

All accepted de Valera's invitation, except Craig, who replied to his 'namesake in Dublin Senate' that he had 'already accepted the Prime Minister's invitation to London Conference'.[16] For 'sheer impertinence it could hardly be beaten' claimed Craig's wife.[17]

Craig was not involved in the talks between de Valera and Lloyd George following the truce in July. He informed Cope: 'I'm going to sit on Ulster like a rock, we are content with what we have got – let the Prime Minister and Sinn Fein settle this and if possible leave us out.'[18] He wanted to make Northern Ireland 'a new impregnable Pale'.[19] Craig believed that 'no coercion of Ulster' was among Lloyd George's non-negotiable commitments. On 18 July, however, Lloyd George put forward 'five suggestions to Craig and his ministers as to how they might accommodate de Valera's requirement of Irish unity with local autonomy for the north devolved from Dublin.[20] Craig and his colleagues emphatically rejected them and Lloyd George backed down. Two days later, Lloyd George made his proposal to de Valera of offering Southern Ireland a dominion settlement. De Valera rejected the proposals, instead demanding 'that Ulster should become a part of the Irish Dominion. Failing this, he demanded, as his only alternative, complete independence for Southern Ireland.'[21] Lloyd George suggested that Craig meet with de Valera again, as another meeting was the only way to make 'him realise that Ulster is a fact which he must recognise, not a figment bolstered up by the British Government as a counter to Sinn Fein. He does not understand this. Till he understands it, I fear that a settlement will always be unattainable.'[22] Craig replied that he would only meet de Valera if he 'accepted the principle of Ulster's independent rights, and that he gave a written statement to that effect.'[23] This stance was repeated when de Valera invited him to attend a conference in Castlebellingham in County Louth in late July.[24]

De Valera remained adamant that 'we cannot admit the right of the British government to mutilate our country, either in its own interest, or at the call of any section of our population.'[25] Importantly, he also stated, 'we do not contemplate the use of force. If your Government stands aside, we can effect a complete reconciliation. We agree with you "that no common action can be secured by force".'[26] He followed up by stating in the Dáil on 22 August that they 'had not the power, and some of them had not the inclination, to use force with Ulster. He did not think that policy would be successful.'[27] At the same meeting, he also declared:

> as far as dual nationality was concerned, they never recognised it, but that fact would not prevent the British government from establishing it. For his part, if the Republic were recognised, he would be in favour of giving each county power to vote itself out of the Republic if it so wished. Otherwise they would be compelled to use force.[28]

The one 'certain result' of the county option would have been the gain of counties Tyrone and Fermanagh to the south at the expense of the north, something the Earl of Midleton 'believed that the Sinn Féin leadership was especially covetous of' and that there would be 'no more trouble' if they were transferred.[29] During the impasse between de Valera's talks with Lloyd George in July and the negotiations in October, Sinn Féin established a committee to 'collect, compile and arrange … statements of fact and argument bearing on the position of Ulster'. It had the remit to address the 'challenge which Ulster posed to the Sinn Féin cabinet' and 'devise a policy tolerable both to their own supporters and to the British government and which could also be imposed on the Ulster unionists'.[30] The suggestion made by some northern Sinn Féin members to set up an advisory body of experts on the north to support the negotiation team in London was not taken up, however.[31]

Much has been written about the Anglo-Irish negotiations from October to December 1921. That the Sinn Féin plenipotentiaries had a number of disadvantages in comparison to the British delegation was clear. Chief amongst these was the vast experience of the British parliamentarians over the Sinn Féin negotiators. The Sinn Féin negotiation team consisted of Griffith, Collins, Robert Barton, Éamonn Duggan and George Gavan Duffy. The British team consisting of people like Lloyd George, Winston Churchill and Lord Birkenhead was accustomed to stringent debate and opposition in Westminster, unlike the Irish delegates, who were part of what was essentially a talking shop – the Dáil. Lloyd George claimed the Irish delegates 'are simple; they have none of the skill of the old nationalists; these men are not accustomed to finessing'.[32] Most of the British parliamentarians had no respect for the Irish, with Bonar Law declaring 'the Irish were an inferior race'.[33]

During the negotiations, the two primary issues discussed were Ulster and the crown. Were the talks to fail, 'the British were determined that the break should come on the issue of sovereignty, while the Irish were intent that it should be Ulster'.[34] The Irish were successful in reopening the Ulster question and rekindling matters that the unionists thought were settled. Lloyd George admitted they had a weaker case on Ulster, stating 'while British soldiers might die for the throne and empire, I do not know who will die for Tyrone and Fermanagh'.[35] The Irish delegation began with the position that 'the unimpaired unity of Ireland is a condition precedent to the conclusion of a Treaty of Association between Ireland and the nations of the British Commonwealth'.[36] On 17 October, the Sinn Féin proposals on Ulster contained concessions that weakened their hand from the outset; their proposals were in line with de Valera's utterances in the preceding weeks. According to John McColgan:

> The Unionists were offered the option of joining with the South or of maintaining local autonomy (over an area to be determined by plebiscite) subject to overriding authority from Dublin. Thus, instead of demanding complete Irish unity at the start, Sinn Féin opened negotiations giving away ground on Ulster. This approach probably prejudiced their chances of forcing the break on Ulster.[37]

It has also been argued that by this move, 'Sinn Fein had ... implicitly accepted partition by arguing that the state of Northern Ireland should be subservient to Dublin rather than London.'[38] During the negotiations, Lloyd George had to expend as much energy in soothing unionist (both Ulster and Conservative) fears as he did in negotiating with Sinn Féin. Although Craig and Bonar Law were not 'the elephants in the room', they were 'the elephants outside the door'.[39] Lloyd George told Griffith, 'we could not coerce Ulster. There was the same strain in the argument of de Valera as I have [heard] here this morning, that Ulster would come in if we let her alone ... It is a mistake to assume that the population of Ulster for the time being is opposed to partition. It is not.'[40] Nevertheless, once the Irish delegation stated that their allegiance to crown and empire was contingent on Ireland's 'essential unity', Lloyd George and others within the British government appeared open to changing Northern Ireland's status if Sinn Féin would accept allegiance to the crown.[41] Austen Chamberlain, one of the British delegates, explained to his wife that 'the six counties was a compromise, and, like all compromises, is illogical and indefensible'.[42] After the negotiations had concluded, correspondence was published between Lloyd George and Craig, where the former said in November that 'two dominions in Ireland was impractical and indefensible'.[43] He 'decried the idea of a partition that would involve "cutting the natural circuits of commercial activity", and said that "when such frontiers are established they harden into permanence".'[44] Lloyd George unsuccessfully tried to squeeze Craig into accepting an all-Ireland parliament. Craig did not budge; instead, he 'proposed that Northern Ireland should become a dominion "based on 'equality of status' with the South", a proposal that came "as a shock to those accustomed to receive their passionate assurances of union"' and demonstrated that unionists were somewhat flexible in their relationship with the union.[45]

Craig had become increasingly wary of Lloyd George since the latter's five suggestions in July of local autonomy for the north within a Dublin parliament. He was aware of Lloyd George's cunning and duplicity and also of Northern Ireland's vulnerability. Ulster unionists noticed a cooling of their relationship with senior figures within the Conservative Party. John Andrews, northern labour minister, condemned the attempted 'disgraceful betrayal of Ulster' by members of the British government.[46] Lloyd George's overtures in July prompted the northern cabinet to agree

> that everything in the situation pointed to the desirability of Northern Ireland consolidating its position as quickly as possible, and it was decided to carry on with the establishment of the new Parliament rapidly. The Prime Minister undertook to write to the Chief Secretary in regard to the early appointment of the Civil Service Committee, which had been suspended pending the establishment of some form of Government in Southern Ireland.[47]

Under the Government of Ireland Act, a civil service committee was set up to allocate civil service staff to the northern and southern jurisdictions. The committee could only function once both governments were established and had nominated their representatives to the committee.[48] With no southern government in operation, Craig protested that the north was being 'left in mid-air' and suggested setting up a government in Southern Ireland ruled by the Lord Lieutenant or as a crown colony, or, alternatively, scrapping the idea of a civil service committee altogether.[49] As the year progressed, he pressed harder for the transfer of services to Northern Ireland. Craig had appeared open to cooperating with Sinn Féin earlier in 1921, particularly through the Council of Ireland. He talked of a future of competition and rivalry between Northern Ireland and Southern Ireland and of using the Council of Ireland to address all-Ireland problems. At a lunch in Belfast in February 1921, he spoke of his 'hope not only for a brilliant prospect for Ulster, but a brilliant future for Ireland'.[50] That same month, Craig stated, 'The rights of the minority must be sacred to the majority ... it will only be by broad views, tolerant ideas and a real desire for liberty of conscience that we can make an ideal of the Parliament and the executive'.[51] One of the first actions of the Northern government was to select its twenty members to sit on the Council of Ireland, led by Craig (see Chapter Four). In declining to meet de Valera at a conference, he pointed out that they could instead meet at the council once it convened.[52] Craig also appeared receptive to an all-Ireland council of finance, suggested by Arthur Griffith during the treaty negotiations.[53] This openness changed, however, once he spoke to Churchill and Birkenhead. The return of Bonar Law, 'an Orangeman and a fanatic', back to the political scene after an absence due to ill-health also added to Craig's resolve.[54] Griffith noticed that by mid-November, Craig had 'become more intractable as a result of the people he had met here in London'.[55]

Craig refused to concede any ground to Lloyd George and instead won a major concession from him. On 5 November, Lloyd George agreed to transfer services to Northern Ireland without the existence of a government in the south. The Lord Lieutenant was empowered to appoint, on a temporary basis, Southern Ireland's representatives of the civil service committee, and services were scheduled to be transferred to the north between 22 November 1921 and 1 February 1922.[56] That Lloyd George, the wily negotiator, would grant rather than receive concessions from Craig suggests that his commitment to an all-Ireland solution was not wholly sincere. The Irish delegation were aware that the northern jurisdiction was not fully functioning when the negotiations began in October; services being withheld by the British demonstrated that partition could be negotiable, but they appeared unaware of how to use this to their advantage. The significance of services being transferred to the north seemed lost on almost all of those in Dublin too.[57] The main opposition in Dublin came from the civil service itself. From 9 November, the Dublin Castle departments were commanded to assign officers for temporary transfer to the north. Whilst Craig sat on his rock of Ulster, 'the civil service sat on the rock of the Civil Service Committee ... confident that whatever would emerge from the London negotiations would be at least as good as existing terms and might be even better'.[58] To prevent the enforced transfer of staff to Belfast, the civil service representative body, the Irish Civil Service Association, took a case to the High Court, further stalling the transfer of staff.[59] This did not greatly perturb Craig or Clark, who had been filling the northern civil service with Ulstermen they considered loyal.[60] In fact, it suited them not to have too many staff transferred from Dublin, particularly those staff members who did not want to be there. Craig was satisfied that finance and, most importantly, law and order, had successfully been transferred, with agricultural services to be transferred by 1 January and education services by 1 February 1922.[61] The transfer of powers of law and order gave the Northern government control over the RIC in the six counties and allowed it to remobilise the Specials.[62] Clark's role in Dublin Castle was discontinued, and he became Permanent Secretary to the Ministry of Finance and head of the civil service in Northern Ireland.[63] The judiciary was transferred to Northern Ireland on 1 October, with a formal opening of the new courts taking place three weeks later.[64]

With the possibility of reaching a settlement by pressurising Craig now ended, Lloyd George looked to squeeze the Sinn Féin delegation instead. His secretary, Tom Jones, dangled the idea of a boundary commission in front of Griffith and Collins. Collins was against the proposal, as 'it sacrificed unity entirely'. When he enquired why the British would not concede to local plebiscites, cabinet member Austen Chamberlain could only reply meekly, claiming that 'you could not put a more difficult question to us in the light of the history of recent years'.[65] Griffith, however, 'was not alarmed'.[66] He believed the Ulster cabinet would not accept such an offer. Initially, the openness in relation to accepting a boundary commission was a tactical move 'to deprive "Ulster" of support in England by showing it was utterly unreasonable in insisting to coerce areas that wished to get out'.[67] Griffith did believe there would be benefits to it, writing to de Valera that the Boundary Commission 'would give us most of Tyrone, Fermanagh, and part of Armagh, Down, etc.'.[68] Griffith naively interpreted his assurances regarding a boundary commission as a ploy to help Lloyd George secure Irish unity. Instead, his assurances resulted in an animated Lloyd George using them against him as the negotiations reached their conclusion, leading to Griffith and the rest of the Irish delegation signing the Anglo-Irish Treaty on the morning of 6 December 1921.

The Anglo-Irish Treaty's main provision relating to Ulster was Article 12. It stipulated that if Northern Ireland opted not to join the Irish Free State, as was its right under the treaty, a boundary commission would determine the border 'in accordance with the wishes of the inhabitants, so far as may be compatible with economic and geographic conditions'.[69] Although Northern Ireland was nominally included in the Irish Free State, 'in reality the inclusion of a clause allowing the north-east to opt out of Dublin jurisdiction, something they were to do at the first opportunity in December 1922, was merely window-dressing to disguise the established fact of partition'.[70] Central to the problem with the Boundary Commission was its ambiguity. No 'timetable was mentioned or method outlined to ascertain these wishes; how exactly economic and geographic conditions would relate to popular opinion, and which would prove most important'.[71] No plebiscite was asked for, the clause was open to a number of different interpretations and no time was specified for the convening of the commission. The ambiguity suited Lloyd George perfectly. On one hand, he could give the impression to Sinn Féin that large tracts of Northern Ireland would be transferred to the south. On the other hand, he could give the impression to Craig that it would rationalise the cumbersome border, with perhaps the inclusion of Protestant strongholds to the north. The duplicity of Lloyd George in 1916 in his dealings with Carson and Redmond was clearly forgotten. The Sinn Féin delegation blundered greatly in acceding to such a vague and indefinable clause. Frank Pakenham contended that the blame on the Irish part 'must rest either on the legal intelligences of 1921 which failed to see evil lurking in Clause 12, or on those of 1925 which permitted the decision of Mr. Justice Feetham [see Chapter Six]'.[72]

Ulster unionists were vehemently opposed to the Boundary Commission, despite Craig being one of the first to suggest such a concept during the embryonic stages of the Government of Ireland Bill (see Chapter Two). Firstly, they were not party to the treaty and yet were now obliged to adhere to its clauses. It reignited the sense of uncertainty and once again put Northern Ireland's future in doubt, or at least significant parts of it. Craig told Lloyd George that he would refuse to cooperate with the commission, as there was 'no precedent in the history of the British empire for taking away territory from an established government without its sanction.[73] At a northern cabinet meeting the following month, the unionist government reflected on Craig's refusal and weighed up their options on participating, or not, in the Boundary Commission. Although non-participation would make the government 'very popular' in Northern Ireland for a time, having no input meant that 'Ulster would lose a larger area than if she had a representative on the Commission', and resistance would be ineffective 'unless we were prepared to take up arms against British troops'. Such a move would see them 'probably lose the support of the Unionist Party in Great Britain'.[74] If they did take part, Bonar Law assured them that either Lord James Clyde or Lord Dunedin, Andrew Murray, both politicians and judges within the Conservative Party, would act as the northern commissioner. Edward Carson also consented to act as Northern Ireland's commissioner, stating that 'a little modification of the boundary might be advantageous'. Craig 'thought the best course would be not to show our hand at the present time but to consider the matter very carefully during the few months that might elapse before the Boundary Commission would be established'.[75] A significant amount of time elapsed by the time the commission finally met in 1924.

Nationalist leaders in the six and twenty-six counties were overly optimistic, as it would transpire, regarding the outcomes that would be achieved from the Boundary Commission, believing many areas in Northern Ireland would be transferred to the Irish Free State, including 'Derry and its western hinterland, most of Tyrone and all of Fermanagh, south Armagh and south Down'.[76] Denis Gwynn wrote that the 'suggestion of a Boundary Commission seemed naturally to imply that the Ulster Unionists would not be allowed to retain the full Six-County area if they did refuse to enter the Free State'.[77] To many nationalists, the treaty 'was a temporary settlement, regarded by many as extorted by threat of immediate war'.[78] The optimism over the Boundary Commission in many ways explains the small fraction of time devoted to partition (just nine out of the total 338 pages of the treaty debates) during the acrimonious Dáil debates on the treaty.[79] Both the pro- and anti-treaty sides supported the Boundary Commission as a means to end or at least limit partition. Both sides 'were complacent about the vague terms of reference for the Boundary Commission and the lack of provision for plebiscites even in border areas'.[80] Sovereignty was the primary cause of the split that followed the treaty. Even de Valera's alternative proposal to the treaty, Document No. 2, originally included the same clauses on the north as the original treaty.[81] Many nationalists along the border believed their transfer to the Irish Free State was imminent. They were lulled into a false sense of security, believing they could continue to ignore the northern jurisdiction and its institutions. Their hopes would soon prove illusory.

Up until 1922, partition was an administrative inconvenience that had little impact on the lives of people. The border 'had not yet become a frontier between two mutually antagonistic states'.[82] From 1922, with a new government established in the south, the effects of partition became more apparent. Both Irish governments were 'forced to devote much attention to relations with each other and to the question of the boundary between their two states'.[83]

CHAPTER SIX

Politics

From its birth, Northern Ireland faced significant political challenges. In the eyes of many on the island, including one-third of the population within its own territory, it lacked legitimacy. Although signing the treaty meant that Sinn Féin had formally accepted partition, the inclusion of Article 12, gave hope to nationalists, who believed that much of the northern territory would be transferred to the Free State, leaving the remainder as an unviable rump. One of the objectives of the treaty, at least on the British side, was to normalise relations between both Irish jurisdictions. In many ways, the treaty led to the opposite. The shadow of the Boundary Commission hung over Northern Ireland. Nationalists felt they could continue to ignore and obstruct the northern jurisdiction, particularly in areas of nationalist majorities. The commission merely added to the vulnerability and paranoia of unionists. Craig stated as much to Churchill in May 1922:

> The Boundary Commission has been at the root of all evil. If you picture Loyalists on the borderland being asked by us to hang on with their teeth for the safety of the Province, you can also picture their unspoken cry to us, 'if we sacrifice our lives and our property for the sake of the Province, are you going to assent to a Commission which may subsequently by a stroke of the pen, take away the very area you now ask us to defend?'[1]

The prospect of some levels of cooperation in 1921 evaporated, replaced by a siege mentality to protect the north's interests from the south and from those disloyal elements within its territory. The focus of the following chapter, security, was the primary concern of the northern government. Almost all political decisions arose from the need to secure and strengthen its borders and defeat its opponents through military and political means. The northern government was able to take whatever measures it saw fit. In the northern House of Commons, there was no opposition, with the Sinn Féin and UIL MPs abstaining from parliament. As the House of Commons elected members of the senate, only unionist senators were present.[2] Other than providing financial support, the British government mainly adopted a *laissez faire* approach, allowing the devolved northern government to manage its own affairs unimpeded.

The make-up of the cabinet of the first northern government was also a significant factor in determining how the southern and internal opposition were dealt with. All cabinet members were drawn from the upper layers of Protestant Ulster society. James Craig, son of a millionaire, was a man of independent means. Lord Londonderry and Edward Archdale owned large estates of land. John Andrews was chairman of his family's linen company and a director of two other companies. Hugh Pollock was managing director of a company of flour importers whilst Richard Dawson-Bates was a prosperous solicitor.[3] They all had close links to the Orange Order, a trend that was to continue for many decades. By 1968, everyone who served in the cabinet had been a member.[4] In 1921, the average age of the cabinet was fifty-four, and owing to Craig's reluctance to make changes, the average age had increased to sixty-two by 1938. At the outbreak of the Second World War, only twelve people had served in the northern cabinet from 1921 to 1939.[5]

Cabinet ministers tended to be 'dogged, reliable and conservative, rather than imaginative and innovative'.[6] James Lichfield, a senior civil servant seconded to Northern Ireland, believed 'the only Cabinet Minister of real value was Craig himself'. Pollock and Londonderry, though deeply conservative in relation to social and financial matters, were more open-minded and outward-looking than their colleagues. Archdale, Andrews and Dawson-Bates all showed a reluctance to treat Catholics equally. All aspired to have the minimum number of Catholics, if any, working in their departments.[7] After Dawson-Bates heard 'with a great deal of surprise, that a Roman Catholic Telephonist has been appointed', he refused to use the telephone for important business until he succeeded in getting the employee transferred.[8] His 'paranoia knew no bounds'.[9] He was in favour of a ban on Catholics entering the northern civil service.[10]

The original cabinet consisted only of men. In the history of the northern parliament (1921 to 1972), Dehra Parker became the first and only female cabinet member in 1949, when she was appointed Minister for Health and Local Government.[11] In 1918, Irish women who were over the age of thirty with certain property rights were granted the vote. In 1922, 'the Free State had extended the franchise to all those over twenty-one, while women in the North, along with their British counterparts, had to wait until 1928'.[12] The northern cabinet unanimously decided not to extend the franchise to women over twenty-one in 1924.[13] Shortly after the northern government was established, the executive committee of the Ulster Women's Unionist Council sent a letter to Craig, asking for 'the inclusion of women in the different departments of the Northern Parliament'. A resolution was passed

> to bring before the Government the importance of the services women can and are anxious to render to their country, especially in such matters as Education, Care of Children, Local Government, Agriculture and Labour. We ask, therefore, that our desire to be included in the above named Departments be seriously considered, either as Advisory Committees, or Women to consult with Ministers and Officials, or as Women Officials.[14]

Craig replied that they could 'rest fully assured that when opportunity presents itself, the fullest co-operation and assistance will be requisitioned from your Council'. He was unable to make many female appointments to the civil service at that time, as services had not yet been transferred. However, he promised that 'when the Services are transferred we will not be neglectful of the claims of the remainder on our list to such appointments as may be available'.[15]

Women on the nationalist side, although supporting their political representatives, had fewer opportunities to participate; this was exacerbated by the policy of abstentionism. Cumann na mBan, the Irish republican women's paramilitary wing, suffered low morale in the north, being outlawed by the northern government in 1922. The Ladies' Auxiliary of the Ancient Order of Hibernians was probably the most popular female nationalist organisation in the north during the inter-war years.[16] For the six counties, between 1898 and 1940, female representation on local councils was, on average, around 1.4 per cent. Within local government, they were able to exercise more influence as poor law guardians than anywhere else. Instead of dealing with gender issues, women activists tended to focus on support for, or opposition to, the northern jurisdiction. In a sectarian society, gender was 'relegated to the margins of discourse and policy', in many ways illustrated by Dehra Parker.[17] Her 'political *leitmotif* was unionism: in thirty-five years in parliament she never voted against the government, and in the early years of Stormont, she consistently voted for measures that would strengthen the majority at the expense of the nationalist minority'.[18] She was one of the first to call for the abolition of PR in local elections, condemning the tyranny with which nationalist councils 'ground the minority under their heel ... We have had to sit there and listen to our King being insulted, to our Government being derided. We have been told that killing was no murder unless committed by the foreign invader'.[19]

The local elections of 1920 had been deeply embarrassing for the unionists, who lost many local authorities and seats to nationalists and the labour movement (see Chapter Two). Most nationalist-controlled local authorities within Northern Ireland chose a policy of non-recognition of the new jurisdiction, some more vociferously than others. On the day of King George V's state opening of the Belfast parliament on 22 June 1921, Thomas Corrigan, secretary of Fermanagh County Council, pulled down a Union Jack flag from Enniskillen courthouse.[20] A delegation from Fermanagh County Council who met the Dáil cabinet in August informed them that 'Fermanagh, by a large majority ... resolved that it would not submit to the partition parliament in Ulster'.[21] Tyrone County Council dithered on non-recognition and 'shuffled pragmatically between the Dáil and Belfast'.[22] Derry City renounced the Belfast parliament on 25 August 1921 but did not 'declare definitive allegiance to the Dáil'.[23] Both Tyrone and Fermanagh declared allegiance to the Dáil on 28 November. Five days later, Tyrone County Council justified its actions and rejected the 'arbitrary, new-fangled, and universally unnatural boundary', pledging 'to oppose it steadfastly and to make the fullest use of our rights to mollify it'.[24]

The northern government, recently emboldened with the transfer of security powers, decided to act against the 'recalcitrant County Councils',

Tyrone and Fermanagh. It considered withholding grants, selecting specific members to act as the 'whole County Council' or appointing 'a special Commissioner to take over the responsibilities'.[25] It chose the latter option and suspended both councils, with the police taking over the headquarters in Omagh and Enniskillen and impounding their records.[26] Faced with suspension, the 'ever pragmatic nationalist politicians' from Tyrone County Council, 'temporarily and under protest, accepted the northern government'. When W.T. Cosgrave, the Dáil local government minister, queried the council's U-turn, it replied that 'in view of the altered political situation, and with a desire to promote a peaceful settlement', all communication would 'for the present', be sent 'to the Northern Minister of Local Government'.[27] Fermanagh County Council, on the other hand, remained defiant and suspended for a year.[28] The suspensions coincided with the signing of the treaty on 6 December. A day later, a northern nationalist delegation met Eoin MacNeill, the Dáil speaker and Sinn Féin MP for Derry, in Dublin's Mansion House to discuss the implications of the treaty for the nationalists in the north.[29] MacNeill assured 'his fellow Ulstermen that although the danger they faced "is a real danger, it is an artificial one. It has not got the strength of permanency". He expanded on this by asking them to pursue a fully-fledged policy of non-engagement with the northern parliament to include non-payment of taxes and non-recognition of the courts.'[30]

This stance saw a public split for the first time between the Nationalist Party and Sinn Féin 'during their time in control of Londonderry Corporation'. The Sinn Féin councillors put forward a motion in January 1922 to pledge allegiance to the Dáil. Opposing the motion, the mayor, Hugh O'Doherty, 'held the view that declared allegiance to the Dáil was counterproductive while the constitutional situation remained in a state of flux. To do so now would alienate unionist opinion, split the nationalist bloc in Derry and bring the full force of the Northern Ireland government down on the corporation.'[31] He used his right as chairman to bypass the motion by not aligning with the Dáil whilst still repudiating the Belfast parliament. This pleased neither Sinn Féin nor the northern government. In total, twenty-one nationalist-controlled authorities, including those of Newry, Armagh, Strabane, Cookstown, Downpatrick, Magherafelt and Keady were suspended by April 1922.[32]

Sir Edward Carson inspects a Colt Browning machine gun at an Ulster Volunteer Force (UVF) rally. Home Rule was fiercely opposed by Ulster unionists who threatened the use of violence by forming the militia, the UVF in 1913 to halt its implementation. (Courtesy of the National Library of Ireland)

'The Nation Mutilators' cartoon published in the *Catholic Bulletin* in December 1917 showing John Redmond in league with Sir Edward Carson on the issue of partition. Redmond and the Irish Parliamentary Party's popularity were in terminal decline for their continued support of the First World War and for their perceived humiliating concessions in accepting some form of partition. (Courtesy of Dublin City Library and Archive)

Walter Long was a key figure of David Lloyd George's British cabinet in formulating Irish policy. He was the main architect of the Government of Ireland Act 1920, which led to the partition of Ireland. (Courtesy of the National Portrait Gallery, London)

Sir Ernest Clark. His work as Assistant Under-Secretary assigned to Belfast was crucial in creating the structures of a functioning government for Northern Ireland when it came into being in the summer of 1921. Future Northern Ireland Prime Minister Basil Brooke described Clark as the 'midwife to the new Province of Ulster'. (Courtesy of the National Portrait Gallery, London)

The Robinson and Cleaver Department Store in Belfast decorated for the visit of King George V and Queen Mary to open the Northern Ireland Parliament on 22 June 1921. (Courtesy of the National Library of Ireland)

On the same day as the Northern Ireland Parliament was officially opened on 22 June 1921, the Irish Republican Army (IRA) attacked a troop train returning from the official opening of the Belfast Parliament, derailing it at Adavoyle on the Louth/Armagh border. Four men and eighty horses were killed. Pictured are IRA members celebrating in a captured British Army armoured car involved in the derailment. (Courtesy of the National Library of Ireland)

THE CABINET OF NORTHERN IRELAND.

The cabinet of the first Northern Ireland government. Left to right: Edward Archdale (Minister of Agriculture and Commerce), Richard Dawson-Bates (Minister of Home Affairs), Lord Londonderry (Minister of Education), Sir James Craig (Prime Minister), Hugh Pollock (Minister of Finance), John Andrews (Minister of Labour) and Wilfred Spender (Cabinet Secretary). (Courtesy of the Linen Hall Library)

Sir Denis Stanislaus Henry, a Catholic, was the first Lord Chief Justice of Northern Ireland. Henry was responsible for establishing the new judiciary of Northern Ireland, almost from scratch. (Courtesy of the National Portrait Gallery, London)

The Northern Ireland Prime Minister James Craig outside Dublin City Hall after meeting the Chairman of the Irish Free State Provisional Government, Michael Collins in February 1922. (Courtesy of the RTÉ Stills Library)

The Boundary Commission's first sitting in late 1924. The commissioners were Eoin MacNeill (first left), Joseph R. Fisher (second left) and the chairman, Justice Richard Feetham (first right). (Courtesy of the National Library of Ireland)

A young Belfast refugee sitting outside Marlborough Hall in Dublin in 1922. Waves of sectarian violence accompanied the birth of Northern Ireland. A consequence of the violence was the displacement of thousands of people from their homes in Belfast, with many of them moving to Dublin. (Courtesy of British Pathé)

A Gordon Brewster cartoon published in the *Evening Herald* in May 1928 showing the crippling effects the Civil Authorities (Special Powers) Act had on the nationalist minority in Northern Ireland. 'Under the Civil Authorities (Special Powers) Bill the Government retains the right to arrest and imprison without cause shown; if Ministers desire, papers can be compelled to suppress the publication of news of which exception is taken, and comment can be made a punishable offence' is inscribed in ink. (Courtesy of the National Library of Ireland)

Frances Kyle and Averill Deverell, the first women to be called to the Bar in Britain or Ireland in November 1921. Kyle, originally from Belfast, pursued her professional career in Northern Ireland, whilst Deverell, from Greystones in County Wicklow, pursued her career in the Irish Free State. (Courtesy of the Mary Evans Picture Library)

Unionists west of the Bann river demanded further punishment of nationalist-controlled councils. These demands led to some of the most significant decisions the government would make leading to long-lasting repercussions. In addition to suspending councils, it looked to take back control of them. It did this by abolishing PR, compelling councillors to pledge an oath of allegiance to the crown and gerrymandering regions to 'reduce radically the number of local councils held by nationalists'.[33] With no opposition present to delay its progress, the bill to abolish PR was ready to become law by 5 July 1922. Michael Collins, who had been chairman of the provisional government of the Irish Free State since January 1922, complained to Churchill, 'Do you not see ... the true meaning of all this?' He argued that the bill's purpose was 'to oust the Catholic and Nationalist people of the Six Counties from their rightful share in local administration' and, in anticipation of the Boundary Commission's work, 'to paint the Counties of Tyrone and Fermanagh with a deep Orange tint'.[34] Churchill agreed with Collins and persuaded the Lord Lieutenant of Ireland, Viscount FitzAlan, to withhold royal assent. Craig and his cabinet then threatened to resign, forcing Lloyd George's coalition to climb down and after a two-month delay, royal assent was given on 11 September 1922.[35] It is clear that the decision to abolish PR 'was taken solely in the interests of unionism while also serving to alienate the nationalist minority'.[36] Craig also decided to abolish PR for parliamentary elections, coming into effect for the 1929 election to the northern parliament, claiming that PR

submerges and clouds the issue. At Election times, the people do not really understand what danger may result if they make a mistake when it comes to third, fourth, fifth or sixth preferences. By an actual mistake, they might wake up to find Northern Ireland in the perilous position of being submerged in a Dublin Parliament. What I hold is, if the Ulster people are ever going – and I pray they may not – into a Dublin Parliament, they should understand that they are voting a Dublin Parliament, and not be led by any trick of a complicated electoral system, such as Proportional Representation.[37]

The decision to abolish PR for parliamentary elections did not have a significant impact on nationalist representation in the northern House of

Commons, as they went from holding twelve to a slight reduction of eleven seats in most subsequent elections.[38] The abolition of PR for parliamentary elections impacted most negatively on the labour movement, with elections largely becoming 'sectarian headcounts' on the legitimacy of Northern Ireland and the border.[39]

The abolition of PR was followed by the rearrangement of local government boundaries. A one-man commission under Judge John Leech held inquiries in contested areas, 'where it appears that substantial inequalities exist in regard to populations and valuations'.[40] Unsurprisingly, 'the majority of these areas in question contained a Catholic and nationalist majority'.[41] Nationalists were sceptical, seeing the commission as 'purely and simply a proposed gerrymander of the area' and a means to 'hand over control to the Ascendancy party'.[42] With few exceptions, nationalists refused to meet the commission, resulting in unionists dictating 'the positioning of boundaries with meticulous care to their own complete satisfaction'.[43] In the Clogher Rural District in Tyrone, the seat share went from being almost equal between unionists and nationalists to eleven for unionists and five for nationalists. Dungannon Urban Council, also in Tyrone, normally expected to return three nationalists. Under the new ward boundaries, however, it changed to a return of two unionists and one nationalist.[44] In Enniskillen, County Fermanagh, the nationalist majority of 56 per cent of the population obtained seven seats, whilst the unionists won fourteen seats.[45] In arguably the most blatant example, in Lurgan Borough Council, County Armagh, according to John O'Brien, 'the gerrymander was such that just 551 Unionists votes secured 15 seats while 5,499 Nationalist votes were unable to secure even one seat'.[46] With many nationalists boycotting the 1924 local elections, the true impact became apparent at the 1927 local elections. In 1920, 'opposition parties won control of twenty-four local authorities out of twenty-seven, but by 1927 Unionists had a majority in all but twelve councils. Unionists recovered Londonderry Corporation and the county councils of Fermanagh and Tyrone'.[47] Unionists defended their actions by stating that boundaries were redrawn to account for the rateable value and population, as 'those who paid the most rates were entitled to the biggest say in the conduct of local government'.[48] This dubious defence of the rich being entitled to stronger representation than the poor benefitted unionists, who were, on average, richer than nationalists.[49] Unionist control of local and national government 'was consolidated by direct and indirect economic discrimination in employment, both in the public and private sectors, and in the distribution of public-consumption benefits, especially public housing'.[50] Buckland asserts that the 'tendency towards discrimination on matters of law and order developed almost accidentally out of the confused troubles of the years 1921–2, but how, in respect of education and representation, discrimination became an integral part of government policy'.[51] The electoral changes in Northern Ireland were scathingly attacked by the Dublin-based North-East Boundary Bureau, who claimed that the 'ultimate aim is the practical disenfranchisement of minorities generally and particularly of the great Nationalist minority of 34 per cent'.[52] The bureau was established in 1922 'to take all necessary steps for the collection and compilation of data in connection with the Boundary Commission', one of many attempts by the Free State government to minimise the impact of partition.[53]

The provisional government, the transitional government for the twenty-six counties until the Irish Free State officially came into being on 6 December 1922, led by Michael Collins, had to try to prevent a civil war within its own jurisdiction and react to conflict in the northern jurisdiction almost from the very moment of its inception. Collins, 'almost alone amongst the leadership of Sinn Féin, had come to accept the reality of partition and strove to do something to undermine it'.[54] Lloyd George complained to Churchill, 'we could get Mr Collins to talk about nothing else'.[55] He pursued a dangerously duplicitous path of pursuing peace through pacts with James Craig in January and March of 1922 on the one hand, and sanctioning 'a policy of military activity along and across the border' on the other.[56]

In the first pact of 21 January between Collins and Craig, Collins agreed to discontinue the Belfast Boycott whilst Craig promised to 'facilitate, as far as economic conditions allowed, the return of expelled catholic shipyard workers to their jobs'.[57] The Belfast Boycott was discontinued, but Craig failed to secure the return of many Catholics; just twenty out of over 7,000 Catholics were reinstated in Belfast shipyards by the end of January.[58] A large-scale system of relief was sought from the British government to deal with unemployment, and both endeavoured to find 'a more suitable system than the council of Ireland ... for dealing with problems affecting all Ireland'.[59] Craig believed, in its proposed form, that the council would be more of an irritant to both sides and 'would find it very difficult to prevent very acrimonious discussion if the members of the Council included Mr. Coote and similar representatives on one side, and the Countess Markievicz and other irresponsible representatives on the other'.[60] William Coote, an MP for Fermanagh and Tyrone, had urged Protestants to fire all Catholic employees that same month.[61] Craig told Collins that an 'All Ireland Parliament was out of the question, possibly in years to come – 10, 20 or 50 years – Ulster might be tempted to join with the South', and wanted to know if it was Collins's 'intention to have peace in Ireland or whether we were to go on with murder and strife, rivalry and boycott and unrest in Northern Ireland'. According to Craig, Collins 'made it clear that he wanted a real peace and that he had so many troubles in Southern Ireland, that he was prepared to establish cordial relations with Northern Ireland, to abandon all attempts to coercion, but hoping to coax her into a union later'.[62] Collins, showing a less than wholehearted commitment to the Boundary Commission, agreed with Craig for them to 'deal with the question of the boundaries without help or interference from any British authority', and to nominate representatives reporting to Collins and Craig directly with a view to 'mutually agree' on borders.[63] Their agreement on the boundary was even more vague than Article 12 of the treaty. The main conclusion Collins drew from the conference with Craig was 'that north and south will settle outstanding differences between themselves. We have eliminated the English interference.'[64]

The pact was broken within days over unrealistic expectations and a significant escalation of violence in the north. Although broken, the pact was still noteworthy in some respects. Collins was now considered the spokesperson for northern nationalists, at least by the British. And whilst Craig claimed the pact showed that the provisional government accepted partition and the legitimacy of the Belfast government, his 'agreeing to the meetings involved in some sense a recognition that the Dublin government had some say over what occurred north of the border'.[65]

The months following the first pact saw violence reach new levels of brutality. It was a civil war in Northern Ireland in all but name. Winston

Churchill, as Secretary of State for the Colonies, was responsible for Ireland within the British cabinet. He urged Collins and Craig to meet again, resulting in a conference in London on 29 and 30 March. The second pact, signed on 31 March, had more concrete proposals. It was agreed 'to reform the Belfast special constabulary and to recruit catholics into that force'. Once IRA activities ceased in the six counties, special constabulary reforms would extend beyond Belfast. The British government committed to supplying 'a relief grant, not exceeding £500,000' to Northern Ireland. The northern government again promised to help restore Catholic shipyard workers to employment and both sides agreed to commence prison releases.[66] Churchill triumphantly claimed, 'Peace today is declared.' The reality was markedly different, more akin to Lord Hugh Cecil's observation that the agreement was 'a statue of snow'.[67] The agreement broke down almost from the outset. There was much opposition from unionist quarters. Field Marshall Sir Henry Wilson, former chief of the imperial staff, military adviser to the Northern Ireland government and unionist MP for North Down, was fiercely opposed, asking at a meeting with northern ministers, 'Who is governing Ulster, you or Collins?'[68] Immediately after the pact, violence accelerated, and the final pact between Craig and Collins lay in tatters.

The pacts with Craig were in many ways a public front for Collins, who by his other actions, sought to destabilise the northern jurisdiction. As well as arming the IRA for engagements in the north, Collins led a policy of non-recognition of the six counties, which caused deep frustration for the British and Northern Irish governments.[69] One of the primary policies of non-recognition involved the payment of salaries in Northern Ireland for those teachers who refused to recognise the six counties' Ministry of Education and 'the Provisional Government ... holding examinations in the Intermediate Schools under Roman Catholic management in various parts of Northern Ireland' (see Chapter Eleven).[70] The provisional government was also extremely tardy in transferring civil service personnel and files to Belfast. There were approximately 120 officials seeking to be transferred to the Northern Ireland government, but their transfer was held up by the provisional government. This caused 'serious inconvenience to the Northern Government'.[71] The Department of Agriculture alone 'was unwilling to transfer files covering a long list of topics, including agricultural schools, crop disease, flax, egg marketing, food and drugs legislation, and the establishment files of the transferred staff'.[72] Files from the Land Registry were still not transferred to Northern Ireland by March 1923, leading one civil servant to claim, 'It really is monstrous that this obstruction should continue.'[73] Relations with the northern government were, according to Diarmuid O'Hegarty, the southern cabinet secretary, 'anything but friendly and it was the settled policy that no facilities should be afforded to the Government of Northern Ireland'.[74] Collins sent a directive to his cabinet colleagues, instructing them 'to have a scheme prepared for non-cooperation in every possible way with the Northern Parliament, and in addition, a scheme towards making it impossible to carry on'.[75]

Collins met with opposition from within the provisional government for his policy on the north. His 'cabinet colleagues were, in the weeks before his death, moving to shut down any further provocative actions and instead impose "a policy of peaceful do-nothingness"'.[76] Once he was killed in August 1922, a new policy prevailed. The policy was to recognise the northern government and discontinue obstructionist policies.[77] Seamus Woods, the officer commanding the 3rd Northern Battalion of the IRA in Belfast, claimed, 'Of all the Dublin government ministers, Collins had been most deeply concerned about the fate of northern Catholics.'[78] Leading the new initiative was Ernest Blythe, Minister for Local Government and Ulster-born Protestant. Research from David Fitzpatrick has revealed that, for a time, Blythe led a double life as a member of both the IRB and the Orange Order when he was a journalist for the unionist newspaper, *North Down Herald* (1909–13).[79] He was 'probably the only member of the Provisional Government who had a realistic insight into how the Ulster Protestant mind worked'.[80]

The steps of the new policy on the north included:

(a) Payment of teachers in the Six Counties should immediately be stopped. From the point of view of finance, educational efficiency, and public morality it is indefensible. In the case of the primary schools, we should take the step of approaching Lord Londonderry through a suitable intermediary and arranging that the teachers who remained with us shall not be penalised.

(b) We should stop all relations with local bodies in the Six Counties and should try to arrange that those which have been suppressed should be restored on condition of recognising the Northern Government.

(c) Catholic members of the Northern Parliament who have no personal objection to the oath of allegiance should be urged to take their seats.

(d) Ample precautions should be taken to prevent border incidents from our side. Any offenders caught by us should be definitely handed over to the Northern authorities, a condition precedent being of course that flogging should be dropped.

(e) As it is quite evident that the Catholics of the Six Counties cannot by use of arms protect themselves we should on receiving satisfactory assurances from the British, urge them to disarm.

(f) Prisoners in the North should be requested to give bail and to recognise the courts.

(g) The "Outrage" propaganda should be dropped in the Twenty Six Counties. It can have no effect but to make certain our people see red which will never do us any good. If it could be got into the English papers it would be useful; but it certainly should not be forced into the Irish papers. Much of it, particularly in regard to prisons is, like all prison propaganda, false.

(h) All kinds of minor nagging should cease.[81]

According to Donnacha Ó Beacháin, 'The government memorandum was, in effect, a lengthy farewell note to the northern nationalist community, who were now urged to fend for themselves.'[82] This was apparent when, in October 1922, a deputation of nationalists from Northern Ireland arrived in Dublin seeking funds from the provisional government, receiving 'short shrift from Kevin O'Higgins, the new minister for home affairs: "We have no other policy for the North East than we have for any other part of Ireland and that is the Treaty policy".[83] That same month, W.T. Cosgrave, the new chairman of the provisional government, told a delegation of northern nationalists that this government took 'very strong action' against people who 'refused to give it their allegiance, and that if we were to discourage them from giving their allegiance to Craig's administration he would provide a weapon that could be used by his enemies in both the north and the south'.[84] Craig and Cosgrave

> got on better at a personal level than Craig and Collins had, but direct governmental contact with Northern Ireland was never very forthcoming. Dublin would base its Northern Ireland policy on the Treaty and the Boundary Commission. While it would treat the North with courtesy, it would do nothing that would help to consolidate the position of the Northern Ireland government.[85]

Cahir Healy, a Sinn Féin politician based in the north and internee on the converted prison ship, the *Argenta* from 1922 to 1924, summed up how many northern nationalists felt: that they were 'abandoned to Craig's mercy ... Personally, we must look after ourselves, I think'.[86]

Another step by the Free State government in March 1923 had arguably the biggest impact in cementing partition: the imposition of customs duties on imported goods (see Chapter Nine). The creation of a customs barrier was key in translating partition into a reality.[87] It did so in a bid to achieve fiscal independence from Britain and generate revenue for the exchequer. It was also an attempt to apply economic pressure on the nascent Northern Ireland jurisdiction. In announcing the imposition, the government stated that 'pending a decision as to the future boundary line, a temporary frontier will be placed along the boundary line between the six Northern and twenty-six Southern counties'.[88] The temporary frontier on imported goods lasted for over seventy years, only rescinded due to the introduction of the Single Market throughout the European Union in 1993.

The decision to erect customs barriers before the Boundary Commission had convened showed, perhaps, a lack of faith in the commission and made it more difficult to make subsequent changes to the border. Despite this and the devastating impact the civil war had on the Free State, 'the Irish government had not buried its head regarding the Commission'.[89] The civil war was a contributory factor in the delay in its convening, as were the non-cooperation of the northern government and several changes of government in Britain.[90] Between 1922 and 1924, there were three general elections and four governments in Britain.[91] The North-Eastern Boundary Bureau was set up in October 1922 to prepare the case for the Free State at the Boundary Commission, with Kevin O'Shiel, Assistant Legal Advisor and native of Tyrone, appointed as head of the bureau.[92] The bureau conducted an extensive publicity and propaganda campaign, which included 'exploring every possible aspect of the Silesian, the Schleswig-Holstein and the Hungarian [recent] Plebiscites, and also the special position of Alsace-Lorraine (the attempt made to Germanise it, etc. etc.)' and setting up a local division with a large number of people employed, at 'considerable expenditure'.[93] Many pamphlets were distributed to the border areas most likely to be transferred; they presented economic and political arguments to advance the Free State case.[94] Despite the considerable work conducted by the bureau, 'ultimately the Commission refused to consider its work, which amounted to some fifty-six boxes of files'.[95]

The Free State government was the first to appoint its commissioner, Eoin MacNeill, the Minister of Education, in July 1923. Almost a year later, in June 1924, the British government appointed the chairperson of the Boundary Commission, Richard Feetham, a judge based in South Africa. With the northern government refusing to appoint its commissioner, the British intervened by selecting Joseph R. Fisher, a barrister and former editor of the Belfast unionist-leaning newspaper, the *Northern Whig*.[96] The northern government could not have selected a better candidate to advance the unionist cause. Stanley Baldwin, the British Prime Minister at the time, told Craig in 1923, 'If the Commission should give away counties, then of course Ulster couldn't accept it and we should back her. But the Government will nominate a proper representative [for Northern Ireland] and we hope that he and Feetham will do what is right.' Fisher was that 'proper representative', who even 'privately advocated the inclusion of Donegal into the Northern statelet'.[97] Thompson Donald, a unionist MP, was speaking for many unionists when he declared, 'we will take Donegal, whether you like it or not'.[98]

The commission met for the first time in November 1924. Feetham, with a very vague clause from the treaty to work from, decided not to conduct a plebiscite, 'choosing instead to assume a quasi-judicial approach' and ruling out wholesale transfers. From December 1924 until July 1925, the three commissioners conducted informal and formal hearings, interviewing more than 500 witnesses based on written statements submitted in advance.[99] The claims ranged from small areas such as Castle Saunderson in County Cavan and Keady in County Armagh to claims that all of Ulster should be included in Northern Ireland and that there should be no partition of Ireland whatsoever.[100] The locality of Drummully in County Monaghan was almost completely cut off from the rest of Monaghan by the Fermanagh districts of Clonkeelan and Derrysteaton. Representations were made to the commission by nationalists in Drummully to have 'enough of Fermanagh moved to the Free State to restore them to their town, they rather despondently added that, failing this, Drummully should be transferred to Northern Ireland'. Likewise, Drummully unionists said 'they would favour any end to the anomaly by being placed entirely on one side or the other'.[101] Drummully residents told the commission 'that as a consequence of partition their area was almost a land peninsula, its sixteen townlands inaccessible without twice crossing the border'.[102] Many claims were made based on economic and geographic grounds, with much emphasis placed on Donegal's dependency on Derry, and vice versa.[103]

The work completed by the commission would not be fully revealed to the public for decades due to a leak of the recommendations by the pro-unionist newspaper the *Morning Post*, in November 1925. Much to the surprise of many nationalists, no large-scale transfers were on offer. In fact, 'a rich portion of East Donegal' was to be transferred to the north. The leaked report recommended the shortening of the border by fifty miles, transferring 286 square miles to the south and seventy-seven square miles to the north, which would have moved 31,219 people to the Irish Free State and 7,594 in the opposite direction.[104] The Free State 'had never considered the possibility that its territory would be handed back to the north'.[105] The leak caused outrage in Dublin. People in Donegal were particularly crestfallen, as 'Donegal was blockaded: they could not leave the county without passing through the Six Counties'.[106] It was deeply humiliating for

MacNeill and the Free State government. Unlike Fisher, who was believed to be responsible for the leakage, MacNeill did not even inform his cabinet colleagues of the progress of the commission. With the furore caused by the leak, MacNeill resigned from the commission, the Free State government and the Dáil, claiming as he departed that 'he wasn't the most suitable person to be a commissioner'.[107] Pleading ignorance of the commission's findings, Cosgrave claimed it 'would be a farce and a travesty if the forecasts which had been published were correct'.[108] Realising the danger the crisis posed to the government, he dashed over to London to have the report shelved. He was accompanied by Kevin O'Higgins, who claimed: 'the Free State government could survive politically on the basis of the present border only if they got either "an amelioration of the conditions under which the nationalists were at present living in North-East Ireland" or some other concession that could "deaden in the twenty-six counties the echo of the outcry of the Catholics in North-East Ireland"'.[109]

O'Higgins declared that he would prefer for northern nationalists to be helped. A determined Craig resisted attempts that would have helped Catholics, including 'proposals to disband the Special Constabulary, reinstate proportional representation and end discrimination'.[110] Lord James Salisbury, leader of the House of Lords, suggested that Joseph Devlin should be appointed as an Ulster liaison officer to Ulster Catholics, a sort of ombudsman. Craig rejected this too, preferring for the Free State to be relieved of part of the British national debt.[111] The Free State government accepted Craig's suggestion and was 'absolved of its responsibility under Article 5 of the Anglo-Irish Treaty to pay the British exchequer ten million pounds a year as its share of the British national debt'.[112] This showed the extent to which the Free State government 'was prepared to purchase its own independence at the expense of Irish unity'.[113] The border remained as it was, and as it is to the present day. The Free State government also agreed to the disbandment of the Council of Ireland, the one tangible avenue that cooperation, perhaps union, could have been forged.[114] Craig 'suggested joint meetings of the two governments in Ireland "at an early date" so that both governments could deal with charges brought by one against the other'.[115] Cosgrave agreed, but the two men never met each other again. The next meeting between the heads of both Irish governments occurred forty years later, when Seán Lemass met Terence O'Neill in 1965.

Craig returned to Belfast happy and contented after the tripartite agreement between the British, Free State and northern governments. He had kept his promise of not giving an inch, and the troublesome Council of Ireland was disbanded. Craig claimed in 1934 that he was an Orangeman first and a politician and MP afterwards, 'all I boast is that we are a Protestant Parliament and a Protestant State'.[116] Although his government had succeeded in securing its borders, it made no effort to be conciliatory towards the substantial Catholic minority. The violence may have been curbed in the north, but there was little peace. After 1925, the nationalist community had to accept, 'whether they liked it or not, that they were citizens of Northern Ireland'.[117] Devlin and Thomas McAllister, MP for County Antrim, decided to enter the northern parliament followed by three more nationalists in 1926; by 1928 there were ten. The Boundary Commission crisis in late 1925 alienated most northern nationalists from the Free State government. Cahir Healy stated, it was 'amazing ... that the liberties and rights guaranteed to the nationalists by Article 12 should be scrapped, and the people sold into political servitude for all time'.[118] Cosgrave was fooling few people by calling the agreement a 'damn good bargain'.[119] Spender later claimed that Cosgrave did not believe it was a good bargain; when meeting with Craig, he 'burst into tears and said that Lord Craigavon had won all down the line and begged and entreated him not to make things more difficult for him'.[120] The Free State government and its Sinn Féin predecessor had failed politically, just as it had militarily, in preventing partition and unifying the island of Ireland.

CHAPTER SEVEN

Security

Northern Ireland experienced very violent beginnings. Between 1920 and 1922, waves of violence, including many sectarian killings, engulfed the six counties. It is estimated that over 550 people were violently killed in the six counties during this period. Approximately 300 of the dead were Catholics, over 170 were Protestants and over 80 were members of the security forces.[1] Belfast accounted for the vast bulk of the deaths, with just under 460 killed and over 1,100 people wounded.[2] Catholics, one-quarter of the population of Belfast, suffered over 70 per cent of the deaths in the city. Catholic relief organisations estimated that 'in Belfast, between 8,700 and 11,000 Catholics had been driven out of their jobs, that 23,000 Catholics had been forced out of their homes, and that about 500 Catholic-owned businesses had been destroyed'.[3] Those forced from their homes had to seek refuge elsewhere, in places such as Dundalk in County Louth and in Dublin and Glasgow. The nationalist community referred to the period as the 'Belfast pogrom', where 'Orange mobs and crucially, regular and auxiliary members of the police force carried out this premediated campaign of murder and expulsion'.[4]

Unionists saw it differently. They saw the threat posed by the IRA and the disorder it had caused in the south and west of Ireland and were determined to prevent the contagion spreading to the north. They were deeply distrustful of Dublin Castle and of the RIC, a mainly Catholic police force. They took matters into their own hands and armed themselves.[5] By early 1922, one in six Protestant males were members of the Ulster Special Constabulary.[6] From November 1921, the northern government officially took over responsibility for law and order, establishing its own police force, the RUC, in 1922. The northern government's obsession with security saw it make many decisions to protect itself, most notoriously through the

Civil Authorities (Special Powers) Act of April 1922.[7] The British army also remained in situ and active, particularly when violence peaked in the first half of 1922. The IRA's strength in the north had increased significantly in 1921, augmented further by the newly formed provisional government's assistance in early 1922. All of these forces pitted against each other were responsible for Northern Ireland's brutal beginnings.

With the truce of July 1921, most parts of Ireland by and large saw a cessation of violence. Although bound by the truce, hostilities escalated in the north, with more people killed in Belfast 'during the last five months of the year than in the first seven'.[8] Initially, confusion was prevalent between the northern government and Dublin Castle over who was responsible for security matters in the six counties. This ended with the transfer of law and order responsibilities to the northern government on 22 November. The 'RIC stationed in the six counties was placed at the disposal of the Northern Government ... Its administration, however, remained with the Inspector General in Dublin'.[9] The Specials were remobilised again. The void left by the demobilised Specials from July to November had been filled by loyalist vigilante groups and a revived UVF, under the leadership of Fred Crawford.[10] Crawford had succeeded Wilfrid Spender, who became cabinet secretary to the northern government. In anticipation of the transfer, the northern government sought to bring the vigilante elements under the Specials' umbrella.[11] On 9 November, Charles Wickham sent a circular to all county and city commandants of the Specials:

> Owing to the number of reports which have been received as to the growth of the unauthorised Loyalist defence forces, the Government have under consideration the desirability of obtaining the services of the best elements of these organisations.

> They have decided that the scheme most likely to meet the situation would be to enrol all who volunteer and are considered suitable into Class 'C' and to form them into regular military units.[12]

The 'Wickham circular' was leaked, and Michael Collins raised the issue during the Anglo-Irish negotiations in London. It was deeply embarrassing for the British government, as security had not been transferred to the northern government by that stage, and it was a breach of the truce and the Government of Ireland Act, which prohibited the northern government from raising a military force.[13] Wickham defended the action by claiming unauthorised loyalist defence forces, numbering 21,000 in November and with plans to expand to 150,000, needed to be brought under government control.[14] The circular was withdrawn, but the northern government continued with the recruitment from unauthorised forces as originally planned.[15] When security powers were transferred to the north, the 'force at the disposal of the Authorities included about – 2,500 R.I.C. over 4,000 "A" Constabulary, nearly 20,000 "B" Constabulary, and "C" Constabulary now being raised'. Until a force of 3,000 additional 'A' Specials had been raised, the government required the 'assistance' of British troops in the 'Cities of Belfast and Derry'.[16] It was unusual that the northern government, a regional one, was 'in possession of a paramilitary police force over which the central government had so little direct influence.[17]

Meanwhile, the IRA's numbers had grown significantly in the latter half of 1921 (see Chapter Four). The Belfast brigade of the IRA, which had only 367 members in June, grew to 632 by August. In the rest of County Antrim, the IRA's numbers swelled from 111 in June to 260 in August. By December, the IRA had trebled in size in six months, to 835 in Belfast and 302 in Antrim.[18] Throughout the whole six counties, the three IRA divisions had a nominal active strength of 2,157 before the truce. This had risen to well over 4,000 by October, still considerably below loyalist numbers.[19] To accommodate the new recruits, training camps were established across the north in isolated areas such as the Sperrin Mountains. Some from Belfast travelled south to County Wicklow for further training. Key members of the IRA from the south, including Emmet Dalton, Ernie O'Malley and Dan Breen, travelled north to provide training.[20] It was felt within unionist circles that the revived UVF did little to curb the growth of the IRA during this period.[21] Even with increased numbers, the IRA in the north suffered an arms shortage. By late 1921, 'the arms held by the IRA in Belfast, Antrim and East Down combined consisted of just 92 rifles, 170 shotguns, 41 automatic pistols, 186 revolvers and 5 Thompson sub-machine guns; by contrast, the 1st Southern Division in Cork had 870 rifles, 3,950 shotguns, 381 automatic pistols, 1,076 revolvers and 10 Thompsons'.[22]

The enlarged IRA and loyalist forces led to a renewed confrontation in late November. The IRA matched the actions of its enemies and started to engage in overtly sectarian acts. In late November, bombs were thrown into trams carrying shipyard workers in Corporation Street and Royal Avenue in Belfast, killing eight and wounding nine.[23] The *Belfast Newsletter* called the bombing on Corporation Street 'an appalling outrage ... the cries of the wounded were heartrending'.[24] With Catholics still expelled from the shipyards, clearly all the casualties were Protestants. There was discomfort within the IRA in relation to their new tactics, with one member saying 'there was a bit of a stink about it'.[25] The loyalist reprisals resulted in fifteen people killed in one day alone, 22 November, with St Matthew's Church in Ballymacarrett taking the brunt of the attacks.[26] Violence in late November resulted in thirty deaths (sixteen Protestants and fourteen Catholics) and ninety wounded (fifty-nine Protestants and thirty-one Catholics).[27] The *Belfast Newsletter* issued an appeal from Craig 'to support the Relief Fund for the dependents of Loyalists killed or injured during the outrages committed in the city'.[28] The bombing of the trams led to two cabinet conferences of the northern government, where it was decided to conduct vigorous searches in the affected areas, increase the amount of armoured and Lancia cars on the streets and 'utilise' more 'A' Specials.[29] On 1 December, the Minister of Home Affairs, Dawson-Bates, brought before the cabinet the general scheme of a bill that should be prepared 'which would enable the Powers of the Restoration of Order Act to be carried out by the Constabulary Authorities, instead of by the competent Military Authority'. It was agreed though that 'this Bill should not be brought before the House until the emergency arose'.[30] The bill would take shape as the Civil Authorities (Special Powers) Act, introduced in April 1922.

The trouble died down in the beginning of December but recommenced from 17 December, leading to three more deaths and twenty-three injured during the following week.[31] The re-instigation of violence was caused to a large extent by the confusion surrounding the Anglo-Irish Treaty, signed on 6 December 1921. Ominously, the northern government 'ordered an end to the Truce, following a week later with instructions to disregard the liaison arrangements', an arrangement that had been in place between the British authorities and the IRA during the truce.[32] The treaty left northern republicans confused and dismayed. For the nationalist community in the north, the sovereignty issue was of secondary importance compared to the issue of partition.[33] The role of the proposed Boundary Commission was of primary interest. Whilst nationalists living in the border regions, particularly in Fermanagh and Tyrone, were optimistic that they would be quickly transferred to the Free State, those living in Belfast and east Ulster knew they would remain in Northern Ireland, regardless of the generosity of the Boundary Commission. One IRA member stated that 'The Treaty was a tragedy when it came. We all knew that. We knew in the North that we had been left out.'[34] Robert Lynch asserts that attitudes to the treaty by the IRA in the north were far more complex than those that developed in the south:

> For the Northern IRA their primary concern lay in undermining the increasing permanency of partition and they would welcome support from whichever side of the Treaty divide seemed most able to accomplish this end. This pragmatic attitude meant that the organisation in the North resembled, more than any other part of the Sinn Féin movement, the pre-Truce IRA and were essentially beyond categorisation as either pro- or anti-Treaty.[35]

Eoin O'Duffy was able to allay the fears of the northern IRA commanders to an extent, although there was still some confusion, as some believed that the Falls Road in Belfast could vote itself out of Northern Ireland.[36] O'Duffy was Deputy Chief of Staff of the IRA and Ulster liaison officer since the truce. Sharing a platform with Michael Collins in Armagh in September 1921, he had notoriously said that the IRA may 'have to use lead' against those who were 'against Ireland and against their fellow countrymen.'[37] The intervention of Collins was pivotal in securing the support for the treaty of many northern IRA members. He assured the northern IRA that they were high on his list of priorities. Becoming the 'unofficial leader of the northern Catholic minority', Collins dictated much of the actions of the northern IRA for the first half of 1922.[38]

An attempted escape from Derry Jail by IRA prisoners on the night of 1–2 December 1921 had major repercussions. It was the catalyst (see below) for a marked increase of hostilities early in the new year. The botched attempt involved two friendly warders who were provided with 'chloroform to incapacitate the guards on the prison gates' by the IRA.[39] On the night of the escape, fourteen prisoners opened their cells with duplicate keys, overpowered the warders and administered the chloroform to two police constables, 'but without sufficient knowledge of its effects' which 'caused them to ingest fatal doses'.[40] As they scaled the prison wall, the prisoners were spotted by a special constable, who raised an alarm. The prisoners were captured soon after.[41] Three were sentenced to death by the new Lord Chief Justice of Northern Ireland, Denis Henry: one of the warders, Patrick Leonard, as well as two IRA members, Thomas McShea and Patrick Johnston.[42]

A month later on 14 January, Dan Hogan, commanding officer of the 5th Northern Division of the IRA, was one of several Gaelic footballers from Monaghan arrested by the Specials in Dromore in County Tyrone. They were on their way to the Gaelic Athletic Association's (GAA) Ulster senior football final in Derry City, 'where they intended to rescue' the three men under death sentence in Derry Jail by making a detour on the way to the match.[43] When arrested and found to have arms, they 'claimed that this was a breach of the truce and … were armed for self defence, as they had to pass through Protestant areas'.[44] Hogan's brother, Michael, had been killed whilst playing for Tipperary in Croke Park on 'Bloody Sunday', 21 November 1920. When Collins asked for the football prisoners to be released, Craig advised that they apply for bail, something Collins could not agree to, 'as it would recognize the northern courts'.[45] The northern cabinet subsequently agreed to the release of the prisoners, 'provided the Provisional Government were prepared to acknowledge the validity of the Ulster Courts'.[46]

The arrests gave Collins an opportunity to show his new hard-line policy to his IRA colleagues. He was under pressure from those opposed to the treaty in the south and from northern Sinn Féin and IRA members who claimed life under the Specials was 'hell'. Collins was warned by James Mayne, a Sinn Féin member from Cookstown in County Tyrone, that 'the Irish Party was swept aside' because of partition, and if Tyrone was thrown to the 'Ulster wolves an agitation will arise that will shake the foundation of the Free State'.[47] In early January a 'shadowy new body' called the 'Northern Command', also named the 'Ulster Council', was established to coordinate IRA activity in the six counties and along the border. It was headed by Collins under the auspices of the IRB, whose supreme council he was president of.[48] Firstly, he despatched two of his 'Squad' members to England to assassinate the two hangmen assigned to execute the Derry Jail inmates; but both hangmen had already left for Ireland.[49] Next, he ordered a 'major IRA incursion across the border into the counties of Tyrone and Fermanagh on the night of 7–8 February: some forty prominent loyalists were seized and taken south. They included the eighty-year-old Anketell Moutray, Orange county grand master in Tyrone, who was to exasperate his captors by singing metrical psalms and "God Save the King" without ceasing.'[50] Collins and the provisional government's Minister of Defence, Richard Mulcahy, who had also approved the raid, denied knowing anything about it.[51] It had been planned for 24 January but was postponed in order to give the Craig–Collins Pact, agreed on 21 January, a chance to work.[52] The kidnapped loyalists were taken across the border to be held as hostages for the Derry Jail and 'football' prisoners. As it happened, 'the British government had ordered the reprieve of the Derry men, over the heads of the Northern government, on the very day of the raid.'[53]

The kidnappings caused a furore in the unionist community. Craig issued a statement to the 'People of Ulster', condemning the 'dastardly outrages' that 'will never be forgotten – it merely strengthens our determination that what Ulster has she holds'. He also blamed the British government, saying if they had 'shown courage and prescience this could never have occurred. I place the responsibility on their shoulders for having demobilized the Special Constabulary in consequence of the Truce.' He 'arranged for the immediate distribution of the arms necessary to protect our border.'[54] On the same day, his brother Charles asked Lloyd George in Westminster for assistance to 'be given to the local authorities to hunt down the perpetrators of these outrages', as they had very likely 'come from the Free State, and after committing the outrages, having returned there.'[55]

The northern government subsequently bolstered the border areas with many more Specials. Arms arrived from the British authorities via Carrickfergus in County Antrim. In February 1922:

The distribution of the arms to the whole B force was made ... by convoys of furniture vans escorted by armoured cars of the A

Specials. Each man was issued with a rifle and bayonet, webbing equipment and a hundred rounds of ammunition. At the same time, uniforms were issued to the whole B force. This consisted of 1914/18 type army tunics, trousers and puttees dyed dark green and with the appropriate badges and buttons ... In country districts the Special Constabulary were now allowed to keep their arms in their houses.[56]

In Tyrone, five 'A' Special platoons joined the existing platoon in Aughnacloy. Similar reinforcements took place in other border counties. The 'roads crossing into the Free State were then made impassable by blowing up bridges or digging trenches and were covered by constabulary posts. Only the main roads were left open and on these there were permanent road blocks.'[57] In 1922, the Specials were also provided with wireless communication, allowing them to perform as mobile support units.[58] In some places, 'sniping from across the border was so heavy that farmers were forced to evacuate, leaving Specials to feed cattle and poultry'.[59] One group of reinforcement Specials left Newtownards by train, via Belfast en route to Enniskillen on 11 February. The train crossed the border and stopped in Clones in County Monaghan, where the nineteen Specials boarded a train bound for Enniskillen. Alerted to their presence, the local IRA commandment, Matt Fitzpatrick, arrived at the station with his battalion. On entering the train, Fitzpatrick was shot dead. There are conflicting reports on who fired the first shots, 'with both sides claiming vociferously that they were the innocent victims of an unprovoked attack'.[60] Once Fitzpatrick was felled, the other IRA members outside the train immediately responded, and a hail of bullets was fired at the Specials' carriages. Four Specials were killed with many more Specials and civilians wounded.[61] Some of the Specials were captured and subsequently taken to Carrickmacross, also in Monaghan.[62]

Following this, violence erupted in Belfast, resulting in the deaths of thirty-four people between 13 and 15 February. A particular incident was one of the most horrific of all that occurred during those two years of violence in Belfast: 'in Weaver Street off York Road in north Belfast ... a grenade was thrown at a group of Catholic children playing – two died instantly and four more subsequently died from their wounds'.[63] The following day, the *Freeman's Journal* described the sickening scenes on Weaver Street:

The children were playing in Weaver street about 8:30pm. Some were skipping and some were swinging ... on ropes tied to lamp-posts. Others were singing, sitting on the doorsteps of their homes. There was childish joviality everywhere ...

Suddenly there was a terrific explosion. The laughter of the children ceased and cries of agony rent the air. Parents were dazed. All over the street the children who, a moment before, were skipping and swinging, care-free, were lying bleeding. Pools of blood wetted the pavement, and a scene of heart-rending confusion ensued.

Mothers ran out of their houses in distraction, mingling their cries with the agonised screams of their suffering children. The little ones were brought into their homes, where little could be done for their wounds ...

When the wounded reached the hospital [the Mater] the entire staff was ready to receive them. Catherine Kennedy was dead on arrival, and the little girl, Johnstone, dying. Most of them had lost consciousness, but many were groaning and writhing in agony ... Each child was carried into the hospital by the ambulance men, some of whom, hardened by contact with suffering, had been so moved by the scenes they had witnessed in Weaver street, that they could ill repress the tears that welled into their eyes as they tenderly bore the groaning little ones into the building.[64]

Winston Churchill described the Weaver Street bombing as 'the worst thing that has happened in Ireland during the past three years'.[65] Whilst condemning the 'dastardly deed, involving the lives of children' in Weaver Street, 'a Sinn Fein area', Craig was quick to point out that 'the greatest tension has existed in Belfast since the kidnapping of Loyalists and the murderous attack on the police at Clones' and the 'trouble began with firing on workers and Loyalists going to their work, the firing coming from a Sinn Fein locality.[66] He followed up by claiming the outbreak of violence in Belfast 'was a direct effort of the IRA to stir up trouble and make our Parliament impotent.[67] He insisted from Churchill 'permission to send a column of 5,000 Specials across the border to rescue the hostages' and 'demanded that the British army reoccupy a series of towns on the southern side of the border. He wanted more British troops sent to the six counties as well'. He also wanted 230 police cars and lorries, 150 machine guns and three armoured cars.[68] Churchill did not grant most of Craig's demands, 'warning that such measures might provoke the resignation of the Provisional Government and leave the anti-Treatyites in control in Dublin'. However, he did send another three battalions of British troops to the north, promising a further six battalions if needed.[69]

Hogan and some of the other IRA prisoners were released by the British government, overriding the northern government again, and Collins responded in kind by releasing twenty-six loyalists. A border commission was established: an ad-hoc peacekeeping agency assigned to arbitrate in any future border dispute, consisting of representatives from the British army, the IRA and the RIC. It achieved very little, fading out of existence by the end of April.[70] An all-out war between north and south was averted, but the violence continued, remaining on the brutal path since February. The months of February and March 1922 witnessed levels of violence in the north that had not been experienced before. Between 11 February and 31 March, fifty-one Catholics were killed with 115 wounded, and thirty-two Protestants were killed with eighty-six wounded.[71]

The most notorious incident in March was the 'MacMahon murders' of 24 March. After the IRA killed two Specials on May Street in Belfast on 23 March, the home of Owen MacMahon, a Catholic publican, was attacked early the next morning. Five men dressed in police uniforms broke into the house using a sledgehammer. They proceeded to shoot the male members in the house, resulting in six deaths: Owen MacMahon and his sons Frank, Patrick and Gerald, as well as Edward McKinney, who worked for MacMahon; another son, Bernard, died a week later. The youngest boy, Michael, aged twelve, survived by hiding behind a sofa and feigning death.[72] It was widely believed that John Nixon, RIC district inspector, was responsible for the killings. He was suspected of leading an assassination gang within the RIC who hunted down and killed Catholics as reprisals for police killings.[73] It was a landmark event that was widely condemned in Ireland and Britain, with the public believing 'it transcended all the previous "rules" for reprisals'.[74] The *Manchester Guardian* claimed it 'outdoes in horror anything that has yet occurred even in that city of many murders'.[75] The IRA sought revenge. Cumann na mBan 'issued a statement warning of retaliatory action if any more attacks on Catholics took place'.[76] On 31 March, a bomb was thrown into the home of Francis Donnelly, a Protestant, on Brown Street, severely wounding him and his two daughters. His two boys, aged twelve and two, died from their injuries. As they left, 'the attackers fired revolver shots at Donnelly's wife who was nursing a baby'.[77] Members of the provisional government were so incensed by the MacMahon killings that they considered breaking the treaty. Mulcahy, the defence minister, blamed the British government for financing the Specials, 'a sectarian police force engaged in a very extensive campaign of murder and violence'.[78] After the incident, both the pro- and anti-treaty sides of Sinn Féin called for joint action on the north.

March had seen a higher death toll than February, with sixty-one people killed in Belfast alone. One witness 'remembers the cross-firing that was kept up day and night'.[79] Soon after this, Craig and Collins signed their second pact. Like the original pact, it was ineffective almost as quickly as it was signed. The all-too-familiar pattern was followed: 'On 1 April an RIC constable from Brown Square barracks in Belfast was shot dead. Less than an hour later uniformed police broke into Catholic homes in Arnon Street and Stanhope Street and in reprisal beat a man to death with a sledgehammer, mortally wounded a child, shot three men dead and injured two other children.'[80] Nixon's 'murder gang' was deemed responsible. It would be an exaggeration to suggest that Northern Ireland was in peril of retaining its status as a devolved entity during the height of the IRA attacks on its territory. Northern Ireland was beleaguered, though, and the British government was frustrated with the inability of the northern government 'to maintain control of its allotted area and the role of many of its security forces in a number of high profile atrocities'. The British were 'also tired of the crippling costs of maintaining such a large, and one-sided, security apparatus'.[81] Even though the northern government controlled the Special Constabulary, the British government financed it with vast sums of money. In a memorandum from May 1922, it was estimated, that for the Specials alone, the British had covered the cost of 'full webbing equipment' for 8,000 'A' Specials, 25,000 'B' Specials and 15,000 'C' Specials, 23,000 rifles, 15,000 bayonets, 242 guns, 50 Vickers guns, 3,000 RIC revolvers, camp equipment, 150 bicycles and spare parts, signalling equipment, 10 million rounds of ammunition, mills bombs for barrack defence and motor transport.[82] An additional 4,900 rifles were handed to the Belfast government from army stocks, available since the truce of July 1921.[83] The northern government even asked the Royal Air Force (RAF) for planes and bombs. This request was turned down angrily by Churchill, who stated 'it is not the business of the Ulster Police to have an air force'.[84] In May 1922, Craig estimated the annual cost of covering security for Northern Ireland to be £2.75 million, with a special supplementary amount of £2.1 million needed for the threats posed in 1922.[85] The British government also supplied uniforms for the new police force, the RUC, which had been established to replace the defunct RIC. Churchill stated that he 'did not want khaki uniforms' for the RUC and promised to assist the northern government in obtaining blue clothing by utilising the large stock of partly worn RIC uniforms in Dublin.[86]

The RIC was formally disbanded in May and replaced by the RUC at the beginning of June as the north's new regular police force. The disbandment of the RIC in the Free State followed a similar timeline.[87] Wickham became the RUC's first Inspector General. This was unpopular with many hard-line loyalists, who felt Wickham, as an Englishman, 'was not sufficiently committed to their cause'.[88] The 3,000-strong force was to consist of one commissioner in Belfast, six county inspectors, thirty-five district inspectors, one medical officer, fifty-eight head constables, 400 sergeants and 2,489 constables. Wickham asserted that more staff were needed, claiming that since the Special Constabulary 'was formed in October, 1920, leave has been unknown; normal hours of work are from 9:30 am, to 7:30 pm, or later. If efficiency is to be maintained it can be accomplished only by the provision of the minimum necessary staff'.[89] It was hoped that 'when times become normal', the force would be reduced significantly.[90]

In January 1922, Dawson-Bates, the Minister for Home Affairs had appointed a fifteen-person committee, including two Catholics, to investigate the organisation, recruitment, conditions of service, strength and cost of the future police force.[91] The committee took evidence from different parties. It was agreed that the police force should be centralised and not the responsibility of county councils, as some could not be trusted. It was stated that it 'would be an absolutely impossible view that the county council of Fermanagh should take over the police force, owing to their political complexion. They would recruit their own men for the purpose of carrying out their own views.'[92] Even though some called for the establishment of a separate women's police force, the committee decided there should not be an increase in the number of policewomen for the new force, standing at just two for the entire RIC in the north.[93] A women's section of the Specials had been arranged to organise the supply of nurses, typists and clerks under the leadership of Lord Londonderry's wife, Lady Edith.[94] The committee agreed that there should be a minimum height required of five feet eight inches, with one witness claiming, 'A small policeman may be all right, but there always seems to be something wrong with him. I really do not think people have respect for a small policeman, although he is very often just as good as a big one.'[95] The committee concluded that the new force should be based around the existing organisational structure of the RIC, with personnel coming from the RIC and Specials.[96] There were some doubts about hiring from the RIC, as it was claimed that 'nine-tenths of them were recruited outside the Northern Area.'[97] In the south, there were examples of many RIC officers being ordered to leave certain areas, such as Cavan, Wicklow, Galway, Kildare, Donegal and King's County (present-day Offaly), by the IRA. There were accusations of female relations of ex-RIC constables being 'grossly mistreated in some parts of the country', such as Galway.[98] Many moved to the six counties. Most of the doubts about suitability were reserved for the Specials. One witness claimed, 'I think there is only one special constable in six will make a policeman, whereas I would be inclined to say that only one RIC man in six makes a bad policeman.' Another said that only 10 per cent of them 'could write an intelligible report ... If a man is any good he has found a job outside the Specials. It is only the unemployed we are getting in the Specials. The greater number of them were unemployed.'[99] The committee felt that there was little cooperation between the RIC and the Specials, with many in the RIC objecting 'to the type of man they meet in that organisation as recruited from the corner-boy class'.[100] Many felt the ratio of RIC to Specials should be 70:30; however, it was ultimately decided to compose the RUC of 50:50, as long as the Specials received a full six months of training.[101]

Originally, the new force was to be called the Ulster Constabulary. A recommendation was made 'for approval to include "Royal" in the title, which was later granted by George V on 29 April'.[102] The new name was yet another obstacle in attempting to allocate 1,000 places (one-third of the new force) to Catholics to reflect the population of Northern Ireland.[103] The Catholic recruits were to be drawn from ex-RIC officer ranks and the civilian population. Nine of the fifteen from the committee complained about the high numbers reserved for Catholics. Nonetheless, the Catholic allocation remained at one-third, at least nominally.[104] One of the witnesses, Colonel Tillie from Derry, suggested 'that much good might be achieved by informal talks between the County Representatives of the RIC, Special Police, etc., and the County Organisers of the IRA'. He believed that if there was no informal consultation with the IRA, 'the new force will be entirely composed of Protestants without any Roman Catholic representation in it, unless what you get from the old RIC'. The committee ruled against meeting with the IRA, 'an illegal organisation' who they believed were not representative of the majority of Catholics who only wanted peace and were constitutional in their politics.[105] Whilst the Specials remained exclusively Protestant in composition, in the end, Catholics comprised one-sixth of the numbers of the RUC, not one-third as allocated. Most of them were former members of the RIC. No attempt was made 'to increase this proportion and by 1936 there were only 488 Catholics out of 2,849 in the RUC and only 9 Catholics among the 55 officers holding the rank of district inspector and above'.[106] This had declined to about one in ten by the late 1960s: 'Catholics did not join because they did not regard the police as legitimate … When they joined, the atmosphere was rarely inclusive: institutional affiliations between police units and Orange lodges confirmed Catholic perceptions of the RUC as Protestants with guns.'[107] One of the first obligations of the new police force was to enforce the newly enacted Special Powers Act, a law that further alienated the minority community.

The Special Powers Bill was approved by the northern cabinet on 13 March 1922, receiving royal assent on 7 April. The original bill had proposed the establishment of special courts to take the place of court martials; however, this was omitted, as it would reflect poorly 'upon the Judiciary', which was still in its infancy.[108] The new act gave the Minister of Home Affairs, Dawson-Bates, sweeping powers. It 'provided for the death penalty, flogging, arrest without warrant and the prohibition of inquests'. It also permitted Dawson-Bates 'to make further regulations – each with the force of a new law – without consulting Parliament, and to delegate his powers to any policeman'.[109] George Hanna, a unionist MP, believed the bill was too complicated, saying there were 'nine sections of the bill and thirty regulations. One section would have been sufficient: "The Home Secretary shall have the power to do whatever he likes, or let somebody else do whatever he likes for him". That is the whole Bill.'[110] The *Manchester Guardian* strongly condemned the bill, writing:

> Whilst envenomed politicians in the Ulster Parliament are voting themselves power to use torture and capital punishment freely against citizens whom they forbid to defend themselves while they scarcely attempt to protect them from massacre, some of their own partisans in Belfast carry wholesale murder to refinements of barbarity hardly surpassed in the Turkish attacks on Armenians in Constantinople.[111]

Joseph Devlin illustrated the predicament the nationalist community was faced with: 'If Catholics have no revolvers they are murdered. It they have revolvers they are flogged and sentenced to death.'[112] The Special Powers Act was renewed annually until 1928, renewed for five years until 1933, and then made permanent. According to Brendan O'Leary, it was 'one of the most draconian pieces of legislation ever passed in a liberal democracy'.[113] Michael Collins complained bitterly to Churchill about the Special Powers Act, saying it gave 'virtually unlimited' coercive powers to Dawson-Bates, 'notorious for his antipathy to our people'. He warned that 'the situation in the six counties could not be graver, if these offensive, not protective measures are taken against our people ... I cannot be responsible for the awful consequences which must ensure.'[114] Collins was desperate to avoid a conflict with the anti-Treatyites in the south. With both sides of the treaty vehemently opposed to partition, the one area he could get unity on was the north.

Some commentators have argued that 'in supporting aggression on the border during those months Collins pursued the short-term aims of, first, not ceding the initiative on the north to anti-Treatyites and, second, securing the northern IRA for the pro-treaty position or at least some form of neutrality'.[115] The anti-Treatyites also looked to demonstrate their credentials on the issue of partition since the start of 1922, leading to a situation whereby both sides of the treaty split in the south vied against each other to 'prove who was the more reliable ally of beleaguered northern nationalists'.[116] Most northern IRA units remained loyal to Collins. However, the desperate plight of northern nationalists weakened the provisional government's position. The northern IRA was unable to stand alone – it needed assistance from the south. Loyalty was conditional on commitments being met.[117] The news in the south for the first six months of 1922 was dominated by the treaty and the Belfast 'Pogrom'. Incidents such as those on Weaver Street and of the MacMahon family were highlighted to show the 'barbarism' and 'terror' Catholics were experiencing in Belfast, with 20,000 reported to have fled the city.[118] One of the 'most identifiable consequences of partition' was the 'forced displacement of people', those on the 'wrong' side of the border. Thousands of Irish people chose to or were forced to leave the north or south due to partition. The northern government and bodies such as the Ulster Women's Unionist Council, contributed to a refugee fund set up to help southern loyalists who had relocated to the north.[119] The full figure of refugees who fled the north is unknown, but it certainly is higher than the 1,650 'officially recognised' refugees stated to be in the Free State between January and August 1922, according to the southern government.[120] Many moved to Scotland and England, while others relocated to towns along the border, particularly bigger towns such as Dundalk.[121] Dublin saw large numbers of refugees arrive throughout the first half of 1922, and this became a problem for the provisional government.

In April and May, the anti-Treaty IRA took over a number of unionist-owned properties in Dublin to house Belfast refugees, including the Freemason's Hall on Molesworth Street, the Kildare Street Club, the Young Men's Christian Association (YMCA) building on O'Connell Street, and the Orange Order Hall on Parnell Square.[122] The YMCA also had one of its buildings commandeered by the Specials in Belfast.[123] On taking over the

Orange Order Hall, republican activist Maud Gonne said, 'What more suitable place than the house belonging to the Orangemen could be found to house the victims of the Orange terror?'[124] Not to be outdone by the anti-Treatyites, the provisional government rehoused 500 refugees in Marlborough Hall, Glasnevin and granted £10,000 to help them.[125] Up to that point, the provisional government had ignored the refugee crisis. Cosgrave, as Minister for Local Government, was responsible for the issue. 'He would remain unsympathetic and suspicious of the reality of the northern refugee crisis, treating it as a political and financial problem rather than a simple humanitarian one.'[126] The provisional government only responded once the anti-Treatyites had initially filled the vacuum.

The anti-Treatyites also defied the provisional government on the Belfast Boycott. The boycott was discontinued by the first Craig–Collins pact on 21 January. The provisional government considered bringing the boycott back in March due to 'the continuance of atrocities', but made no definitive decision.[127] The IRA Executive, elected at the first anti-Treaty army convention on 27 March, reinstated it regardless. In early May 'a party from the anti-Treaty Four Courts garrison demanded that Woolworth's Department Store on Henry Street pay a £200 fine for breach of the Belfast Boycott'.[128] Similarly, Switzer's, the department store, was forced to write a cheque to the 'Director of Boycott'.[129] In County Louth, the anti-Treaty IRA put up many posters 'warning certain persons who had accounts in Ulster bank to withdraw funds under threat'.[130] The provisional government believed the 'rebel forces' were using the Belfast Boycott as a means to commit illegal actions. The seizing of property in Dublin by the anti-Treatyites in the name of the 'Belfast Boycott' was the direct catalyst that started the civil war in Dublin. On 26 June a raiding party from the Four Courts, which had been occupied by the anti-Treaty IRA since April, seized four cars from Ferguson's, a well-known Belfast firm that had a garage on Baggot Street, in punishment for their doing business with Belfast. Leo Henderson, who led the raid, was arrested by pro-Treaty troops. The anti-Treaty leadership seized National Army general J.J. 'Ginger' O'Connell in retaliation. They held him hostage in the Four Courts, to be released in exchange for Henderson. The following day, the cabinet resolved to have 'Notice served to Four Courts and Fowler's Hall to evacuate and surrender all arms or military action would be taken'.

Military action was taken the next day with the attack on the Four Courts, thus starting the civil war.[131] Before this, an offensive on the north had been attempted, more as a way to avert civil war in the south than as a genuine attempt to help the nationalist community in the north.[132]

The 'Northern Offensive' of May 1922 transpired to be the last military attempt by the Free State to destabilise the north. It involved pro- and anti-Treaty troops from all over Ireland. Collins, in supplying weapons to the northern divisions of the IRA, 'could not ship to them the weapons with which the British were supplying his National Army in Dublin'. He decided to take weapons from the anti-Treaty IRA, to be used in the north, and give them the British weapons in return.[133] Southern IRA members coordinated excursions into the six-counties from Donegal, and the northern divisions were supplied with new weapons and equipment.[134] The offensive was a failure almost from the start, with mistakes, non-transfers, recriminations in public and disagreements between both sides of the IRA divide.[135] Once the unity between both sides waned, Collins's commitment to the offensive also faded. The three southern-based pro-Treaty divisions (1st and 5th Northern and 1st Midland) were told to hold back from travelling north.[136] The offensive still went ahead. Belfast was engulfed in dozens of serious fires, and railway stations and mills were destroyed.[137] At the end of May, both pro- and anti-Treaty IRA troops seized an area around the Belleek–Pettigo triangle, on the border of Donegal and Fermanagh, including areas within the northern jurisdiction. British troops intervened to force them out.[138] With overwhelming numbers and the use of artillery, the British offensive on the Belleek–Pettigo triangle resulted in the deaths of three IRA men, perhaps seven, with another forty to fifty captured. There were some British and Specials casualties too.[139] After a policeman was killed and a mill burned down in Desertmartin by the IRA, 'seven Catholics were murdered in reprisal and following the burning of some of their businesses and homes, all the Catholic residents of this Co. Londonderry town were driven out'.[140]

Reprisals, although not as numerous, were perpetrated by the IRA too. In response to attacks carried out by the 'B' Specials in south Armagh, members of the 4th Northern Division of the IRA killed six Protestants, injured several others and burned a dozen properties in the townlands of Lisdrumliska and Altnaveigh in County Armagh on 17 June 1922.[141] By the end of June, support from the south had ceased, and the supply of men and arms had dried up. The civil war had begun. Spender, the northern cabinet's secretary, remarked that 'lootings and hold-ups have nearly ceased ... The conflict in Southern Ireland had drawn away many of the most active politicians from Ulster.'[142] The northern divisions of the IRA were disbanded, with many moving south to join the Free State army. One of the primary reasons for the move south was the large-scale enforcement of the Specials Powers Act after the assassination of an MP, W.J. Twaddell, on 22 May.

Twaddell was shot dead on the way to his outfitter's shop, 'the only MP to be assassinated in Northern Ireland until the murder of the Reverend Robert Bradford in 1981'.[143] After his death, the northern government ordered the round-up of some 500 Sinn Féin sympathisers; 300 of them were interned on board the *Argenta*, moored first in Belfast Lough, then later in Larne Bay.[144] Although most of the people interned were not activists, many northern IRA members who had not been arrested decided to flee south before they were. Wickham declared that 'in Belfast the spectacle of the floating internment palace in Belfast Lough before their vision acts as a warning to Sinn Féiners to curb their enthusiasm for their evil activities'.[145] When the IRA in Belfast undertook an arson campaign in the city in June, the response from the authorities was ferocious. Leading IRA member in Belfast, Seamus Woods, reported, 'The enemy are continually raiding and arresting; the heavy sentences and particularly the flogging making the civilians very loath to keep wanted men or arms.'[146] The IRA in the north retreated. By 1924, there were just over 600 IRA activists, down from over 4,000 in late 1921. The northern authorities banned 'commemorations, the sale of *An Phoblacht* and the wearing of Easter lilies'. Republicans were a minority among the nationalist population. Nonetheless, the IRA still remained alive in Northern Ireland, with 400 members in Belfast alone by 1934.[147]

The commencement of the civil war in the south was a stroke of great luck for the northern government, one of many following the third Home Rule Crisis of 1912. The conflict in the south brought some stability to the north – a stability attained at a heavy price. So many – from both communities – were impacted deeply by the violence that came with the birth of Northern Ireland. That the Catholic community suffered more, there can be no doubt. Judging by scales of the deaths as well as wounded, evictions, internments, floggings and different forms of discrimination, the Catholic community bore the brunt of the north's violent beginnings. Although Catholics were reluctant to recognise Northern Ireland or participate in its institutions, no attempt was made to assimilate them either. Stability may have been achieved in the north by 1923, but it was done so in what remained a deeply bitter and divided community.

CHAPTER EIGHT

Law

Arguably, nothing demonstrated the complexity of creating a jurisdiction from scratch more so than the law. Under the Government of Ireland Act 1920, the judiciary of Ireland was divided into two – north and south. This was muddled by the superseding of the Government of Ireland Act in the south by the Anglo-Irish Treaty of 1921. Not only were there two jurisdictions with different judiciaries, one jurisdiction had more powers than the other. There was also a parallel system of justice in place, the Republican (or Dáil) Courts, at the time when Ireland was partitioned. Whilst the Free State was presented with most aspects of a functioning legal system, Northern Ireland was faced with the gargantuan task of creating a whole new justice system for a new entity. The civil disturbances that came with the birth of Northern Ireland also distracted the northern government's 'attention from the important business of instituting, housing and funding the new legal system'.[1]

Since the Acts of Union of 1800, a court system for the whole island of Ireland was retained, lasting until the constitutional settlements of 1920–22.[2] Although Ireland was part of the union with Britain, it was administered separately with a viceroy, a ministry, a civil service run from Dublin Castle and a judiciary.[3] The Government of Ireland Act 1920 provided that, 'The Supreme Court of Judicature in Ireland shall cease to exist.'[4] Under the act, Supreme Courts of Judicature were created for Northern Ireland and Southern Ireland.[5] Both judiciaries were to remain reserved services. All matters relating to their functions 'were to remain under the control of the Imperial Parliament'.[6] There was also a High Court of Appeal for Ireland. This court 'was an all-Ireland jurisdiction and lasted from the 15 December 1921 to the 5 December 1922, the day before the new Free State constitution came into force'.[7] In introducing the Government of Ireland Bill to the

House of Commons in February 1920, Lloyd George claimed the Irish judiciary 'was to remain under the Imperial authorities until the proposed two legislatures could come to an understanding. The present view, however, is that there must be separate judiciaries for the two Irish entities.'[8] The two Irish judiciaries were scheduled to be inaugurated on 1 October 1921.

The Northern Ireland Supreme Court had two divisions: the High Court of Justice and the Court of Appeal. The Court of Appeal was further divided into a King's Bench Division and a Chancery Division. In charge of all the work of the northern judiciary were 'five judges: two Lord Justices of Appeal, two High Court Judges and a Lord Chief Justice.'[9] The person chosen to be the first Lord Chief Justice of Northern Ireland was a Catholic, Sir Denis Stanislaus Henry. His appointment was agreed by the northern government at the beginning of August, along with that of Northern Ireland's first Attorney-General, Richard Best. In making the announcements, Craig stated his 'intention was that those announcements of new appointments should be gradually made during the next month so that the people of Ulster might see that progress was being made' and that 'the Courts ought to be ready to function immediately after the Appointed Day'.[10] Up to that point, with transfer of services delayed and the British government in talks with Sinn Féin, the Northern Ireland project looked stillborn. The nationalist-leaning newspaper, the *Irish News*, mockingly stated on 6 August that the northern parliament was

> inherently unworkable … Appointments have been made carrying large salaries; and we now learn that the absurd Northern judiciary has been given a send off with the elevation to the non-existent bench of Mr. Denis Henry, KC, as Lord Chief Justice … Sir James Craig's Government cannot undertake any work with any degree of permanency attaching to it because there can be no permanency in this Partition.[11]

Very little emphasis was made of Henry's Catholicism, with just the *Daily Mail* regarding the appointment as highlighting 'the complete absence of any religious disability to the highest appointments in Ireland. The newspaper pointed out that three of the most important posts in Ireland were now held by Catholics: Henry as Chief Justice, Fitz Alan as Lord Lieutenant of Ireland, and the Lord Chief Justice of Ireland, Justice [Thomas] Maloney'. Craig said years later, 'I have never yet known a country prosper where appointments to the judiciary were made on religious grounds. As long as I have anything to do with it, that aspect will never enter into my mind.'[12] When, in 1930, five years after Henry's death, after a charge was made that no Catholic had been elevated to the bench, Craig replied that 'since the death of our old friend, Denis Henry', it had 'not been possible to find a Catholic lawyer fully-qualified to hold a judgeship', clearly inferring that Catholics could aspire to judiciary appointments if they met the requirements.[13] Despite Craig's assertions to the contrary, the history of Northern Ireland's judiciary suggests appointments to its ranks were barely attainable for aspiring Catholics. After Henry's death in 1925, 'no other Catholic was appointed to the highest court until 1949. As late as 1969 Catholics held a mere six out of sixty-eight senior judicial appointments, and judges and barristers had to take archaic oaths of loyalty' to the British crown, a large deterrent for many Catholics.[14]

Whilst Henry was a Catholic, he was not a nationalist, holding an almost unique position by being a Catholic Ulster Unionist MP before he was appointed Lord Chief Justice.[15] Although it was not uncommon for Catholics to be unionist in political outlook in the south and west of Ireland, it was considerably less so in Ulster.[16] Born in Derry in 1864 into a 'strongly conservative and pro-Union' family, he built his reputation as a barrister on the north-west circuit of Ireland, an area extending from Westmeath to Derry, Tyrone and Donegal.[17] He was known as the father of the north-west circuit. The Northern Ireland parts of the north-west and north-east circuits were merged into one after partition to form the northern judiciary.[18] He became MP for Londonderry South through a by-election victory in May 1916, the first electoral contest after the Easter Rising. He had previously narrowly missed out on entering parliament for the Tyrone North constituency, by nine votes in 1906 and by just seven votes in 1907.[19] Once elected, he was soon promoted to Irish law officerships: Solicitor General in 1918 and Attorney General in 1919. As Attorney General, he served under Chief Secretaries Ian MacPherson and Hamar Greenwood during a time of great upheaval in Irish politics and society.[20] He was responsible for introducing the draconian Restoration of Order in Ireland Act, which became law in August 1920, and established military courts-martial with the power to impose the death penalty.[21] His tenacious 'defence of emergency legislation and the official thinking which underpinned it' and his strident opposition to 'any form of compromise with those whom he regarded as little more than rebels bent on destroying the fabric of law and order in Ireland' made him an ideal candidate to head the northern judiciary, 'in an atmosphere no less frenetic, involving equally strident views when the enforcing of new emergency legislation was challenged'.[22]

Henry was sworn in as Lord Chief Justice on 15 August 1921 at the 'unlikely setting' of Portrush Town Hall. He was faced with the unenviable task of ensuring the judiciary appointments as well as a functioning justice system were in place by 1 October, just weeks later. The Supreme Court 'in its original foundation comprised five judges'. This remained the case until after the Second World War, when it was extended to fourteen members. Within the Supreme Court, the High Court consisted of the Lord Chief Justice as president and 'two puisne judges, one of whom was assigned to the chancery division and one to the queen's bench division', and the Court of Appeal consisted of the Lord Chief Justice also as president, 'supported by the two lord justices'.[23] The two Lord Justices were William Moore and James Andrews. The two High Court judges were D.M. Wilson and T.W. Brown. All were Ulstermen, 'with the exception of Wilson', all had 'lived through the rise and development of Unionist opposition to Home Rule, and all bar Andrews had stood for election in the Unionist interest'. Andrews' brother John was Minister for Labour in the first northern government. Another brother, Thomas, was managing director of Harland and Wolff and responsible for the design of the *Titanic*, on which he perished in 1912.[24] They were all 'well acquainted with the law in Ulster. Henry had dominated the North-West, Moore and Wilson had worked in the North-East'.[25] Although some had experience as 'county court judges and resident magistrates', Moore was the only one with senior judicial experience. He was the 'only member of the southern judiciary who signified a desire to serve as a judge in Northern Ireland'.[26]

Henry also had to oversee the appointment of officials and secure a courthouse by 1 October. Moore wrote a memorandum in late 1922 outlining the enormous undertaking that the establishment of a justice system from scratch entailed.[27] Much of the burden fell to Henry. From 1921,

> Henry did not spare himself in constant anxious work in setting up the courts and their administration, involving him in endless discussion and negotiation with the governments in Belfast and London, with the bar and the Law Society, council officials, his southern counterparts and many others. Added to his judicial work this made up a formidable workload and his son was of the opinion that this contributed to his death in 1925 at the early age of 61.[28]

Under the Government of Ireland Act 1920, it was the duty of the imperial government to provide a suitable dwelling for the Supreme Court and its staff. To acquire a site and erect a suitable building was not possible by 1 October. [29] Several sites were proposed for the permanent courthouse, including Stormont and the Royal Belfast Academical Institution at College Square East. Eventually the government purchased the site of the old potato market, and it was here that the new Law Courts opened in 1933.[30] For the twelve years before the permanent courthouse was built, it was necessary to use temporary accommodation. The Antrim County Courthouse on the Crumlin Road in Belfast was chosen as the best available option. Whilst suitable for assize work and periodic courts that met two or three times per year, the courthouse was 'not at all so suitable for the housing of a permanent staff to carry on the permanent departmental work of a permanent High Court'.[31] As well as this, the bulk of Antrim County Council's business, as well as that of the Land Registry and the Belfast Local Bankruptcy Court, were conducted at the County Courthouse. Henry met with representatives from Antrim County Council, the Lord Mayor of Belfast and the Town Clerk, and successfully secured the building by 1 October. However, the conditions for the staff were very cramped. The temporary courthouse lacked a waiting room for jurors and contained no separate accommodation for women jurors. There were also no facilities available for the press. For Henry and Craig, 'the absence of a Supreme Court building could have symbolised the Nationalist assertion that the structures of the new state were impermanent'.[32]

Henry also established the court offices with the two main divisions of the Registrar and Chief Clerk's offices and minor ones of the Taxing Master and Accountant General. The court offices were 'more or less founded on the English System and quite unlike that of Dublin.'[33] Once Henry had decided on the categories of the court offices, he was 'unable to set about appointing officers to fill these positions until the establishment of the office with its consequent salary and pension rights had been approved by the Imperial Treasury'. Before 1 October, he had difficulties in even nominating a messenger for the judiciary.[34] Henry had many meetings and discussions with treasury officials in Dublin from September to November 1921, and this involved 'considerable correspondence and delay' when speedy decisions were needed, a trend experienced with many other civil service departments.[35] Members of the legal civil servant branch in the Four Courts in Dublin were eligible to transfer themselves to the northern courts, with many applying 'but with the attached condition that they should receive promotion on transfer. This was impossible to concede as of right and such applications were withdrawn.'[36] Ultimately, five people arrived from Dublin: J.G. Breakey, J. O'H. Devine, R.C. Hill, H.C.S. Torney and R.H. Torney. In total, there were sixty-four officials appointed in the court office 'from Registrar to Messenger'.[37] Most officials came from the six counties, something desired by Craig. Henry personally conducted many interviews and arranged the desks, furniture, dies, seals, presses and forms for the new judiciary.[38] There was an issue with the judicature fee stamps, however, as there was no stamp office at the Law Courts in Belfast as there was at the Four Courts. With stamps only obtainable at the Custom House, for some time, documents issued at the court offices involved 'the attendance of the Solicitors at the Courts to get the documents and ascertain the fees payable on them, the taking of them to the Custom House to have the stamps impressed and bringing them back again to the office to be signed, certified and issued'.[39] This one seemingly trivial point illustrates the many teething problems associated with establishing a new justice system.

The new justice system for Northern Ireland became operative on 1 October 1921 and was formally opened three weeks later on 24 October. It was another day of ceremony, reminiscent of the opening of the northern parliament four months earlier, and another day to demonstrate the viability of the northern jurisdiction. Many were in attendance from all 'branches of the industrial, commercial, and professional activities of Belfast'.[40] Judges assembled in 'full Robes and full bottomed Wigs' listened as the Lord Chief Justice Henry declared, they would 'do our best to carry on the Traditions handed down to us by the great Judges who adorned the Irish Bench'. He acknowledged the 'very many difficulties in connexion with the Institution of an entirely new series of Courts and Offices' and thanked Antrim County Council and Belfast Corporation for allocating space and accommodation for the new courts. He also was appreciative of the help received from Thomas Molony, the Lord Chief Justice of Ireland, who had 'given us his help in placing at our disposal the services of his skilled Officials, and in giving us access to all the Books and Documents we required'.[41]

The judges in situ during the birth of Northern Ireland had an extremely difficult task. The 'conditions in which they had to work for some years were most unsatisfactory' and 'the future of the new state and their own future remained in doubt for a material length of time'.[42] From the start of the judiciary, Henry created a commission to serve Belfast, made circuit arrangements and contributed to the functioning of the High Court of Appeal for Ireland. The commission dealt with crime for the city of Belfast and met on four occasions each year. By July 1922, it had met three times, with Henry, Moore and Andrews presiding on one occasion each.[43] In total that year, 'according to the criminal lists at the Belfast city commission, there were 97 cases of murder, 59 of attempted murder and 37 of felonies endangering life'.[44] In the same year, the Special Powers Act had transferred 'many of the powers for preserving peace and maintaining order from the judiciary to the executive'.[45] The courts were still inundated with severe criminal cases, such was the level of violence in the city that year. Henry also established a Circuit of Northern Ireland with a rota involving the Lord Chief Justice and his two Lord Justices taking a share in the work of the commission and assizes. Although it was not obligatory for the Lord Justices to carry out such work, 'there are not enough puisne judges to carry on the necessary work in Belfast', according to Moore.[46] Henry also attended four sittings of the High Court of Appeal for Ireland, up until it disbanded in December 1922.[47] An anomaly arose in early 1921 within the Government of Ireland Act in relation to the High Court of Appeal. It was discovered by Sir John Ross, the last Lord Chancellor of Ireland, that the High Court of Appeal could 'never sit in cases from Northern Ireland', as the required minimum of two northern judges for the appeal sitting could not happen, as four of the five northern judges would have been involved in the original case, disallowing their participation in the appeal. The issue never arose in the south due to the far greater number of judges located there. It was eventually amended to allow for a minimum requirement of one northern judge to participate in appeal sittings.[48]

Many of the cases the judges convened over on the circuit were in relation to the new border and the confusion it caused. Judges on both sides of the border were faced with complex issues over territory without any precedents to work with. In the case of a Donegal man being sued at the King's Bench Division of the High Court in Belfast in November 1921, with Henry presiding, it was debated whether the case would be more cost-effective to be tried in the north or to have the writ served out of the jurisdiction by registered letter.[49] Similarly, in the south, there was confusion over where people who resided in County Down (in the north) should be tried for allegedly running over a boy with a motor car in County Louth (in the south).[50] In 1925, at the Monaghan Circuit Court, the judge had to rule on the jurisdiction of a case involving a man who went to sleep with 'his head in the Free State and his feet in Northern Ireland'.[51] When Henry and Justice Wilson travelled around the six counties for the first circuit in March 1922 for the spring assizes, most of the cases were related to the ongoing unrest that had consumed Northern Ireland. The circuit route started in Antrim, then to Down, Armagh, Fermanagh, Tyrone and Derry.[52] At the Tyrone assizes, he sentenced a large number of defendants to penal servitude for possession of arms, bombs, unlawful assembly, holding up vehicles and shooting at police officers.[53] Soon after, as some were sentenced to penal servitude in the Derry assizes for similar offences, they declared that they refused to recognise the court, owing their allegiance to Dáil Éireann instead. At the same assizes, the press reported that 'every case ... save one, in which a man was charged with stealing ducks, Catholic Jurors were challenged by the Crown and ordered to stand by'.[54] It was a common occurrence for the crown's authorities in the north to routinely challenge 'Catholic jurors when Catholics were on trial'.[55] Henry was also involved in some highly controversial cases as Lord Chief

Justice. In July 1922 'he ruled against the plaintiff in a landmark case [O'Hanlon v Governor of Belfast Prison] challenging the legality of the unionist government's Special Powers Act'.[56] In a case of special constables killing three Catholics in June 1922, Henry 'agreed that the security forces had been fired on. He rejected the claims for compensation, and found that the deaths arose out of unlawful assembly'.[57] As Lord Chief Justice of Northern Ireland, Henry continued with his support for the forces of law and order.

At the official opening of the northern judiciary in October 1921, Henry recognised the 'many inconveniences since the opening of our Courts' on the Solicitors' Profession'.[58] The Incorporated Law Society of Ireland, the regulatory body for solicitors, was opposed to the division of the Irish judiciary under the Government of Ireland Act and supported an amendment by the MP Colonel Walter Guinness, at the committee stage of the bill, 'to continuing one Judicial system for the whole of Ireland'. The Society feared that it would be split along with the judiciary.[59] At the half-yearly meeting of the society in November 1920, it reported that in May 1920

The Northern Law Society, with whom this Society had always been on the best of terms and who were represented by five members on the Council, passed a resolution that steps be taken to procure, amongst other things, the introduction of provisions into the bill, or by regulations to be made under it, whereby the Northern Law Society should have the same status, constitution and powers, etc., in respect of Northern Ireland as the Society had at present for the whole of Ireland.[60]

This 'came as a great surprise, and it was earnestly hoped ... that the Society might continue to exercise its functions in the future, as it had done in the past, throughout the whole of Ireland'.[61] S.G. Crymble, president of the Northern Law Society, declared at the opening of the northern judiciary that 'The Institution of the Supreme Court of Northern Ireland has rendered it necessary that a new Incorporated Law Society should be established, and the Members of our Profession should be brought under your Lordship's jurisdiction and control'.[62] Much to the disappointment of the Incorporated Law Society of Ireland, the Northern Law Society succeed in obtaining a charter in June 1922.[63] The charter gave the northern body the same powers for the north that the Incorporated Law Society of Ireland previously had for the whole island. Under the charter, the Northern Law Society could appoint 'Lecturers for the instruction of their Students, arrange a syllabus of subjects of Examination as qualification for Admission to their Profession, and all other requisite arrangements: so that Apprentices in their Offices need no longer spend their time in Dublin, or pay any fees or Stamps there.'[64]

The relations between the Bench and the Bar in the northern judiciary were considered quite strong, with the judges and the Attorney General offering the Bar Council a gift of £100 on the birth of the new circuit. The Bar of Northern Ireland appointed a committee on 26 October 1921 to draw up a constitution and rules. The Bar Council was elected and a library committee was appointed on 12 January 1922. Subscribing to the Bar library gave members privileges 'of the Library, Robing Room, and Luncheon Room in the Courts'. There were fifty-seven subscribing members by late 1922. The Bar also formed a Circuit of Northern Ireland, and all 'existing members of the late North-East and North-West Circuits were eligible for the New Circuit'. One of the greatest initial challenges for the Bar was 'the crying necessity for an adequate Law Library'. There was an 'urgent want of a Law Library available to Bench and Bar in the Court House, containing the Reports for the last sixty years'. Queen's University permitted the Bar to use its library, 'but this, from its situation so far away, does not meet the difficulty'.[65] The Government of Ireland Act had practically severed the Bar of Ireland into two bodies but 'all the then existing Members of the Bar had the right of Audience in both areas of Ireland preserved to them'.[66] By 1926, 'there were between 60 and 70 barristers who regarded themselves as permanently practicing in Northern Ireland'.[67] One of those was Frances Christian Kyle, the first woman to be called to the Irish bar in November 1921.[68]

The passing of 'the Sex Disqualification (Removal) Act in 1919, which applied generally throughout the United Kingdom, had the effect of removing an actual legal barrier in the way of women seeking to enter any profession, including that of the law'.[69] Kyle was immediately followed by Averill Deverell on the same day. Both women made headlines around the world for being the first women to be called to the Bar in Britain or Ireland.[70] That day was also the first call of a divided Irish Bar. Kyle, originally from Belfast, pursued her professional career in Northern Ireland, whilst Deverell, from Greystones in County Wicklow, pursued her career in the south.[71] Kyle, like all other students from Northern Ireland at the time, still had to study at King's Inns in Dublin to qualify as a barrister. This arrangement continued until 1925.

The link 'provided by King's Inns between the benchers and bars of Northern Ireland and Southern Ireland remained, and at first it seemed that, unlike the remainder of the legal system, this link would not be broken'.[72] Sir John Ross, the Lord Chancellor, claimed in 1921, 'There is one thing that would never be split up, and that was the Honorable Society of the Benchers of King's Inns'.[73] King's Inns, eager to remain united, understood the need to recognise the changed political and legal circumstances. The 'resolution envisaged a largely autonomous structure in Northern Ireland for the education and discipline of bar students under the auspices of King's Inns, while seeking to preserve the ultimate right of the benchers in Dublin to determine any matters in dispute'.[74] The Bench and Bar in the north felt it was 'impracticable at present to form a new Inn in Belfast even if desired, partly from lack of funds, and partly because at first not more than about ten students in the year as a maximum might be expected'.[75] An agreement was reached between Dublin and Belfast:

(1) That the Lord Chief Justice of Ireland would call to the Bar of Southern Ireland all students called to the Bar in Northern Ireland, and the Chief Justice would similarly call to the Bar of Northern Ireland all students so called in Southern Ireland.

(2) That the Benchers of King's Inns would appoint and pay a professor of law to deliver lectures in Northern Ireland.

(3) That it would no longer be obligatory on Northern students to attend lectures in Dublin.

(4) That all Term examinations (except the final) for such students should be held in Belfast.

(5) That Northern students would only be required to keep four dining terms instead of twelve in the King's Inns.

(6) That the existing Benchers in Northern Ireland with an added number should act as a Committee of the Benchers of King's Inns in respect of all matters of discipline and education in Northern Ireland subject only to an appeal to the whole body of Benchers in the event of any member of the Bar being disbarred.

(7) That the Librarian of the King's Inns provide the Bar in Belfast with the penultimate edition of all leading text books in the King's Inns Library.[76]

J. Martin Ellison was appointed King's Inns Professor for Northern Ireland, and 450 textbooks were sent from Dublin to the library committee of the northern Bar.[77] It was 'intended to send a set of law reports as well, but this was frustrated by the seizure of the Four Courts by the anti-treaty faction of the IRA on Good Friday 1922 and the subsequent destruction of the building'.[78] The northern committee contributed to King's Inns by assigning two of its members to act as examiners during final exams from 1922 to 1925. Also, a northern committee nominee, John McGonigal, was elected a bencher to King's Inns in 1923.[79]

Reconciling two distinct political and judicial entities under the King's Inns umbrella proved difficult, and strains began to show. The solicitors' profession in Northern Ireland was required to pay stamp duty to King's Inns on solicitors' articles of clerkship. Although the amount of money in question was small, £312 in 1923–24, the northern government 'did not wish to have to remit sums paid in Northern Ireland to Dublin'.[80] The northern finance minister, Hugh Pollock, raised the issue with Henry.[81] A far more significant division arose over 'the decision of the benchers of King's Inns to allow a number of leading politicians and others to be called to the bar despite their not having passed some or all of the prescribed examinations'.[82] The northern committee was not satisfied that some of those exempted 'had reached the proper standard of education ... some of them they considered were not qualified, nor in some cases were they satisfied with the grounds for such exemption'.[83] There had been precedents for exemptions, particularly for First World War service. The northern committee was irked that the 'war service was, in some instances, in the forces opposed to the crown' and 'felt that the actions of the benchers in Dublin imperilled the system of reciprocity between King's Inns and the English inns of court whereby each recognised the qualifications of the other as satisfying the requirements for call'.[84] Those exempted included Kevin O'Higgins, Minster for Justice in the Free State, and the Ceann Comhairle (speaker) of Dáil Éireann, Michael Hayes.

After the inauguration of a new court system in the Free State in 1924, Thomas Molony retired as Lord Chief Justice and was replaced by Hugh Kennedy, 'an advanced constitutional nationalist who saw dominion status as an avenue to the development of a distinctly Irish, as opposed to English-inspired, structure of the state and its institutions'. His attitude towards the northern judiciary was almost certainly less accommodating than Molony's.[85] Molony had previously been strongly rebuked by W.T. Cosgrave for ordering the transfer of Land Registry titles to Northern Ireland without the consent of the provisional government.[86] King's Inns ignored the northern committee's threats to leave and even inflamed the situation by proposing that the Irish language should be compulsory for a call to the Irish bar.[87] This requirement was eventually introduced in 1929. Notice was sent to King's Inns on 31 July 1925 that the northern bar was severing connections with it. An application was made to 'the Benchers of Gray's Inn, London, that the Northern Bar might be affiliated to that body. Gray's Inn intimated in reply that they could accept students only on the ordinary conditions – namely, that they should keep the usual Terms and become barristers of that Inn.'[88] The northern Bar subsequently decided to establish an Inn of Court of Northern Ireland, which was inaugurated at the Belfast Law Courts on 11 January 1926.[89] The main common link between both Irish justice systems was thereby finally broken.

Although the Government of Ireland Act 1920 was rejected by the people of the twenty-six counties, the necessary steps were still taken to bring it into force in the south. Accordingly, on 1 October 1921, on the same day the northern judiciary came into being, 'the old Supreme Court of Judicature in Ireland ceased to exist, and was replaced by the new Supreme Court of Judicature in Southern Ireland'.[90] With the accession to power of the provisional government in January 1922, 'it found itself in possession of two separate systems of courts … Dáil Courts, operating under the decrees of the revolutionary cabinet, and the Supreme Court of Judicature in Southern Ireland, the County Courts, and the Courts of Petty Sessions, all of which had been transferred to the new administration'.[91]

In 1919, the Sinn Féin counter-government had established a 'system of tribunals and courts dealing initially with disputes over land, and extending into the field of criminal law. The system ultimately paralleled the British court system, operating at its expense in terms of caseload'.[92] By September 1920, these Dáil (also called Republican or Sinn Féin) Courts had created a judicial structure of Parish Courts, District Courts and a Supreme Court.[93]

Such was their impact that the *Irish Times* claimed 'the whole countryside now brings their rights and wrongs to the courts of Sinn Fein'.[94] They were less successful in the north, where the 'political realities of the Northern situation prevented the Dáil Courts winning the kind of acceptance by the community which they had in the South'.[95] There, the Dáil Courts were 'largely confined to south Armagh, south Fermanagh, mid-Tyrone and the adjacent mountainous areas of south Derry, all without sizeable unionist populations'.[96] Some pro-Sinn Féin solicitors based in the north tended to cross the border to use the courts. Those in Derry used the District Court in Carndonagh in County Donegal.[97] The Dáil Courts were most successful in the north during the truce period from July 1921, where court sittings were convened more regularly and more openly, mainly due to the absence of the British military, including one held provocatively 'near the Crown court in Bishop Street' in Derry.[98]

Once the provisional government took power in 1922, it was 'faced with alternatives: it could either consolidate these Dáil Courts, or it could utilise the ordinary courts which had been handed over. The latter course was adopted'.[99] The establishment of new courts for the Free State was delayed until 1924, with the existing structures remaining in place until then. Cosgrave set up a 'committee to advise on the establishment of the new judiciary'. The committee was chaired by Lord Glenavy (formerly Sir James Campbell), a former Lord Chancellor, Lord Chief Justice as well as a staunch unionist. Other members of the twelve-strong committee included Hugh Kennedy and Cahir Davitt (son of Land League founder Michael and formerly a judge in the Dáil Courts). Cosgrave wrote a letter to the committee in January 1923, offering some advice:

> In the long struggle for the right to rule in our own country, there has been no sphere of the administration lately ended which impressed itself on the minds of our people as a standing monument of an alien government more than the system, the machinery and the administration of law and justice which supplanted in comparatively modern times, the laws and institutions till then a part of the living national organism. The body of laws and the system of judicature so imposed upon this Nation were English (not even British) in their seed, English in their growth, English in their vitality. Their nomenclature were [sic] only to be understood by the student of the history of the people of Southern Britain ... there is nothing more prized among our newly won liberties than the liberty to constitute a system of judiciary and an administration of law and justice according to the dictates of our needs and after a pattern of our designing.[100]

The committee barely heeded Cosgrave's advice. There were no dramatic changes made to the court structures of the British system, nor was there much change in the modes of dress or address, with robing and wigs remaining. Hugh Geoghegan contends that a 'gentle revolution took place, rather than a radical revolution', as it was felt that, although the appointments of judges were considered 'political appointments', they were independent in their work. He also believed the legal establishment had no desire for a revolution.[101] The Courts of Justice Act 1924, establishing the new Free State court system, was preceded by the Dáil Éireann Courts (Winding-up) Act 1923. The Dáil Courts, 'the homegrown regime', were disbanded in favour of essentially retaining the structures of the British justice system.[102]

The division of the Irish judiciary under the Government of Ireland Act demonstrated the true impact of partition. Splitting the legal system in Ireland was a mammoth undertaking that impacted greatly on judges, barristers, solicitors and everyone else involved in the legal professions. Legal confusion arose in relation to jurisdiction over border regions, the differing political statuses of Northern Ireland and the Irish Free State, and in future relations between north and south. Whilst the Free State was presented with the structures of the past (i.e. British and home-grown), the northern judiciary had little to work with: it had no courthouse, no staff, not even books. Such were the divergent paths the north and south were taking that the one common link, education at King's Inns, was broken with the justice systems mirroring the politics of both jurisdictions by cutting off all avenues of cooperation.

CHAPTER NINE

Business and Trade

The first decades after the partition of Ireland consisted of 'prolonged periods of economic stagnation and decline' for both Irish jurisdictions.[1] During the inter-war period, economic depression prevailed, forcing thousands into unemployment and emigration. Northern Ireland was hard hit by recessions in its traditional industries: shipbuilding, linen and agriculture. For the linen industry, 'this decline was permanent'.[2] There was little effort made by both jurisdictions to cooperate economically with each other during this period. The Ulster academic, Norman Gibson, suggested in 1959 that the negative economic consequences of partition were 'primarily because of our own stupidity and our refusal to co-operate on common economic problems'.[3] Sinn Féin and its successors introduced measures that guaranteed a divergence between both jurisdictions on trade, with its Belfast Boycott campaign from 1920 and the Irish Free State's introduction of customs barriers in 1923.

The Belfast Boycott, which began haltingly in 1920 (see Chapter Three), was enforced more rigorously from 1921. The appointment of a director and the allocation of £2,500 gave the campaign impetus to apply economic pressure on the north-east of Ireland. An 'advisory committee was formed, inspectors appointed, and enforcement committees created around the country to ensure the boycott was obeyed'.[4] By March 1921, 'there were 184 committees dotted around the country, by May, there were 360'.[5] It still was enforced intermittently from 1921, and 'it becomes active, dies down, and revives in different districts owing either to direct orders or local conditions'.[6] However, the director, Joseph MacDonagh, was 'relentless and efficient' and ensured its effectiveness in many areas.[7] The boycott essentially involved members of the IRA intercepting and destroying products that 'originated in the north-east, and southern traders were banned from doing business with their northern counterparts'.[8] In the words of Peter Hart, the IRA enforced the boycott with 'threats, guns and kerosene'.[9] In Monaghan, where the boycott was effectively policed more than anywhere else in the country, 'shopkeepers were cautioned by the IRA not to deal with Belfast firms, and members of the public were warned not to enter the shops of those who were supplied from Belfast'.[10]

To prevent goods from entering regions, trains were raided by the IRA. In Inniskeen, Monaghan, despite 'much local condemnation', local IRA members raided trains and burned the goods within them.[11] Many of the raids took place in areas close to the border, in places such as Tyrone and Louth.[12] On a number of occasions, the IRA wantonly destroyed foodstuff that could have been used by refugees. A case in point was in Offaly, where 'five barges of much needed food heading north were seized and destroyed along with £200 worth of clothing made in Belfast'.[13] Sometimes the raiders were unable to resist the temptation and commandeered items for themselves. A Monaghan brigade, who 'captured a key of whiskey that was going from Belfast to Dundalk … could not burn the whiskey – it would be sacrilege – we took it away and buried it'. Later 'some of the boys' were found 'having a quiet squig'.[14] Instead of burning captured Gallaher's cigarettes and tobacco, an IRA unit claimed that 'when a lot of our men had been arrested and interned in Ballykinlar [County Down], the tobacco and cigarettes were sent to them, but before doing so we extracted the cigarettes from the packets and put them into "Slainte" packets with a few "Slainte" cigarettes on top'.[15]

Blacklists were published of local and national firms to be boycotted. Members of Cumann na mBan played a large role in 'persuading shops not to stock goods manufactured in Belfast and issuing blacklists of firms handling Belfast goods: woman the consumer had become woman the activist'.[16] A body enforcing the boycott, 'the Belfast Advisory Committee', also issued 'White Lists': lists of firms who were not considered responsible for expelling Catholics from their workforces, and therefore should not be boycotted.[17] To circumvent the blacklist order, railway officials at Richill station in County Armagh 'were engaged in relabelling Belfast goods before re-consigning them to merchants in the south and west of Ireland'. Goods manufactured in Belfast were invoiced 'to show that they came from County Armagh, which was not on the boycott list'.[18] The IRA burned the Richill station shortly afterwards.[19]

The most common form of punishment inflicted on firms trading with Belfast companies or banks was financial. Fines were imposed. There was 'usually little resistance offered and fines were paid relatively freely'.[20] Goods, not homes or business premises, were burned or destroyed, although some homes and businesses were targeted in the almost 800 arson attacks throughout Ireland in the first six months of 1921, 'particularly common along the Ulster border'.[21] An example of another form of punishment meted out was during an incident in March 1921, in which workers from Belfast firms in Louth were threatened by the IRA and given twenty-four hours to return to Belfast.[22] A month later, shots were fired into a shop that was believed to be uncooperative with the boycott in Carrick-on-Shannon in County Leitrim. One of the gunmen was accidently shot dead by his own gun whilst breaking a window.[23] The Great Northern Railway was forced to close its routes from Dundalk to Enniskillen due to the kidnapping of drivers who delivered Belfast goods.[24] A Dublin representative of a Belfast drapery was kidnapped by the Irish Volunteers at his home in Dublin.[25] The president of the Belfast Chamber of Commerce declared that 'no Belfast representative' was 'safe to go to [the] South'.[26]

With little tangible evidence, many in the IRA and Sinn Féin believed the boycott was achieving results. Nationalist-leaning newspapers fed this notion. The *Freeman's Journal* claimed in February 1921 that Edward Carson was urged to reconsider his decision to resign as Ulster Unionist leader 'to appease the fears of Ulster traders'. A member of Portadown Chamber of Commerce declared that 'the building of a barrier round the six counties was certainly not going to be for the good of the commerce of Belfast and Ulster'. Many wholesale firms claimed they were badly hit, losing 75 per cent of their trade outside of Ulster. Northern salespeople on the road frequently returned with no orders. The paper asserted that the ascendancy leaders, landlords and 'Orange chiefs … busy preparing for the pigmy parliament' lost little by the boycott, but 'the business men, the prop and mainstay of Ulster, are in a state of great anxiety'.[27] Joseph MacDonagh boasted that 'except in Antrim and Down it was impossible for a Belfast merchant to sell as much as a bootlace in any other part of Ireland'.[28] In May 1921, the RIC Inspector General claimed that 'the Belfast

Boycott was spreading. It is useless to pretend that this is not extremely serious and it is significant to note that some large English firms are now yielding to it and promising to obey the orders of Dáil Éireann.'[29] Liam Gaynor, an IRA member from Belfast who played a large role in enforcing the boycott, made a number of claims regarding its effectiveness, including a wild statement that he had instructed Harry Boland, a colleague of his on the IRB Supreme Council who had toured the United State with de Valera, 'to institute a boycott of linen throughout the United States. This was done, and millions of pounds worth of business were subsequently lost by Belfast linen firms.'[30] A far more plausible assertion by Gaynor is that the boycott helped to 'strengthen the morale of our fighting forces.'[31]

Sinn Féin used the Belfast Boycott as a ploy to garner more votes in the 1921 general election to the northern parliament. Its negative impact on Ulster was exaggerated. One Sinn Féin supporter claimed that 'the merchant princes and capitalists of Belfast had come to realise that the boycott was hitting them and had found out that Ulster could not get on without the other three provinces.'[32] During the truce, the IRA was able to devote more time to enforcing the boycott, and people who 'were previously "on the run" are now at their homes and have found in the Boycott a ready means to hand of injuring Ulster.'[33] Craig claimed, in a meeting with Hamar Greenwood, that during the truce, the 'boycotting of protestant firms was more rife in Ulster than ever before.'[34] The manager of the Newry branch of the Northern Banking Company wrote a letter to Craig in September 1921 asking the northern government to 'drive … the Southern Banks out of the North'. With little powers transferred at that point, the northern government could do little, 'but as soon as powers were transferred drastic action was foreshadowed'.[35] Once in a position to do so, a boycott committee was established by the north, headed by Thomas Moles, which instructed the Minister of Home Affairs, Dawson-Bates, 'to apply the law against [the] Boycott as far as possible'.[36]

With the signing of the Anglo-Irish Treaty in December 1921 and the subsequent establishment of the provisional government the following month, the rescinding of the boycott formed part of the first Craig–Collins Pact of 21 January 1922 (see Chapter Six). This was agreed to 'with a view to encouraging a better feeling between the Six Co. area and the rest of Ireland'. Collins pointed out to Craig 'that the raising of the boycott was without prejudice to the setting up of tariffs by the Irish government in the event of such action being considered desirable at a later stage'.[37] In return, Craig promised to facilitate the return, where possible, of expelled Catholic shipyard workers to their jobs. Craig claimed that Collins believed the boycott 'had not been altogether a success in Southern Ireland' and he 'would be glad to put an end to it as it was found that it was being used by tradesmen as a means of undermining their rivals, and was leading to great bitterness amongst Sinn Féin ranks'. Craig conceded to a request to halt legal proceedings for offences relating to the boycott if 'the Boycott were properly removed'. He believed the discontinuation of the boycott 'merely foretold what would eventually have taken place' but told Collins 'that its cessation by his direction would be more satisfactory to both sides'.[38]

The removal of the boycott resulted in the staff from the boycott directory losing their jobs. Michael Staines, the director since January 1922, informed the staff that their 'services are no longer required' from the end of February. The eighteen staff members were unhappy with their dismissal, saying the work was 'highly distasteful and fraught with great risk'; some who suffered imprisonment 'for their connection with the Boycott campaign' demanded either 'transfers to other departments or adequate compensation'. They believed 'that the Belfast Boycott as a weapon, was in a large measure, responsible for bringing N.E. Ulster to a reasonable frame of mind ... securing guarantees for the Catholic victims of Belfast Bigotry'. They claimed the treatment they received by the provisional government 'compares very unfavourably with that promised by the Irish Government to the Crown Forces and other British Government Officials who served against the Irish Republic during the war'.[39] The cabinet eventually agreed 'to offer three months' wages to buy off the boycott staff'.[40]

Shortly after the provisional government rescinded the boycott, the anti-Treaty IRA imposed it again, much to the embarrassment of the government (see Chapter Seven). At the Cumann na mBan convention on 5 February, Mary MacSwiney, TD, asked 'the women to join in the re-imposition of the Belfast Boycott unless the prisoners in Northern Jails for political offences were at once released'.[41] Cumann na mBan members in Donegal, led by Eithne Coyle, responded by raiding trains and burning Belfast newspapers 'on the Derry and Lough Swilly line'.[42] Within months, there were many incidents of 'unauthorised persons' enforcing the boycott, causing the provisional government to issue a warning that 'the demands referred to are made without lawful authority and should be disregarded and payment refused'.[43] Despite the warning, the boycott continued in many parts of the country.

Ulster traders responded by forming a group, 'the Ulster Traders' Defence Association', to impose a counter boycott, claiming that 'although officially discontinued by the Provisional Government', the boycott 'is at present being carried on more bitterly than ever'. A poster issued by the Ulster Traders' Defence Association maintained:

> They give lip service to the ideal of Irish Unity, and yet they snap the most important link between North and South by attempting to destroy trade inter-communication ... They have produced an atmosphere of bitter hostility to Belfast by unscrupulous propaganda ... They have stolen and burnt Ulster goods. They have maltreated Ulster travellers. They have intimidated merchants desirous of buying Ulster Goods.
>
> The closing down of all firms in Dublin having any connection with Belfast is now practically complete, and the Provisional Government has failed to protect Belfast firms having premises in Dublin, even when such premises are situated in the heart of the city.
>
> The Ulster Traders' Defence Association exists to defend trade interests ... The Southern Boycotter is determined to ruin your trade, but he cannot injure it to any greater extent than you can hurt his. Show him that you can play at the game too.
>
> REFUSE TO BUY HIS GOODS AS HE REFUSES TO BUY YOURS.[44]

Ulster people were urged not to buy any southern goods, including clothing, meat, butter, biscuits, furniture, stout and whiskey.[45] The appeal was heeded by many in the north.[46] With the start of the civil war in the south, the enforcement of the boycott became even more uneven and sporadic, eventually petering out. However, its legacy of driving a psychological wedge between north and south continued far longer.

Economically, the boycott did have a negative impact on trade in Belfast and other areas in the north. Ernest Clark wrote a memorandum on the effects of the boycott in November 1921. In it, merchants were cited as saying that 'the sum of six million capital employed is affected; and the loss of turn over amounts to five million pounds per annum, and the loss of profit on this turn over is possibly ten per cent'. Clark personally believed those figures should be discounted by one-third. He also noted 'the loss of wages and profit in companies with transport, and the loss of wages to the persons employed in manufacture, transport and agency'.[47] In all probability, Belfast trade with the south never recovered to its pre-boycott level, which had been halved by 1924.[48] The northern government considered pressing 'the Imperial Government to pay compensation' to distributors for their losses caused by the boycott, but ruled against it as 'it would be almost impossible to distinguish genuine claims from false ones'.[49] Clark also noted that the boycott had a negative economic effect on those imposing it, with goods 'presumably purchased in the cheapest market prior to the Boycott' now bearing an increased 'cost to the consumer' and diminished profits for traders.[50] This was borne out in Monaghan, where 'it was estimated that the working man in Monaghan town who observed the boycott had to pay 5s. per week extra for the cost of living'.[51]

On banking, Clark believed it was 'a mistake to suppose that this withdrawal of deposits and credits in the Southern Branches of the Northern Banks really hampers their banking activities. The North itself provides by its deposits and credits all the funds which the Northern Banks require to finance Northern trade'.[52] David Johnson claims the boycott had an impact on the business of northern banks in nationalist areas. Northern-based banks, such as Ulster Bank, Northern Bank and Belfast Bank, saw business diminished with decreased deposits and some sub-branches having to close in the south. The Belfast Bank lost one-fifth of its deposits outside of Northern Ireland and decided to close all of its southern branches in 1923.[53] However, Eoin Drea refutes Johnson's assertion, claiming that the boycott was not as significant for Ulster Bank as Johnson suggests.[54] He further asserts that 'the coming into existence of the Irish

Free State and Northern Ireland did not impact upon the operational structure of Ulster Bank. It continued to be run as a unitary business across the 32 counties.[55] Even though Ulster Bank was unionist in outlook and opposed to the 1921 Anglo-Irish Treaty, pragmatism saw it retain its presence in the Irish Free State. This presence involved assisting in the funding of the new government south of the border, despite the bank disliking 'intensely the idea of making any advances to the Free State'.[56]

The boycott had minimal impact on Northern Ireland's three main industries: agriculture, shipbuilding and linen. Ernest Blythe, a firm opponent of the boycott from its initial imposition, believed the 'wholesale distributing trade is quite a minor factor' and claimed the boycott had no effect on northern farmers, as their 'market is not in our territory'.[57] As well as claiming that the boycott resulted in 'millions of pounds' worth of business' losses for the linen industry, Liam Gaynor also claimed they were successful 'in the stoppage of orders for Belfast-built ships' with 'South American Companies'.[58] Blythe disagreed, saying the 'boycott would threaten the northern ship-building industry no more than a summer shower would threaten Cave Hill'.[59]

Whilst its economic aims to hamper trade in Belfast met with mixed results, the boycott's aim to unify Ireland was an unmitigated disaster. Winston Churchill believed 'it recognised and established real partition, spiritual and voluntary partition, before physical partition had been established'.[60] P.S. O'Hegarty, writing in 1924, had no doubts about its damaging effects: 'it raised up in the South what never had been there, a hatred of the North, and a feeling that the North was as much an enemy of Ireland as was England ... it was an utter failure inasmuch as it did not secure reinstatement of a single expelled Nationalist, nor the conversion of a single Unionist'.[61] Michael Collins also realised that the boycott was ineffective and believed a better way 'to fight the Northern parliament' economically would be to 'set up an effective tariff-barrier in its stead'.[62] The Free State government decided to do this in 1923.

Arguably, the single most significant factor in cementing partition was the imposition of customs duties on imported goods by the Free State government in April 1923. The creation of a customs barrier was key to translating partition into a reality.[63] Arthur Griffith had previously argued for a fiscal policy separate to Britain, stating, 'The question of customs is not – let us repeat and emphasise – a question of raising tariffs against England. It is a question of preventing Ireland from having her fiscal policy upset every time a new fiscal doctrine appeals to the English electors as good for England.'[64] The provisional government sponsored the North-Eastern Boundary Bureau and produced an anti-partition pamphlet entitled 'IF "ULSTER" CONTRACTS OUT', before the north, as predicted, contracted itself out of the Irish Free State in December 1922. It stated that the Free State had the same rights as Great Britain and Northern Ireland 'to safeguard its commercial and industrial interests'. Ireland's economic life 'has deteriorated continuously under the British fiscal system'; it was geared for 'England's industrial and commercial interests', with agriculture in Ireland 'declining as the industries of Great Britain increased'. In 1920, nearly 80 per cent of Ireland's imports were received from Britain, and over 99 per cent of Ireland's exports were sent to Great Britain. In a nutshell, Ireland was too dependent on Great Britain.[65] It further asserted that Ireland's place in British policy was to be 'the fruitful mother of flocks and herds'. Ireland 'commits the economic heresy of importing foodstuffs for her own use and exporting the small quantity she grows', 'buying the finished beef and selling the live animals … Ireland exports at the point of lowest economic value and imports at the point of highest economic value.' It concluded by stating that 'even with the costs involved', there was 'an urgent need for a complete recasting of the existing fiscal system … there is a need for Ireland to erect customs frontiers to gain a separate fiscal policy'.[66] The decision was made in 'the dying days of the Irish civil war, with predictions that the Irish Free State government would carry a deficit of £20 million … but it remained to be seen if raising revenue through tariffs would be undermined by loss of trade'.[67]

As well as seeking fiscal independence from Britain and generating revenue for the exchequer, the policy was also an attempt to apply economic pressure on the nascent northern jurisdiction. The North-Eastern Boundary Bureau claimed the erection of a customs barrier would 'gravely imperil' the 'future prosperity' of Northern Ireland and would 'extinguish the enormous distributing trade Belfast does with the rest of Ireland'. The north would have to import flax from countries such as Russia, France and Belgium instead of having access to flax from the Free State. The north's 'other industries such as bacon-curing, tobacco, milling, tanning, etc.'

would also suffer. Such was the Free State's optimism in the customs barrier that it hoped economic pressure would force the north to end partition.[68]

For fiscal independence to be enforced successfully, it was necessary to surround the Free State with a complete 'Customs ring'.[69] Cosgrave saw 'no possible escape, if the North severs herself from the Irish fiscal unit and joins the fiscal unit of Great Britain' other than imposing a customs barrier, 'no matter how friendly we may wish to be with the North'.[70] This posed few problems for goods coming in and out of the main ports. It was the 'land frontier' (i.e. the boundary between Northern Ireland and the Irish Free State meandering some 270 miles from Carlingford Lough to Lough Foyle) that gave rise to most of the complications. In announcing the imposition, the government stated that 'pending a decision [by the Boundary Commission] as to the future boundary line, the frontier will be temporarily placed along the boundary between the Six Northern Counties and the Twenty-six counties at present included in the Irish Free State'.[71]

The Free State government announced in late February 1923 that customs barriers would be enacted on 1 April, leaving very little time for people and businesses to prepare. The arrangements were agreed between the Free State government and the British government, not the northern administration, who had no control over customs and excise. The negotiation 'provides perhaps the most direct example of British and Irish officials collaborating on activating the means of living apart'.[72] In practical terms, the importing and exporting of merchandise across the border was prohibited except through designated routes and at designated times. Stations were open for the clearance of merchandise between 9 a.m. and 5 p.m. daily, except on Sundays.[73] Farm produce was exempted, as was the removal of household furniture and small domestic supplies of non-dutiable goods.[74] Customs regulations stated that farm produce 'carried by Farmers for Marketing will be specifically treated. It will be allowed to be imported or exported by any road, whether approved or not, and will be exempt from the full requirements as to Report'.[75] Cross-border roads were designated as 'authorized', 'concession' or 'unauthorized/unapproved'.[76] Many 'unapproved' roads were earmarked for closure. Some roads, using explosives, were 'cratered' and made impassable.[77] The British and Free State governments published the list

Table 2.   Approved/authorised roads, nearest boundary posts and customs stations

Approved Roads	Boundary Post	Customs Station
Moville–Londonderry	Pennyburn	Londonderry
Buncrana–Londonderry	Pennyburn	Londonderry
St. Johnstown–Londonderry	Creevagh	Londonderry
Lifford–Strabane	Strabane Bridge	Strabane
Castlefinn–Strabane	On road between Clady and Strabane	Strabane
Ballyshannon–Belleek–Enniskillen	Belleek	Enniskillen
Manor Hamilton–Enniskillen	Belcoo	Enniskillen
Swanlinbar–Enniskillen	On road between boundary and Enniskillen	Enniskillen
Clones–Newtown Butler	On road between boundary and Newtown Butler	Newton Butler
Monaghan–Auchnacloy	On road between boundary and Auchnacloy	Auchnacloy
Monaghan–Middletown–Armagh	Middletown	Armagh
Castleblaney–Keady–Armagh	On road between boundary and Keady	Armagh
Dundalk–Newtown Hamilton–Armagh	On road between boundary and Newtown Hamilton	Armagh
Dundalk–Killeen–Newry	On road between boundary and Newry	Newry
Greenore–Carlingford–Newry	On road between boundary and Newry	Newry

Source: UK National Archives – HO 267/49 – Customs & Excise, March 1923.

of the 'authorized' or approved roads along with the relevant boundary posts and customs stations for each road (see Table 2).

Every railway line crossing the border was approved for the importation and exportation of merchandise. People wishing to move merchandise across the border had to submit a carrier's report to customs officials, who tracked the actual goods against the documented amount and then gathered the relevant fees. Each report had to contain 'mark and numbers on the packages, the number of packages, description of the goods, net quantity of the goods, and value of the goods'.[78] Although there was free movement of people across the border, those who crossed had their person and personal effects examined to prevent smuggling. Goods carried 'by travellers for their personal consumption during a journey, or to privately-owned household effects, or to small private purchases of groceries' were not restricted.[79]

There was widespread disapproval of the decision in the north and south, particularly from those closest to the border who would be most affected by the imposition of customs barriers. Business groups such as the Chambers of Commerce in the Free State and the Dublin Mercantile Association vehemently opposed the decision, calling it a 'suicidal policy', claiming it would lead to dire economic consequences.[80] Some Free State tobacco manufacturers were optimistic that their businesses would benefit as their competitors in the north and elsewhere would be burdened with increased costs.[81] The Dundalk tobacco manufacturer, P.J. Carroll, objected to the erection of customs barriers 'on the grounds that it would disrupt its access to the United Kingdom market' and 'they would have to drop their business outside the state altogether or set up a manufacturing plant outside the state. If they set up such a plant, numbers employed in Dundalk would be reduced by half'.[82] Most tobacco retailers and smokers feared the introduction of customs barriers would lead to less choice at higher costs.[83] One Dundalk distillery put all of its 150 employees on notice, their employment to be terminated on 1 April unless the customs taxes proposed were modified.[84] One Monaghan newspaper, the *Northern Sentinel*, deplored 'all the inconveniences of the present situation and the hampering effects on the commerce of the county that an artificial and entirely indefensible division has created'.[85] Many felt that the new customs barrier would lead to an increased cost of living for consumers as well as considerable confusion and lengthy delays in the handling of traffic.

James Craig called for the Free State to postpone for all time a customs barrier, claiming, 'Those in the South who proposed to erect that barrier wall, and not the North, would be responsible for partition. There was no such thing as partition if they had not a Customs barrier between the North and the South'.[86] John Andrews, the northern labour minister, declared a customs barrier would be a two-edged sword, which our Government and the Imperial Government could easily wield with disastrous results against the Free State. I hope, however, that such a situation will never arise. I would much prefer to see the two Governments going forward in friendly rivalry, each striving for the welfare of its own part of our island home.[87]

Pollock, the northern finance minister, also claimed such a decision would only cause further damage to the Free State, as 'Ulster, being more self-contained, and enjoying the unrestricted market of forty millions of people, can afford, although regretfully, to be deprived of close commercial associations with the three millions of the South'.[88]

As 1 April drew closer, the physical signs of the new measures began to appear. Declaration forms were issued at railway stations. Proclamations appeared in newspapers, and signs and posters were displayed in prominent places. Construction began on customs huts and stations along the border, many of them initially temporary in nature. The first customs post in Muff, County Donegal, was a tepee-like cloth construction.[89] A crude wooden structure surfaced in Clones in Monaghan.[90] One hut near Emyvale, also in Monaghan, was burned by armed men.[91] Staff were brought in to man the new stations. Railway companies hired extra staff to meet the extra demands. Many officials deployed north of the border were Scotsmen and Englishmen who had previously held similar roles in the recently created demilitarised zone in the Rhineland.[92] The northern government received applications from people interested in working as customs officials, with many of the applicants being ex-RIC or soldiers who had served in the First World War. One applicant claimed that he worked in the Baltics on 'frontier delimitation purposes when the Latvian and Esthonian [sic] Governments agreed to trust me with the delimitation of their national frontier'.[93] Confidential instructions were issued to RUC and Special constables who were to be employed in customs work. The instructions included information on approved and unapproved routes, protocols to use when searching people and their property and strategies to prevent smuggling.[94]

As well as being April Fool's Day, in 1923, Easter Sunday fell on 1 April, the day the new customs barrier came into operation. Traffic was light due to it being a holiday, and little disruption was caused by the new measures.

A man who claimed he had nothing to declare in Dundalk was subsequently found to have in his possession a box of 100 cigarettes. He was duly warned of the grave nature of his offence and told not to do it again. Another merchant caused some amusement when he had to undo a 'bale' of lady's underwear in front of passing onlookers.[95] Once the Easter break was over, the real effects of the customs barrier began to be realised. The new arrangement led to increased congestion at ports and border controls, with goods awaiting clearance leading to heavy loses and disruption to businesses. The customs barriers also resulted in the closure of some border companies who were reliant on cross-border trade. The consequences of the new measures were most keenly felt by the border counties, where Donegal was economically cut off from Derry, and Down from Louth.[96] Although both jurisdictions opted for a relatively open border with no barbed-wire entanglement to seal the frontier, it severely curtailed the movements of residents along the border. Railway services suffered considerable disruptions, with some lines zigzagging the border on numerous occasions and customs examinations expected for each crossing. A train running from Clones to Cavan had to cross the border six times in eight miles. Common sense soon prevailed, and it was decided to curb examinations to just the first point of entry beyond the border.[97]

The trade barriers introduced in 1923 had a negative impact on trade between north and south, but less than widespread perceptions have contended. Trade had always been more reliant on east–west trade (Britain) rather than north–south trade.[98] As previously stated, border counties and towns were more affected than others. Those counties and towns experienced a slower rate of growth than they should have because of the border.[99] According to Catherine Nash, Bryonie Reid and Brian Graham in their book, *Partitioned Lives: The Irish Borderlands*:

> despite the conventional conceptualization of the Irish border through the lens of the debate on the Boundary Commission and the politics and symbolism of partition, it was the imposition of new regulations and people's responses to them that constituted the border in this period. The political entered everyday life, not through the boundary commission or the ideological ramifications of partition, but through the ways in which the borderlanders came

to terms on a mundane, daily basis with the existence of the customs barrier which impeded and constrained their established social and economic networks.[100]

Undoubtedly, the introduction of the customs barrier helped cement partition. Up to this point, partition was seen by many as merely an administrative burden that barely impacted on the daily lives of people. However, the introduction of customs barriers made it tangible and real. Movement and trade were now curtailed across the border, impeding long-established economic and social ties. It formalised the border, making it easy for the Boundary Commission to retain the status quo in 1925.

Businesses, trade associations and charities were all impacted by the partition of Ireland. In Cormac Ó Grada and Brendan M. Walsh's study of the economic impact of the border in 2006, *Did (and Does) the Irish Border Matter?* they claim 'it did, but less than popular perceptions imply'.[101] Fearful of the impact partition would bring to their businesses, some firms opened offices in both jurisdictions. A.A. Watt & Co. Ltd., a distillery, opened another office in the Irish Free State in 1923 to 'cope with problems created by partition'.[102] The insurance industry was particularly affected by partition. In April 1921, the *Freeman's Journal* wrote about the confusion caused by it:

> While it was apparent from the first that many of the administrative problems under Partition would be practically insoluble, the attempt to grapple with the details goes to prove that the complexities and difficulties arising out of the working of the scheme will be even more numerous and involved than was anticipated in the severest criticism.[103]

To illustrate the confusion caused by partition, the article claimed it was nowhere more apparent than in the administration of health insurance (see Chapter Three). The partitioning of health insurance involved three parties; the insurance commissioners, the approved insurance societies or companies, and the insured people themselves. The approved insurance societies protested strongly against their partition, claiming that dividing 'the work of the societies would dislocate the whole machinery of national health insurance'.[104] The northern government wanted to take over the national health insurance services for its area by 1 January 1922.[105] With the date pushed to 1 March, the societies attempted other stalling tactics, including referring to Article 12 of the Anglo-Irish Treaty and claiming the transfer would be impractical, as 'the boundaries of Northern Ireland have not yet been finally decided upon'.[106] The confusion persisted long after the national health insurance schemes were eventually transferred in 1923. A meeting of the Derry Diocesan Catholic Friendly Societies, which operated close to the border, explained the difficulties they faced: 'With the constant change of employment and residence at the hiring fair periods; and complicated by employers purchasing stamps in an area under a different Government to that which governs their residential area, and employees working in one area and having their residence in another'.[107]

The largest industry in Ireland, agriculture, had worked effectively under an all-Ireland agriculture department before partition (see Chapter Three). Even though the department was divided, responsibility for fisheries and the administration of the Diseases of Animals Acts were reserved for the Council of Ireland under the Government of Ireland Act.[108] After the signing of the Anglo-Irish Treaty, the new Free State Minister for Agriculture, Patrick Hogan, sought to maintain the all-Ireland nature of his department by delaying the transfer of services to the Northern Ireland agriculture ministry and by attempting to administer the Diseases of Animals Acts for the whole of Ireland until the Council of Ireland was set up.[109] The department was a particularly complex one, making it extremely difficult to divide. Before partition, the branches of the Department of Agriculture and Technical Instruction included agriculture, technical instruction, statistics and intelligence, accounts, transit and markets, veterinary, fisheries and an agricultural wages board.[110] According to the department, there were examples where 'the staffs are not interchangeable, in some instances consisting of one specialist only'.[111] Teething problems were overcome and both departments, north and south, did learn to cooperate with each other in areas of common interest, such as disease control. In a rare occurrence, both agriculture ministers met in 1926 to discuss areas of common concern.[112]

Many associations linked with agriculture also looked to retain their all-Ireland structures. The Irish Technical Instruction Association, consisting of unionists and nationalists, 'refused to recognise the law's bill of divorcement. It resolved ... to maintain itself as an All-Ireland Association for the discussion of matters common to North and South.'[113] The *Irish Times* claimed in May 1921 that the Ulster Farmers' Union 'advocated a single organisation of farmers for the whole of Ireland. Curiously enough, all the resistance to this proposal comes from the "anti-partitionist" farmers of the South.'[114] This was rebuked by the Irish Farmers' Union, who claimed it had consistently attempted to convince the Ulster Farmer's Union to affiliate and form an all-Ireland body, but without success.[115] The Irish Shorthorn Breeder's Association remained an all-Ireland body after partition 'so that matters affecting the interests of breeders in both the Free State and in Northern Ireland might be discussed and dealt with by an organisation representative of the entire country'.[116] There was also no partition in the Irish Creamery Managers' Association. The only change in its structures was the appointment of a committee 'in the Northern area to negotiate with the Northern Government in matters which affected that area alone'.[117]

Historian John Whyte claims that many organisations remained all-Ireland in structure after partition for reasons such as historical inertia, self-interest and self-esteem. 'People are more flexible than their political ideologies might lead one to expect: they are willing to accept different territorial frameworks for different activities.'[118] In many instances, there is no clear indication as to why one body is governed over another except for 'the accidental preferences of the small group of people responsible for founding each body may have been decisive'.[119] For example, the Royal Irish Academy is an all-Ireland body, yet the Irish Historical Society and the Ulster Society for Irish Historical Studies are divided on geographical lines, though the latter society does cater for the historical province of the nine counties of Ulster, not just the Northern Ireland territory. Both cooperate closely, however, and have jointly published the *Irish Historical Studies* journal since 1937.[120] Both bodies also established an all-Ireland body, the Irish Committee of Historical Science, 'with the consent, approval and financial support' of both Irish governments.[121]

Whyte claims that charitable and welfare bodies tend to recognise the international frontier mainly because they were formed after partition and a large aspect of their activities comprises negotiating with governments:

'it is probably more convenient for those involved in such matters to concentrate on one government than try to spread their energies across two, with divergent legal codes, levels of financing, and social welfare systems'.[122] Many formed before partition were reluctant to split on a north–south basis. The Irish Union of the YMCA, a predominantly Protestant-run association, was deeply impacted by partition. It was unable to hold an all-Ireland conference for years due to the 'present disturbed and lawless state of the country'.[123] The Specials commandeered the building of Mountpottinger YMCA in Belfast. The anti-Treaty IRA occupied the YMCA building in Dublin in April 1922 (see Chapter Seven), and many YMCA huts had to close in 'South-Ireland, Mid-Ireland and Dublin districts'.[124] The YMCA building at 43 Upper Sackville Street (present-day O'Connell Street) in Dublin 'was practically destroyed on the night of July 3rd [1922], during the fighting between the Free State troops and the Republicans'.[125] But it was still committed to retaining its all-island structures. Its national committee consisted of two people from the north, mid (including Dublin) and south Ireland.[126] The changed political circumstances were recognised by changing the name of the northern district to the Northern Ireland division.[127] Its female counterpart, the Young Women's Christian Association, also remained an 'all-Ireland Association recognising no boundary … its work and activities were to be found in all parts, from Antrim to Kerry'.[128] The Ulster Girl Guides was formed in March 1920, as the Government of Ireland Bill was being debated in Westminster. 'Dublin was to be the head quarters for all Ireland, and they were to have one vast organization.'[129] The first meeting was presided over by the Duchess of Abercorn, wife of the first Governor of Northern Ireland. She was also president of the Ulster Women's Unionist Council. The charity organisation, the Stewart Institution for Imbecile Children, even though based in Dublin with accommodation for just 130, accepted children 'from all parts of Ireland; there was no partition'.[130]

A special feature of professional associations is the number of all-archipelago bodies that exist that are affiliated to kindred bodies in the UK. The primary reason for this is that the market is seen as one: 'Irish doctors, engineers, architects, surveyors and so on have gone in large numbers to Britain, and are anxious to avoid taking any step which would make that freedom of movement more difficult.'[131] There are many different types of accountant institutions governed by all-archipelago bodies, including the Association of Certified Accountants, the Institute of Cost and Management Accountants and the Chartered Institute of Public Finance and Accountancy.[132] However, the Irish Chartered Accountants has remained an all-Ireland body. The association's president acknowledged in 1927 that partition did render it 'impossible to discuss most matters of interest by reference to the country as a whole'.[133] The Pharmaceutical Society of Ireland wanted to remain an all-Ireland body but was forced to split as new regulations adopted by the society 'could not be approved because the Northern Government had no control over the Society making them'.[134] The society suggested that 'it should be left as the licensing body for the whole of Ireland, and that merely an executive body should be set up in Belfast for local administrative purposes, but the Government there did not see eye to eye with that proposal' and subsequently set up a separate pharmaceutical-licensing body for the six-county area.[135] Demonstrating the arbitrary nature of approaches to all-Ireland governance, another healthcare body, the Irish Dental Association, remained all-Ireland.[136]

Business and trade were as deeply impacted by partition as most facets of society were. The decisions to impose a boycott on Belfast firms and erect a customs barrier between north and south had far-reaching consequences. Those decisions introduced a physical manifestation of partition that had not existed before. They enhanced the physical and psychological partition of the island and were wholly unsuccessful in their attempts to unify the country. A peculiar aspect of partition in Ireland, compared to other divided jurisdictions, is the number of organisations who have chosen to ignore it. Many business, trade and charity groups formed before 1921 remained all-Ireland bodies, including unionist-leaning ones, and to this day. There was no compunction or obligation for most organisations to follow suit once the new international frontier was created with the partition of Ireland. With the confusing nature of partition and the uncertainty surrounding its viability, it is little wonder that most bodies remained all-Ireland entities. Retaining all-Ireland structures was also a feature within many sporting bodies, trade unions and religious organisations.

CHAPTER TEN

Religion

Religion has played a central role throughout Irish history, including in the period leading to the partition of the island. The spectre of partition posed vast problems and some opportunities for the Catholic Church and the main Protestant churches. A study of the impact of partition on the main religions in Ireland must also include a study on the impact of partition on education, as the majority of educational institutions were controlled by religious bodies, the subject of the following chapter.

With the partition of Ireland, the Catholic Church saw itself being subject to both the best and worst outcomes with the creation of both states. It would go on to exert huge control over the Irish Free State on one hand and become the main voice for the large but powerless minority in Northern Ireland on the other. The Catholic Church remained an all-Ireland body; there was never a question of it dividing itself along partitionist lines. Only two of its dioceses in Northern Ireland, Dromore and Down and Connor, were located entirely within the new jurisdiction. Four others – Derry, Clogher, Armagh and Kilmore – were located partly or mostly on the southern side.[1] The Primate of All Ireland was the Archbishop of Armagh and, as a body, the Catholic hierarchy in Ireland met regularly.[2] Of all the organisations that were all-Ireland bodies before partition, religious organisations had the highest number that remained so after the founding of the two jurisdictions. By 1973, there were sixty-four Church or Church-related organisations from all religions on the island of Ireland. Of those, forty-eight were all-Ireland, with two based solely in the Republic of Ireland, one based in the United Kingdom and the other thirteen all-archipelago bodies. There was no religious body exclusively based in Northern Ireland.[3] This has not changed much since 1973.[4]

Since Home Rule had arisen as a political issue from the 1870s onwards, the Catholic Church was linked with the movement. It formed an alliance, the 'Clerical–Nationalist Alliance', with the Irish Parliamentary Party in the 1880s. The Church supported the party on land reform and Home Rule issues in return for the party supporting the Church on educational matters.[5] By the time of the third Home Rule Bill in 1912, the Church was considered to be firmly in favour of Home Rule. A priest from Strabane, speaking on behalf of a Home Rule candidate for North Tyrone in 1911, said that 'anyone who voted for the Unionist candidate would be "recreant to his country" and would be "held responsible at the day of Judgement"'.[6] Such rhetoric greatly exacerbated those opposed to Home Rule.

Religious tensions were further aggravated by two papal pronouncements published shortly before the introduction of the third Home Rule Bill. The first, the *Ne Temere* decree of 1908, declared that all mixed marriages not celebrated before a Catholic priest would be invalid.[7] This decree led to a much-publicised controversy. In 1908, Alexander McCann, a Belfast Catholic, married Agnes Barclay, a Presbyterian, in her own church. They had two children. The local priest urged them strongly to have the marriage validated in a Catholic ceremony, something Agnes refused to do. Alexander then deserted her, taking the two children and all her belongings with him. The McCann case became a national issue, hotly debated in parliament, at public meetings and in the media.[8] The second pronouncement, *Motu Proprio, Quantavis Diligentia*, issued in October 1911, forbade lay people from suing ecclesiastics in the Law Courts unless they had permission from their bishop.[9] The two Vatican decrees were used extensively by unionists as a tool to oppose Home Rule, claiming it would lead to Rome rule. All the main Protestant churches shared this concern.[10]

The Catholic hierarchy appointed Cardinal Michael Logue and Bishops Patrick O'Donnell and Denis Kelly to study the 1912 Home Rule Bill.[11] Although 'dexterous and shrewd, Logue was by no means the most intelligent or administratively competent of bishops. As well as being at times slow and indecisive, he had a tendency to state the obvious.'[12] He was considered a moderate nationalist but did comment, 'on the whole, as far as religious interests are concerned, I would rather live under the Imperial

Parliament than under a Home Rule Parliament. The former might be brought sooner or later, to remove religious grievances and disabilities, the latter simply cannot.' The third clause of the bill prevented the proposed Home Rule parliament from giving 'a preference, privilege, or advantage' to any religion.[13]

Once John Redmond was informed by Herbert Asquith that he was considering local autonomy for Ulster on a temporary basis, Redmond sent emissaries to consult the Catholic hierarchy to gain their support, seeing them as a vital interest group. As the proposed temporary exclusionary period for the Ulster counties expanded from three to six years, with Carson demanding permanent exclusion, Logue was not optimistic about the future (see Chapter One).[14] The Church was presented with a dilemma by the 1916 Easter Rising. It was opposed to physical force, a view most forcefully expressed by Bishop Kelly, who denounced the Rising as 'murder pure and simple'.[15] Its views did start to change though, following the execution of the Rising leaders. Reflecting the general population, the Church moved towards an advanced nationalist position from 1916 to 1921.[16] The Catholic hierarchy participated in the renewed efforts instigated by Lloyd George as the fallout from the Easter Rising was being realised from the summer of 1916 onwards. Lloyd George's new proposals, recommending the exclusion of the six counties, was rejected by the hierarchy, as they feared the exclusionary provisions would become permanent. In the weeks preceding the conference, anti-partition meetings were organised in Ulster, with many of the Catholic clergy organising and participating in the meetings and writing anti-partition letters to the press. Mary Harris, in her book, *The Catholic Church and the Foundation of the Northern Irish State*, commented that 'it was the spectre of a Protestant-controlled Education Office in Belfast more than the concession of additional "acreage" which made the Northern bishops prefer to remain "under English rule" for fifty more years'.[17] Despite Catholic hierarchy opposition, a resolution was carried by 475 votes to 265 to accept the proposals.[18] Once Redmond realised he was being duped in July 1916 and that the proposed settlement would be made permanent, the Irish Parliamentary Party rejected the proposals it had voted in favour of a month previously. Even though much of the hierarchy's advice had been ignored and the Irish Parliamentary Party initially voted in favour of Lloyd

George's proposals, much of the unionist press blamed the Catholic Church for the 'wreckage' of the settlement.[19]

At this juncture, the political influence of Bishop O'Donnell (a keen supporter of the Irish Parliamentary Party) within the hierarchy began to wane just as Bishop Joseph MacRory's began to rise. MacRory, Bishop of Down and Connor was a vociferous opponent of partition. He would become disillusioned with the Irish Parliamentary Party and increasingly drawn to supporting Sinn Féin.[20] Paul Bew, Peter Gibbon and Henry Patterson contend that he eventually became one of 'the two most important northern leaders' of the nationalist minority of the new northern jurisdiction, along with Joseph Devlin.[21] As the Irish Parliamentary Party's lustre began to diminish, another bishop whose diocese would straddle the border, Bishop Charles McHugh of Derry, gave his views on the party: 'Is the spirit of Ireland dead, or has her manhood departed that she can stand listlessly by and see all the endurance, all the organised effort of centuries brought to nought, and her birthright battered for less than a mess of pottage by those who had entrusted to them the sacred duty of guarding and defending her?'[22]

McHugh produced an anti-partition manifesto against 'the dismemberment of our country' in May 1917, signed by Logue, seventeen other Catholic bishops and the Church of Ireland bishops of Ossory, Tuam and Killaloe. Four Catholic bishops – MacRory, O'Donnell, Kelly and the Archbishop of Cashel, John Harty – were amongst the 101 members of the Irish Convention that met from 25 July 1917 to 5 April 1918 in another attempt to resolve the Irish question. The convention brought the Catholic hierarchy face-to-face with Ulster unionists, where many long-standing grievances were aired. Whilst O'Donnell made a favourable impression among unionists by downplaying the significance of *Ne Temere* and *Quantavis Diligentia* and proposing extra Unionist representations in an all-Ireland Home Rule senate:

> MacRory, who had the prevention of partition as his main object in the Convention, spoke for Irish rights with a minimum of tact ... While he stated that he sought a settlement that would 'bury the hatchett', Plunkett [Horace, convention chairman] commented to the King that he couldn't help feeling MacRory had made 'rather free use of the hatchet he proposed to bury'.[23]

No agreement was reached at the convention. Lloyd George blamed the Catholic bishops, stating, 'to be defeated by Maynooth is indeed an added humiliation.'[24] It would mark the last serious constitutional attempt to achieve a solution.

Further wedges were driven between unionism and nationalism with the anti-conscription campaign and the Westminster election of December 1918, with the Catholic Church playing a prominent role in both. The possibility of a split Catholic vote in Ulster between Sinn Féin and the Irish Parliamentary Party and the fear of consequently losing seats to Ulster unionists, led Cardinal Logue to intervene between both strands of nationalism. He was responsible for dividing Ulster seats between both parties and, as noted by many unionist commentators, in the process was offering clear recognition to a republican party.[25] This tacit approval of Sinn Féin would only increase with the onset of the War of Independence. Despite recognising the legitimacy of Sinn Féin in many ways, Logue was no supporter of them. He favoured dominion status for the whole country and believed Ireland should remain within the British empire with a parliament similar to that of Canada or Australia.[26] Whilst there were differences of opinion within the Catholic hierarchy over the declaration of a republic by the first Dáil in 1919, at the beatification of Oliver Plunkett, the seventeenth-century Archbishop of Armagh, in Rome in May 1920, Logue, O'Donnell 'and a number of other Irish bishops attended a reception hosted by the speaker of the Dáil on behalf of "the government of Ireland". Towards the end of that gathering the orchestra struck up "A Nation Once Again" and "The Soldiers Song", at which "archbishops, bishops, priests ... sang the stirring anthem amid enthusiastic scenes". [27] The whole proceedings were viewed with horror by the unionist press, as articulated by the *Belfast Newsletter*:

> The Pope, some of the leading officials at the Vatican, and a number of R.C. bishops from this country have spent a week in praising and blessing an Irish rebel [Oliver Plunkett] who was hanged for treason, and there is no doubt that the proceedings were intended to encourage the present rebellion, although they know it is accompanied by assassination and outrages of every kind.[28]

The Government of Ireland Bill, when introduced to the House of Commons in February 1920, was roundly condemned by the Catholic Church. Logue referred to the bill as 'worse than useless'.[29] When asked for his comment on the appointment of a Catholic, Lord FitzAlan, as Lord Lieutenant, Logue said that 'he received the news in the same manner as he would the appointment of a Catholic hangman'.[30] The Catholic hierarchy particularly resented, in their view, the British government's coercion of the whole of Ireland for the sake of Ulster unionists. They issued a statement on 19 October 1920:

> The governing classes across the water, instead of encouraging Ulster Unionists to coalesce with the rest of the country, have used that section for centuries as a spear-head directed at the heart of Ireland. The whole British administration sat complacently while a provisional [Unionist] government was formed and an army drilled in Ulster … [Then, during the First World War] the highest offices in the gift of the State were for the contingent rebels of Ulster in contrast with the bullet for Irish insurgents. [Now] all Ireland must be coerced for the sake of the North-East, and especially Tyrone, Fermanagh and Derry City.[31]

The outbreak of sectarian violence in Derry and Belfast in the summer of 1920 only added to the Church's fears for the impending new northern jurisdiction. In the same statement of October 1920, the Catholic hierarchy referred to the violence engulfing Belfast at that time:

> In no other part of Ireland is a minority persecuted. Only one persecuting section can be found among the Irish people; and perhaps recent sad events may, before it is altogether too late, open the eyes of the people of England to the iniquity of furnishing a corner of Ulster with a separate government, or its worst instrument, a special police force, to enable it all the more readily to trample under foot the victims of its intolerants.[32]

The removal of predominantly Catholic workers from the Belfast shipyards led to increased violence, with churches, church leaders and church property seen as legitimate targets. During violence in Lisburn following the assassination of Swanzy (see Chapter Three), the Union Jack flag was hoisted at the entrance of the Catholic church and 'To Hell with the Pope' and 'No priests here' written on the wall of the severely damaged parochial house.[33] Bishop MacRory moved from his house in Andersonstown (west Belfast) to St Malachy's College for his own safety. In December 1920 he appealed for help for the expelled workers to Cardinal O'Connell: 'Fully fifty thousand Catholics are now on the verge of starvation in my diocese, which is no longer in Ireland, not even in Ulster – for that historic province has been mutilated – but in the nameless satrapate made up of the six amputated counties.'[34]

Logue, who claimed he had never experienced more anxiety in his forty years as a member of the hierarchy, condemned Lloyd George for talking about the safeguarding of Ulster without talking about the safeguarding of the minority in Ulster.[35] As partition fast approached, the Church believed that in the new state, Catholics would be reduced to 'the status of hewers of wood and drawers of water'.[36]

Many members of the Church played an active role in the election to the new northern parliament in May 1921. In the build-up to the election, bishops such as Logue, MacRory and Edward Mulhern of Dromore made many comments condemning the looming partition of the island.[37] MacRory asked priests to appeal to people to vote for the anti-partition ticket. He was also instrumental in convincing de Valera to agree to an electoral pact with Joe Devlin (see Chapter Four).[38] Logue was invited to the state opening of the northern parliament by King George V in June 1921 but refused to attend on 'the grounds that he had a prior engagement'.[39] Instead, he, along with the rest of the hierarchy, issued a statement condemning the new parliament:

> Every horror has been intensified, and we are now threatened with even darker doings because our countrymen spurn; as they rightly do, the sham settlement devised by the British Government. In defiance of Ireland a special Government has been given to one section of her people, remarkable at all times for intolerance, without the slightest provision to safeguard the victims of ever-recurring cruelty; and a Parliament of their own is set up in the

midst after a year of continuous and intolerable persecution directed against the Catholics of Belfast and the surrounding areas, at a time when the campaign of extermination is in full blast and a public threat is uttered to leave the Catholic minority at the mercy of Ulster's special constables. Until repression ceases, and the right of Ireland to choose her own form of government is recognised, there is no prospect that peace will reign amongst us.[40]

Members of the hierarchy played a prominent role in bringing about the truce of July 1921. Bishop Mulhern passed a letter to de Valera from Lloyd George, inviting the Sinn Féin leader to London for a conference.[41] The hierarchy welcomed the peace conference, which began in October, and hoped for a better settlement than the Government of Ireland Act. They contributed to the treaty negotiations through the Committee of Information on the Case of Ulster, established in September 1921. The committee secretary, Seán Milroy, initially contacted twenty-eight people for information, including bishops MacRory, Mulhern, McHugh and O'Donnell as well as eight northern priests. This reliance on the Catholic Church demonstrated recognition of the Church's expertise in northern affairs whilst also highlighting the weakness of the Sinn Féin movement on the ground in the north.[42] Most bishops were convinced that the Anglo-Irish Treaty was an acceptable compromise.[43] There was, however, much misgivings on the treaty provisions for continued partition. It rankled with some hierarchy members that the Dáil members during the treaty debates expressed more concern for the issues of sovereignty and the oath of allegiance than for partition.[44] However, utterances from Griffith and Collins reassuring the bishops that the Boundary Commission would pave the way for greater independence and an end to partition did help to alleviate those concerns.[45]

The provisional government formed in the south in early 1922 became reliant on Bishop MacRory for advice on the north. Collins, looking to define northern policy, invited MacRory to a cabinet meeting in late January. Its advisory committee on Northern Ireland contained three bishops and ten priests based in in the north. Members of the clergy were also prominent in the three committees set up to promote reconciliation after the second pact between Collins and Craig.[46] The Catholic Church's support for the new government in the south and its policy of non-recognition of the northern government was seen by unionists as a further example of the Church's sedition to the northern state. The provisional government had continued a non-recognition policy that had been adopted by the Church since Northern Ireland came into being in the summer of 1921. As well as not accepting Craig's invitation to attend the opening of the northern parliament, Logue also refused to participate in the Lynn Committee to forge the education policy for the north (see Chapter Eleven). Ernest Clark's overtures for MacRory to participate in a meeting of community representatives to restore order in Belfast in July 1921 was only met with reluctant consent, such was the distrust of any involvement with the new state, even where such involvement could help to alleviate some of the suffering experienced within the Catholic community.[47]

The Church caused considerable embarrassment for the northern government by its statements to the press on the ongoing sectarian violence in Belfast. It refuted the claims that the initial violence was caused by the IRA, strongly criticising the northern jurisdiction and its policing apparatus as the primary culprit of the violence. The hierarchy issued a statement in April 1922 condemning the northern government, comparing it to

> the government of the Turk in his worst days than anything to be found anywhere in a Christian State ... Not only have Catholics been denied for over 20 months their natural right to earn their daily bread, and thrown on the charity of the world, but they are subjected to a savage persecution which is hardly paralleled by the bitterest sufferings of the Armenians. Every kind of persecution, arson, destruction of property, systematic terrorism, deliberate assassination, and indiscriminate murder reign supreme.[48]

In response to the media onslaught by the Church, the northern government was assisted by the 'Ulster Association for Peace with Honour'. The association set up an energetic publicity committee, which met 134 times during its first year, to support Craig in his stand against attacks by the Church on the northern jurisdiction.[49] The security forces in Northern

Ireland were also criticised by the Church for holding up Logue and O'Donnell for unnecessarily long periods on 6 and 15 June 1922.[50]

The northern administration passed a number of pieces of legislation soon after its formation that guaranteed an antagonistic response from the Catholic Church. The passing of the Special Powers Act and the subsequent internment of suspect Catholics led the *Irish Catholic* to condemn the judicial system of Northern Ireland and call the prison ship, the *Argenta*, 'The Floating Coffin Ship'. The newspaper was subsequently banned for a month.[51] The Local Government Act, abolishing PR for local elections and obliging those who held local government positions to declare an oath of allegiance, received an indignant response from Catholic chaplains. At the time, there were Catholic chaplains in twenty-four workhouses, six lunatic asylums, two military barracks and various district hospitals. Just as teachers in Catholic schools faced a similar dilemma, chaplains who refused to sign the oath of allegiance were dismissed or forced to work without pay. By December 1922, practically all chaplains had declined to sign, claiming their duties were of a religious nature and that they could not agree to sign any document declaring political allegiance.[52] Canon D. McDonnell, chaplain at the Belfast workhouse, said that the government would have his support as long as it legislated '"for the common good, irrespective of creed or class" and that this should be sufficient'.[53] By early 1924, most chaplains had succumbed and signed the declaration of allegiance. The Promissory Oaths Act of 1923 required that civil servants and teachers in independently run schools also take an oath of allegiance. Although bitterly opposed to the act, teachers were forced to acquiesce, leading the republican newspaper, *An Phoblacht*, to condemn the Catholic Church for influencing 'their flocks to bow tamely to the humiliating decrees of the Orange Junta'.[54]

In another hard-hitting statement in October 1923, the hierarchy called on Catholics to no longer 'lie down under the degrading thraldom to which the Belfast parliament seeks to subject them'. They claimed that 'a deliberate conspiracy has been set on foot to deprive the Catholics in the North-East of even the elementary rights of citizens'.[55] The bishops called on Catholics to 'organise openly on constitutional lines to make an end of this monstrous and corrupt tyranny'.[56] With the clergy playing a major role, protest meetings were held all over the north the following month.

One priest, Fr Philip O'Doherty, said at one of these protest meetings that 'this Lilliputian Parliament was hardly two years in existence and "No Pope" or rather "To hell with the Pope" was stamped on every line of legislation'. Some unionists considered the bishops as being responsible for civic unrest.[57] Protest meetings were also held for political prisoners on hunger strike who were still interned, with clergy members playing a prominent role in such meetings. Although the protests did not succeed, they offered a forum for Catholics to vent their frustrations and demonstrate nationalist cohesion.[58]

When the Boundary Commission finally met in November 1924, the Catholic Church played an active role in providing recommendations and conveying the opinions of Catholic inhabitants in the border areas. Some priests took private censuses in areas of Tyrone in 1922 and again in 1925. Almost thirty priests gave evidence to the Boundary Commission, and bishops in the north were visited by the commissioners. The main argument put forward by the Church was that the inhabitants in their areas wanted to be transferred to the Free State. Some clergy members expressed outright opposition to partition.[59] Once it was decided to retain the status quo and leave the area of Northern Ireland as it was, many clergy members residing in border areas reacted with amazement and fury. Protest meetings were organised, with the clergy again playing a prominent role. Many accused the Free State government of making partition permanent.[60] Although MacRory expressed grave reservations about the outcome of the Boundary Commission, O'Donnell, who became cardinal soon after the decision, remarked, 'The area of the Six Counties is now fixed as the area of Northern Ireland, and everyone within it has to make account of that fact.'[61] This was a pivotal moment for the Catholic Church in the north. It no longer viewed northern politics within the context of politics on the whole island. Led by O'Donnell, the Church looked to work with northern structures and obtain reforms from within. There was no longer a point in looking for redemption from the Free State. They would only be able to do so alone.[62]

That the Protestant churches did not split after the partition of Ireland is somewhat surprising, as widely divergent views were expressed between northern and southern members regarding the division of the country. Although there were some Protestant supporters of Home Rule, most wished to maintain the union with Great Britain. Despite that the first leaders of the Home Rule political movement, Isaac Butt and Charles Stewart Parnell, were Protestant, within the Church of Ireland, there was almost unanimous opposition to their position.[63] Many believed that Protestants would be imperilled under Home Rule. Special General Synods were held by the Church of Ireland as Home Rule Bills came before the House of Commons in 1886, 1893 and 1912. At the 1886 General Synod, a resolution was passed, 'representing more than six hundred thousand of the Irish people, consider it a duty at the present crisis to affirm our constant allegiance to the Throne, and our unswerving attachment to the legislative Union'.[64] Church of Ireland Primate Robert Bent-Knox claimed that the second Home Rule Bill of 1893 was 'bristling with dangers', stating, 'it would be better to call it a Bill to suppress the Protestant faith – a Bill to subjugate this country to Papal dictation'.[65] An anti-Home Rule motion was passed at the Methodist Conference of 1892 by 195 votes to eleven. At the Presbyterian General Assembly of 1893, 304 delegates supported a motion opposing Home Rule. Eleven delegates opposed the motion, however, with 341 abstaining.[66]

As a new century dawned with the Ulsterisation of unionism prevailing, Church of Ireland numbers dwindled considerably outside the north-east of Ireland. In some instances, Protestants were 'seeking in Canada and elsewhere a freer atmosphere and fuller scope for their energies where no religious disabilities bar their progress'.[67] All of the Protestant churches became identified with Ulster unionism yet still maintained an all-Ireland institutional presence. This was particularly an issue for the Church of Ireland and the Methodist Church, who had significant membership numbers outside of Ulster.

The attitude of these two denominations to political events had to account for the potential ramifications for their members living in the south and west of the country. This was less problematic for the Presbyterian Church, whose membership had long been concentrated in the north-east. Additionally, the leadership of all the churches had to consider the possibility that the unionist campaign would fail and that they would be obliged to come to terms with a Dublin administration dominated by nationalists.[68]

According to the 1911 Irish census, 34.32 per cent of Church of Ireland members resided outside of Ulster, with just over 20 per cent of Methodists and only 4 per cent of Presbyterians also residing there.[69] In 1910, eleven former moderators of the Irish General Assembly of the Presbyterian Church published a manifesto in which they contended that the interests of all the people of Ireland were best safeguarded by the union with Great Britain.[70] The weekly Presbyterian newspaper, the *Witness*, was a strong supporter of Ulster unionism and more vociferous in opposing Home Rule than the press of the other Protestant denominations.[71]

A Presbyterian elder, Thomas Sinclair, was responsible for drafting the text of the Solemn League and Covenant, which was signed by 471,414 men and women on Ulster Day, 28 September 1912. It was the province's most prominent manifestation of opposition to Home Rule.[72] The drafting committee included senior clerics from the three main Protestant religions: the Church of Ireland Dean of Belfast Cathedral, the Moderator of the Presbyterian General Assembly and a former vice-president of the Methodist Conference.[73] The text of the covenant relied heavily on religious language and imagery. Clergy from all of the three main Protestant denominations played a leading role on Ulster Day itself, cementing the view amongst many, that unionist politics had the blessing of the leaders of the Protestant Churches. Properties owned by the three Protestant Churches featured prominently as venues for signings of the covenant in different locales; 193 church-owned properties were used across the province.[74] Many clergy members were responsible for organising events for their local areas, and Church leaders were prominent among the first signatories in City Hall in Belfast. Of 1,225 active Protestant clergy ministering in Ulster at the time, 798 are identified as signing the Covenant, a rather low percentage of 65 per cent of those who were eligible to sign.[75]

At the Church of Ireland General Synod of April 1912, a resolution had been passed granting 'unswerving attachment to the legislative union now subsisting between Great Britain and Ireland'.[76] Only five out of 403 opposed the resolution.[77] Despite this apparent unity of stance, there were clear differences between northern and southern clergy members during the Home Rule Crisis of 1912, a crisis that would develop further as partition loomed on the horizon. Northern members became open to the exemption of Ulster or part of Ulster from Home Rule, whereas southern members did not want to be a small scattered minority in a divided island. 'If home rule could not be defeated, their aims were to preserve the unity of Ireland with safeguards for the unionist minority.[78] Differences within the Church became apparent during Ulster Day itself. Charles Frederick D'Arcy, the Church of Ireland Bishop of Down, Connor and Dromore, without consulting the other Ulster bishops, announced that there would be special services in the churches of his diocese on the morning of Ulster Day. John Baptist Crozier, who was the Primate, and the other Ulster bishops 'much put out by Down's actions' agreed that on the 22 September, there should be 'prayers on the whole matter of home rule'. This, they hoped, would mean avoiding an identification of the Church with the proceedings of Ulster Day.[79] D'Arcy 'rejected criticisms that the church should not be involved in a political campaign ... he believed that the "deep conviction in the heart of the Ulster protestant" was as much religious as political, and that Ulster unionists were being oppressed, misrepresented, and driven to extremism'.[80] On the morning of Ulster Day, he preached to a packed congregation at St Anne's Cathedral before signing in Belfast City Hall; he was the fourth person to do so.[81] The five other Church of Ireland bishops whose dioceses covered Ulster also signed the covenant. The Archbishop of Dublin, Joseph Ferguson Peacocke, 'was very much afraid that if the members of the Church of Ireland were associated with the decisions of the Belfast meeting, the Hibernians and the Land League might raise hostility against them throughout the other provinces'.[82] The Bishop of Cork, Charles Dowse, also criticised the Church of Ireland's involvement with Ulster Day, stating 'that the great majority of the laity in the south object to being in any way identified with the Ulster movement'.[83]

Dr Henry Montgomery, Moderator of the Presbyterian General Assembly, and Dr W.J. Lowe, the General Assembly Clerk, were, like D'Arcy, amongst the first signatories in City Hall on Ulster Day.[84] There was also some opposition to Home Rule amongst Presbyterians. When the Presbyterian General Assembly, as well as the Methodist Conference, met in the summer of 1912, the highly charged political atmosphere meant that the question of Home Rule was considered too controversial to be put to a vote.[85] There was a vote taken the following year, with 921 voting for a resolution and agreeing to 'determined and unyielding opposition to Home Rule'; forty-three voted against, with 165 abstaining.[86] Some Presbyterian ministers 'who opposed the campaign against Home Rule and their church's part in it found their position so uncomfortable that they went abroad to pursue their ministries elsewhere. A substantial majority remained, however, to persist in dissent.[87] Unlike the Church of Ireland, where it was expected that the clergy would take leadership roles on political issues, political involvement by Presbyterian and Methodist ministers was generally frowned upon, with laypeople from both denominations leading the demonstrations against Home Rule.[88]

Most of the Methodist leaders signed the Covenant on Ulster Day, some with their own blood. The Methodist Conference was 'determined at all costs to maintain the solidarity of the Church both North and South'.[89] The trend of conference resolutions during the third Home Rule Crisis was that they were 'the friends of all, and the enemies of none'.[90] There were some southern and British supporters of Home Rule within Methodism, but most wanted to maintain the union with Great Britain. A motivating factor for Methodist ministers to remain neutral was related to their assignments. Ministers were moved to new areas every three years, with many moving from Ulster to other provinces in Ireland where anti-Home Rule sentiment would not be well-received.[91]

Members of the Protestant clergy took a dim view of the Easter Rising belligerents, with the Archbishop of Dublin, John Henry Bernard, writing a letter to *The Times* stating that 'this is not the time for amnesties and pardons, it is the time for punishment swift and stern'.[92] Bernard was a unionist but one who could be considered a pragmatic unionist.[93]

> At the close of 1916 he was vigorously impressing on unionists that the home rule act of 1914 was a political fact which they could not ignore, and he strove for an Irish settlement which would give Ireland a measure of autonomy, sufficient, in Bernard's opinion, to satisfy reasonable nationalists while maintaining the unity of Ireland and preserving many links with Great Britain.[94]

Bernard, along with the Primate, Crozier, and the Provost of Trinity College, John Mahaffy, represented the Church of Ireland at the 1917 Irish Convention.[95] Crozier and Mahaffy submitted a minority report in opposition to the convention's findings 'dissenting from that of the majority on the grounds that its provisions would imply either the coercion of Ulster ("unthinkable") or the partitioning of Ireland ("disastrous"). Instead, the minority report proposed a federal solution, based on Swiss or Canadian models'.[96] In May 1917, three Church of Ireland bishops, the bishops of Tuam, Ossory and Killaloe, together with seventeen Catholic bishops, signed an anti-partition declaration (see above). This move provoked an immediate riposte from Crozier and the four other bishops from Ulster, who expressed the view that Home Rule would be 'disastrous to the best interests of Ireland and dangerous to the empire', adding that no scheme of Home Rule could be carried 'without the exclusion of Ulster'.[97] The 'use of "Protestant" as a synonym for "Ulster Unionist" also attracted significant criticism from clergy members resident in the other three provinces, who claimed that many Protestants in the South objected to being identified with northern resistance', with many in fact favouring Home Rule.[98] Protestant clergy members who were critical of Ulster unionism included Charles Dowse, Church of Ireland Bishop of Cork, and William Crawford, former vice-president of the Methodist Conference. Crawford, also the principal of Wesley College in Dublin, 'criticised Ulster unionists for trying to impose their wishes on the majority population of the country. He espoused the need for toleration and conciliation and urged Irish protestants to show goodwill'.[99]

Although it became acceptable as a compromise to northern clergy members, there was little support for partition within the Church of Ireland. D'Arcy, speaking in 1919, accepted that the relationship between the two regions of the Church (north and south) was not always ideal and that 'a certain aloofness exists'.[100] However, he urged closer union between northern and southern dioceses, claiming 'the inclusion of communities so contrasted, yet so complimentary to each other, is "a splendid heritage" for any Church'.[101] In the same article in which D'Arcy's comments appeared, the *Irish Times* saw little future for a unified Church of Ireland with partition on its way, claiming 'from the day when it is enforced the Church of Ireland will no longer be the Church of Ireland. The judgement of Solomon will cleave her body with the sword of an Act of Parliament'.[102] The same paper had claimed earlier in 1919 that partition would 'divide the Church of Ireland and the Presbyterian and Methodist Churches not only against one another, but against themselves'.[103] D'Arcy, on becoming Primate of all-Ireland in 1920, addressed the issue of partition and the effects it would have on the Church of Ireland:

If, for purposes of administration, he asked, 'Ireland were divided, were they to anticipate any corresponding feature in the Church? There were Churchmen in the South of Ireland who were apprehensive on this point. They feared that North and South might drift apart. They thought the Church might suffer partition. The Primate emphatically declared that he did not believe that the creation of an administrative boundary, such as was proposed in the Bill, could have any such effect. If it had, it would be proof of a very feeble flickering life in the Church. The division of the United States of America into distinct states did not partition the various Churches which existed in that great country. The separation of the provinces of Canada did not split up the Churches of Canada. The various territories which united to form the Commonwealth of Australia did not demand separate Churches for themselves. Those who anticipated the partition of the Church of Ireland were really crediting their Church with a very low degree of vitality ... he thought so highly of their Church that he was persuaded that the new situation, if it should come to pass, would but afford further proof of that tenacious life which had enabled her to exist and persist through all the confusions of the most troubled of all histories.[104]

The *Church of Ireland Gazette* believed the Primate was being overly optimistic:

We venture to think that political partition would have a more serious effect upon the Church than his Grace would appear to indicate. We do not anticipate a formal schism; but we do regard as an inevitable consequence a drifting apart in heart and in mind ... A political partition of Ireland cuts far deeper than State frontiers in the United States or in Canada. It is a formal recognition of distinct nationality.[105]

Although describing partition as 'distasteful', the Presbyterian General Assembly declared that 'under no circumstances will we consent to come under the rule of a Dublin parliament'.[106] For the sake of peace, Presbyterians reluctantly accepted the Government of Ireland Act.

As Catholics became the minority in Northern Ireland, Protestants became an even smaller minority in the south. Church of Ireland members in the three southern provinces were badly shaken by the breakdown of law and order that came with the War of Independence and the subsequent civil war. As R.B. McDowell states in his book, *The Church of Ireland 1869–1969*:

> Certainly there was no declared hostility to protestants on religious grounds. But the Protestant was often a unionist in areas where a unionist was a rara avis. In the spring of 1922, after a number of protestants in the south had been compelled by threats to leave their homes and some in county Cork had been murdered, the members of the general synod resident in the twenty-six counties appointed a deputation to interview the provisional government.[107]

The person who led the deputation, the Archbishop of Dublin, John Gregg, described the killing of Protestants in west Cork as 'a declaration of war upon a defenceless community'.[108] He was referring to the killing of eight Protestants, in their homes, in Dunmanway, Ballinen and Clonakilty at the end of April 1922.[109] Peter Hart contended that the IRA killed 200 civilians in County Cork between 1917 and 1923, over seventy of whom were Protestant, a contributory factor to the sharp decline of Protestants living in Cork.[110] The deputation, on being received by Michael Collins and W.T. Cosgrave, asked if the provisional government was 'desirous of retaining' the Protestant community in the country.[111] Collins and Cosgrave assured them that the government would do everything to protect all citizens of the state.[112] Gregg was instrumental, not only in maintaining the unity of the Church of Ireland but also in integrating the Protestant community into the new Irish Free State. He declared that 'whatever our religious or political outlook may be, here is our home, and we have a right to be here'.[113] Although there was some violence perpetrated against Church of Ireland members in the south, most parts of Ireland remained unaffected, with most people on good terms with their neighbours. Within the Presbyterian Church, the

> Reports of the State of the Country Committee to the General Assembly contained allegations that a campaign of extermination

was being pursued in the south. In 1922 the Assembly was told that 'many members of our church have been shot or intimidated or deprived of their property and compelled to leave the country'. At the same time southern Presbyterian ministers stated in debate in the Assembly that they did not believe that any of their people were being attacked because of their religion.[114]

Some Methodists were also killed, and others were forced to leave Ireland during the War of Independence and the civil war. A Wesleyan soldier was killed as he entered the Methodist church in Fermoy on 7 September 1919 and others were wounded in the attack.[115] The Methodist Conference had to be moved from Cork to Belfast in 1921 due to the 'unsettlement of the South'.[116] On the whole, however, 'few barriers were raised against the preaching of the Methodists, and of religious persecution there was practically none'.[117]

With the partitioning of Ireland, the three main Protestant religions retained their all-Ireland structure. Even though the majority of Church of Ireland members resided in Northern Ireland

the machinery of the church remained largely based in the south. Of the thirteen diocesans only five worked and three lived in Northern Ireland. The divinity school and the headquarters of the representative church body remained in Dublin and the general synod continued to meet there. This meant that the Church of Ireland remained a unifying force in Irish life, northern churchmen interested in ecclesiastical administration being kept in touch with Dublin.[118]

Most Church of Ireland members accepted the Irish Free State reluctantly; they still clung to old loyalties and symbols as much as they could. They looked on as the Irish Free State government took the Catholic Church's lead on issues such as divorce and birth control.[119] The *Irish Times* claimed in 1928 that the Church of Ireland had lost its voice and did not speak out at all on issues of concern to its members in the Irish Free State – gone was the 'old authority, the old courage ... the old confidence'.[120] Due to the major constitutional changes that affected the island of Ireland in the early

1920s, a new legal foundation needed to be created for the Irish Methodist Church to be able to continue as an all-Ireland body. Bills were passed in the Irish Free State and in Northern Ireland in 1928. 'This Methodist Church Act of 1928 was the first instance in which the two parliaments acted identically and simultaneously', allowing the Methodist Church to continue its work throughout the whole island.[121] Regardless of their misgivings, Presbyterians gave the Irish Free State recognition as a legitimate state. The General Assembly encouraged Presbyterians in the south 'to co-operate whole-heartedly with their Roman Catholic fellow-countrymen in the best interests of their beloved land'.[122]

The leaders of the Protestant Churches saw their congregation numbers dwindle significantly in the twenty-six counties with the onset of partition. In September 1922, the Church of Ireland Bishop of Kilmore 'told the annual Diocesan Synod that "the Church had suffered severely" and that emigration from the south and the west had been "calamitous"'.[123] The censuses of 1911 and 1926 (the censuses taken before and after partition) show the rapid decline in population of all Protestant denominations in that period. The First World War and the withdrawal of British crown forces contributed to this decline, but the War of Independence, the subsequent civil war and the partition of Ireland were also major factors in Protestants emigrating from the new southern state.[124] Protestant Episcopalians (members of the Churches of Ireland, England and Scotland) fell from 249,535 in 1911 to 164,215 in 1926, a decline of 34.2 per cent. Presbyterians declined from 45,486 in 1922 to 32,429 in 1926, a decline of 28.7 per cent. Methodists fell from 16,440 in 1911 to 10,663 in 1926, a decline of 35.1 per cent. In the same period, the Catholic population of the twenty-six counties decreased by just 2.2 per cent.[125] A private census of 'Free State Protestants who had migrated north to County Fermanagh between 1920 and 1925 listed almost 150 Monaghan families, comprising over 450 persons, some driven out by the dislocation of unionist trade, and others who left voluntarily, determined to live under British rule'.[126] Somerset Saunderson, a Protestant and unionist leader from Cavan, declared in 1922, 'Now ... I have *no* country!'[127] Unquestionably affected by the revolutionary violence, the Free State was 'reasonably sensitive' to their position. They 'were over represented in both the Senate and the Dáil ... they retained ownership of a disproportionate share of land in the state and retained a dominant position in industry, finance and the professions'. Even though the Protestant population had reduced to 7 per cent by 1926, they 'still produced 40 per cent of lawyers and over 50 per cent of bankers, and over a quarter of large farms were still in Protestant ownership'.[128] Whilst experiencing significantly less discrimination than Catholics in the north, the 'small Protestant minority, though mostly free from physical persecution after 1922, suffered increasingly from the legal incorporation of Catholic moral precepts'.[129] Many Protestants in the south felt isolated and politically impotent.[130]

The one religion in Ireland that saw the greatest institutional changes due to partition was Judaism. It was no longer organised on an all-Ireland basis. While 'Jews in Northern Ireland remained affiliated to Jewish structures in Britain, those south of the border ... were fortunate enough to enjoy the prudent leadership of the Chief Rabbi of Saorstát Eireann, Dr Isaac Herzog'.[131] Born in Poland in 1888, he moved to Belfast in 1915 as rabbi of the Jewish community there. A regular visitor to Dublin, he was appointed Chief Rabbi of the Jewish Community in Dublin in 1919 and Chief Rabbi of the Irish Free State in 1925.[132] His son, Chaim, became Israel's president in 1983.[133] At the beginning of the twentieth century, the nascent Jewish community members in Ireland were sympathetic to the British empire, seeing the British monarch as a guarantor of their liberties.[134] Sympathies soon started to change. The Judaeo Home Rule Association was founded in 1908.[135] Jews such as Jacob Elyan became active in the wider Home Rule movement through the United Irish League. John Redmond believed a Jewish Irish Parliamentary Party MP in Westminster would challenge the unionist cry of 'home rule is Rome rule', and asked Elyan to stand for election.[136] Elyan declined due to ill-health.

By the time of partition, many Jews were involved in Irish nationalist politics, 'to a greater extent than is recognised', according to Dermot Keogh.[137] Chaim Herzog claimed his father was 'an open partisan of the Irish cause' and that 'the Jewish community as a whole gave a lot of help to the Irish'.[138] Many Jews opposed the partition of Ireland. Herman Good, who would later become a judge and a leading figure in Irish Jewish affairs, speaking in 1928 as a law student, argued 'that the only possible reason for supporting the partition of Ireland was 'a complete lack of sense of Irish nationalism', adding that 'a sense of Irish nationalism had yet to be born in the six counties ... where the people had not yet become free'.[139]

Other religions and faiths, such as Islam, Hinduism and Buddhism, did not have institutional infrastructures when Ireland was partitioned, thus experiencing little upheaval from the political divide. For example, Islam in Ireland only started to organise in the Republic of Ireland from the 1950s with the founding of the Dublin Islamic Society by students of the Royal College of Surgeons.[140]

The partition of Ireland caused seismic shifts for all the major religions. Although the Catholic Church and the three main Protestant denominations retained their all-Ireland structure, they did so under very changed circumstances, as they then had to operate within two widely different jurisdictions. This was most clearly demonstrated through the issue of education within both states, where the major religions played a pivotal role.

CHAPTER ELEVEN

Education

Education in Ireland had been somewhat united before partition under the umbrellas of the Board of Commissioners for National Education, established in 1831, and the Board of Commissioners for Intermediate (secondary) Education, established in 1878. Edward George Stanley, Chief Secretary for Ireland, founded the Board of Education in 1831 with the intention 'to unite in one system, children of different creeds'.[1] The reality, however, transpired to be different over the next century, with the major churches taking a dominant role in the running of education, setting it on a denominational course where united and 'mixed' education was merely a pipedream.[2] Education would be coloured by intense rivalry between the Catholic Church and Protestant denominations long before partition drove a wedge even further within education on the island.

The two boards acted as intermediaries between the state and schools and provided funding to the schools. Once a national school was recognised by the National Education Board, the school received 'a percentage of capital costs to establish and maintain a school. In addition, the board paid teachers' salaries, published and provided textbooks, operated a system of inspection and generally attempted to play quite an interventionist role in the promotion of elementary education.'[3] The churches were the main providers of national schools, with 9,000 schools in operation before partition. More than 60 per cent of national schools in the early years of the twentieth century were single-teacher schools, with an average of fewer than fifty pupils in attendance on a daily basis.[4] The small school sizes were partly due to the Catholic Church's preference for single-sex schools.

The Intermediate Education Board was far less interventionist. It also had far fewer schools, with just 356, consisting of 27,500 students in 1920.[5] Schools received funding based on the results pupils obtained at the annual examinations, which were set and conducted by the board. There was a high failure rate, with 49 per cent of students failing to pass even one subject in 1919–20. It was recommended that the three grades of examination available at intermediate level be replaced with just two – an intermediate certificate examination for students aged fifteen to sixteen and a leaving certificate examination for students aged seventeen to eighteen. Although not implemented before partition, both jurisdictions would implement examination systems based on those recommendations.[6]

The Board of Commissioners of National and Intermediate Education were appointed by the Lord Lieutenant, and by 1921 were composed of 'equal numbers of Catholics and of members of the various Protestant denominations ... the half and half system'.[7] Annual reports of the boards were addressed to the Lord Lieutenant. Each board appointed their own full-time staff. One resident commissioner directed the affairs of the National Education Board, whilst two assistant commissioners were responsible for the Intermediate Education Board. Most commissioners 'were drawn from the upper ranks of the churches, the judiciary and the universities. In 1919-20 they comprised five bishops and an ex-Moderator of the Presbyterian General Assembly, seven lawyers including the Lord Chief Justice of Ireland, the Provost of Trinity College and several other academics and members of the Irish "nobility".[8] The main Protestant denominations had been opposed to the national education system at the time of its inception in 1831, but by 1920, the Protestant churches were deeply ingrained in the national education system and were far more open to denominational mixing and educational reform than the Catholic Church.

There was strong initial support for Stanley's national education initiative within the Catholic Church. After the Synod of Thurles in 1850, the Church insisted that only Catholics attend Catholic schools. Catholic 'children were to be educated in Catholic schools with a Catholic ethos. Teachers were to be trained in Catholic teacher-training colleges and appointed by Catholic clerical managers, who would also supervise their textbooks.'[9] The church demanded denominalisation within education. It was opposed to Catholics attending 'mixed' schools and campaigned against the introduction of 'model' schools that aimed for a 'united education'. Twenty-eight such schools had been established by the National

Board by the early 1860s. The Church's campaign was successful: 57.4 per cent of national schools had some degree of interdenominational mix in 1867, with only 25 per cent by 1913.[10] The Church 'viewed the educational system as a moral rather than as a strictly educational responsibility, and believed that the system of clerical control over each primary school was a moral necessity'.[11] It was also opposed to compulsory schooling, as it felt that this would lead to free education, followed by lay and purely secular education.[12] The average attendances at primary schools in the decade before the two Irish political entities were formed was 70 per cent. The Irish Compulsory Attendance Act of 1892 only applied to urban areas, 'a fatal flaw in an agrarian country'.[13] The Church was wary of educational reform and of change. It mistrusted the British administration, conscious of previous historical attempts at proselytism and Anglicisation.[14] It tolerated the national system, as it had *de facto* control over Catholic schools.

The religious instruction allowed under the educational system was acceptable to the main religions in Ireland. The placement of the Irish language within education was a different matter, however, between the Catholic and Protestant churches. The National Education Board claimed in 1919 that 232 schools were bilingual, that Irish was taught as an extra subject in 1,525 schools and that twenty-three colleges conducted vacation courses for Irish. The board claimed an inspector and six organisers were employed to promote the teaching of the language.[15] This was not satisfactory for the Gaelic League, who campaigned to make the Irish language an official language of the curriculum. It felt the National Education Board was antagonistic to the language.[16] Even though Irish was the vernacular of 25 per cent of the population in 1831, no place was found for the language under the new education system. The Gaelic League and its forerunner, the Society for the Preservation of the Irish Language, believed one of the most effective ways of stalling the anglicisation of Ireland was through the education system. It bemoaned the policy of the National Education Board to remove Gaelic myths from education and engender an image of the British empire equal to that of the ancient Greek empire.[17] Led by Douglas Hyde, founder and first president of the Gaelic League, successful campaigns were fought to maintain the Irish language as an intermediate education subject in 1899 and make the language compulsory for matriculation at the new National University of Ireland in 1909.[18] The Gaelic League, in its campaigns to cement the place of the Irish language in Irish education, received public support from the Catholic Church, including from leading members of its hierarchy, such as Cardinal Michael Logue.[19] Although many Protestants were involved in the Gaelic League, including its president, Hyde, there was little evidence of promoting the Irish language within Protestant schools, nowhere more so than in Ulster. Gaelic games also were almost exclusively played in Catholic schools.[20] Many unionists claimed that sedition was being inculcated in Catholic national schools. Prominent advanced nationalists associated with the teaching profession included Pádraig Pearse, Éamon de Valera, Eoin MacNeill and Thomas Ashe. Christian Brother schools came in for criticism from many quarters because of the way they taught history. The *Londonderry Sentinel* declared in June 1920 'that the fires of treason and rebellion are fed from generation to generation in Irish elementary schools (for which the English taxpayer has helped to pay) has been known for a long time to those familiar with this country'.[21] The differences between the two traditions in relation to language, culture, politics and their role within education would be realised in the different approaches taken by the northern and southern administrations following partition.

Education offered a stark reminder of the divide within Irish society, most clearly demonstrated through the issue of educational reform, with, in the main, Catholic nationalists pitted against Protestant unionists. Education had received very little governmental investment in the first twenty years of the twentieth century, meaning that some schools were in dire financial straits. Many intermediate schools were in bad need of repair, and underpaid teachers moved to England in droves. According to Seán Farren, 'nothing happened in the period between 1904 and 1920 to materially improve this situation. So, as was the case for hundreds of national schools, many unsuitable, insanitary and poorly equipped intermediate schools were to become part of the educational inheritance of the new Irish states.'[22]

To compound matters, the rapid increase of Belfast's population put a huge strain on school accommodation, with estimated shortages of available school places reaching over 20,000.[23] The main Protestant churches were unable to raise the necessary finances and concluded that the introduction of a local rate for education would be the best solution to solve the school accommodation shortage. The British government, leading unionist politicians and many within the teaching profession favoured the introduction of rates and saw 'local authority involvement in the provision and management of schools as essential, if education in the country was to be adequately funded and developed'.[24] Opposition from the Catholic Church was swift and fierce. Rates on education were seen as double taxation, with Ireland already more heavily taxed than anywhere else within the United Kingdom at the time.[25] The Church believed that the involvement of local authorities would significantly erode its power in education. Church of Ireland Bishop of Down and Connor, Charles D'Arcy, claimed that Catholic schools, like Protestant ones, were suffering from severe overcrowding, a claim denied by his Catholic counterpart, Joseph MacRory. MacRory vehemently opposed Catholics having to pay rates needed to prop up Protestant schools, stating in a pastoral that 'it is strange that while Catholics, the poorest section of the community, were prepared to do voluntarily what was necessary for education, their richer fellow-citizens were not, and pointed to the injustice of a rate which Catholics would have to pay for schools they could not attend'.[26] A bill was introduced in 1919 to establish a Belfast education authority to introduce rate support and local authority involvement in education. The bill was withdrawn, however, as the British government proposed to introduce its own bill, the MacPherson Bill, named after the Irish Chief Secretary.

Ian MacPherson had been appointed Chief Secretary on 13 January 1919, shortly before the outbreak of the War of Independence. His education bill 'proposed to replace semi-independent education boards with a Department of Education, to set up an advisory committee and county education committees'.[27] The bill proposed rate support for maintaining, heating and lighting schools, support for poorer students looking to advance to secondary school, reform of the intermediate education examination system and improved remuneration for teachers.[28] The bill was supported by virtually all interested parties, with the exception of the Catholic Church and nationalist politicians. The Irish National Teachers' Organisation (INTO), the union representing national school teachers, despite the majority of its members being Catholic, supported the bill. INTO president T.J. Nunan described opposition to the bill as unintelligent, saying he would prefer an elected as opposed to an appointed board of education. Some Catholic commentators charged that this was a betrayal not just of the Church but also of the Irish nation.[29] The bill was also welcomed by secondary school organisations of the Protestant tradition – the Irish Schoolmasters Association, the Association of Irish Schoolmistresses and the Incorporated Association of Assistant Masters (IAAM). The Association of Secondary Teachers in Ireland (ASTI) 'passed a resolution withholding approval of the Bill because it did not provide for adequate security of tenure and for an impartial Board of Appeal against dismissal'.[30]

The Catholic Church condemned the proposed Department of Education, describing the bill as 'the most denationalising scheme since the Act of Union'. The hierarchy was 'convinced that the enactment of the measure would deprive the Bishops and Clergy of such control of the schools as is necessary for that religious training of the young which [Pope] Leo XIII declared to be a chief part of the care of souls'. MacRory described the bill as 'hopelessly vitiated, rotten at the core, by reason of the anti-Irish and anti-Catholic character of the Department of three upon which it proposes to confer all the real power'.[31] The Ulster bishops were particularly hostile to the MacPherson Bill because of 'proposals, then being widely discussed, for a separate administration in all or part of Ulster with control of education amongst its functions'.[32] The division over the bill reflected the wider divide in Irish society at the time, with nationalists supporting the Catholic Church's opposition to the proposed measures and unionists firmly in favour of them. Many local authorities that Sinn Féin controlled, whose role in education would have been enhanced, nevertheless opposed the bill, as it was considered anti-Irish.[33] Joe Devlin, Irish Parliamentary Party MP, was also opposed: 'to give over the control of primary education into the hands of a body of the character and the past record of the Belfast City Council would be an appalling disaster to the Catholic interests of that city'.[34] Logue, in a novena in March 1920, said that 'Parents are bound to make sure, by every means in their power, that their children are brought up and educated as faithful Catholics, in a Catholic atmosphere, and under the care and direction of their pastors, whose strict right and leading duty is to watch over, direct, and safeguard the religious education of the lambs of their flock'.[35] The Church also played the Irish card, saying that education 'should be a native plant of native culture ... It should be a growth from within not an importation from without ... So it was in Ireland when our schools were famous; so it has not been in Ireland since England took upon herself to say what kind of schooling, if any, we must have.'[36]

The Catholic Church's campaign was successful and the bill lapsed. The bishops' stance seemed to confirm the worst fears of Protestants on the influence of the Catholic Church. Unionist newspapers, including the *Belfast Newsletter* and the *Northern Whig*, lamented the role of the Church in stopping the introduction of a modern education system. The *Northern Whig*'s editor, Robert Lynn, commented that the Irish layman was 'considered good enough to run a Home Rule parliament or a comic opera republic, but they could not be allowed to look after their schools'. He also said that Irish education was fifty years behind Britain's education due to the reactionary policy of Catholic bishops, remarking that 'Ireland is to be educated according to the decision of Pope Leo XIII, and the aim of Irish education is to be, not the training of young Irishmen to play their part in life as self-respecting, honest, loyal citizens, but to be docile and submissive slaves of Mother Church and her Bishops.'[37] Lynn would later play a pivotal role in the future education system of Northern Ireland.

Although the Catholic Church's campaign was a contributory factor in the withdrawal of the bill, the main reason for its withdrawal was the introduction of the Government of Ireland Bill. With partition pending, it made little sense to forge ahead with MacPherson's bill, as argued by the *Irish Times*:

> The Home Rule Bill must play havoc with the Education Bill. The latter proposes one great scheme of educational co-ordination for the whole of Ireland. There will be one national department for primary, another for secondary, and a third for technical education; and all three will be united at the top by the supervision of an Irish Minister. Under the Government's Home Rule Bill this plan must go completely by the board ... Mr. MacPherson's education scheme would be quite practicable in a united Ireland. It would be, as he will surely discover, utterly impracticable in a partitioned Ireland.[38]

The MacPherson Bill may not have succeeded on an all-Ireland basis. However, it would eventually provide the framework for the future education system of Northern Ireland, as feared by the Catholic bishop of Kildare and Leighlin, Patrick Foley:

I think we may regard the Education Bill as dead, as far as our part of the Country is concerned, but God help the poor Catholics in the N.East, where the new parliament will be put into operation. Possibly they will be fairly well treated in other respects, but it is very likely that Carson's non bill will be revived, and passed without delay by the N.E. Parliament.[39]

As the Government of Ireland Bill was moving towards the statute books, and with it the creation of two new jurisdictions in Ireland, the impact it would have on education was widely debated. The *Freeman's Journal* claimed that education would be the area most affected by partition, predicting that the education system of Northern Ireland would be 'completely different from what it was in the past'. The paper also believed it would prove difficult to partition the national boards without further legislation, as they were not a department, but chartered corporations 'holding property all over Ireland in trust'. The same article saw big obstacles in the provision of teacher training:

There is no Protestant training college and no Catholic training college for male teachers in the whole of the six counties. The Ulster Protestant teachers have been trained mainly in the National Board's College at Marlborough street and in the Church of Ireland's Training College in Kildare place. Withdrawal of the Ulster Presbyterian teachers in training and the Ulster Protestant Episcopalian teachers will seriously weaken these institutions. In fact it is doubtful if the Marlborough Street College will be worth continuing. The Ulster Catholic male teachers resort chiefly to St Patrick's Training College, Drumcondra, and unless that institution is recognised by the Northern Education Department as a training college for the Ulster schools in the future it also must be weakened.[40]

There was a fear that some intermediate education grants, such as the Birrell and Duke grants (named after Chief Secretaries Augustine Birrell and Henry Duke), would disappear and the southern parliament would face disproportionate financial burdens to support the universities, and with 'the interval of confusion and uncertainty which will certainly mark the transition period, poverty and insecurity will swell the tide of teachers emigrating to England.'[41] Teachers met in Belfast in March 1921 to discuss the consequences of partition on education for the six counties. Most were in favour of immediately establishing a permanent education department for Northern Ireland but also stated 'it would devolve upon the individual representatives of the various organisations whose ramifications extend throughout all Ireland to keep in sympathy and close touch with the general ideals of those associations'.[42]

The election to the northern parliament in May 1921 saw education become one of the main issues on both unionist and nationalist sides. It was believed by many Catholics that they would be taxed by a Belfast parliament to build schools for wealthy Protestants who had neglected their duties. The new parliament would plan the destruction of Catholic schools.[43] Unionists also campaigned on education, with one speaker from Ballymena claiming they were 'faced with Home Rule or Rome Rule dominated by the Roman Catholic Hierarchy of the Church of Rome. Were they going to permit themselves and the destinies of their children to be placed in the hands of the Hierarchy of the Church of Rome?' Unionist candidate William Twaddell claimed that no clergyman should have the power of managing schools. He protested that the Catholic clergy would not allow their people to read the Bible and that Catholics had been teaching the 'Hymn of Hate' in Catholic national schools. He added that 'the managers of Protestant schools did not teach the "Hymn of Hate" nor give the children the blackest pages in Irish history to read'.[44] James Craig, soon to be Northern Ireland's Prime Minister, also intervened and made no secret of his desire to curtail the Catholic Church's influence over education.[45]

When Northern Ireland came into being, in education terms it

inherited nothing more than the schools and colleges which had been operating within its six counties. These amounted to 2,040 national schools, 75 intermediate schools, 12 model schools, 45 technical schools, one teacher training college (St. Mary's, a Roman Catholic college for girls in Belfast), Queen's University, also in Belfast, and the quite small Magee College in Derry. Because the Boards of National and Intermediate Education had been based in Dublin, no local administration existed within Northern Ireland.[46]

The *Freeman's Journal* claimed that within the civil service for the national boards, there was no appetite amongst them to 'strike their tents and march to the Promised Land in the North'.[47] It was an enormous task for the new Northern Ireland Minister of Education, Lord Londonderry, to build from the ground up a new education system for the fledgling state, a task which he relished. Born in London, Charles Stewart Henry Vane-Tempest-Stewart, seventh Marquess of Londonderry, was among the richest landowners in the United Kingdom. He served as education minister and leader of the Northern Ireland senate from June 1921 to 1926. At Stormont, he cut an aristocratic figure. His contemporaries noted that 'he apes his ancestor, the great Lord Castlereagh, wears a high black stock over his collar, and a very tightly fitting frock coat and doesn't look as if he belongs to this century at all'. He addressed his civil servants like domestics and emphasised points 'by striking the ministerial table with his riding crop'.[48] To officials in the education ministry, Londonderry loomed as one of the kingdom's last imposing noble figures. He would appear in the morning 'meticulously groomed; his face almost shone, as if he had been shaved twice and then polished with pumice by his valet'.[49] Always more interested in British than Irish politics, he served as Secretary of State for Air in the Westminster cabinet from 1931 to 1935, giving him responsibility for the RAF. He 'preserved the RAF from excessive treasury cuts, and encouraged the building of a new generation of fighters and the development of radar'. These measures proved highly important when the Second World War began. However, his close attachment to some leading members and his favourable opinions of the Nazis throughout the 1930s have not helped his post-war reputation.[50]

Donal Akenson outlined the many obstacles Londonderry needed to overcome in his new job:

The difficulties facing Lord Londonderry in establishing a ministry of education in Northern Ireland should not be underestimated. The region was at war, there were severe educational deficiencies, and there existed no trained cadre of educational administrators in Belfast because previously the central administration had been located in Dublin. The ministry of education was established on 7 June 1921, but it was some time before control of the educational services was actually transferred from the Dublin authorities to the northern ministry. This delay in acquiring operative powers stemmed from the refusal of the southern government to cooperate fully in working the government of Ireland act, 1920. As late as September 1921 Londonderry still did not have any idea when the actual transfer of authority would take place, and only in early November was 1 February 1922 finally set as the transfer date. Even after the southern government had grudgingly agreed to allow the bifurcation of Ireland's educational services, according to Ulster authorities there were difficulties in securing the transfer of personnel to the north and avoidable delays in the transfer of necessary files and documents.[51]

One of his first actions as minister was to establish the Lynn Committee, named after its chairman, Robert Lynn, to propose structures for the future of education in Northern Ireland. Lynn 'was not altogether open-minded or tactful in matters involving the cultural patterns of the Roman Catholics'. He said the Irish language was 'purely a sentimental thing. None of these people who take up Irish ever know anything about it. They can spell their own names badly in Irish, but that is all. I do not think it is worth spending any money on.'[52] The committee did not receive cross-community support, with the Catholic Church refusing to participate in the committee. Explaining the reasons for the Catholic Church's non-participation, Cardinal Logue said:

I regret I do not see my way to nominate members of the Commission on education which Your Lordship proposes to appoint. I should be glad to co-operate in any effort for the improvement of education, but judging from the public utterances of some members of the Belfast Parliament and their sympathizers I have little doubt that an attack is being organized against our schools. I fear that the Commission proposed by Your Lordship, I am sure with the best intentions, will be used as a foundation and pretext for that attack.[53]

The Church had been offered four out of thirty seats on the committee but believed, with the MacPherson Bill showing the incompatibility of both sides on education, further discussion would be pointless.[54] This, Akenson believed, was a mistake:

By refusing to sit they surrendered their last shred of influence at the very time when the basic character of Ulster's educational development was being determined ... The refusal of the Catholic religious authorities to exert their influence upon the Lynn committee and subsequently upon the Londonderry act was especially unfortunate because, despite the civil war which was raging in Northern Ireland, the Unionist government was making a determined effort to govern in a non-sectarian manner, an attempt which was abandoned in the mid-1920s.[55]

Both Farren and Harris disagree with Akenson. The influence of four members in a committee dominated by unionists and Protestants would be minimal. If Logue accepted the invitation, it would have legitimised the new state, something nationalists were unwilling to do. The committee first convened at the time of the truce and the subsequent negotiations between Sinn Féin and the British government. At this time, there was a genuine expectation amongst nationalists that there would be an entirely new constitutional arrangement implemented to replace the Government of Ireland Act.[56]

Londonderry genuinely wanted the Catholic Church to be centrally involved. He sought 'one great body and in one band all the great educational forces of the country, so as to elaborate a system which will be satisfactory in every respect ... a system which will be the admiration of all other countries.'[57] Despite a number of attempts to convince Logue to reconsider, there was no involvement from the Church. He did, however, appoint one Catholic to the committee, Andrew Nicholas Bonaparte Wyse, who, as one education journal noted, 'does not belong to Ulster and whom the Roman Catholics of Ulster would not regard as representing them'.[58] He went on to become permanent secretary to the Northern Ireland education ministry from 1927 to 1939, the only Catholic to be in charge of a civil service department in the north.[59]

The committee produced an interim report in June 1922. This would form the basis of Londonderry's Education Act, which became law in October 1923. Although there was no involvement from the Catholic Church, the committee did try to be somewhat mindful of Catholic views.[60] The interim report recommended the creation of local education committees to act as education authorities. These education authorities would become the main providers of education services. Emphasis was placed on the need to maintain a positive and close relationship between the schools and the religions they were associated with, 'wherever church schools would be transferred, account would be taken of this relationship in the deeds of transfer'.[61] There was not a lot of controversy arising from curriculum reform, except for the recommendation to make the Irish language an optional subject. This proposal was to keep it in line with other secondary languages, such as French. This was greeted with hostility from the nationalist community as further evidence of the regime's antipathy towards nationalist's cultural values, relegating their language to the same status as continental ones. 'The committee argued that all schools should be obliged to inculcate appropriate civic values, at the core of which lay loyalty to the northern state and to the British Empire.'[62] All history books would also need to be approved by the ministry. The teaching of civics would include instructions on loyalty to Northern Ireland's constitution and the British empire, and the flying of the Union Jack was recommended to be flown in all schools on suitable occasions.[63] Although claiming to be mindful of Catholic views, many of the committee's recommendations would suggest otherwise. Its stance could be explained by the antipathy that both the nationalist community in Northern Ireland and the new provisional government in the twenty-six counties displayed towards the northern state and its education system.

During the teething phases of partition, there was still a need for cooperation between both jurisdictions on certain educational matters. By

1922, the Intermediate Education Board was still setting and administering examinations for the whole island of Ireland. The Permanent Secretary of the northern Ministry of Education had requested that the commissioners in Dublin do so for 1921–22.[64] Northern Ireland civil servants pointed out 'that Ulster's share of the cost of examinations for the Intermediate Classes would probably be between £3000 and £4000 if carried out jointly with Southern Ireland and might be double this amount if carried out by Northern Ireland separately'.[65] James Craig preferred to end the reliance on the south, saying 'it would have a most unfortunate political effect … it would be better to face the future at once and take over full responsibility'.[66] The arrangement stopped after a new regulation was introduced by the board in Dublin to permit candidates to answer questions in Irish in subjects other than Irish itself. Reaction to this change was quite hostile within the education ministry in Belfast, with Londonderry stating, 'I will not for one moment allow the use of the so-called Irish language in the Intermediate Examinations for Northern Ireland.'[67] He then announced that because of this and other changes, the examinations would be cancelled for Northern Ireland.

Whatever chance of cooperation there was evaporated once many teachers of Catholic schools embarked on a campaign of non-recognition of the northern education ministry in early 1922 with the explicit support of the newly formed provisional government of the Irish Free State. The issue had arisen in October 1921 when Catholic intermediate schools refused to recognise the ministry. 'When the northern ministry warned Fr John McShane of St Columb's College, Derry, that failure to supply information on any school to the ministry might result in loss of funds by that school, McShane indignantly forwarded the ministry's letter to Dáil Eireann's Minister of Education, stating that he considered the letter "a direct violation of the truce".'[68]

The full transfer of education to the north was scheduled for 1 February 1922, with all teachers to be paid by the north from that date. Michael Collins was prepared to finance the northern schools who refused to recognise the Belfast ministry:

A well-publicised and widely reported meeting of Catholic teachers in Strabane in late February called upon the provisional government of the Irish Free State to continue to administer the schools throughout Ireland and pledged themselves not to accept salaries from the northern government. They also called upon the southern government to reimburse them for the financial losses incurred through their non-cooperation with the northern ministry of education. Similar resolutions were passed in the same week by a large number of Catholic teachers meeting at Omagh.[69]

The northern Ministry of Education reported that there were 'salary claims received for all national schools except 8 in January 1922'. There was then a 'big fall in claims for February. Claims from 170 schools outstanding, all under Catholic management'.[70] John Duffin, a Belfast teacher, became chief organiser of the non-recognition campaign in the North.

He began by convening a meeting of teachers in Belfast at which there was much support for the campaign. The number of primary schools involved in the campaign showed a progressive increase for each of the first few months of 1922, stabilising around May. Out of 740 Catholic schools, 270 opted for non-recognition ... all Catholic Intermediate schools in Northern Ireland refused to recognise the northern ministry. Armagh and Newry technical schools also looked to Dublin as did St Mary's Teacher Training College.[71]

The provisional government also provided interim grants to the Catholic intermediate schools in the north.[72] At its peak, more than one-third of Catholic schools supported the boycott. To serve the non-cooperating northern intermediate schools, 'the Dublin government set up twenty-two examination centres in Northern Ireland, and 738 candidates sat for their examinations'.[73] According to Londonderry, the provisional government had the audacity to ask 'that the protection of His Majesty's Forces may be extended to their officers' whilst overseeing the examinations.[74] Although the Catholic Church took a neutral stance publicly, it offered considerable encouragement to the Dublin government's non-recognition campaign.[75] Whilst the campaign was ongoing, there was still some hope for an agreement on a thirty-two-county commission for education.[76] Even though Carson had hoped that education would not be partitioned, cherishing an all-island system similar to what was proposed under the MacPherson Bill, Londonderry and the northern administration were firmly against such an arrangement. Londonderry was scathing in his criticism of the provisional government's obstructionist policy, declaring:

> it will not succeed. It can have one effect only, and that will be to widen, beyond hope of repair, the breach that already exists between the North and the South. If there is any field of administration in which, more than any other, joint and harmonious action between the North and the South might be expected to produce good results in the direction of bringing the Irish people together it is the educational field.[77]

By the summer of 1922, with the civil war commencing in the south, the momentum of the campaign was stalled. The campaign lost its biggest advocate from the provisional government with the death of Collins in August. Ernest Blythe, speaking that same month on the teachers' non-recognition campaign, commented:

> Payment of teachers in the Six Counties should immediately be stopped. From the point of view of finance, educational efficiency, and public morality it is indefensible. In the case of the primary schools, we should take the step of approaching Lord Londonderry through a suitable intermediary and arranging that the teachers who remained with us shall not be penalised.[78]

The provisional government decided to cease payment to teachers in September, with the last payment being made in November 1922. Echoing southern policy in all other areas, the northern teachers would receive little more than verbal support from 1922 until the 1970s. The nationalist community was 'on its own'.[79] Catholic teachers and managers then sought aid from the Ulster ministry and offered to comply with its regulations. After a period of negotiation, the ministry agreed it would again make grants to the schools, but that as a precondition, the manager and teaching staff had to sign a declaration that they would in the future carry out the rules and regulations of the ministry. No payment was made to the teachers for the period of non-cooperation, but for salary, pension and promotion purposes, the teachers were not penalised.[80]

By 'certain school teachers' not accepting their salaries, it resulted in a 'windfall' of £166,000 for the northern government, which was used for 'special expenditure' within the education ministry.[81] The primary outcome of the boycott was to worsen relationships between both communities. Many unionists believed that Catholic teachers 'leaned strongly towards sedition'.[82] Farren claims, 'it also had the further effect of reducing the possibility of co-operation at an educational level between the two Irish administrations in such areas as teacher training where the possibility of maintaining an all-Ireland framework had existed'.[83]

With just one teacher training college located in the north from the outset of partition – St Mary's, the Catholic college for female students in Belfast – the northern administration hoped for cooperation with the south in relation to teacher training. None was forthcoming.[84] The southern government introduced sweeping changes to education from 1922, with a large emphasis on Irish and Gaelic culture, something wholly unappealing to the northern administration. There was a big dilemma for Protestant teachers, both male and female, and Catholic male teachers. Previously, Catholic teachers had normally studied in St Patrick's College in Dublin or De La Salle College in Waterford. Presbyterian students usually went to Marlborough Street College in Dublin, whilst Church of Ireland teachers went to Kildare Place, also in Dublin.[85] The Belfast government subsequently established a non-denominational college for teacher training: Stranmillis College in Belfast. There was still a dilemma for Catholic male teachers who were unable to study in Irish Free State institutions, as the northern education ministry 'insisted that Northern Ireland teachers would have to be trained in the North as the southern system and curriculum were at a significant variance'.[86] They were also unable to attend Stranmillis College, as no Catholic school would employ them. A compromise was eventually reached that allowed Catholic male teachers to train in St Mary's College in Strawberry Hill in London, with the northern education ministry agreeing to pay their fees and maintenance.[87]

Another compromise was reached regarding the attendance of Catholics at Queen's University, Belfast. The Catholic Church allowed their congregation to attend the university on the condition that they did not live in university residences. There was no alternative university in Belfast, and there were some Catholics on the Queen's University senate. The university offered separate chairs for Catholics in mental and moral science, Celtic languages and literature. There were also links with the Mater Infirmorum Hospital. In 1920, there were 192 Catholic students at Queen's. During 'term time Fr (James) King (chaplain) gave religious instruction for half an hour a week, and an examination was held at the end of the year. All students residing in the city were visited. All attended to their religious obligations and their general conduct was good. They were clearly closely monitored.'[88] This was in sharp contrast to the Church's view on Trinity College Dublin, where Catholics were not allowed to study. The Church had an extremely antagonistic relationship with the Dublin university, believing its aim was to anglicise its students.[89]

The 1923 Northern Ireland Education Act, 'the Londonderry Act', which spawned from the Lynn Committee's findings, was a major piece of legislation. Writing in 1936, historian Nicholas Mansergh considered it to be 'perhaps the most significant legislative achievement of the northern parliament'.[90] The act repealed in whole or in part seventeen earlier pieces of legislation and introduced significant structural changes to the ownership, management and financing of schools in Northern Ireland. Local education committees were to be comprised of local authority members as well as other members of the public with an interest in education.[91] Existing schools were invited to transfer the control and management of schools to local committees. Trustees who did not wish to transfer their schools could retain 'voluntary' status. However, to gain capital grant aid, there needed to be two local authority members for every four trustee members on each local education committee.[92] The act relegated religion to a minor role; it would no longer be part of the required curriculum. Unsurprisingly, there was widespread opposition from the Catholic Church. The Church's main problems with the act were the weakening of religious instruction and the perceived loss of church control that the act envisaged. Northern bishops remarked:

An education measure has been passed under which Catholic schools are starved unless indeed they go under a control that is animated by the dominant spirit towards Catholics ... It is doubtful whether in modern times any parallel can be found for the way in which the Catholic minority in the North of Ireland is being systematically wronged under the laws of the Northern Parliament. This ever advancing aggression on Catholics is a grave menace to the peace of the whole community.[93]

More surprisingly, and alarmingly for Londonderry and the northern administration, was the opposition from the Protestant churches. The Protestant churches, like the Catholic Church, took grave issue to the diminution of religious instruction but also to the loss of Church control over teacher appointments.[94] One unionist MP accused Londonderry of attempting to put 'Socialists and Roman Catholics into your schools ... putting in men who burned the Bible'.[95] Under fierce pressure from the Protestant churches, James Craig, who was 'ever fearful of disastrous election results', was responsible for an amended education act in 1925, conceding to many of the Protestant churches' demands.[96] In all, the act was amended five times between 1925 and 1935.[97] The 1923 act was fundamentally changed from the secular system that Londonderry had hoped for. The 'great majority of northern Catholics and Protestants would not be educated together at any level outside university and most schools remained denominational in character and practice. With his act in tatters Londonderry's relationship with Craig worsened and probably contributed to his resignation in January 1926'.[98]

Another act of 1923 that posed a moral dilemma for many Catholic teachers was the Promissory Oaths Act. The act required teachers to take an oath of allegiance, to swear to 'render true and faithful allegiance and service to His Majesty King George the Fifth, His heirs and successors according to the Law and to His Government of Northern Ireland'.[99] Refusal to take the oath would lead to the withdrawal of salaries and bonuses.[100] Many were bitterly opposed to the teachers' oath, and some priests suggested that children be withdrawn from schools. As with the campaign to boycott the northern administration, most teachers conceded that they had little option but to take the oath in order to earn a living.

Both Northern Ireland and the Irish Free State were able to show greater scope for separate expressions of how education was to be handled in a divided rather than united country. Such separate expressions were clearly demonstrated in the very different approaches taken to education within both jurisdictions. Whereas Northern Ireland introduced widespread changes that essentially sought to democratise education, the Irish Free State made very few structural changes to the system it had inherited from the British. The primary structural change was the abolition of the National Education Board in 1922 and the Intermediate Education Board in 1923, to be replaced by the Department of Education in 1924. The transfer of power from the boards to the new department had not been 'smooth nor sharp', with disputes and disagreements colouring the handover.[101] Other reforms included:

'Payment – by – results' at secondary level had been abolished, reforms in teacher training to take account of the new school programmes at primary level had been introduced, provision for additional scholarships to assist less well off pupils proceed to second level education had been made, and a new and long sought for School Attendance Act to make schooling compulsory between the ages of six and fourteen.[102]

The marked difference from the system of old was the aim to use the education system to revive the Irish language and Gaelic culture in general. The policies of the new education minister, Eoin MacNeill, showed a commitment and acquiescence to the education policies of the Catholic Church and the Gaelic League.[103] The government adopted 'a radical set of proposals' for the Irish language from the outset:

In the higher classes of the national schools, Irish and English were to be obligatory, and History, Geography, drill and signing were to be taught through Irish. In the lower 'infant' classes, all the teaching was to be conducted through Irish. There was, it is true, an escape clause which allowed that 'in the case of schools where the majority of the parents of the children object to having Irish or English taught as an obligatory subject, their wishes should be complied with'. But the government pressed ahead vigorously with this programme in the primary schools and, also, took steps to advance

Irish as a regular subject and as a medium of instruction in the secondary schools (making Irish an obligatory subject for the passing of state public examinations became an important if, in time, contentious part of this strategy).[104]

The teaching of history also played a key role in the government's policy to create an 'Irish Ireland':

The role of history was to foster a sense of national identity, pride and self-respect, taught through the medium of Irish, by demonstrating that the Irish race had fulfilled a great mission in the advancement of civilisation. Thus, both the Irish language and Irish history were to be interwoven in the twin aims of creating a Gaelic state and of legitimising that state through the appeal to history.[105]

The teaching of history was also used to promote a Catholic worldview. One of the chief architects of the Free State education system, T.M. Corcoran, Professor of Education at University College Dublin, 'did not accept that history was a subject of secular instruction: he clearly and unequivocally saw history as a branch of religious instruction, of ethics, of Catholic sociology, and held that through the teaching of history, Catholic principles could find an entrance into the substance of other subjects'.[106] As well as glorifying Ireland's past, a strong sense of Anglophobia permeated the education system. An attempt was made to move away from Anglo-Irish literature and instead reconnect with European literature. There were mere fleeting references to Anglo-Irish writers in school syllabuses.[107]

The Gaelicisation of Irish education led to some confrontations with the Protestant churches. The Church of Ireland was opposed to compulsory Irish, claiming 'English is the home language of most of our families as it is the language of the Bible, the prayer book and church formularies'.[108] The Church also complained 'that the Irish phrase books for primary schools contained "some – many of them too much – Roman catholic doctrine" and that "the books by P. Pearse" on the teachers' training course were open to grave objections'.[109] A compromise was reached, with the education minister agreeing to substitute texts if equivalent books were suggested.

On the whole, the Protestant churches were effectively in control of their schools, with little intervention from the education department.[110]

Before partition, education in Ireland had witnessed significant divisions between nationalists, unionists, Catholics and Protestants. These divisions only worsened after partition, with both jurisdictions adopting very different approaches to education. The north instigated major reforms that looked to democratise education, whilst the south imposed minimal structural reforms but fundamentally changed the education system in its attempt to Gaelicise Ireland. The divergence in paths was also clearly illustrated by the obstructionist tactics of the south and the failure of both jurisdictions to cooperate on areas of common interest such as teacher training and examinations.

CHAPTER TWELVE

The Labour Movement

John Whyte, in his paper, 'The Permeability of the United Kingdom – Irish Border – A Preliminary Reconnaissance', claims that the interrelationships of trade unions in Ireland are complicated. Many are all-Ireland or all-archipelago.[1] This in many ways reflects their history and the complex relationship the labour movements in Ireland and Britain have had with the Irish question and partition.

By the end of the nineteenth century, the trade union movement in Ireland was dominated by large British unions, to which some local Irish unions were affiliated.[2] By 1900, 75 per cent of Irish trade unionists were members of British-based unions.[3] Attempts at unity within the trade union movement between the two main industrial cities, Belfast and Dublin, and between Catholics and Protestants, were hindered by issues relating to sabbatarianism and the backing for nationalist causes and martyrs, but were aided by support for explicit matters to do with trade unionism.[4] According to Charles McCarthy:

> In 1892 when the Belfast council held a labour demonstration in support of striking linenlappers and a monster procession included thirty or more protestant and catholic bands; 'orange and green rosettes decked the breast of the District Master of the Orange Lodge in common with that of the vice-president of the Irish National Federation (Irish Federated Trade and Labour Union).[5]

An all-Ireland umbrella body, the Irish Trades Union Congress (ITUC), was launched in Dublin in 1894.[6] The ITUC was nationalist in outlook, supported Home Rule and strongly opposed partition. The British labour movement, which had strong links throughout Ireland, also supported

Home Rule and opposed partition. The British Labour Party held its annual conference in Belfast in 1907.[7] It 'supported the philosophy of Irish nationalism in a well-meaning but essentially unthinking and emotional manner, secure in the knowledge that the party was in too minor a political position to have to do anything meaningful about it'.[8]

At the time of the third Home Rule Crisis in 1912, divisions began to appear within the trade union movement, particularly in Belfast. Some, like William Walker, were opposed to Home Rule and believed the Irish labour movement should affiliate to the British labour movement.[9] A decision of the ITUC annual congress in 1912 to form an Irish Labour Party and to declare independence for Irish trade unionism met with opposition from many quarters, particularly those affiliated to British-based unions.[10] Membership of amalgamated (British) Irish-based unions was on the wane, however, and by 1914 the majority of unions in attendance at the ITUC annual congress were Irish.[11]

The newly formed Irish Labour Party protested to Asquith and Birrell about the possible exclusion of Ulster in 1914 and 'circularized trades councils with an anti-partition manifesto. British Labour replied that party officers agreed with the ITUC on Ulster.'[12] The Irish Labour Party argued that partition would weaken the working class. The leading socialist republican, James Connolly, believed there was one circumstance in which his 'vision of the future harmony of the Irish working class would be destroyed. This was if Ireland were to be partitioned. Partition would be disastrous, because it would keep alive the national issue at the expense of class questions.'[13] He famously observed that it would mean 'a carnival of reaction both North and South'.[14] It has been argued that it was 'the fear of partition which was one reason why Connolly was in favour of desperate measures in 1916'. He also 'had first-hand experience of Belfast politics and its working class as a union organiser there from 1911 to 1913. This experience informed his interpretation of working class divisions in northeast Ulster and their political consequences'.[15] Likewise, union leader James Larkin, 'who liked to call himself an Ulsterman, was beside himself with anger at the prospect' of partition.[16] The ITUC annual congress in June 1914, with twenty delegates from Ulster and four from Britain in attendance, condemned partition by eighty-four votes to two, with eight delegates unrecorded.[17] At that meeting, 'a Cork delegate predicted a commercial boycott of Belfast in the event of partition, and another, with equal prescience, warned: "the North would [then] tell Nationalists to look South for employment ... bitter divisions would arise".[18] In Belfast, although most workers were unionist in outlook, the majority of the leaders of the labour movement, although not nationalist, were fearful of being locked in an Orange state and were opposed to partition. Emmet O'Connor has stated, 'Whereas *labour* [workers] was mostly Unionist, and by extension Conservative, *Labour* [activists] was very much a part of the British trade union movement, and that movement supported the Liberals, and later the BLP, who in turn were allied intermittently with the Irish Parliamentary Party (IPP).'[19]

The third Home Rule Crisis saw the birth of 'Labour Unionists', predominantly working-class unionist clubs that were incorporated within the Ulster Unionist Council.[20] Labour unionists held a 'monster demonstration' against Home Rule in the 'Ulster Hall on 29 April 1914, convened by former officers of the Shipwrights' Association and the Amalgamated Society of Engineers'.[21]

During the war years, the ITUC and Labour Party continued its opposition to partition. Resolutions were passed against partition in the Annual Congresses of 1916 and 1917, believing such a move would be 'disastrous to the working class movement'.[22] The ITUC contended that partition would 'create two problems in Ireland instead of one'.[23] The ITUC sent a delegation to meet Lloyd George in 1916 to protest against the exclusion of Ulster when he was tasked by Asquith to find a resolution to the Home Rule impasse immediately after the Easter Rising (see Chapter One). He was surprised that the trade unions of Ireland met as one congress and told the delegation, 'Nobody liked partition well enough to choose it, but they were faced with the certainty that Ulster could not be forced into an Irish Parliament.'[24]

As most in Ireland moved away from seeking a Home Rule solution to one of complete independence from Britain, divisions in labour and the trade unions increased significantly on a north-south basis. The ITUC and Labour Party made a number of decisions that were seen as supportive of Sinn Féin. This was met with opposition from many quarters in Ulster. The Irish trade union movement played a prominent role in the anti-conscription campaign of 1918, along with Sinn Féin and all of nationalist

Ireland, in opposition to compulsory conscription to the war front, most conspicuously by its organisation of a national strike on 23 April.[25] The Irish Labour Party also decided, after much contentious debate, not to contest the 1918 general election in order not to complicate the 'national' question, helping to pave the way for Sinn Féin's landslide victory.[26] The democratic programme, read out at the inaugural meeting of the First Dáil in January 1919, was a collaboration between Sinn Féin and the Labour Party, with labour activist Thomas Johnson responsible for writing the bulk of the document.[27] Such actions alienated labour and trade union activists in Ulster, especially when sectarian strife began to boil over in the north.

A Belfast Labour Party emerged out of a conference of trade unions and Independent Labour Party (ILP) representatives in 1917.[28] 'Dublin unions, such as the Brick and Stone layers, the Irish National Teachers' Organisation, and the Drapers' Assistants, lost northern branches after the general strike against conscription' in 1918.[29] At the Irish Convention of 1917–18 (see Chapter One), the trade councils of Dublin, Belfast and Cork were offered seven of the ninety-five seats. The ITUC was not consulted. The Dublin and Cork trade councils declined, but Belfast agreed unanimously to accept the invitation to participate and ended up signing 'the Convention's majority report, favouring Dominion Home Rule'.[30] Labour in Belfast also ignored the party in the rest of the country and ran four candidates in the 1918 general election.[31] A sign of the rift within trade unionism in Ireland was demonstrated at the ITUC annual congress in Derry, where very few of the 220 delegates came from either Derry or Belfast.[32] To curb the haemorrhage of members from Ulster, the ITUC congress suggested that its national executive should consist of three members and a secretary from Dublin, three members from Belfast and two from Cork.[33] In 1919, the Belfast Labour Party still 'applied to join the British Labour Party, only to be told to redirect its enquiries to the Irish Labour Party'.[34]

Despite misgivings about being associated with the all-Ireland Labour Party and ITUC, most labour activists in Ulster were firmly opposed to partition. There had been 'solidarity across the sectarian divide … at the beginning of 1919 when engineering and shipyard workers campaigned, unsuccessfully, for a reduction in their working hours'. Whilst the four-week 'strike was unsuccessful', there were hopes of a thriving socialist movement in Belfast.[35] Three of its four candidates in the 1918 general election 'were Home Rulers, as were the majority of its 22 candidates in the municipal elections of 1920'.[36] The Belfast Labour Party won twelve of the sixty seats in Belfast in the municipal elections of 1920. The 'outgoing Corporation of 52 Unionists and eight Nationalists yielded to a council of 37 Unionists (including six UULA [Ulster Unionist Labour Association] men), 12 Labour councillors, one Independent Labour Unionist, five Nationalists, and five Sinn Feiners. Labour formed the official opposition'.[37] In the nine counties of Ulster, supporters of unionism were in a minority.[38] According to Austen Morgan:

> This labourist expression was, among voters, compatible with forms of loyalism (and nationalism in the case of catholics), but social reform was the important issue for the leadership of the labour movement and activists. Belfast labour subscribed, in the main, to [Woodrow] Wilsonian democracy, and, while it never became nationalist or separatist, it was certainly not unionist, the idea of Carson running Ulster being rejected on social and political grounds. These predominantly protestant men (and some women) would have accepted a negotiated solution such as dominion home rule, rejecting the partition which had been inevitable since before the war.[39]

The Irish labour movement's anti-partition stance was echoed by the British labour movement, which totally opposed the Government of Ireland Act 1920. The *Labour Leader* wrote in January 1920 that 'to have two Parliaments in a small country like Ireland' was both an 'affront to national dignity' and 'a practical impossibility'.[40] In July 1920 the British Trades Union Congress (TUC) passed a resolution in support of an all-Ireland parliament with 'full Dominion powers in all Irish affairs'.[41] This stance soon waned as the British Labour Party edged closer to power and realised that sympathy and support for Irish nationalism would not win votes in Britain.[42] It became clear that if the British Labour Party wanted to attain power, 'it had to distance itself from the revolutionary politics which had rapidly come to dominate Irish nationalism since 1918'.[43] Before then, in the autumn of 1920, spearheaded by Arthur Henderson, the British Labour Party 'proposed that Ireland be allowed to solve its own problems and that the British Army should be withdrawn. A constituent assembly would then draw up a constitution for all Ireland with adequate protection for minorities.'[44] The executive of the Irish Labour Party and ITUC accepted this position in January 1921.[45] Unity in Irish labour was fragile, however, with the ITUC blamed for doing little to foster closer cooperation.[46] The ITUC showed little appetite to address northern issues. Its 'response to the expulsion of Catholics and left-wing Protestant workers from their jobs in 1920 was embarrassingly feeble'.[47] James 'Dungaree' Baird, a Labour councillor on Belfast Corporation, 'who wore his work clothes in the splendid City Hall', helped to form the Expelled Workers' Relief Committee. When he asked the ITUC and the British TUC for help, neither were particularly forthcoming. Most assistance for expelled workers came from Catholic-nationalist and Sinn Féin sources. The ITUC assisted with the enforcement of the Belfast Boycott, though.[48] At the Irish Labour Party and ITUC annual meeting in August 1921, held in Dublin's Mansion House, an address was made by Sinn Féin president, Éamon de Valera, who happened to be negotiating with the British on the same day in the same location. He remarked, 'were it not for the solidarity of Labour behind the national cause in Ireland … the Irish cause would not be where it was that day'.[49] An anti-partition manifesto was unanimously passed at that meeting too.[50] The unionist-leaning newspaper, the *Belfast Newsletter*, declared that those actions 'emphasised the complete subservience of the Labour party in Ireland to Sinn Fein'.[51]

There was also a drive in Dublin to replace the amalgamated unions with Irish-based ones, particularly since the founding of the Irish Transport and General Workers' Union (ITGWU) in 1909. In 1917, the Irish National Union of Vintners, Grocers and Allied Trade Assistants was founded, breaking from the National Amalgamated Union of Shop Assistants. In 1920, the Irish Electrical Industrial Union sprang from the Amalgamated Engineering Society.[52] There was a push for trade unions to move further north too. In the border county of Louth, the ITGWU and the British-based Amalgamated Transport and General Workers' Union survived and grew in both Drogheda and Dundalk, with the older pre-partition trade unions, the Workers' Union of Ireland (WUI) and the National Union of Dock

Labourers, losing out.[53] The WUI 'had already established a firm presence among general workers outside Belfast. With textile operatives, the story was similar. The ITGWU recorded some success in recruiting Protestant and Catholic workers in Monaghan and Caledon, County Tyrone, but otherwise its resolute Ulster campaign found itself sided into the nationalist ghetto.'[54] Trade unionists based in the six counties of Ulster that would form Northern Ireland remained loyal to British-based unions, which in 1920, made up 80 per cent of union membership there; 15 per cent were members of local-based unions and just 5 per cent of Dublin unions.[55]

The Labour movement's association with Sinn Féin was used against the Belfast labour candidates, who ran as independents, in the 1921 election to the Northern Ireland parliament.[56] For the election to the southern parliament, the Labour Party, as in 1918, did not contest the election, allowing Sinn Féin to win 124 out of 128 seats unopposed. Edward Carson had integrated the UULA, a pressure group established in 1918, uniting trade unionists within a wider unionist movement, 'into the Unionist political machine after the war in an attempt to spike the guns of Labour'. It 'began to work closely with the fiercely Loyalist ex-servicemen's associations in focussing Protestant workers' attentions on what they saw as the exigencies of the National Question'. Labour 'representatives were ousted from top positions in trade unions and were replaced by Loyalists. What seemed to be the nascent development of class politics in Belfast relapsed into a familiar tribal pattern'.[57] The northern labour candidates were anti-partitionist, but for socialist rather than nationalist reasons.[58] Their message was lost by the sectarian nature of the election, and once loyalists prevented them from holding an election rally in the Ulster Hall, they folded their campaign.[59] All labour candidates performed disastrously and lost their deposits.[60] Three of the four candidates – John Hanna, James Baird and Harry Midgley – 'were Protestants and thus all the more reprehensible in the eyes of those Loyalists to whom they were the archetypal "Lundies" [traitors]'.[61] Austen Morgan asserts that 'it was the IRA war's coming north which reversed the balance in the protestant working class between labourism and loyalism', leading to the almost total whitewash of labour candidates at the election.[62] By 1921, with the north engulfed in sectarian violence, there was no platform for a socialist voice at the 'Partition Election'. It has even been claimed that the 'Partition of

Ireland was a conscious act on the part of British Imperialism chiefly intended to divide the working class along sectarian lines'.[63] Arthur Griffith claimed, during the treaty negotiations, that the violence in the north was due to 'the activities of Belfast politicians' and 'the ambition of Belfast capitalists to keep labour disunited'.[64]

The Irish labour movement was not a homogenous group. Comprising Protestants and Catholics, unionists and nationalists, and socialist internationalists, a delicate juggling act was required within the political party and the trade unions following the onset of partition. The labour movement in the north sought to avoid contention and remain united by focusing on labour and trade union issues, including wages and conditions for workers. Charles McCarthy believed the labour movement in the north was held together by 'the unifying force of socialism, with its uncompromising international ethic, which seemed to be so strong an influence on many of the trade union leaders down through the years, despite the fact that very many of the rank and file members were not only indifferent to such ideas but were often hostile to them'.[65]

O'Connor contends that:

> clinging to core interests has enabled a united, secular Labour movement to function in a confessional society among the very people most divided by sectarianism. Historically, keeping contention out of the unions was in turn made possible by the marginality of nationalism, the self-exclusion of Unionists – as distinct from Protestants – and their management by a self-selecting elite, committed to Labourist values. In fact unions were less concerned about divisions between Catholics and Protestants than the antagonism between Labourism and Unionism. With a mainly Protestant, anti-Unionist leadership and a mainly Protestant, Unionist membership, mutually dependent for their bread and butter, but otherwise at odds, they found themselves walking a tight line between their organisational interests and the politics of their members.[66]

Some who were involved in the Belfast Labour Party, such as William McMullen, sought to move away from the British Labour Party, whilst others such as Sam Kyle, Hugh Gemmell and Harry Midgley 'concentrated on supplying a non-sectarian opposition to the governing unionists with British Labour as their model and ideological base'.[67] The issues of social reform kept them united. With such divergent views on partition, the topic was avoided as often as possible. When Harry Midgley ran in the Westminster election in 1923 in West Belfast, he tried to appeal to unionists and nationalists by being duplicitous on the issue of partition: 'On the Shankill Road he stressed his Protestantism and his army service in the Great War, while in the Falls he hit out against the internment of prisoners and appeared to share the aspirations of his audience to a United Ireland'.[68] Whilst many of their members were unionists, most of the leaders of Belfast labour were anti-partitionist; they did not give any credibility to the Northern regime.[69] One of the first signs of the Northern Ireland jurisdiction being perceived as a reality was the decision of the Belfast Labour Party to organise itself on a six-county basis in 1924, as the Northern Ireland Labour Party (NILP).[70] Although independent, it modelled itself on British labour and was closely linked with the Irish Labour Party 'by virtue of a number of trade unions and other organisations being affiliated to the ITUC of which the Irish Labour Party was part'.[71] Whilst technically it was a breakaway from the Irish Labour Party and ITUC, covertly, ITUC officers may have given their approval. Luke Duffy, chairman, and Thomas Johnson, secretary of the ITUC, had visited Belfast in February 1924 and discussed the creation of a party for the six counties.[72] The NILP was able to cross the sectarian divide, garnering support from Protestants and Catholics. With 'Devlinite nationalism hesitant about practising minority politics, and republicanism even more disorientated', the NILP was seen as an appealing political option for many nationalists.[73] After the Ulster Unionist Party, it was the 'only other coherent group in the Commons' in Belfast.[74] The political prospects for the labour movement in Northern Ireland were to a large extent thwarted by the abolition of the PR voting system, first for local elections and then for Northern Ireland general elections (see Chapter Six). The labour movement was most negatively affected by the decision, even more so than the nationalist minority, with elections thereafter largely becoming 'sectarian headcounts' on the legitimacy of Northern Ireland and the border.[75] The NILP took three of the fifty-two seats in the 1925 Northern Ireland general election under PR, and only one or two generally for the next twenty years once PR was abolished. It took none at all from 1949 to 1958. It was a Belfast-centred party, winning just one seat outside the city in a Stormont election, in south Armagh in 1938.[76]

The ITUC remained an all-Ireland body, primarily because there was no feasible alternative in the north and there was little interest in forming an Ulster TUC.[77] The British TUC 'was not going to jeopardise the position of its affiliates in the Free State by extending its remit to Northern Ireland ... and had even less enthusiasm than the ITUC to speak for a region where trade unionism had become embroiled in sectarian conflict'.[78] British trade unions 'with a substantial cross-border membership continued to locate their Irish offices in Dublin, and Loyalist aggression made officialdom more inclined to maintain lifelines to London and Dublin'.[79] William O'Brien, General Secretary of the ITGWU, emphasised in 1925 'the fact that the working class in Ireland recognises no political or geographical border. Partition ... prevails almost exclusively in the political sphere'.[80] R.J.P. Mortished, Assistant Secretary of the Irish Labour Party and ITUC, speaking in 1926, claimed, 'the existence of an All-Ireland Labour organisation, holding annual Congresses attended by delegates from all parts of the country, without distinction, and represented by a National Executive which included citizens of Belfast and Derry, as well as Dublin and Cork, is the surest existing sign that the present political partition of Ireland is not inevitably final'.[81] The NILP affiliated to the ITUC in 1927 and formed a joint council with the Irish Labour Party in 1930. Emmet O'Connor contends that 'meetings were few and discussions confined to general exchange of views'.[82] The labour movement in the north moved from a position of fervent to nominal opposition to partition as Northern Ireland's security became more assured.[83] Midgley gained more power in the 1930s within the movement and also veered more towards a unionist stance.[84] The *Belfast Newsletter*, in an editorial written in 1934, highlighted the primary dilemma facing the NILP. With its close links with the British labour movement and its affiliation with the ITUC and cooperation with the Irish Labour Party, it had to decide whether to work towards 'an Ulster "partitioned" from the Free State or "partitioned" from the United Kingdom'.[85] Until it stopped avoiding this key issue in such a divided society, it would remain politically weak. By skirting the issue of partition, it was open to attacks from both unionists and nationalists.[86] The increased level of unionism within the labour movement in the north led to ruptures with the movement in the Irish Free State, which broke off relations with the NILP during the late 1930s.[87]

The ITUC was committed to retaining its all-Ireland structures. Recognising that its trade unions and members based in Northern Ireland needed to be treated differently, a Northern Ireland committee (NIC) of the ITUC was established to speak 'for all trade unions in the north and all trade unionists'.[88] Acknowledging that the Northern Ireland government was likely to be hostile to the northern committee, as it saw the northern committee as a Free State organisation, the ITUC granted the northern committee a large degree of autonomy. Local representatives chaired conferences in Belfast, instead of the ITUC president; the northern committee was able to hire a full-time officer with an office; and, the northern committee was given the authority to make appointments to Northern Ireland government boards.[89] According to Francis Devine and Emmet O'Connor, 'while it remained technically a sub-committee "empowered to act for the National Executive in matters peculiar to the Six County area", the NIC gradually assumed a *de facto* autonomy'.[90]

The partitioning of Ireland posed similar problems for the main trade unions in education, INTO and ASTI, as it did for most trade unions that straddled both new jurisdictions. Both INTO and ASTI are run on an all-Ireland basis, despite education being administered separately in each jurisdiction. INTO was founded in Dublin in 1868 to represent national school teachers throughout Ireland.[91] Before partition, its all-island nature was tested by potential splits. In 1884, a number of northern associations seceded from INTO and set up a new organisation in 1886: the Northern Union of Irish National Teachers. In 1888, the central executive of INTO voted to amalgamate with the northern union, and after a joint meeting between both bodies in Dundalk, a settlement was reached.[92] The possibility of a break away by the Protestant members of the organisation was threatened in 1899. This was avoided though, by the establishment of the Irish Protestant National Teachers' Union, which 'would concern itself with the managerial question and any other matter which specially affected them as Protestant teachers, while all other professional matters would form a common platform for all members, as had previously been the case'.[93]

The most serious breach in the unity of the organisation took place in 1918–19, when four northern branches withdrew from INTO and established a new body called the Ulster Teachers' Union, composed of Protestant teachers. 'The withdrawal was inspired entirely by political motives'.[94] The main reasons cited were INTO's affiliation to the ITUC, that body's recommendation to withdraw labour candidates from the 1918 general elections to favour Sinn Féin candidates and INTO's participation in the one-day anti-conscription strike in April 1918.[95] Four branches – Coleraine, Lisburn, Londonderry and Newtownards – severed their connections with INTO in 1919 and took steps to establish the Ulster Teachers' Union. All the Catholic teachers and a substantial number of Protestant teachers in the area remained loyal to INTO, however.[96] According to Thomas J. O'Connell, who wrote a history of INTO in its centenary year of 1968:

> For a number of years strained relations existed between the Union and the INTO … As the years went by a spirit of co-operation gradually grew up; old rivalries were forgotten and both bodies now co-operate in matters of common interest. Since 1920, eight members from branches in Northern Ireland, four of whom were Protestants, have been unanimously elected as President of the INTO.[97]

Speaking at the INTO annual congress in March 1921, just as partition was being implemented, the newly elected president from Belfast, John Harbison, declared that 'no matter what changes might take place in the country, legislative or political, there was going to be no partition in their ranks'.[98] To retain its all-Ireland structures INTO realised, just like the ITUC, it needed to offer its northern members a large degree of 'home rule'. Once Northern Ireland was established, a northern committee of INTO was formed to

> manage its special affairs in Northern Ireland. It has its own official journal and holds annual conferences to which the President and other members of the Executive and Finance Committee are invited. Subscriptions and other fees are sent to Head Office as in

the case of all INTO branches, and payments of benefits as well as the expenses of the administration in Northern Ireland are paid from the general funds of the INTO.[99]

ASTI was formed in Cork in 1909 to cater for secondary school teachers in Ireland. It added an Ulster provisional council in 1914 to its Leinster and Munster councils.[100] A rival body, based largely in Belfast, the IAAM was formed in 1916. It was predominantly Protestant and did not admit women to its fold. ASTI affiliated with the ITUC in 1919, and a federation was formed between ASTI and INTO that same year with the establishment of a joint advisory committee.[101] Like INTO, ASTI saw a huge haemorrhaging of its Protestant members, with many dissatisfied with the political direction of the organisation. Most of them resigned and joined the IAAM and the Irish Union of Assistant Mistresses. The Belfast women's branch of ASTI seceded as a body in early 1920 due to ASTI's affiliation to the ITUC.[102]

The teachers' unions desired to retain their all-Ireland structure after partition and made a concerted effort to accommodate their members based in the new jurisdiction of Northern Ireland, mirroring the tactics of other trade unions and the ITUC. The Labour movement was faced with many challenges when the country was partitioned. The movement included a divergent group of people who had to operate under enormous sectarian and political pressures. Partial union was achieved, particularly within trade unionism, by clinging to core interests within the movement and offering a large degree of autonomy to northern labour activists, recognising the vastly different circumstances they operated under.

CHAPTER THIRTEEN

Infrastructure and Services

By drawing a line and creating a physical border spanning almost 300 miles, some of the most challenging issues faced by both jurisdictions after partition related to infrastructure and service-based issues. Even after 1925, when many believed the border issue was settled, concerns relating to the railway infrastructure, the territorial ownership of bodies of water and the postal services demonstrated the uncertain and confusing nature of partition.

Speaking in August 1922, J.T. Farrell of the Railway Clerks Union stated that:

> No employees were more affected by the problem of partition than railway employees ... the Great Northern Railway crossed the border at 11 different points, the Londonderry and Lough Railway had its head and neck in the north-east and its tail in the twenty-six counties. They had the same in connection with the Donegal line, and the Dundalk and Greenore railway had one leg in either direction. The Irish Railway Commission, and that held in Belfast to a large extent, ignored the political difficulties arising from the situation. The question was one that would have to be solved, and it was one of the strongest indications of the evils of partition brought about by the Act of 1920.[1]

The complexity of the railway infrastructure and ownership within Ireland was compounded dramatically by the creation of a border. Five railway companies were directly affected by the new border by serving both sides of it: the Great Northern; the County Donegal; the Londonderry, Lough Swilly and Letterkenny; the Sligo, Leitrim and Northern Counties; and the

Dundalk, Newry and Greenore Railways.[2] This was further exacerbated by the Free State's decision to impose a customs barrier in 1923. Before the creation of the two Irish political entities, the prospect of amalgamating the many private railway companies had been discussed for as long as there had been different railway companies. The railway companies were temporarily under government control during the First World War. This arrangement ended in 1921.[3] Under the Government of Ireland Act 1920, the railways were a reserved service to be treated as an all-Ireland concern that would come under the control of the Council of Ireland once it was established between the north and south jurisdictions. With the Anglo-Irish Treaty of 1921 superseding the Government Ireland of Act for the twenty-six counties, railways remained a reserved service in Northern Ireland. This meant the Free State government could legislate on railways within its jurisdiction, but the northern government could not for its area – all railway legislation affecting the north must come before the imperial parliament in Westminster. In 1923, when the Londonderry and Lough Swilly Railway Bill came before Westminster, it was deemed unpassable, as that railway company operated on both sides of the border and the imperial parliament could not legislate for the Free State territory.[4] The northern government was happy 'to leave this matter entirely to the Imperial Members in view of the awkward precedents which might be originated'.[5] Relationships between the two Irish governments only complicated matters further. The Free State government, intrinsically opposed to partition, sought unification of the railway companies, whilst the northern government, looking to assert its independence from Dublin in every feasible way, wanted the Free State government to have no say or control of any railway issue within the northern jurisdiction. When Joseph McGrath, the Free State's Minister of Industry and Commerce, publicly called for the unifying of all Irish railways on an all-Ireland basis in December 1922, John Andrews, Minister of Labour for Northern Ireland, responded, 'Mr. McGrath has no more right to interfere with or propose legislation affecting Northern Ireland railways than I have to interfere with or propose legislation affecting the railways in Southern Ireland.'[6]

The Free State government was forced to decide on the future of the railways, for its own jurisdiction at least. Disruptions caused by the civil war, the threat of strikes and the unviability of some of the smaller railway companies led to serious problems for the industry. During the civil war, 'railway lines countrywide were attacked by the anti-Treaty faction fighting against the Free State Government'.[7] The uncertainty of train travel in the south resulted in some people preferring to get a boat from Cobh in County Cork to Liverpool in England to reach destinations in Northern Ireland – a considerably longer and more complicated journey, but one that was safer.[8] The Free State government initially hoped the railways would group together, and if not, it would introduce legislation to unify them. The biggest dilemma was caused by the railway companies that straddled both sides of the border, particularly the Great Northern Railway, which had one-third of its lines in the Free State and 50 per cent of its shareholders registered in the south.[9] The delineation at the border was uncertain, too, until the Boundary Commission's decision of 1925. Whilst the Free State's preferred option was for a unified railway service throughout Ireland, the northern government looked at the possibility of amalgamating the railway companies in Northern Ireland with British railway companies.[10] Craig and Cosgrave met in July 1923, with government conferences continuing into 1924, at which it was agreed that the Free State would legislate for railway companies based solely in the Free State territory, and the northern government would not look to amalgamate railway companies in Northern Ireland with British ones.[11] The Free State government duly introduced legislation to the Dáil, the Railways Act 1924, which unified all Free State railway companies, except the Listowel and Ballybunion monorail. In total, twenty-six companies merged to form the Great Southern Railways.[12] For railway companies based solely in the north or working across both sides of the border, it was agreed to continue with the 'present well-established and competitive system of private management'.[13] This practice continued up until the 1950s when, in one of the few occasions of cross-border cooperation, both governments agreed to purchase the Great Northern Railway in 1951, to be run by a joint board nominated by the two governments.[14]

At the onset of partition, the most vigorous challenge to the railway industry came from a large increase in the use of roads by motor vehicles. Responsibility for roads in Ireland was vested in local authorities by the Local Government Act 1898. In 1909, 'vehicle and driver taxation were introduced by the new Road Board, whose authority passed to the Ministry for Transport in 1919'.[15] After partition, responsibility for roads and bridges (except railway bridges in the case of Northern Ireland) were transferred to the respective Irish jurisdictions. One of the first tasks of both governments was to invest heavily in road maintenance, given the significant increase in road traffic experienced during the inter-war years. For example, in Northern Ireland, licensed motor vehicles increased from 5,000 in 1921 to 66,000 in 1927.[16] For both jurisdictions, the responsibility for road maintenance remained the preserve of local authorities, aided by governmental subsidies and motor taxation. Once responsibility for roads was transferred to the north in late 1921, the British transport ministry gave 'the proceeds of the Motor Licence Duties collected in Northern Ireland' to the Northern Ministry of Home Affairs.[17] Both jurisdictions, with little money, were forced to invest heavily in the road network, such was the state of dilapidation. On one hand, 'the condition of the roads' was 'responsible for considerable damage to the motor vehicle; while on the other hand, the heavy commercial motor vehicle causes considerable damage to the road surface', mainly as 'the road foundations were not designed to carry the heavy traffic which motor transport' was then imposing.[18] The bad quality of the roads made motor journeys over fifty miles uncompetitive when compared to rail travel due to 'the high cost of repairs, replacements and depreciation charges'.[19] In the north and the south, 'road surfaces were upgraded and carriageways improved. Tar replaced macadam. In some instances ... reinforced concrete was used to construct roads.'[20]

The border, and particularly the introduction of customs barriers, posed additional problems for motorists. The Revenue Commissioners in Dublin declared that on and after the imposition of the customs barrier on 1 April 1923, 'motor cars which have been manufactured in Great Britain will be subject, when imported into the Free State, to an ad valorem duty of 33 1/3 per cent'. The *Irish Times* predicted the duty would not come to pass, as it would cripple the motor industry in the Free State and jeopardise the presence of the Ford Motor Company, which employed 1,800 people in Cork.[21] Petrol cost more in the north than it did in England and Scotland, as supplies of petrol were no longer received from Dublin and petrol had to be imported.[22] For motorists, approved roads could only be used to cross the border from 1923. People travelling from Dundalk to Forkhill in south Armagh were no longer able to travel the direct route of four miles due to the absence of an approved road; they had to make a journey of twelve miles instead.[23] Initially, cars were unable to cross the border on Sundays or public holidays as customs stations were closed. It was agreed to remove this impediment for fear of hampering the tourism industry.[24] Donegal County Council requested that the Revenue Commissioners make the Letterkenny road an approved one, 'as the closing of this road, which was one of the principal main trunk roads on [sic] the county, was causing dislocation of traffic, and had resulted in serious inconvenience'. Cumann na nGaedheal TD, Patrick McGoldrick believed the road should remain closed, saying, 'Instead of people in the Free State squealing, they should leave it to the other people to do the squealing … if possible not even a fly should be allowed to pass through.'[25] In 1926, Louth County Council passed a motion calling on the Free State government to impose 'Border-road tolls, by which motor lorry owners from Northern Ireland using Free State roads should be compelled to contribute to the cost of road maintenance in the Free State'.[26] Signposts had to be erected directing motorists to customs stations due to the complicated nature of the customs process, which involved 'on first importation and final exportation of a motor car from N. Ireland to the Irish Free State, four calls have to be made'.[27] There was some cooperation between the two jurisdictions on road and motors issues. For example, motorists were allowed to use one driving license for both jurisdictions.[28]

Cross-border cooperation was harder won on the issue of fishing rights on Lough Foyle and the River Foyle. Disputes over fishing on the Foyle spanned three decades after partition, demonstrating the uncertain nature of the border, the local problems it caused and the actual remit of its physical territory. It also showed the haphazard way in which the border was drawn up. No boundary was delimited at any point for either Lough Foyle or Carlingford.[29] As a result, nobody knew where the border line was on various waterways straddling the border. The issue was further complicated by the different constitutional positions of the two jurisdictions. Under the Government of Ireland Act 1920, north and south jurisdictions were both to remain within the United Kingdom, meaning that the issue of territorial waters would not have arisen. However, the Anglo-Irish Treaty of 1921 'afforded enhanced "dominion" status to all of Ireland – outside the

United Kingdom, albeit within the British Empire. Authority having passed to Dublin, the Treaty then allowed for Northern Ireland, as defined by the previous Act, to opt out, thus returning to its original standing.'[30] Northern Ireland, as expected, opted out of the Free State. However, under the Government of Ireland Act, its jurisdiction was for the boroughs of Belfast and Derry and for the parliamentary counties of Antrim, Armagh, Derry, Down, Fermanagh and Tyrone, not for any territorial waters, which the Free State government argued was part of its territory as a dominion.[31] On the other hand, the Northern government made a claim to the imperial government 'that the whole of the deep waters of Lough Foyle fell within the territorial waters of Northern Ireland'.[32]

This argument was the main defence used in a court case in Belfast in 1923 by a steamship company summonsed when one of its steamers, the *Greyhound*, was accused of selling liquor on Sundays in Belfast Lough, in contravention of a Sunday Closing Act disallowing the sale of alcohol on Sundays, passed by the northern government.[33] The defence ascertained that as the alcohol was sold on Belfast Lough, and that as all territorial waters of Ireland belonged to the Free State, Northern Ireland had no jurisdiction over the Lough. This claim was refuted by the prosecution who argued that the northern parliament had powers to deal with 'lighthouses, buoys and beacons in Belfast Harbour', it, therefore, had jurisdiction over Belfast Lough.[34] The steamship company lost the case and was fined £2.[35] The ruling against the steamship company did not refer to the rights over territorial waters, however. Questions remained unanswered; the *Irish News* pondered, 'Are the Northern Government justified in trespassing on Irish ocean waters to the extent of keeping the Prison Ship *Argenta* moored within 3 miles of Larne?'[36]

The territorial rights over Lough Foyle and the River Foyle was a key factor in causing and maintaining the dispute over fishing rights from the 1920s through to the 1950s. A Free State judge, Louis J. Walsh, claimed in October 1923 that 'the whole of Lough Foyle, up to the high water mark on the County Derry or Magilligan side belongs to the Free State. So that there is no entry to Derry port except through our waters'.[37] This was disputed by the Irish Society which before partition, controlled the provision of licences to fishermen to use the Foyle. It had leased this function to the Foyle and Bann Fisheries Company, who maintained, after partition, that it alone controlled the entire fishing rights, as before.[38] Fishermen from Inishowen in Donegal ignored the Foyle and Bann company and sought licences from the Free State via Moville in Donegal and continued to fish in Lough Foyle. In 1923, after an unsuccessful attempt to seize salmon nets off Inishowen fishermen, the Foyle and Bann company had summonses issued for Moville District Court against the fishermen. The fishermen decided to contest on the grounds that the Irish Society had no exclusive rights, based on a charter issued by King Charles II in the seventeenth century due to the earlier *Magna Carta*, which stipulated that the king had no lawful right to create several fishery in tidal waters.[39] The fishermen won their case. In 1925, in a submission to the Boundary Commission, the Free State government ascertained that a survey commissioned by King George IV in 1825 on borders and boundaries showed that no part of Lough Foyle was included in County Derry.[40]

Despite the fishermen's legal success in 1923, the dispute remained unresolved, partly because no jurisdiction was prepared to, or wanted to deal with the thorny territorial ramifications. The British government simply said 'it was not in a position to express a view'.[41] Further flashpoints saw the issue move centre stage yet again in 1929. Donegal fishermen were asked to surrender their nets by three motorboats belonging to the Foyle and Bann Fisheries Company in June 1929. Guns were used when the fishermen refused. A similar incident happened the following month.[42] In retaliation, boats belonging to the company were deliberately wrecked.[43] On 26 July, Lord Justice Andrews of the Chancery Division of the Northern Ireland High Court 'issued an interlocutory injunction to restrain Donegal fishermen ... from "trespassing" on the waters of the Lough'.[44] The fishermen ignored the proceedings in Belfast. The company messenger travelling to Donegal to issue the writs to the fishermen was told in no uncertain terms to turn back. The writs posted by registered mail were returned, marked 'Undelivered, refused'.[45] The Dublin government considered submitting the issue to the Court of International Justice at the Hague but demurred in the end, leading the *Sligo Champion* to ask, in a biting editorial on the Free State's inaction, 'Is the Saorstat a Nation?'[46] The *Donegal News* claimed the Free State government's apathy was responsible for the incident.[47] The Board of Conservators at Moville, set up by the Free

State to issue fishing licences to Donegal fishermen for Lough Foyle, called a special meeting and demanded that the Dublin government 'protect the territories of Saorstat Eireann and punish any person found infringing on their rights'.[48] The government was also threatened that a failure of Gardaí to protect the fishermen might 'prejudice the public against the Government Party in future elections in Donegal'.[49]

Due to territorial uncertainty surrounding Lough Foyle, neither jurisdiction could enforce its rulings. With the Free State unwilling to assert its territorial claim, the dispute was allowed to linger on for years. According to Peter Leary, 'Attitudes to the Foyle dispute did not, however, fold neatly along the lines of religious denomination or pre-partition politics.'[50] Inishowen fishermen disputing Northern Ireland's claim to territorial waters in Lough Foyle included Catholics, Presbyterians and Church of Ireland members, some of whom had signed the Ulster covenant in 1912 opposing Home Rule.[51] The attorney generals from both jurisdictions worked quietly in the background for some time to reach the agreement the two governments were eager to attain. Finally, in 1950 the two governments agreed to acquire all fishing rights from the Irish Society and set up a joint authority to regulate and conserve the fisheries for the Foyle region.[52] It was the first cross-border body with decision-making powers, brought about not because of an initiative led by either government, but by a determined campaign by fishermen who 'seized the opportunity presented by partition to reassert their claim to fishing rights'.[53]

There also were doubts over the main water supply for Belfast, the Belfast Water Works, remaining in Northern Ireland before the Boundary Commission made a decision, as 'part of the catchment area of the Belfast Water Works, as well as the Reservoir and portion of the pipe line' were 'situated in territory in which the majority of the population desire to be included in the Free State [east and south Down]. The Free State government promised 'to give guarantees to the Northern Government regarding the safety of the waterworks and free access to them' if the land was transferred to the south.[54]

There had been concern over the control of lighthouses, including on Lough Foyle.[55] Under the Government of Ireland Act 1920, lighthouses, buoys and beacons were listed as reserved services.[56] After partition, lighthouses continued to be administered by the Irish Lighthouse

Commissioners in Dublin, something that irked the northern government. Hugh Pollock, the northern finance minister, 'demanded that reserved services administered in the six counties should not be carried out from Dublin'. He also insisted that the 'Belfast Harbour Commission … already has some experience of lighthouse supervision'.[57] The northern administration was eager to have as little to do with the south as possible and it sought to assert its independence at every opportunity. When the British government proposed to create a new Irish Office to deal with the Irish jurisdictions, the northern government strenuously objected and insisted that the Free State should remain under the remit of the Colonial Office, with the north remaining a responsibility of the Home Office.[58] On the administration of lighthouses, the northern cabinet suggested that 'the Belfast Harbour Commission should take over the management of the Lighthouses in Northern Ireland'. It was agreed to 'get into touch with the Londonderry – and Newry – Harbour Authorities securing their acquiescence'. If that failed, it was proposed that the Scottish Lighthouse Authorities should take over the management of lighthouses for Northern Ireland.[59] Later, the northern government suggested that Trinity House in London (the official authority for lighthouses in England and Wales) should instead administer lighthouses for the north.[60] With all efforts failing, the northern administration had to concede to the status quo, with the Irish Lighthouses Commissioners remaining the body that administered lighthouses for the whole island.[61] Later, the Free State government had an issue with maintaining lighthouses in the north, as it wanted financial aid from the British government to do so.[62]

Arguably, the best example of cooperation between north and south on a governmental level occurred with the Erne Hydroelectric Scheme in the 1940s and 1950s. Cooperation on electricity was not a major priority at the time of the foundation of the two jurisdictions. Before partition, electricity supply across the country was sporadic and in the hands of private and public ventures. The total number of consumers was just a small fraction of the population. According to Maurice Manning and Moore McDowell, electricity in Ireland was developed in 'an uncoordinated, haphazard and slightly eccentric way'.[63] A government committee on natural resources produced a report in 1921 suggesting the increased use of water for generating electricity and highlighted in particular the 'possibilities of the

Rivers Shannon, Erne, Bann and Liffey'.[64] The report was discarded after the creation of two jurisdictions. The rivers Shannon and Liffey were solely in the south, whereas the River Erne was partially, and the River Bann solely in the north. There was some level of cooperation between both administrations from the onset of partition 'in the operation of the sluice system which controlled the water levels in Upper and Lower Lough Erne'.[65] The Erne river and lakes catchment area is 1,560 square miles, of which 830 are in the south, and the other 730 in the north.[66] 'North-south co-operation on drainage was ... institutionalised in the form of a Lough and River Erne Drainage District, constituted in 1863, managed by a drainage board annually, and operating four sluices, two in the North and two in the South'.[67]

The Electricity Supply Board (ESB), the electricity provider for the south from 1927, planned a major project to harness the power of the Erne waters to generate electricity. To optimise the Erne's potential for generating electricity, the ESB needed the cooperation of the northern government. From 1938, the ESB started official and unofficial communications with the Belfast government.[68] The ESB project offered significant attractions to the administrations on both sides of the border: electricity for the south, and drainage of the Erne catchment area for the north.[69] The southern government was fully behind the scheme, with two of its ministers, Seán MacEntee and Seán Lemass, publicly citing the benefits to both jurisdictions.[70] Regardless of the obvious benefits to the northern government, it took many years before an agreement was reached. The northern administration pursued a policy of non-cooperation with the southern government for political reasons.[71] According to Michael Kennedy, 'ESB planning began on the Erne scheme in 1942, but the first cross-border (government) contacts were not made until 1943. Not until early 1946 did Belfast agree to allow the dredging by the ESB to take place within Northern Irish territory.'[72] Another hurdle had to be overcome. Under the Government of Ireland Act 1920, Northern Ireland could only engage in projects solely within its jurisdiction. Amending legislation was needed from Westminster to allow the northern government to cooperate with the south on the Erne project.[73] There were deep divisions within the northern cabinet. It took the influence of the Prime Minister, Sir Basil Brooke, whose constituency in Fermanagh stood to benefit greatly from the drainage of the Erne, to get the cabinet to agree on the scheme.[74] Brooke succeeded, and the ESB Erne's scheme was allowed to proceed 'in a spirit of co-operation and goodwill on all sides'.[75] The Erne Hydroelectric Scheme showed that the north and south could work together on cross-border issues. They could agree on issues relating to the land the two jurisdictions shared. However, even with such an obviously mutually beneficial scheme, it still took years before the bad faith that had endured for decades was overcome.

The postal services were, like the railways and lighthouses, a reserved service under the Government of Ireland Act 1920. Again, with the Anglo-Irish Treaty overriding the Government of Ireland Act for the twenty-six counties, the Irish Free State took control of its postal services whilst the imperial parliament in Westminster retained control of the postal services for Northern Ireland. This fact, and the nature of mail routes and post offices, caused many teething problems as partition set in. Writing in January 1922, soon after the Anglo-Irish Treaty was signed, Judge Louis J. Walsh, who ruled in favour of fishermen from Inishowen to fish in Lough Foyle in 1923 (see above), questioned the authority of the all-Ireland reserved services created under the Government of Ireland Act. Commenting specifically on the registry of deeds, Walsh said:

> Under the Partition Act the Belfast Parliament was refused control of it. Under the Treaty it should be now, so far as the twenty-six counties are concerned, in the hands of the Provisional Government. But it is an all-Ireland service that has not been partitioned. Therefore, its administration must be as a whole. Therefore, it seems to me that our new Government is actually ruling Northern Ireland already.[76]

He also asked, 'What will be done with the Post Office in Carsonia [Northern Ireland]? The South will have a postal service of its own. Will the Belfast sorters leave the night mail at Bessbrook and Adavoyle, and the train be there invaded by the Free State Postal and Customs officials?'[77] The northern government found it very difficult to assert its independence from the rest of Ireland on the issue of postal services. Examples of its dependence on cooperating with the Free State included: residents in border areas in the north being reliant on Free State post offices to deliver their mail, sensitive mail for security forces being routed through Free State post offices and mail from Britain being delivered via the Holyhead–Kingstown (now Dún Laoghaire) route to different locales in Northern Ireland.

In 1923, the RUC officer commanding in Urney in County Tyrone complained that official letters for his platoon were being sent via Strabane to Clady station in the Free State (County Donegal), 'from thence they are brought to Clady Village, which is in Northern Territory, a distance of about a quarter of a mile'.[78] He suggested that the platoon should receive its mail from the Sion Mills post office 'and avoid the danger of tampering with any official letters in the Free State'.[79] The cost to change the delivery post office from Clady station to Sion Mills was estimated at £27. It was, therefore, decided to have a messenger from the camp collect their post from Sion Mills instead at a cost of £1.10 per annum.[80] A reverend F.W. Grant from Kinawley in County Fermanagh complained personally to Craig that his post was going to Ballyconnell in County Cavan, in the Free State. He threatened that unless Craig resolved the issue, even though he had 'been a life-long consistent Unionist', he intended 'putting the whole matter into the hands of Mr. Joseph Devlin [the nationalist leader from Belfast]'.[81]

Complicating the confusion over mail routes and the jurisdiction remit of post offices was the inability of the northern government to make any decisions on postal services. Such decisions were required to be made by the Postmaster General in London. The northern government established a function within its Ministry of Commerce to make representations to the British Postmaster General.[82] The majority of residents of Belcoo in County Fermanagh petitioned the Ministry of Commerce for a post office in Belcoo in late 1922. The town had been served by the Blacklion post office in County Cavan up to that point. Belcoo and Blacklion are contiguous, just separated by a bridge. They were informed that the ministry could not make any decisions on postal services and that the petition would have to be sent to the Postmaster General in London.[83] The Belcoo residents sought their own post office, as it was inconvenient to receive their mail from Blacklion; they were liable to pay the higher postage charges in force in the Free State; and due to the safety concerns caused by many incidents of civil disturbance that had occurred in Blacklion for much of 1922.[84] In December 1922, sixty armed men raided shops and private houses in Blacklion, taking away large quantities of goods. The disturbance was heard in Belcoo, just across the border.[85] A month later, Free State army troops caused further disturbances in Blacklion, with one drunken soldier crossing the border into Fermanagh armed with a rifle.[86] In May 1923, the Belcoo residents were informed their petition was successful and they would be granted a post office.[87]

The Belcoo post office opened. However, 'the arrangement in force necessitates the conveyance of letters posted in the Belcoo Office to Blacklion for sorting and despatch from Belcoo Railway Station by an official attached to the Blacklion Office', which 'neutralizes in a considerable degree the advantages expected by the Belcoo residents from the establishment of a separate Post Office there'.[88] The residents requested that either the 'sorting and despatch of outgoing letters should be entrusted to the sub-Postmaster of Belcoo' or to arrange for distribution and collection of letters in the townlands of Creenahor and Moneyorgan 'in that area to be undertaken by postmen of the Imperial Postal Service'.[89] This request was turned down for a variety of reasons; the proposed changes at Belcoo would cost £330 per annum, to be paid by Northern Ireland. The Boundary Commission had still not decided on the boundary: 'The Post Office is not disposed to take any movement which would suggest an attempt to force a decision on the boundary question'; and the 'Imperial Post Office would have to secure the sanction of the Free State Post Office to make any alterations to Belcoo'.[90] Once the boundary question was settled in 1925, the northern government was reluctant to halt the arrangement with the Free State postal services that allowed Free State post officers serve some northern areas and vice versa due to the increased expenditure that would be involved and the loss of an efficient service that such a move would entail.[91]

Claire Fitzpatrick has ascertained in her study on the all-red (British Empire) mail route pursued by Craig's government that 'gaining control over the post and communications was important for establishing Northern Ireland as distinct from the rest of Ireland while confirming its membership of the United Kingdom. Postal services signified cohesion of the state, a common linking of peoples'.[92] At one of the first northern government cabinet meetings, Ernest Clark stated that on the issue of postal services, 'Northern Ireland should be made a self-contained unit corresponding direct with London, instead of along the present channel through Dublin.'[93] Until April 1922, the whole island was served by the Holyhead–Kingstown mail service.[94] The northern government, through the Postmaster General in London, decided where possible, to divert all mail destined for Northern Ireland by the Holyhead–Kingstown route to the Stranraer–Larne service instead, foregoing the route through the Free State, in essence creating a "red" route.[95] The decision came in for much criticism, particularly from areas in the north that were negatively affected by the move, with mail now taking longer to arrive. The *Frontier Sentinel*, based in Newry in County Down, 'argued that it was "extraordinary" that people were prepared to "scrap a service" which has given "every satisfaction and little fault"'.[96] Under pressure from the Belfast business community and by the fact that 'the service via Kingstown' ensured 'an arrival in London at 5:45am whereas via Larne and Stranraer the mails did not arrive in London until 7:15am', Craig decided on 1 March 1927, 'for the time being we should agree to the mails being allowed to go via Kingstown and Holyhead'.[97] The dream to circumvent the Irish Free State for mail services continued, with many hoping the use of airships and flying boats from Liverpool would solve the problem in the future.[98] The incident demonstrated that practical and financial considerations could still take precedence over politics in the fledgling jurisdiction. It is important to note, as Fitzpatrick has, that when 'Northern Ireland as an entity was uncertain the clamour was great, when its status was secure [after the Boundary Commission decision in 1925], the clamour diminished.'[99]

The impact of partition on the infrastructure of the island of Ireland and the services that had served it on an all-Ireland basis beforehand showed the scale of the changes needed to create a border. The confusion and uncertainty that such a cleavage caused was aptly demonstrated by the effects it had on railways, fisheries and postal services. This was further amplified by the different political statuses of both Irish jurisdictions. Customs, practices and services had to be changed overnight to accommodate two political jurisdictions instead of one. In some instances, where economic sense prevailed, as with postal routes and the Erne

Hydroelectric Scheme, it was eventually possible to achieve cooperation between both entities. In other cases, the psychological partition was too difficult to overcome, with the two jurisdictions growing further and further apart from each other.

CHAPTER FOURTEEN

Sport

All sports had to adapt to the new scenario of two different jurisdictions on the island, regardless of whether they were united or not. The sports that remained or became unified after partition saw some issues caused by the creation of two political entities, primarily centred around anthems, flags and other emblems. Most sporting bodies that governed on an all-Ireland basis were mindful of the changed political landscape and looked to adopt policies that would appease all. Some sports were more successful in doing this than others.

The GAA regularly liked to portray itself as a non-political body.[1] Through its organisation of a mass protest against permits from the British authorities on 'Gaelic Sunday' in 1918, its support for the Irish republican prisoners' dependents fund and the active military participation of many of its members, it clearly was a political body and one closely aligned with Sinn Féin and its military arm.[2] Although it was cross-border in almost everything that it did, it was not cross-community.[3] In reality, there was no place within the GAA for anyone from the unionist tradition. The GAA was trenchantly opposed to partition.[4] Opening a GAA ground in Rosculligan, County Cavan, in 1923, the GAA president, Dan McCarthy, who was also a TD in Dáil Éireann, said the association 'should not recognise partition' although the GAA was 'open to all Irishmen'.[5] The GAA never countenanced anything other than remaining an all-Ireland body, and given its homogenous (Catholic) make-up, there was little danger of internal divisions relating to partition and sectarianism. Its policy on partition was similar to that of leading nationalists in the south: it chose to ignore it. There is no mention of partition in the minutes of the Ulster GAA Council from 1921 to 1922. Secretary of the Ulster GAA Council, Eoin O'Duffy, was one of the leading figures of the IRA in Ulster by mid-1921. The term 'Northern Ireland' was avoided in meetings and documents. Like most other nationalists, there were hopes the border would be short-lived.[6]

According to David Hassan, almost immediately after partition, 'GAA activities in Northern Ireland became embroiled in controversy, mostly on account of clashes with the Royal Ulster Constabulary (RUC), the north's new police force.'[7] As the new northern administration adopted a siege mentality, numerous GAA members were interned without trial between 1922 and 1924 on the prison ship *Argenta*.[8] This led to a lapse in GAA fixtures in 1922 in south Armagh and south Down for fear of people being interned. Very few Gaelic games were played in the rural areas of the six counties in 1922. Most famously, members of the Monaghan Gaelic football team were arrested by 'B' Specials in Tyrone on their way to the Ulster football final in Derry in January 1922 (see Chapter Seven), which almost led to the resignation of Craig and his government. 'Thus the first Northern Ireland government narrowly avoided being brought down by a GAA team.'[9] Also, in August 1922, 'the Derry football team ... was detained overnight on route to Cavan.'[10] The hibernation of the GAA in some counties lasted for years.[11] A motion was tabled by Ulster officials in April 1923 'to direct the attention of Congress to the importance of keeping the GAA alive in the North-East counties'. The GAA Central Council in Dublin rejected the proposal to appoint a full-time paid special organiser for the six counties. According to Dónal McAnallen, 'There was already in these counties a sense of abandonment by the rest of Ireland in the sporting realm as in other matters – a theme that would recur for many years.'[12]

Partition also led to many practical difficult decisions for the GAA. Its long-standing ban on members of the crown forces was retained but reinterpreted: members of the new police force, an Garda Síochána, and the Irish army of the Irish Free State were admitted to the GAA, but RUC members and Specials were barred from the outset as front-line United Kingdom forces.[13] In 1922, the GAA leadership also covertly removed the ban on oath-swearing public servants after the Free State gained sovereignty. The Promissory Oaths Act (Northern Ireland) 1923, required all public servants, including school teachers, to swear allegiance. Some northern nationalists initially refused to do so. The Central Council confirmed, after a query from Ulster, that 'the taking of the oath did not debar teachers from participating in GAA affairs'.[14]

The Free State caused a bigger problem in 1923 when it introduced a customs barrier at the border. Those crossing into the twenty-six counties had to obtain customs passes from thereon in. The lengthy form-filling and fee payments affected the GAA possibly more than anything else.[15] The creation of a customs border and security posts generated problems for GAA clubs such as Crossmaglen Rangers in south Armagh, cutting the club from its natural hinterland of places such as Dundalk and Castleblaney, south of the border.[16] Even though the GAA was vehemently opposed to partition, it appeared to favour the Ulster counties that were not in the six counties of Northern Ireland. Venues in counties Monaghan and Cavan dominated the hosting of major Ulster championship ties, based on the belief that they would draw bigger crowds. Only three Ulster senior football finals took place in the six counties from 1921 to 1945. This was reflected on the field, with Monaghan and Cavan completely dominating there also.[17] Cavan alone won seven Ulster senior football championship titles in the 1920s, eight in the 1930s and nine in the 1940s.[18]

Local councils in Northern Ireland became forums of unionist discrimination against the GAA, with very few playing fields being allocated to the association. Gaelic games were not seen as sports but as nationalist political symbols. 'Belfast rule became more adverse than Westminster rule for Gaelic sports'.[19] According to McAnallen, while 'the vast majority of northern GAA members remained outside the IRA ranks, more than enough of them were involved in trying to bring down the state for the state to treat the association with suspicion'.[20] The GAA in Northern Ireland had no option but to play its games without causing immediate disruption after the onset of partition. A manifestation of this hibernation came in 1929 when the GAA declined a request that was 'made by the nationalist-sponsored National League of the North for participation by the Association in the selection of parliamentary candidates for the Northern Ireland parliament'.[21]

Through its ban on 'foreign games', the GAA fiercely opposed the sports it saw as foreign (in reality, sports it saw as British). Its mouthpiece, the *Gaelic Athlete*, depicted soccer and rugby as 'exotic imitations' of

Britishness, describing Irishmen who played those codes as 'blatant Imperialists for all Ireland to roll itself up in the Union Jack and sing and toast "Irish Nationality" with a leer on its lying lip'.[22] In many ways, the GAA did not face the difficulties sports such as soccer did. It did not have to change its hand with the onset of partition. It remained an organisation almost solely catering to Catholics and nationalists. It did not have to find solutions to accommodate different communities. Even though by some of its actions, it accepted the realities of partition, it faced no internal challenges by publicly opposing it.

Thwarted by northern opposition for some years initially, rugby was eventually unified in Ireland under the Irish Rugby Football Union (IRFU) umbrella in 1879.[23] Any inclination for the northern branch to disaffiliate from the IRFU after partition was prevented by the actions of the parent body in Dublin, who made great strides to accommodate its northern members. Other than occasional complaints of annual general meetings always being held in Dublin and an unfair allocation of tickets for international matches being offered to Ulster people, the northern branch was very happy with how it was treated by the IRFU.[24] Whilst much of official Ireland looked to forget its part in the First World War, the IRFU united in commemorating rugby players who had fought and died in the war with a memorial installed at Lansdowne Road.[25] Echoing its success in inter-provincial matches against Leinster and Munster, Ulster players were well-represented in the Irish international teams selected after partition.[26] To the detriment of upgrading Lansdowne Road in Dublin, the IRFU sanctioned and allocated funds for the erection of a new rugby stadium in Belfast at Ravenhill.[27] The new ground accommodated over 20,000 people, including 4,000 covered stand seats. This allowed the IRFU to continue its tradition of hosting international matches in Belfast and Dublin, unlike the rugby unions in England and Scotland, who did not countenance internationals outside of London or Edinburgh respectively. Effusive in praise, the IRFU northern branch claimed, 'At the present time in Dublin they had the finest body of sportsmen it was possible to get, and any proposition for the good of the game was fairly and reasonably met by the Irish Union.'[28] International matches were briefly withheld from Belfast in 1926 when the northern government imposed an entertainment tax that added a £500 cost to host matches in Belfast.[29]

The northern branch was also happy with its representation on the IRFU governing body. It held two of the five seats on the international selection committee and it had equal representation to Leinster on the IRFU council.[30] Of the sixteen presidents of the IRFU elected between partition and the outbreak of the Second World War, nine were from Leinster, six were from Ulster and one from Munster.[31] All past presidents were allowed to sit on the IRFU council, thus giving them significant leverage. At one stage, there were twenty past presidents on the thirty-eight-member council, something opposed by Leinster, Munster and Connaught, but not by Ulster.[32] The willingness to accommodate Ulster may certainly be explained by the make-up of the IRFU council, where the overwhelming number of members were Protestants from the upper-middle class who were inclined to have unionist sympathies. For example, of the nine presidents of the IRFU from Leinster between partition and the outbreak of the Second World War, seven were Protestants, many of them with 'strong links with one of the Free State's most ostentatiously unionist institutions, Trinity College Dublin.'[33] According to Liam O'Callaghan, those involved in governing rugby within Ireland had other 'potent social binding' agents, such as education, work, church and leisure activities.[34] These factors were crucial in ensuring unity within rugby after partition.

In fact, during the years immediately following partition, most opposition to the IRFU did not come from Ulster but from Munster, Connaught and large pockets in Leinster. Many in the Irish Free State believed that rugby in Ireland was governed by a Protestant upper-middle-class minority who were too unionist in outlook.[35] The IRFU's prohibition of matches on Sundays, its preference for a rugby union or Union Jack flag over the Irish Tricolour and its toasting of the British king, even cancelling fixtures on the death of King George V, proved controversial decisions that demonstrated the IRFU administrators had more in common with the majority opinion of Northern Ireland than with that of the Irish Free State.[36] Whilst the IRFU's 'unionism' irked many in the Irish Free State, they did not have enough internal power to effectively oppose the IRFU. In essence, the IRFU remained an all-Ireland body after partition due to the similarities in identity shared by an overwhelming number of those who governed the game north and south and the willingness of the IRFU council to accept the changed political position by accommodating Ulster.

The sport of bowls, like soccer, was governed from Belfast. The Irish Bowling Association (IBA), from its foundation in 1904, was dominated by Belfast clubs. The modern version of the sport was introduced to Belfast through Scottish immigrants.[37] The IBA was formed by six clubs from the north-east in Belfast in 1904. The first Dublin club to affiliate was the Kenilworth club from Rathmines in 1906.[38] Such was the dominance of Belfast that according to the IBA constitution and rules booklet from 1914, it was stipulated that 'Matches between Dublin and Clubs outside Belfast shall be played on Saturday in Belfast … The final shall be played in Belfast on the last Saturday in August, on a neutral green to be selected by the IBA Committee.'[39] Like rugby, cricket and hockey, bowls tended to be dominated by upper-middle-class Protestants, sharing the same identity throughout Ireland.

With the onset of partition, instead of dividing along political lines, the IBA sought increased cooperation with the south. Speaking in October 1922, the IBA president, Thomas McMullan claimed that 'if we had bowling greens in all the towns in Ireland and ceased to talk politics at every opportunity we would soon create a better spirit than that which prevailed at present'. He hoped 'that the serious troubles in the South would soon end, and that the South would become as prosperous as the North'.[40] McMullan's call for increased unity throughout Ireland in bowls contrasted sharply with his political views as an Ulster unionist MP in the newly created Northern Ireland parliament.[41] It was a striking feature of post-partition Ireland that many leading unionist politicians who were involved in sports' governing bodies, whilst strongly opposing Irish unity politically, were promoters of unity and all-island cooperation in sport.[42] This double-handed approach of firmly held political opinions coexisting with softer cultural approaches was common in post-partition Ireland.

Despite the attempts of the IBA to grow the game in the south, Belfast clubs still dominated the sport by the late 1920s. The IBA Senior Cup was only won for the first time by a team outside of Ulster in 1961, when the Leinster club from Dublin won the competition.[43] Of the thirty-three clubs affiliated to the IBA in 1929, twenty-seven were from Belfast, four from rural Ulster and the remaining two from Dublin.[44] The IBA committees were also dominated by members from Belfast, with John Rowland the first member from the Irish Free State to be appointed to the international selection committee in 1932.[45] All of the annual and committee meetings were also held in Belfast. Dublin's request to host an international match in 1925 was turned down, as three-quarters of the team were from Ulster.[46]

To grow the sport in the south, the clubs in Dublin amalgamated to form the Irish Free State Bowling League in 1927 which was affiliated to the IBA.[47] Soon after, the IBA decided to host the 'home nations' international match series in Dublin in 1930. The decision taken at an IBA meeting the previous year was not without opposition.[48] Despite the disapproval, the matches were held in Dublin in 1930, formally opened by the Free State Governor General, James McNeill and accompanied by the IBA president, Major William Baird.[49] Baird, the owner of the unionist-leaning *Belfast Telegraph* newspaper group, witnessed the Irish Tricolour being flown at the opening ceremony.[50] It is not known if the IBA objected to the flying of the Tricolour, but the association soon introduced its own flag of green, black and blue to be flown at international tournaments.[51] For matches played in the south, the IBA suggested that the green, black and blue flag be used with the letters B, L and I superimposed on the flag, representing the Bowling League of Ireland, the new name of the Irish Free State Bowling League after the introduction of *Bunreacht na hÉireann*, the new constitution in the south, in 1937.[52]

Boxing was a sport pursued mainly by male working-class Protestants and Catholics and had strong military and security connections.[53] The governing body for boxing in Ireland at the time of partition, the Irish Amateur Boxing Association (IABA), remained an all-Ireland body. Headquartered in Dublin, as boxing grew in popularity in Belfast, the IABA decided to alternate its annual meetings and venues for international events between Dublin and Belfast. The IABA chairman, Dr Robert Rowlette from Dublin, justified the decision: 'There could be no doubt that in the past it had been a hardship upon Belfast to have always to travel for the annual meeting to Dublin, no doubt at much inconvenience. The new arrangement would tend to equalise that, and he had no doubt it would be for the general good of the sport.'[54] With the creation of two new jurisdictions in Ireland, the RIC, Ireland's all-island police force, was disbanded, replaced by an Garda Síochána in the Irish Free State and the RUC in Northern Ireland. The two new police forces, reflecting political opinion at large, practically ignored each other. As affiliated bodies within the IABA, however, they both cooperated with and competed against each other in the boxing arena, including instances where members from each force crossed the border for boxing events.[55] In one such middleweight contest, the RUC's Jim Magill defeated Garda Jack Chase in an official box-off to represent Ireland at the 1932 Olympic Games in Los Angeles. Magill was, however,

> prevented from travelling when the Ulster Council of the Irish Amateur Boxing Association (IABA) refused to endorse his selection. The accepted wisdom was that the Council was informed by the Stormont [Northern Ireland] government that it would be 'inappropriate' for a member of the RUC to compete under the Irish tricolour representing the Irish Free State, despite the fact that Magill was a seasoned Irish international.[56]

Despite such incidents, the IABA never strayed from being an all-Ireland body. Echoing the federalist approach adopted by many other sporting bodies that remained all-Ireland, in 1926 the IABA was reorganised to include a central council made up of three representatives from each newly created provincial council.[57] The provincial councils were granted a large degree of autonomy, and inter-provincial championships were inaugurated to stimulate interest in boxing.[58] The new structures saw a remarkable turnaround in success for the IABA. Affiliated clubs increased from twenty-seven in 1928 to sixty-six in 1929.[59] The Ulster council, with increased autonomy, was happy to remain within the IABA fold, as it also saw strong growth in its number of affiliated clubs.[60] The fact that the IABA was recognised and associated with the Irish Olympic Council, an all-Ireland body, could also explain why boxing remained a united sport on the island.

One sport that achieved a lasting union after partition in Ireland was cricket. Despite cricket being the most popular sport in Ireland in the 1860s and 1870s, with an estimated 500 cricket clubs established throughout the country, there was no national body overseeing the game until 1890.[61] At that time, it was played in most parts of Ireland by Protestants and Catholics from all classes.[62] Over the next thirty years, attempts were made (and thwarted) to have a unified governing body for Ireland, with northern members believing there was a bias against them. The Northern Cricket Union claimed cricket was dominated by Leinster and Munster, Dublin would control the national team selection and venue locations, and there was little appetite to financially contribute to a body where little representation for the north was anticipated by the Northern Cricket Union.[63] On the face of it, from venues chosen and teams selected for Ireland from 1910 to 1914, it appears the Northern Cricket Union had some justifiable concerns. Of the sixteen home matches played in Ireland during that period, thirteen were held in Dublin, two in Munster and one in Bray in County Wicklow. In the same period, Ulster players only featured in fifteen of the twenty-seven matches Ireland played in.[64]

Immediately after the First World War, the Leinster Cricket Union initiated overtures once again to entice the Northern Cricket Union to join an Irish Cricket Union. The Northern Cricket Union agreed to restart the annual inter-provincial match with Leinster, which had lapsed for eight years, but felt 'that the present time was not opportune for discussing the proposed formation of an Irish Cricket Union'.[65] Junior and schools inter-provincials with Leinster were also resurrected. Cricket was affected by the War of Independence, particularly when, at a cricket match in Trinity College Dublin, a spectator, Kathleen Wright, was shot dead by the IRA.[66] The incident led to the Northern Cricket Union cancelling the senior and schools inter-provincial against Leinster scheduled for Dublin that year, 'owing to the present state of affairs'.[67] A year later, it also cancelled the schools inter-provincial due to the 'situation that had arisen in Dublin' with the start of the civil war.[68] The northern body resisted a number of attempts made by Leinster to amalgamate during the years of conflict. Once the security situation calmed down in Ireland, it was ready to consider unification. The smoothing of relations was certainly helped by the increase in representation at international level for Ulster players. Three Ulster players were selected for Ireland for the first time in February 1923, followed by four selected to play against Scotland in May 1923.[69] That same year, Irish cricket authorities agreed to form an Irish Cricket Union, 'composed of an equal number of Northern and Southern Representatives, and having as its first Chairman', Robert Erskine, the Northern Cricket Union's chairman. The northern body was happy with the result, stating it 'has given rise to much satisfaction, and will, it is hoped, result eventually in a regular series of International Matches, in addition to a Gentlemen of Ireland Match for Belfast annually'.[70] Like the other provincial unions, the northern body still ran its own league and cup fixtures for senior and junior levels. Once the North-West (Derry) Cricket Union joined the fold in 1925, cricket in Ireland was unified under one body.[71]

The first decade after partition saw a vast improvement in relations between north and south in cricket. The Irish Cricket Union chose Belfast as a venue for the first time for an international representative game against Wales in 1924, signalling a move towards closer cooperation.[72] The union formed in 1923 was cemented over the following years, leaving cricket as it is today, governed on an all-Ireland basis. A factor that helped cricket governance to unite in Ireland was the change in identity of those who supported the game. By the time of partition, cricket had retreated from its popularity amongst Protestants and Catholics of all classes. A combination of factors saw the game's demise in much of Ireland: attacks from the GAA on what it saw as a 'foreign game', the inability of cricket in Ireland to unite under one governing body for decades and the 'unravelling politics of Ireland' all contributed to Irish cricket shrinking in size and becoming mainly the preserve of upper-middle-class Protestants.[73] Ironically, the contraction of the game in Ireland in many ways facilitated unity from a governance perspective, as it shared a similar identity profile to other all-Ireland sports, such as rugby, bowls and hockey.

Other sports that were, like cricket, divided at the time of partition and later unified included table tennis and show jumping. In 1937, the Northern Ireland Table Tennis Association unanimously agreed to join with the Irish Free State association to form an all-Ireland body. The primary reason for this was both teams' underperformance at the World Championships in previous years, where both teams 'came out somewhere near the bottom in the team contests'.[74] A process in the 1950s that lasted over six years also saw north and south join together in show jumping under the Irish Show Jumping Association. The negotiations were prolonged due to issues over flags and anthems. It was finally agreed to use the four provinces flag, matching saddle cloths and the anthem of 'St Patrick's Day Parade' for international events, with the exception of the nations cup, which used the Irish Tricolour and the Irish national anthem, 'Amhrán na bhFiann', instead.[75] Even with the compromises, some riders were unhappy with the new arrangements.

The Irish Lawn Tennis Association (ILTA) was affiliated to the Lawn Tennis Association in England from its foundation in 1908. With the creation of two political entities in Ireland, the ILTA unanimously agreed to 'be established on independent lines similar to the Governing Associations in the Dominions'.[76] The resolution was supported by all the tennis clubs in Northern Ireland. The decision allowed the ILTA to govern its own affairs, clubs would pay affiliation fees to the ILTA, not to the Lawn Tennis Association, and Ireland would be allowed to enter the Davis Cup.[77] Ireland's entry into the Davis Cup was initially disputed by the Lawn Tennis Association due to the confusion over Ireland being a 'geographical entity'.[78] Some in the Irish Free State, including senator Oliver St John Gogarty, complained that the Irish Tricolour was not used for Davis Cup matches in subsequent years. The ILTA responded that 'if the Tricolour were flown some difficulty might be presented if there were players from the Six Counties'.[79] Even though tennis players from Northern Ireland were eligible to represent Ireland in the Davis Cup, there were some periods of confusion and disgruntlement over their status by their lack of representation on the Irish team.[80] To cement the ILTA's future as an all-island body, it was decided to grant increased provincial control in 1927. Three provincial councils were set up: Leinster and Connaught, Ulster, and Munster, and a general council with its headquarters in Dublin. The provincial councils were delegated to organise inter-provincial matches, inter-club matches and to control all internal affairs of the province. It was also agreed for the general council to consist of ten members from Leinster and Connaught, six from Ulster and five from Munster.[81] The tennis example presents another case of highlighting how the democratic and federalist approach to internal governance was the clearest path to internal unity. Tennis, like many other all-Ireland sports, was mainly the preserve of the upper-middle classes, which also lessened its scope for division.

Hockey in Ireland experienced relatively little turbulence with the partitioning of Ireland. The Irish Hockey Union (IHU) was formed in 1893 with provincial branches established in 1898 and 1899.[82] The IHU was structured similarly to a federation with the four provinces partially autonomous.[83] With the IHU primarily responsible for selecting the international team but little else, there were far fewer opportunities for conflict. The selection committee was made up of five people, with a member from each province plus an additional member elected, which tended to alternate between Leinster and Ulster. International fixtures were also alternated between the north and the south.[84] Hockey was also a homogenous sport, mainly played by upper-middle-class Protestant men and women. Hockey clubs were well spread throughout the island. In 1921, there were fourteen affiliated clubs from Ulster, eleven from Munster, sixteen from Leinster and seven from Connaught.[85] The IHU decided soon after partition for an IHU flag with the crests of the four provinces to be used instead of the Tricolour and the playing of the 'Londonderry Air' ('Danny Boy') to be used as the team's anthem.[86] Although hockey has remained united, there were objections from the Ulster Ladies' Hockey Union at the lack of inter-provincial and international matches being held in Belfast.[87] At a dinner organised by the Ulster branch of the IHU in 1925, committee member A.G. Burney acknowledged that Ulster's relationship had improved considerably with the IHU since the early days when 'Dublin forgot there were any provinces outside Leinster, and when Ulster wanted anything they found it very difficult to get, because they were out-voted'.[88] That season, Belfast hosted the international senior men's match against England for the first time and an Ulsterman, R.A. Burke, held the position of IHU president, the second Ulsterman to do so. In his address that night, Burke claimed:

> Hockey in Ireland knew no border, and he agreed with Mr Andrews that it was a pity that the people of the country could not agree generally as they did in sport; in fact he went further, and said one day sport would unite Ireland within the Empire. It was men of the type of Mr. Andrews that could assist to bring that about.[89]

The Mr Andrews he was referring to was the Northern Ireland Minister of Labour and future Prime Minister, John Andrews. Andrews commented on the peculiar scenario where Irishmen had

> throughout the generations that had gone they had rarely if ever ceased fighting with one another, and side by side with that they as

sportsmen found that they had always been good pals and the very best friends ... for Irishmen, no matter in what part of Ireland they lived, that the sooner they learned to put the spirit that was in sport into their public dealings with one another the better it would be for each and all of them.[90]

Andrews' speech demonstrated the peculiar scenario in Ireland of those who, on one hand supported Irish unity in sport, and on the other, were active participants in one of the two Irish jurisdictions totally opposed to the workings of the other. Hockey, like many all-Ireland sports, was played and administered by a homogenous group, adopted a federalist approach with large degrees of autonomy for its provincial councils and made internal governance decisions that promoted equality and diffused tensions, ensuring the unity of the sport on the island.

Ulster was the driving force behind the development of golf in Ireland, in part because of its strong links to Scotland but also because, as the industrial heartland of the island, the north-east had the population density and structured leisure hours that suited modern sports.[91] It was a game played primarily by Protestants and unionists. Arthur Balfour had played golf in the Phoenix Park in Dublin under police protection during his time as Irish Chief Secretary, from 1887 to 1891.[92]

The Golfing Union of Ireland was established in 1891 along similar lines to hockey and rugby, with the provincial councils managing all provincial affairs.[93] Six of the nine clubs that formed the union were from Ulster, and all of the original founders were from the same province. The first meeting of the union took place in the Northern Counties Railway Hotel in Portrush in County Antrim.[94] The union's meetings also alternated between Belfast and Dublin, reducing the scope for disagreements. Because of their Protestant and unionist connections, golf clubs had a difficult time during the War of Independence and the ensuing civil war. A number of clubhouses were burned down and competitions disrupted.[95] Despite these setbacks, the Golfing Union of Ireland remained an all-Ireland body after partition.

The governing bodies for horse racing, the Turf Club, established in 1790, and the Irish National Hunt Steeplechase Committee, established in 1866, remained all-Ireland bodies after partition. During the First World War and the Irish revolutionary years the Turf Club became more unionist in outlook.[96] Military involvement grew significantly during this period. In 1912, 23 per cent of its members bore military titles, but by 1922, this had increased to 63 per cent.[97] Frank Brooke, the Turf Club's senior steward, was killed in July 1920 during the War of Independence and many great houses with racing connections were destroyed.[98] Remarkably, both unionists and nationalists involved in horse racing quickly overcame their differences once Ireland was partitioned. An example of the sport's ability to adapt and accommodate differing political viewpoints was seen a mere six months after the signing of the Anglo-Irish Treaty. The Turf Club sanctioned a race meeting at the Phoenix Park racecourse that became known as 'the IRA meeting'.[99] The purpose of the meeting was to raise funds to help disabled members of the IRA. Later, the Turf Club was moved to pass resolutions of sympathy on the deaths of the two leading figures of the provisional government of the Irish Free State, Arthur Griffith and Michael Collins, who had both died in August 1922.[100] In the decades that followed,

> horse racing prospered in Ireland as never before and in time received a level of state support that no other sport managed to secure. It also retained the support of the British crown. Year after year, the crown paid the winners of King's Plate races held at the Curragh in Kildare or at Limerick Junction regardless of the political relationship between the United Kingdom and the newly independent Irish Free State.[101]

Horse racing in Ireland showed that people who were directly in opposition with each other politically and militarily could settle their differences, and in a very short period of time. According to Fergus D'Arcy, 'the uneasy sporting alliance of gentry and rural middle class somehow survived: the joy of racing and its rivalry continued to transcend ancient enmities'.[102] The commercial nature of the sport was also a factor in the maintenance of unity. Horse racing was a business for many stakeholders, regardless of class or political view. To divide would have been costly for all involved in the sport in Ireland. It also would have been difficult for horse racing in Northern Ireland to survive alone, with just two racecourses based in the six counties, at Down Royal and Downpatrick.[103]

The sports of greyhound racing and coursing were governed by the Irish Coursing Club on an all-Ireland basis from its establishment in 1916 to 1958. Like horse racing, greyhound racing and coursing had strong commercial interests, making unity more likely. In 1927, greyhound tracks were opened in Dublin, Belfast and Cork, followed by tracks at Limerick and Waterford. In the Free State, under the Betting Act of 1926, 'bookmakers offered on-course and off-course betting'.[104] Circumstances were more difficult for greyhound racing organisers in the north due to Protestant resistance for gambling and difficulties encountered in registering tracks in Northern Ireland. In 1958, a semi-state body, Bord na gCon (the Irish Greyhound Board) was formed to govern greyhound racing.[105] 'One of the most unusual consequences of the establishment of Bord na gCon was that the Board's jurisdiction of the sport was restricted to the Republic of Ireland, while the Irish Coursing Club, which remained an all-island organization, had sole control of the sport in Northern Ireland'.[106]

The legacy of one of Ireland's most famous greyhounds, Master McGrath, who won the Waterloo Cup on three occasions, was negatively impacted by partition. Even though Master McGrath competed years before partition in the 1860s and 1870s and was whelped in County Waterford in the south of Ireland, the legacy of Master McGrath 'was collapsed into a Northern Irish rather than an all-Irish context' after partition.[107] Master McGrath, who resided most of his life in what was then a mainly Protestant town, of Lurgan in County Armagh, acquired a status in the imagination as a representative of the Protestant community. The fact that the dog was owned by a British peer of the realm, Lord Lurgan, would have influenced Catholics in Lurgan and Northern Ireland as a whole to disassociate themselves from the dog.[108] The development of Master McGrath as a symbol of local Protestantism was cemented by the way in which local soccer, rugby, cricket, hockey and golf clubs adopted the town's coat of arms as their club badge, as those sports were mainly patronised by Protestants in the town. The club badges included an image of Master McGrath.[109]

Motor cycling in Ireland is an all-Ireland body under the governance of the Motor Cycle Union of Ireland (MCUI). Like many other all-island sports, each provincial council has enjoyed considerable autonomy in the running of its internal affairs.[110] Unlike the MCUI, motor car racing has been divided north and south since the early days of partition.[111] Ulsterman Harry Ferguson, of Massey Ferguson tractor fame and motor racing pioneer, believed in peace and cooperation between north and south when partition came into being.[112] He even received the support of the Free State Minister of Commerce, Ernest Blythe, in promoting a series of international races across Ireland in 1922. This was also supported by Northern Ireland's government.[113] Due to conflict in the north and south, very little racing occurred in 1922. Racing activity in the north picked up with the aid of the supportive northern government, unlike in the south. There, the civil war and the backlog the conflict created for the Free State government prevented road race bills and speed bills being passed for races to take place.[114] Ferguson and his Ulster colleagues believed the governing body for motor car racing in Ireland, the Royal Irish Automobile Club (RIAC) was 'neglecting the sporting side'. This view was echoed by the MCUI, which, instead of the RIAC, organised the motor car racing and motor cycling racing calendar up until the mid-1930s.[115] It was decided to contact the Royal Automobile Club in London to set up an Ulster division. Even though Ulster split from the RIAC, it was an amicable split. Cooperation on the customs border, supporting each other's races and jointly organising the all-island Circuit of Ireland Rally are just some of the examples of how the north and south in motor car racing, although divided, worked closely together after partition.[116]

Athletics and cycling were the sports where partition was the primary reason for division. Attempts were made from the early 1920s to unite the different athletic bodies operating in Ireland under one umbrella, the National Athletic and Cycling Association of Ireland (NACAI).[117] The man spearheading the move was J.J. Keane. Keane, a GAA activist, echoing GAA exclusion bans, prohibited British soldiers, navy men and police on active service in Ireland from joining the NACAI. This was unacceptable to many Belfast members.[118] This exclusionary rule was eventually removed, and it was decided to hold the national championships on Saturdays and Sundays on alternative years to accommodate Ulster members.[119] The unity was paper-thin from the very outset, with no Ulster delegates present at the NACAI annual congress in May 1924 to ratify the merger. Notably, there was no Ulster representative included in the new executive.[120]

Open conflict broke out at Easter 1925 over an event organised at the stadium of the Belfast Celtic soccer club. As well as athletics, the event included a 200 yards whippet and an open trot handicap. Under the laws of the NACAI and the International Amateur Athletics Federation (IAAF), animal events and the associated gambling that accompanied those events contravened their rules on amateurism.[121] Belfast clubs withdrew from the NACAI and founded the Northern Ireland Amateur Athletics, Cycling and Cross-Country Association in July 1925.[122] 'What was a domestic dispute soon took on an international dimension and became politicised. Unionist-minded administrators and Northern Ireland politicians used the opportunity presented by the dispute to pursue their agenda to achieve separate recognition for Northern Ireland in sport'.[123] Thomas Moles, editor of the *Belfast Telegraph* and Ulster unionist MP, was appointed the new body's president.[124] The unionist members of the northern association deeply resented the Dublin control of the NACAI, the using of the Tricolour for international competitions and the provincial and county structure of the NACAI that aped the GAA structure.[125]

The NACAI was not overly concerned with the secession of many of the northern clubs, believing its international standing would help ease the parent body through murky waters. With the British Amateur Athletics Association forming a branch in Northern Ireland in 1928, a move not blocked by the IAAF, this safety valve was removed.[126] A number of conferences were held over the coming years, but to no avail. Both sides remained intransigent, with the northern association looking to eke out its future under the British umbrella and the NACAI immovable in relinquishing all-Ireland control. It ultimately was a battle lost by the NACAI, which, in its quest to resist partition in a sporting sphere, failed to realise the political reality of partition. After 1934, Ireland's right to compete in athletics in the Olympic Games as a thirty-two-county entity was lost. As a result, athletes within the NACAI did not compete in the Olympic Games for decades.[127] Athletics and cycling, unlike many all-Ireland sports, had to deal with multiple groups from different backgrounds. Both sports were played and administered by Protestants and Catholics from different classes. The athletics and cycling split was, however, dominated by the national political question. It permeated almost every decision made by the NACAI, which simply refused to recognise the political partition of Ireland. It would not 'represent a *mutilated* Ireland in international world competition', resulting in its decades-long international isolation.[128]

Although the split in Irish soccer coincided with the political partition of the island in 1921, the primary reason for the Leinster clubs leaving the Belfast headquartered Irish Football Association (IFA) was more to do with internal politics than national politics.[129] National politics did play a role in fomenting division between Leinster and Belfast, but not as large a role as some commentators have claimed. The main grievances cited by Dublin administrators were the Belfast bias in the selection of players for the international team, the choice of venue for international matches and the make-up of the IFA council and its sub-committees.[130] Many in the south also felt they were short-changed when the IFA offered fund assistance. The parent body did little to encourage the growth of the game outside of the north-east of Ireland.[131]

Both the IFA and the newly formed Football Association of Ireland (FAI) wanted to govern soccer for the whole island of Ireland. Neither body was interested in accepting the new political frontier. The IFA did not see itself as merely governing for the six counties of Northern Ireland – it saw itself as the national association for all of Ireland. It maintained its name, the Irish Football Association, and selected players from the whole island to assert this claim.[132] The FAI also wanted to govern soccer for all of Ireland. It conceded its right to govern within the six counties only when it saw this as the optimum way to achieve international recognition through membership of the Fédération Internationale de Football Association (FIFA).[133] Before 1923, it accepted clubs from Northern Ireland into its fold, including Alton United from Belfast, who won the FAI Cup in 1923.[134]

The conferences held between the two bodies from 1923 to 1932 to achieve unity clearly showed this battle for internal power.[135] The partition of the country was rarely mentioned throughout the conferences. The IFA, the fourth-oldest football association in the world, looked to maintain its status and concede as little as possible. The FAI ultimately would not agree on a settlement unless it was based on total equality, right down to a seat on the International Football Association Board.[136]

The political partition of the island of Ireland posed problems for all sporting bodies in Ireland. The border forced all sports to look at their internal governance structures. Unlike in soccer and athletics and cycling, most Irish governing bodies managed to maintain unity by considerable compromise. Issues of political symbolism were tailored to accommodate diverse political and cultural interests. There was a readiness from many sporting bodies to incorporate inoffensive and neutral flags, anthems and emblems in order to maintain unity. Great efforts were also made to democratise the internal governance structures of those sports. A common trend for most of the sports that remained united was to share national committee representation amongst provinces on a basis of equality. Provincial councils in most cases were afforded large degrees of autonomy to manage their internal affairs, and significant energy was made to accommodate provinces, particularly Ulster, in selections for international contests and venue choices for internationals and committee meetings. Most sports that remained united also did not have the identity issues faced by sports such as soccer. Rugby, hockey, cricket and bowls were primarily the preserve of Protestants from the upper classes. The GAA, as a pan-nationalist association dominated by Catholics, did little to encourage Protestant and unionist membership. Soccer, similar to athletics and cycling, had to cater for different religions and classes. This also provided challenges in maintaining unity for those sports and contributed to their ultimate division.

CONCLUSION

The Impact of Partition

Northern Ireland will be 100 years old in 2021. It has survived as an entity despite the haphazard nature of its birth and the conflicts and disputes over its existence ever since. The border has strangled politics on the island. To this day, it still is greatly misunderstood. Even if unloved, the border has proved incredibly resilient throughout its existence.

The road to partition was long, uncertain and meandering. Between 1912 and 1925, many proposals were put forward to deal with that most intractable of issues, how to solve the Irish question. Initially, the British made attempts to exclude Ulster or parts of Ulster from a Home Rule settlement and for that portion of Ireland to remain part of the union. From 1912 to 1919, the debates focused on the area to be excluded and the time period of that exclusion. During that time, Irish nationalism took a decisive turn towards support for complete independence from Britain. A Home Rule settlement was no longer considered an acceptable solution. The concept of granting two Home Rule parliaments only entered the political domain in 1919, through the Government of Ireland Bill, shortly after the ending of the First World War. Although initially sceptical, unionists soon warmed to the benefits of having their own devolved government. In one of the greatest ironies of Irish history, a Home Rule parliament was inaugurated in the north-east of Ireland before a solution was reached with the rest of Ireland. Six counties of Ulster, not the nine counties as originally proposed by the British government, formed a new political unit, Northern Ireland, in May 1921.

To create a new jurisdiction where one had never existed before was a colossal task. Falling mainly to Ernest Clark, supported by a team of no more than twenty, the machinery of the new administration was put in place from the time of his appointment in September 1920 to May 1921.

With the whole infrastructure of Irish government previously run from Dublin, Clark and his team had to create departments from nothing, and find staff and accommodation for those departments. With the withholding of the transfer of services, the northern government that was up and running by June 1921 had minimal powers and very little to do. Once powers were transferred, the northern government was able to focus on the issue that was most important to its survival: security. Aided by the British, particularly financially, the north became an effective police state, with thousands hired as Specials and RUC officers. The north survived attacks by the IRA in 1922 through its security apparatus as well as that of the British military. Luck also played a part with the start of the civil war in the south, diverting focus from the north.

Ulster unionists experienced extraordinary luck from the time of the third Home Rule Crisis right up to the Boundary Commission decision of 1925. The balance of power in British politics swung completely from Irish nationalism to Ulster unionism in that period. Practically every political decision went their way. They were excluded from a Dublin parliament. The 'sacrifice' they made of agreeing to a devolved government turned out to be far more beneficial for them than remaining solely in Westminster. The more manageable area of six, rather than nine, counties to make up Northern Ireland was agreed to. Their own police force, the Specials, and the partial Ernest Clark were put in place before the Government of Ireland Act 1920 became law. Services were transferred before a settlement was reached with the south. The northern government was allowed to govern as it saw fit, unimpeded by the British, who financed the north's bulging security apparatus and allowed it to limit rights for Catholics, introduce draconian laws and ignore illegal killings by the security forces. Under severe strain from the IRA in the first half of 1922, the start of the civil war in the south helped to secure the north's boundaries. Although refusing to select an appointee to the Boundary Commission, the person selected for them by the British could not have been more agreeable. Ulster unionists, although paranoid and vulnerable, were also decisive. Helped by the British government, who never acted as a neutral go-between as they often proclaimed, unionists stuck to their position of not giving an inch and never wavering.

Meanwhile, Sinn Féin was not decisive. Its approach to the north was simplistic, when it had an approach. It failed to capitalise on the vulnerability of the north, particularly before powers were transferred to Northern Ireland in November 1921. Sinn Féin agreed to the vague wording of Article 12 of the treaty on the Boundary Commission, which ultimately ensured that no northern territory was transferred to the Free State. Sinn Féin opposed coercion but did not engage with Ulster unionists. Sinn Féin tore itself asunder over sovereignty, its championing of northern nationalists ending with the civil war. The Free State introduced customs barriers in 1923, a decision that arguably cemented partition by putting real tangible form to it. Its handling of the Boundary Commission report in late 1925 perfectly encapsulates its policy on partition as willing to accept financial assistance to help its own territory at the expense of the plight of northern nationalists. It also gave up the Council of Ireland easily, which was the one available avenue through which cooperation between north and south could have been attained.

The partition of Ireland was the most significant moment in modern Irish history. The political ramifications of partition still exist within and beyond the island. At its worst, it was directly responsible for hundreds of deaths and injuries, most of them civilians, at the time of Northern Ireland's birth. Thousands were displaced from their homes, mainly Catholics in the north, but also Protestants in the north and south. Masses of people were forced from their jobs. Partition had huge ramifications for almost all aspects of Irish life. Two new justice systems were created, the northern one from scratch. The effects on the major religions were profound, with both jurisdictions adopting wholly different approaches to those religions, as clearly illustrated by both governments' policies on education. There were many day-to-day effects of partition, particularly after the imposition of customs barriers in 1923. Major disruptions were caused in crossing the border, whether from one county to another, from one town to another, or in some cases from one street to another. Checks and stops became the norm, whether by car or by train. Many organisations and societies were divided along partitionist lines, reflecting the new political realities.

And yet, many organisations and groups continued on as before. The partition of Ireland saw a multitude of reactions and approaches from a wide spectrum of groups and organisations. With the confusing nature of partition and the uncertainty surrounding the north's viability for much of its early years, it is little wonder that many bodies remained administered on an all-Ireland basis. The Catholic Church and the main Protestant religions remained all-Ireland bodies. Most trade unions maintained a thirty-two-county presence, as did most sports. One of the major sports that is divided along partitionist lines, soccer, is split mainly because of internal political reasons, not because of the partition of Ireland. Trade bodies, charities and other voluntary groups did not feel the need to split in two. They remained united for a variety of reasons, such as historical inertia, finance, self-interest and pragmatism. For bodies with a homogenous profile, there was little difficulty in remaining united. For those such as soccer and the labour movement, partition highlighted the differences amongst their membership. Many with a diverse demographic still remained united by acknowledging the changed circumstances and by introducing new structures to accommodate members based in Northern Ireland.

Politically, the new jurisdictions moved further and further apart. No organisation or group were beholden to national political decisions – they were free to make their own decisions for their members, without interference in almost all cases. Socially and culturally, there were many differences but also many links between north and south, links that remain to this day.

Endnotes

Introduction

1   S. Milligan, *Puckoon* (London: Penguin Books, 1963), pp. 81–2.
2   Ibid.

Chapter One

1   A. O'Day, *Irish Home Rule 1867–1921* (Manchester: Manchester University Press, 1998), p. 110.
2   R. Fanning, *Fatal Path: British Government and Irish Revolution 1910–1922* (London: Faber & Faber, 2013), p. 13.
3   I. Gibbons, *Drawing the Line: The Irish Border in British Politics* (London: Haus Publishing, 2018), pp. 19–20.
4   J. Loughlin, 'Creating "A Social and Geographical Fact": Regional Identity and the Ulster Question 1880s–1920s', *Past & Present* (No. 195, May 2007), p. 161 and Gibbons, *Drawing the Line*, p. 20.
5   O'Day, *Irish Home Rule*, pp. 183–96.
6   D. Fitzpatrick, *The Two Irelands 1912–1939* (Oxford: Oxford University Press, 1998), p. 9 and R. Lynch, *The Northern IRA and the Early Years of Partition, 1920–1922* (Dublin: Irish Academic Press, 2006), p. 9.
7   A. Jackson, *Home Rule: An Irish History 1800–2000* (London: Weidenfeld & Nicolson, 2003), p. 107.
8   Fanning, *Fatal Path*, pp. 45–6.
9   Jackson, *Home Rule*, p. 118.
10 Fanning, *Fatal Path*, p. 83.
11 E. Phoenix, *Northern Nationalism: Nationalist Politics, Partition and the Catholic Minority in Northern Ireland 1890–1940* (Belfast: Ulster Historical Foundation, 1994), p. xiv.
12 D.G. Boyce, 'British Conservative Opinion, the Ulster Question, and the Partition of Ireland, 1912–21', *Irish Historical Studies* (Vol. 17, No. 65, March 1970), p. 91.
13 Fanning, *Fatal Path*, p. 40.
14 O'Day, *Irish Home Rule*, p. 247.
15 N. Mansergh, *The Unresolved Question: The Anglo-Irish Settlement and Its Undoing 1912–72* (Yale: Yale University Press, 1991), p. 50.
16 A. Jackson, *Judging Redmond and Carson* (Dublin: Royal Irish Academy, 2018), p. 131.
17 Gibbons, *Drawing the Line*, p. 2.

18   Jackson, *Home Rule*, p. 123.

19   Jackson, *Judging Redmond and Carson*, p. 131.

20   O'Day, *Irish Home Rule*, p. 252.

21   Fanning, *Fatal Path*, p. 100.

22   M. Harris, *The Catholic Church and the Foundation of the Northern Irish State* (Cork: Cork University Press, 1993), p. 49.

23   Fanning, *Fatal Path*, p. 104.

24   B. O'Donoghue, *Activities Wise and Otherwise: The Career of Sir Henry Augustus Robinson 1898–1922* (Dublin: Irish Academic Press, 2015), p. 174.

25   Harris, *The Catholic Church and the Foundation of the Northern Irish State*, p. 49.

26   Fanning, *Fatal Path*, p. 104.

27   O'Donoghue, *Activities Wise and Otherwise*, pp. 181–83.

28   Jackson, *Judging Redmond and Carson*, p. 133.

29   I.S. Lustick, *Unsettled States, Disputed Lands: Britain and Ireland, France and Algeria, Israel and the West Bank-Gaza* (Ithaca: Cornell University Press, 1993), p. 207.

30   Fanning, *Fatal Path*, p. 116.

31   P. Buckland, *Irish Unionism: Two: Ulster Unionism and the Origins of Northern Ireland 1886–1922* (Dublin: Gill and Macmillan, 1973), p. 99.

32   Phoenix, *Northern Nationalism*, p. 15.

33   Ibid., pp. 15–16.

34   Fanning, *Fatal Path*, p. 130.

35   Phoenix, *Northern Nationalism*, p. 17.

36   Fanning, *Fatal Path*, p. 135.

37   O'Day, *Irish Home Rule*, p. 268.

38   Phoenix, *Northern Nationalism*, p. 21.

39   Buckland, *Irish Unionism*, p. 106.

40   Harris, *The Catholic Church and the Foundation of the Northern Irish State*, p. 55.

41   Phoenix, *Northern Nationalism*, p. 35.

42   O'Day, *Irish Home Rule*, p. 274.

43   O Donoghue, *Activities Wise and Otherwise*, p. 248.

44   Phoenix, *Northern Nationalism*, p. 35.

45   F.S.L. Lyons, *Ireland Since the Famine* (London: Fontana Press, 1985), p. 385.

46   D. Ferriter, *The Border: The Legacy of a Century of Anglo-Irish Politics* (London: Profile Books, 2019), p. 7.

47   Fanning, *Fatal Path*, p. 162.

48   Lyons, *Ireland Since the Famine*, p. 386.

49   R.B. McDowell, *The Irish Convention 1917–18* (London: Routledge and Kegan Paul Ltd, 1970), p. vii.

50   T. Hennessey, *Dividing Ireland: World War One and Partition* (London: Routledge, 1998), pp. 235–36.

51   M. Laffan, *The Partition of Ireland 1911–1925* (Dundalk: Dundalgan Press, 2004), p. 62.

52   For a full breakdown of the 1918 general election results, see *Irish Times*, 4 January 1919, p. 1 and p. 3.

53   M. Farrell, *Northern Ireland: The Orange State* (London: Pluto Press, 1980), p. 21.

54 O'Day, *Irish Home Rule*, p. 254.

55 Ibid., p. 293.

56 Mansergh, *The Unresolved Question*, p. 119.

57 R. Lynch, *Revolutionary Ireland, 1912–25* (London: Bloomsbury Publishing PLC, 2015), p. 94.

58 Fanning, *Fatal Path*, p. 190.

59 Laffan, *The Partition of Ireland 1911–1925*, p. 63.

Chapter Two

1   Fanning, *Fatal Path*, p. 202.

2   Mansergh, *The Unresolved Question*, p. 121.

3   J. Kendle, *Walter Long, Ireland and the Union, 1905–1920* (Canada: Glendale Publishing Ltd., 1992), p. 3.

4   P. Maume, Dictionary of Irish Biography, available from http://dib.cambridge.org/, accessed 9 April 2019.

5   Ibid.

6   Kendle, *Walter Long*, p. 164.

7   A. Jackson, Dictionary of Irish Biography, available from http://dib.cambridge.org/, accessed 9 April 2019.

8   Kendle, *Walter Long*, p. 174.

9   R. Murphy, 'Walter Long and the Making of the Government of Ireland Act, 1919–20', *Irish Historical Studies* (Vol. 25, No. 97, May 1986), p. 83.

10 Laffan, *The Partition of Ireland*, p. 62.

11 O'Day, *Irish Home Rule*, p. 294.

12 Mansergh, *The Unresolved Question*, p. 123.

13 Fanning, *Fatal Path*, p. 208.

14 Mansergh, *The Unresolved Question*, p. 124.

15 J. Coakley and L. O'Dowd, 'The Irish Border and North-South Cooperation', *Institute for British-Irish Studies* (Working Paper No. 47, 2005), p. 7.

16 Ibid.

17 Ferriter, *The Border*, p. 30.

18 Kendle, *Walter Long*, p. 176.

19 P.J. Dempsey, Dictionary of Irish Biography, available from http://dib.cambridge.org/, accessed 10 April 2019.

20 *The Times*, 24 July 1919, p. 13.

21 *Irish Times*, 26 July 1919, p. 6.

22 *The Times*, 28 July 1919, p. 12.

23 Fanning, *Fatal Path*, p. 208.

24 Phoenix, *Northern Nationalism*, p. 76.

25 Fanning, *Fatal Path*, p. 216.

26 O'Day, *Irish Home Rule*, p. 295.

27 B.A. Follis, *A State Under Siege: The Establishment of Northern Ireland, 1920–1925* (Oxford, Clarendon Press, 1995), p. 2.

28 See O'Day, *Irish Home Rule*, p. 296 and Follis, *A State Under Siege*, p. 1.

29 C. Fitzpatrick, 'Partition, Postal Services and Ulster Unionist Politics 1921–27', *International Journal of Regional and Local History* (1 June 2016), p. 11.

30 M. Kennedy, *Division and Consensus: The Politics of Cross-Border Relations in Ireland, 1925–1969* (Dublin: Institute of Public Administration, 2000), p. 6.

31 Phoenix, *Northern Nationalism*, p. 72.

32 Fanning, *Fatal Path*, p. 204.

33 Mansergh, *The Unresolved Question*, p. 125.

34 O'Day, *Irish Home Rule*, p. 298.

35 Laffan, *The Partition of Ireland*, p. 66.

36 Farrell, *Northern Ireland*, p. 24.

37 T. Dooley, *The Irish Revolution, 1912–23: Monaghan* (Dublin: Four Courts Press, 2017), p. 98.

38 Buckland, *Irish Unionism*, p. 118.

39 D. Gwynn, *The History of Partition (1912–1925)* (Dublin: The Richview Press, 1950), p. 190.

40 Buckland, *Irish Unionism*, p. 121.

41 Dooley, *The Irish Revolution*, p. 98.

42 PRONI – D1098/1/2 – Minute Book of the Ulster Women's Unionist Council Executive Committee, 30 March 1920, 23 April 1920 and 6 July 1920.

43 *Freeman's Journal*, 27 January 1920, p. 1.

44 UK National Archives – PRO 30/67/40 – Papers and Correspondence Relating to the Disruption of the Irish Unionist Alliance and the Formation of the Unionist Anti-Partition League, undated.

45 Fanning, *Fatal Path*, p. 212.

46 Ibid.

47 Mansergh, *The Unresolved Question*, p. 130 and Fanning, *Fatal Path*, pp. 214–15.

48 Follis, *A State Under Siege*, p. 3.

49 Fanning, *Fatal Path*, p. 220.

50 Mansergh, *The Unresolved Question*, p. 138.

51 *Freeman's Journal*, 3 February 1920, p. 3.

52 *Freeman's Journal*, 1 June 1920, p. 2.

53 *Irish News*, 7 January 1921, p. 4.

54 *The Times*, 1 June 1920, p. 18.

55 *Irish Times*, 23 October 1919, p. 4.

56 Ibid., 30 December 1920, p. 5.

57 Ibid., 2 February 1921, p. 4.

58 T. Hennessey, *A History of Northern Ireland 1920–1996* (Dublin: Gill and Macmillan, 1997), p. 8.

59 I. Gibbons, 'Labour and Irish Revolution: From Investigation to Deportation', in L. Marley (ed.), *The British Labour Party and Twentieth-Century Ireland: The Cause of Ireland, the Cause of Labour* (Manchester: Manchester University Press, 2016), p. 76.

60 *Punch*, 7 April 1920, p. 273.

61 Phoenix, *Northern Nationalism*, p. 78.

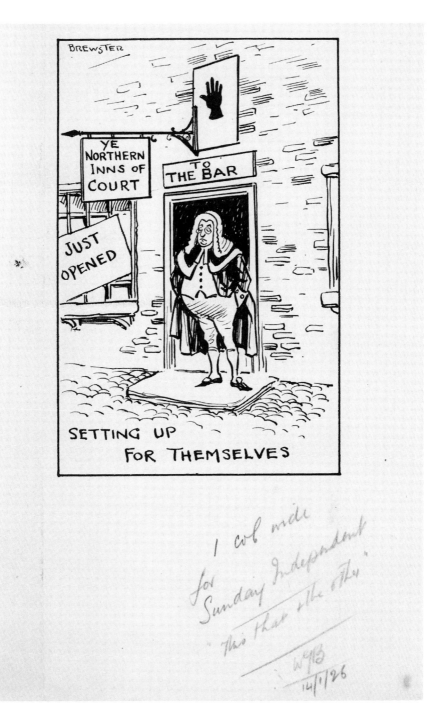

A Gordon Brewster cartoon published in the *Sunday Independent* in January 1926 showing that the Bar in Northern Ireland would no longer have barristers qualify from the King's Inns in Dublin, establishing its own Inns of Court instead. Before 1926, barristers, north and south, qualified through the King's Inns. (Courtesy of the National Library of Ireland)

BELFAST TRADE BOYCOTT

Warning to Irishmen and Irishwomen . . .

In view of the convening of the Partition "Parliament" at Belfast, it has been decreed that NO NOTES OR CHEQUES ON ANY OF THE FOLLOWING BANKS ARE TO BE ACCEPTED UNDER ANY CONDITIONS AFTER THE 7th JUNE, 1921.

THE ULSTER BANK
THE NORTHERN BANK
THE BELFAST BANK

Any such Notes or Cheques seized on or after that date will be confiscated.

All persons in possession of such Notes or Cheques should immediately dispose of them.

By Order,

Belfast Boycott Committee.

A poster warning Irishmen and Irishwomen not to deal with banks headquartered in Belfast. After the expulsion of Catholic workers from the Belfast shipyards in the summer of 1920, Dáil Éireann imposed a boycott on Belfast goods and firms. Whilst its economic effects to hamper trade in Belfast met with mixed results, the boycott's aim to unify Ireland was an unmitigated disaster. (Courtesy of the National Library of Ireland)

A goods train derailed on the Great Northern Railway line from Dundalk to Enniskillen in 1922, where two wagons containing goods were burned. As part of the Belfast Boycott campaign, IRA and Cumann na mBan members raided trains and destroyed goods. The Great Northern Railway was forced to close its routes from Dundalk to Enniskillen due to the kidnapping of drivers who delivered Belfast goods. (Courtesy of the National Library of Ireland)

The Royal Ulster Constabulary (RUC) and customs officers at a border customs post in Killeen, near Newry, around 1930. The introduction of customs barriers by the Irish Free State government in 1923 helped to cement partition, making it tangible and real. Movement and trade were curtailed across the border as a result, impeding long established economic and social ties. (Courtesy of the Museum of the Police Service of Northern Ireland)

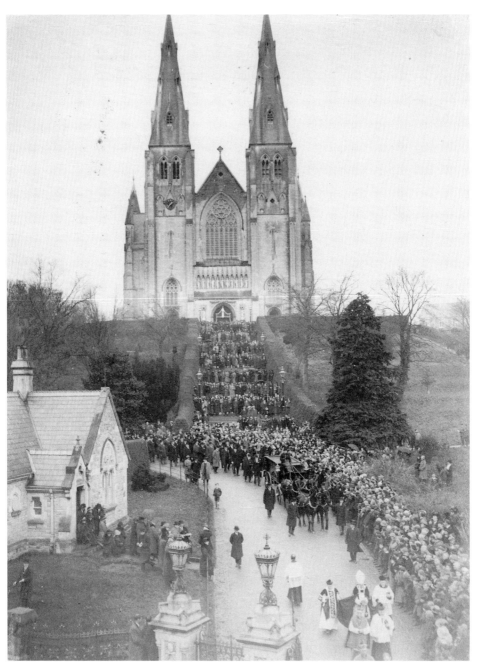

The funeral of the late Catholic Primate of All-Ireland, Cardinal Michael Logue, outside Armagh Cathedral in November 1924. The Catholic Church was trenchantly opposed to partition and remained an all-Ireland body. The main Protestant religions remained 32-county bodies too. Of all organisations that were all-Ireland bodies before partition, religious ones had the highest number that remained so after the founding of the two Irish jurisdictions. (Courtesy of the National Library of Ireland)

Lord Londonderry, the first Minister of Education of Northern Ireland, under a portrait of his ancestor Lord Castlereagh, who it was claimed he aped with his mannerisms from a different century. His attempts to secularise education in Northern Ireland met with fierce opposition from the Catholic and Protestant religions, and were ultimately thwarted. (Courtesy of the Public Record Office of Northern Ireland and Lady Rose Lauritzen)

Members of the executive committee of the Irish Transport and General Workers' Union (ITGWU) and delegates to the Irish Trades Union Congress (ITUC) in Waterford in August 1918. The Labour movement was faced with many challenges when Ireland was partitioned. The movement included a divergent group of people who had to operate under enormous sectarian and political pressures. Partial union was achieved, particularly within trade unionism, by clinging to core interests and by offering a large degree of autonomy to Northern Irish labour activists. (Courtesy of the National Library of Ireland)

Carlingford Lough from Rostrevor in County Down. Demonstrating the haphazard way in which the border was drawn up, no boundary was delimited at any point for either Lough Carlingford or Lough Foyle. Nobody knew where the border line was on various waterways straddling the border as a result. This led to many disputes, particularly over fishing rights. (Courtesy of the National Library of Ireland)

The Lisnaskea Post Office in County Fermanagh. The northern government found it difficult to assert its independence from the rest of Ireland on the issue of postal services. Residents in border areas in the north were reliant on Free State post offices to deliver their mail. Sensitive mail for security forces were routed through Free State post offices and mail from Britain was delivered via the Holyhead–Kingstown (present-day Dún Laoghaire) route to different locales in Northern Ireland. (Courtesy of the National Library of Ireland)

A Gordon Brewster cartoon published in the *Evening Herald* in July 1926 showing that Northern Ireland was stopped from hosting rugby internationals due to the introduction of an entertainments tax in the north that was not in the Irish Free State. This was only a temporary measure with rugby internationals resuming in Ravenhill in Belfast shortly afterwards. The Irish Rugby Football Union (IRFU) went to great lengths to retain its all-island status by accommodating its northern branch. (Courtesy of the National Library of Ireland)

A women's tennis match in County Armagh in 1920. Tennis, like most sports in Ireland, remained governed on an all-island basis after partition. (Courtesy of the Public Record Office of Northern Ireland)

62 Ibid., p. 79.

63 Farrell, *Northern Ireland*, p. 22.

64 Phoenix, *Northern Nationalism*, p. 65.

65 C. Townshend, *The Republic: The Fight for Irish Independence* (London: Penguin Books, 2013), pp. 172–73.

66 Follis, *A State Under Siege*, p. 3.

67 PR had first been trialled in the Sligo borough election of January 1919. See P. Deignan, 'PR & the Sligo Borough Election of January 1919', *History Ireland* (Vol. 17, No. 3, May–June 2009).

68 A. Grant, *The Irish Revolution 1912–23: Derry* (Dublin: Four Courts Press, 2018), p. 92.

69 F. McCluskey, *The Irish Revolution, 1912–23: Tyrone* (Dublin: Four Courts Press, 2014), p. 80.

70 Farrell, *Northern Ireland*, p. 25.

71 B. O'Leary, '"Cold House": The Unionist Counter-Revolution and the Invention of Northern Ireland', in J. Crowley, D. Ó Drisceoil and M. Murphy (eds), *Atlas of the Irish Revolution* (Cork: Cork University Press, 2017), p. 822.

72 Buckland, *Irish Unionism*, p. 142.

73 J. Bardon, *A History of Ulster* (Belfast: The Blackstaff Press, 2001), p. 500.

74 Farrell, *Northern Ireland*, p. 25.

75 Grant, *The Irish Revolution*, p. 94.

76 Lynch, *The Northern IRA and the Early Years of Partition*, p. 25.

77 A.F. Parkinson, *Belfast's Unholy War: The Troubles of the 1920s* (Dublin: Four Courts Press, 2004), p. 23.

78 Grant, *The Irish Revolution*, p. 101.

79 Parkinson, *Belfast's Unholy War*, p. 24.

80 J. McDermott, *Northern Divisions: The Old IRA and the Belfast Pogroms 1920–22* (Belfast: Beyond the Pale Publications Ltd, 2001), p. 31.

81 Parkinson, *Belfast's Unholy War*, p. 24.

82 Lynch, *The Northern IRA and the Early Years of Partition*, p. 20.

83 P. Lawlor, *The Outrages 1920–1922: The IRA and the Ulster Special Constabulary in the Border Campaign* (Cork: Mercier Press, 2011), pp. 21–28.

84 K. Glennon, *From Pogrom to Civil War: Tom Glennon and the Belfast IRA* (Cork: Mercier Press, 2013), p. 27.

85 Parkinson, *Belfast's Unholy War*, p. 27.

86 P. Long, Dictionary of Irish Biography, available from http://dib.cambridge.org/, accessed 10 April 2019.

87 Parkinson, *Belfast's Unholy War*, p. 28.

88 Lynch, *The Northern IRA and the Early Years of Partition*, p. 27 and Glennon, *From Pogrom to Civil War*, p. 30.

89 Parkinson, *Belfast's Unholy War*, p. 33.

90 Ibid.

91 McDermott, *Northern Divisions*, p. 35.

92 P. Bew, P. Gibbon and H. Patterson, *Northern Ireland 1921–1994: Political Forces and Social Classes* (London: Serif, 1995), p. 26.

93 Farrell, *Northern Ireland*, p. 29.
94 McDermott, *Northern Divisions*, p. 35.
95 Lynch, *The Northern IRA and the Early Years of Partition*, p. 29.
96 Ibid.
97 McDermott, *Northern Divisions*, p. 39.
98 House of Commons Debate, 11 November 1920, vol. 134 cols 1452-5, available from http://hansard.millbanksystems.com, accessed 10 April 2019.
99 Follis, *A State Under Siege*, p. 9.

Chapter Three

1 T. Bowman, *Carson's Army: The Ulster Volunteer Force, 1910–22* (Manchester: Manchester University Press, 2007), p. 190.
2 PRONI – D1022/2/3 – File entitled, 'Fermanagh Vigilance Force', 28 September 1920.
3 A. Hezlet, *The 'B' Specials: A History of The Ulster Special Constabulary* (London: Tom Stacey Ltd., 1972), p. 11.
4 Bowman, *Carson's Army*, p. 192.
5 J. McColgan, *British Policy and the Irish Administration 1920–22* (London: George Allen & Unwin, 1983), p. 25.
6 M. Farrell, *Arming the Protestants: The Formation of the Ulster Special Constabulary and the Royal Ulster Constabulary, 1920–7* (London: Pluto Press, 1983), p. 13.
7 UK National Archives – The British in Ireland: Dublin Castle Records – Irish Government. Judicial Proceedings, Enquiries and Miscellaneous Records, 1872–1926, 1920 CO 904/185, p. 103.
8 Lynch, *The Northern IRA and the Early Years of Partition*, p. 34.
9 Glennon, *From Pogrom to Civil War*, p. 32.
10 Farrell, *Northern Ireland*, p. 31.
11 McColgan, *British Policy and the Irish Administration*, p. 26.
12 Fanning, *Fatal Path*, p. 235.
13 Ibid.
14 Mansergh, *The Unresolved Question*, p. 154.
15 McColgan, *British Policy and the Irish Administration*, p. 27.
16 Ibid.
17 Lynch, *Revolutionary Ireland*, p. 101.
18 PRONI – D1022/2/9 – File entitled, 'Special Constabulary: table of progress, S.C. scheme', 30 November 1920.
19 Lynch, *Revolutionary Ireland*, p. 101.
20 Hezlet, *The 'B' Specials*, p. 22.
21 *The Times*, 17 September 1920, p. 8.
22 P. Maume, Dictionary of Irish Biography, available from http://dib.cambridge.org/, accessed 12 April 2019.
23 McColgan, *British Policy and the Irish Administration*, p. 85.
24 J. Reynolds, Australian Dictionary of Biography, available from http://adb.anu.edu.au/biography/clark-sir-ernest-5661/text9557, accessed 12 April 2019.

25 PRONI – D1022/2/2 – Files entitled, 'N. Ireland consecutive draft', including accounts of Clark's first impressions of Dublin and Northern Ireland, undated.

26 Ibid.

27 Ibid.

28 Ibid.

29 Ibid.

30 McColgan, *British Policy and the Irish Administration*, p. 27.

31 PRONI – D1022/2/4 – Files containing copies of papers relating to two conferences between the Chief Secretary of Ireland, Sir Hamar Greenwood, the Standing Committee of the Ulster Unionist Council, and representatives of trade unions and labour organisations, 13 October 1920.

32 Ibid.

33 Ibid.

34 M. Maguire, *The Civil Service and the Revolution in Ireland 1912–1938: 'Shaking the Blood-Stained Hand of Mr Collins'* (Manchester: Manchester University Press, 2009), p. 56.

35 PRONI – D1022/2/4 – Files containing copies of papers relating to two conferences between the Chief Secretary of Ireland, Sir Hamar Greenwood, the Standing Committee of the Ulster Unionist Council, and representatives of trade unions and labour organisations, 13 October 1920.

36 McColgan, *British Policy and the Irish Administration*, p. 31.

37 PRONI – D1022/2/2 – Files entitled, 'N. Ireland consecutive draft', including accounts of Clark's first impressions of Dublin and Northern Ireland, undated.

38 PRONI – D1022/2/17 – Files of Correspondence, mainly between Clark and Sir James Craig, Dealing with Various Aspects of the Setting Up of the Northern Ireland Ministries and Departments – 1921–1922, 8 March 1921.

39 For ample evidence on the sheer volume of work undertaken by Clark and his team to see the new government in Northern Ireland realised, see PRONI – D1022/2/17 – Files of Correspondence, mainly between Clark and Sir James Craig, Dealing with Various Aspects of the Setting Up of the Northern Ireland Ministries and Departments – 1921–1922.

40 Follis, *A State Under Siege*, p. 31.

41 Ibid., p. 25.

42 P. Buckland, *The Factory of Grievances: Devolved Government in Northern Ireland 1921–39* (Dublin: Gill and Macmillan, 1979), p. 9.

43 See PRONI – D1022/2/17 – Files of Correspondence, mainly between Clark and Sir James Craig, Dealing with Various Aspects of the Setting Up of the Northern Ireland Ministries and Departments – 1921–1922 and D1022/2/14 – Copy Correspondence of Clark Concerning Procedural Matters in Connection with Setting up of the Northern Ireland Parliament – April 1921–June 1921.

44 McColgan, *British Policy and the Irish Administration*, p. 55.

45 PRONI – D1022/2/17 – Files of Correspondence, mainly between Clark and Sir James Craig, Dealing with Various Aspects of the Setting Up of the Northern Ireland Ministries and Departments – 1921–1922, 7 April 1921.

46 McColgan, *British Policy and the Irish Administration*, p. 55.

47 Jackson, *Judging Redmond and Carson*, p. 201.

48 McColgan, *British Policy and the Irish Administration*, p. 55.

49 PRONI – D1022/2/2 – Files entitled, 'N. Ireland consecutive draft', including accounts of Clark's first impressions of Dublin and Northern Ireland, undated.

50 T.A.M. Dooley, 'From the Belfast Boycott to the Boundary Commission: Fears and Hopes in County Monaghan, 1920–26', *Clogher Record* (Vol. 15, No. 1, 1994), p. 90.

51 D.S. Johnson, 'The Belfast Boycott, 1920–1922', in J.M. Goldstrom and L.A. Clarkson (eds), *Irish Population, Economy, and Society: Essays in Honour of the late K.H. Connell* (Oxford: Clarendon Press, 1981), p. 287.

52 *Westmeath Independent*, 31 January 1920, p. 4.

53 *Anglo-Celt*, 20 December 1920, p. 1.

54 Laffan, *The Partition of Ireland*, p. 77.

55 Dáil Éireann Debates, Vol. F, No. 16, 6 August 1920, available from www.oireachtas-debates.gov.ie, accessed 13 April 2019.

56 Dublin City Archives – Minutes of the Municipal Council of the City of Dublin 1920, 13 September 1920; Dooley, 'From the Belfast Boycott to the Boundary Commission', p. 91; and B. Hughes, *Defying the IRA? Intimidation, Coercion, and Communities During the Irish Revolution* (Liverpool: Liverpool University Press, 2016), p. 87.

57 Johnson, 'The Belfast Boycott', p. 294.

58 McColgan, *British Policy and the Irish Administration*, p. 53.

59 Follis, *A State Under Siege*, p. 6.

60 *Strabane Chronicle*, 29 January 1921, p. 3.

61 *Irish Times*, 15 November 1920, p. 4.

62 *Donegal News*, 22 January 1921, p. 1.

63 *Irish Times*, 22 January 1921, p. 6.

64 Ibid., 20 January 1921, p. 6.

65 Ibid., 5 April 1920, p. 6.

66 Ibid., 11 February 1921, p. 4.

67 Ibid., 2 March 1921, p. 6.

68 Bureau of Military History, 1913–21, Document No. W.S. 1,099, available from http://www.bureauofmilitaryhistory.ie/, accessed 11 January 2019.

69 Maguire, *The Civil Service and the Revolution in Ireland 1912–1938*, p. 107.

70 *Irish Times*, 22 May 1922, p. 8.

71 Maguire, *The Civil Service and the Revolution in Ireland 1912–1938*, p. 93.

72 M.E. Daly, *The First Department: A History of the Department of Agriculture* (Dublin: Institute of Public Administration, 2002), p. 95.

73 Ibid., p. 92.

74 *Irish Times*, 15 September 1920, p. 4.

75 *Freeman's Journal*, 10 May 1921, p. 6.

76 *Irish Times*, 11 February 1921, p. 4.

77 *Freeman's Journal*, 26 March 1921, p. 4.

78 *Irish News*, 19 March 1921, p. 6.

79 *Freeman's Journal*, 15 April 1921, p. 6.

80 Ibid., 26 April 1921, p. 2.

81 *Manchester Guardian*, 19 April 1921, p. 6.

Chapter Four

1   Bureau of Military History, 1913–21, Document No. W.S. 264, available from http://www. bureauofmilitaryhistory.ie/, accessed 13 April 2019.

2   J.M. Curran, *The Birth of the Irish Free State 1921–1923* (Alabama: The University of Alabama Press, 1980), p. 53.

3   D. McCullagh, *De Valera: Rise 1882–1932* (Dublin: Gill Books, 2017), p. 174.

4   K. Inoue, 'Sinn Féin Propaganda and the "Partition Election", 1921', *Studia Hibernica* (No. 30, 1998/1999), p. 51.

5   *Irish News*, 23 May 1921, p. 7.

6   D. Hall, 'Partition and County Louth', *Journal of the County Louth Archaeological and Historical Society* (Vol. 27, No. 2, 2010), p. 276.

7   Lynch, *Revolutionary Ireland*, p. 96.

8   Inoue, 'Sinn Féin Propaganda and the "Partition Election"', p. 52.

9   *Belfast Newsletter*, 10 May 1921, p. 4.

10 Ibid.

11 Inoue, 'Sinn Féin Propaganda and the "Partition Election"', p. 55.

12 Ibid., p. 54.

13 PRONI – D921/2/1 – Correspondence, Telegrams and Accounts Concerning the South Down Election – 1921, 24 May 1921.

14 PRONI – D1098/1/2 – Minute Book of the Ulster Women's Unionist Council Executive Committee, 4 January 1921, 25 January 1921 and 3 January 1922.

15 Ibid., 25 January 1921.

16 Ibid., 1 March 1921.

17 In the Southern Ireland election of 1921, of the 128 people elected unopposed, six were women: Countess Constance Markievicz, Kathleen Clarke, Ada English, Mary MacSwiney, Kathleen O'Callaghan and Margaret Pearse.

18 Inoue, 'Sinn Féin Propaganda and the "Partition Election"', p. 53.

19 Fanning, *Fatal Path*, p. 255.

20 Farrell, *Northern Ireland*, p. 39.

21 PRONI – D1022/2/17 – Files of Correspondence, mainly between Clark and Sir James Craig, Dealing with Various Aspects of the Setting Up of the Northern Ireland Ministries and Departments – 1921–1922, 28 May 1921.

22 Gwynn, *The History of Partition*, p.193.

23 *Irish Times*, 28 December 1921, p. 7.

24 Laffan, *The Partition of Ireland*, p. 70.

25 *Irish Times*, 28 December 1921, p. 7.

26 A. Greer, 'Sir James Craig and the Construction of Parliament Buildings at Stormont', *Irish Historical Studies* (Vol. 31, No. 123, May 1999), pp. 373–76.

27 PRONI – CAB 4/25, 24 October 1921.

28 Northern Ireland House of Common Debates, Vol. 1 (1921), 7 June 1921, p. 6, available from http://stormontpapers.ahds.ac.uk, accessed 15 April 2019.

29 Hennessey, *A History of Northern Ireland*, p. 9.

30 Buckland, *Irish Unionism*, p. 125.

31 Ibid., p. 125.

32 *Irish Times*, 8 June 1921, p. 6.

33 PRONI – CAB 4/1, 15 June 1921.

34 R. Lynch, *The Partition of Ireland 1918–1925* (Cambridge: Cambridge University Press, 2019), p. 76.

35 O. Rafferty, 'The Catholic Church and Partition, 1918–22', *Irish Studies Review* (Vol. 5, No. 2, Autumn 2007), p. 14.

36 Fanning, *Fatal Path*, p. 258.

37 Ibid., p. 257.

38 Northern Ireland House of Common Debates, Vol. 1 (1921), 23 June 1921, p. 21, available from http://stormontpapers.ahds.ac.uk, accessed 15 April 2019.

39 Lynch, *The Partition of Ireland*, p. 134.

40 D. Hall, 'Politics and Revolution in County Louth, 1912–1923', in D. Hall and M. Maguire (eds), *County Louth and the Irish Revolution 1912–1923* (Dublin: Irish Academic Press, 2017), p. 13.

41 PRONI – CAB 4/4, 23 June 1921.

42 PRONI – CAB 4/7, 4 July 1921.

43 Ibid.

44 Ibid.

45 Ibid.

46 Lynch, *The Northern IRA and the Early Years of Partition*, p. 80.

47 Glennon, *From Pogrom to Civil War*, pp. 68–69 and Farrell, *Northern Ireland*, p. 41.

48 Lynch, *The Northern IRA and the Early Years of Partition*, p. 79.

49 PRONI – CAB 4/9, 15 July 1921.

50 Farrell, *Arming the Protestants*, p. 58.

51 Glennon, *From Pogrom to Civil War*, p. 85.

52 Lynch, *The Northern IRA and the Early Years of Partition, 1920–1922*, p. 81 and Glennon, *From Pogrom to Civil War*, p. 90.

53 Glennon, *From Pogrom to Civil War*, p. 91.

54 Buckland, *Irish Unionism*, p. 132.

55 Buckland, *The Factory of Grievances*, p. 2.

56 Buckland, *Irish Unionism*, p. 134.

57 Hennessey, *A History of Northern Ireland 1920–1996*, p. 9.

58 McColgan, *British Policy and the Irish Administration 1920–22*, p. 54.

59 *Fermanagh Herald*, 4 June 1921, p. 5.

60 *Freeman's Journal*, 15 November 1921, p. 2.

61 *Cork Examiner*, 16 September 1921, p. 5.

62 *Irish Times*, 29 November 1921, p. 6.

63 McColgan, *British Policy and the Irish Administration*, p. 63.

64 PRONI – CAB 4/15, 23 August 1921.

65 *Irish Times*, 27 September 1921, p. 5.

66 Northern Ireland House of Common Debates, Vol. 1 (1921), 20 September 1921, p. 46, available from http://stormontpapers.ahds.ac.uk, accessed 16 April 2019.

67 McColgan, *British Policy and the Irish Administration*, p. 58.

68 Ibid., p. 56.

69 PRONI – CAB 4/15, 23 August 1921.

70 PRONI – CAB 4/12, 4 August 1921.

71 R. Fanning, *The Irish Department of Finance 1922–58* (Dublin: Institute of Public Administration, 1978), p. 80.

Chapter Five

1   J. Bowman, *De Valera and the Ulster Question 1917–1973* (Oxford: Oxford University Press, 1989), p. 31.

2   Ferriter, *The Border*, p. 13.

3   A. Dolan and W. Murphy, *Michael Collins: The Man and the Revolution* (Cork: The Collins Press, 2018), p. 194.

4   Bowman, *De Valera and the Ulster Question*, p. 32.

5   Ibid., p. 34.

6   E. Phoenix, 'Cahir Healy (1877–1970): Northern Nationalist Leader', *Clogher Record* (Vol. 18, No. 1, 2003), p. 46.

7   D. Ferriter, *Judging Dev: A Reassessment of the Life and Legacy of Eamon de Valera* (Dublin: Royal Irish Academy, 2007), p. 149.

8   Bowman, *De Valera and the Ulster Question*, pp. 34 and 52.

9   Fanning, *Fatal Path*, p. 253.

10 McCullagh, *De Valera: Rise*, p. 203.

11 Bowman, *De Valera and the Ulster Question*, p. 47.

12 PRONI – D1022/2/14 – Copy Correspondence of Clark Concerning Procedural Matters in Connection with Setting up of the Northern Ireland Parliament – April 1921–June 1921, 9 May 1921.

13 McColgan, *British Policy and the Irish Administration*, p. 54.

14 Bowman, *De Valera and the Ulster Question*, p. 50.

15 UCD Archives – Ernest Blythe Papers – P24/22 – Office Correspondence Relating to the Peace Negotiations, June–September 1921, 28 June 1921.

16 PRONI – CAB 4/6, 28 June 1921.

17 Bowman, *De Valera and the Ulster Question*, p. 49.

18 Fanning, *Fatal Path*, p. 264.

19 O'Leary, 'Cold House', p. 818.

20 Bowman, *De Valera and the Ulster Question*, p. 51.

21 PRONI – CAB 4/10, 21 July 1921.

22 Ibid., 21 July 1921.

23 Ibid., 22 July 1921.

24 PRONI – CAB 4/12, 4 August 1921.

25 O'Day, *Irish Home Rule*, p. 302.

26 UCD Archives – Ernest Blythe Papers – P24/22 – Office Correspondence Relating to the Peace Negotiations, June–September 1921, 10 August 1921.

27 Dáil Éireann Debates, Vol. S, No. 4, 22 August 1921, available from www.oireachtas-debates.gov.ie, accessed 19 April 2019.

28 Ibid.

29 Bowman, *De Valera and the Ulster Question*, p. 56.

30 Ibid., pp. 56–57.

31 Grant, *The Irish Revolution*, p. 126.

32 Fanning, *Fatal Path*, p. 278.

33 Bardon, *A History of Ulster*, p. 483.

34 McColgan, *British Policy and the Irish Administration*, p. 65.

35 Ferriter, *The Border*, p. 12.

36 O'Day, *Irish Home Rule*, p. 302.

37 McColgan, *British Policy and the Irish Administration*, p. 65.

38 Gibbons, *Drawing the Line*, p. 46.

39 Fanning, *Fatal Path*, p. 282.

40 Ibid., p. 280.

41 Ibid., pp. 284 and 288.

42 Bardon, *A History of Ulster*, p. 483.

43 *Chicago Daily Tribune*, 14 December 1921, p. 9.

44 Ferriter, *The Border*, p. 14.

45 Fanning, *Fatal Path*, p. 296.

46 *The Times*, 22 November 1921, p. 10.

47 PRONI – CAB 4/10, 21 July 1921.

48 Maguire, *The Civil Service and the Revolution in Ireland*, p. 111.

49 McColgan, *British Policy and the Irish Administration*, p. 64.

50 Kennedy, *Division and Consensus*, p. 6.

51 D. Kennedy, *The Widening Gulf: Northern Attitudes to the Independent Irish State 1919–49* (Belfast: The Blackstaff Press, 1988), p. 1.

52 PRONI – CAB 4/12, 4 August 1921.

53 O. McGee, *Arthur Griffith* (Dublin: Merrion Press, 2015), p. 265.

54 Fanning, *Fatal Path*, p. 285.

55 McGee, *Arthur Griffith*, p. 265.

56 McColgan, *British Policy and the Irish Administration*, p. 69.

57 Ibid.

58 Maguire, *The Civil Service and the Revolution in Ireland*, pp. 113–14.

59 McColgan, *British Policy and the Irish Administration*, p. 79.

60 Maguire, *The Civil Service and the Revolution in Ireland*, p. 110.

61 Northern Ireland House of Common Debates, Vol. 1 (1921), 29 November 1921, p. 290, available from www. http://stormontpapers.ahds.ac.uk, accessed 19 April 2019.

62 Grant, *The Irish Revolution*, p. 123.

63 *The Times*, 22 November 1921, p. 10.

64 G. H. Smith, *Sketch of the Supreme Court of Judicature of Northern Ireland: From its Establishment Under the Imperial Act of 1920 Down to the Present Time* (Belfast: Northern Whig, 1926), p. 9.

65 D. Ó Beacháin, *From Partition to Brexit: The Irish Government and Northern Ireland* (Manchester: Manchester University Press, 2019), p. 12.

66 Fanning, *Fatal Path*, p. 293.

67 Bowman, *De Valera and the Ulster Question*, p. 63.

68 Fanning, *Fatal Path*, p. 293.

69 Ó Beacháin, *From Partition to Brexit*, p. 22.

70 Lynch, *Revolutionary Ireland*, p. 102.

71 R. Lynch, 'The Boundary Commission', in J. Crowley, D. Ó Drisceoil and M. Murphy (eds), *Atlas of the Irish Revolution* (Cork: Cork University Press, 2017) p. 828.

72 F. Pakenham (Lord Longford), *Peace by Ordeal* (London: Sidgwick & Jackson, 1972), p. 254.

73 M. Hopkinson, 'The Craig-Collins Pacts of 1922: Two Attempted Reforms of the Northern Ireland Government', *Irish Historical Studies* (Vol. 27, No. 106, November 1990), p. 146.

74 PRONI – CAB 4/29, 10 January 1922.

75 Ibid.

76 P. Murray, 'Partition and the Irish Boundary Commission: A Northern Nationalist Perspective', *Clogher Record* (Vol. 18, No. 2, 2004), p. 182.

77 Gwynn, *The History of Partition*, p. 203.

78 D. P. Barritt and C. F. Carter, *The Northern Ireland Problem: A Study in Group Relations* (Oxford: Oxford University Press, 1972), p. 17.

79 Buckland, *Irish Unionism*, p. 153.

80 Bardon, *A History of Ulster*, p. 486.

81 McCullagh, *De Valera: Rise*, p. 257.

82 Hall, 'Partition and County Louth', p. 261.

83 Laffan, *The Partition of Ireland*, p. 91.

Chapter Six

1 Lynch, *Revolutionary Ireland*, p. 107.

2 Buckland, *Irish Unionism*, p. 124.

3 Bardon, *A History of Ulster*, pp. 496–97.

4 O'Leary, 'Cold House', p. 823.

5 Bardon, *A History of Ulster*, p. 496.

6 Ibid.

7 Ibid., p. 498.

8 Ibid.

9 Lynch, *Revolutionary Ireland*, p. 100.

10 Buckland, *The Factory of Grievances*, p. 21.

11 B. Hourican, Dictionary of Irish Biography, available from http://dib.cambridge.org/, accessed 23 April 2019. Countess Markievicz served as Minister of Labour in the Sinn Féin counter-government from 1919–1921. The next woman appointed to the cabinet in the twenty-six counties was Máire Geoghegan-Quinn in 1979.

12 M. Hill, 'Women in Northern Ireland, 1922–39', in J. Crowley, D. Ó Drisceoil and M. Murphy (eds), *Atlas of the Irish Revolution*, p. 833.

13 PRONI – CAB 4/116, 12 June 1924.

14 PRONI – D1098/1/2 – Minute Book of the Ulster Women's Unionist Council Executive Committee, 20 September 1921.

15 Ibid., 6 October 1921.

16 Hill, 'Women in Northern Ireland, 1922–39', p. 834.

17 Ibid., p. 835.

18 Hourican, Dictionary of Irish Biography, available from http://dib.cambridge.org/, accessed 23 April 2019.

19 Northern Ireland House of Common Debates, Vol. 2 (1922), 17 October 1922, pp. 1047–48, available from http://stormontpapers.ahds.ac.uk, accessed 25 April 2019.

20 Buckland, *Irish Unionism*, p. 152.

21 Phoenix, 'Cahir Healy', p. 38.

22 McCluskey, *The Irish Revolution*, p. 105.

23 Grant, *The Irish Revolution*, p. 126.

24 McCluskey, *The Irish Revolution*, p. 105.

25 PRONI – CAB 4/28, 1 December 1921.

26 Bardon, *A History of Ulster*, p. 499.

27 McCluskey, *The Irish Revolution*, p. 125.

28 Grant, *The Irish Revolution*, p. 126.

29 Phoenix, 'Cahir Healy', p. 38.

30 Grant, *The Irish Revolution*, p. 127.

31 Ibid., p. 128.

32 Bardon, *A History of Ulster*, pp. 499–500.

33 O'Leary, 'Cold House', pp. 821–22.

34 Bardon, *A History of Ulster*, p. 500.

35 Ibid.

36 J. O'Brien, *Discrimination in Northern Ireland, 1920–1939: Myth or Reality?* (Newcastle upon Tyne: Cambridge Scholars Publishing, 2010), p. 9.

37 Barritt and Carter, *The Northern Ireland Problem*, p. 40.

38 J. Whyte, 'How Much Discrimination Was There Under the Unionist Regime, 1921–1968?', in T. Gallagher and J. O'Connell (eds), *Contemporary Irish Studies* (Manchester: Manchester University Press, 1983), available from https://cain.ulster.ac.uk/issues/discrimination/whyte.htm#chap1, accessed 25 April 2019.

39 O'Leary, 'Cold House', p. 824.

40 *Donegal News*, 3 February 1923, p. 5.

41 O'Brien, *Discrimination in Northern Ireland*, p. 10.

42 *Donegal News*, 3 February 1923, p. 5.

43 Bardon, *A History of Ulster*, p. 501.

44 *Ulster Herald*, 7 July 1923, p. 5.

45 O'Brien, *Discrimination in Northern Ireland*, p. 12.

46 Ibid., p. 13.

47 Bardon, *A History of Ulster*, p. 501.

48 Whyte, 'How Much Discrimination Was There Under the Unionist Regime?'.

49 Ibid.

50 O'Leary, 'Cold House', p. 825.

51 Buckland, *The Factory of Grievances*, p. 6.

52 *Ulster Herald*, 29 September 1923, p. 5.

53   National Archive of Ireland (hereafter referred to as NAI) – Department of an Taoiseach – S4743, 26 February 1926.

54   Lynch, *Revolutionary Ireland*, p. 104.

55   Laffan, *The Partition of Ireland*, p. 94.

56   Dolan and Murphy, *Michael Collins*, p. 194.

57   Hopkinson, 'The Craig-Collins Pacts of 1922', p. 147.

58   Glennon, *From Pogrom to Civil War*, p. 100.

59   Hopkinson, 'The Craig-Collins Pacts of 1922', p. 147.

60   PRONI – CAB 4/30, 26 January 1922.

61   NAI – North Eastern Boundary Bureau – NEBB/1/1/3, undated.

62   PRONI – CAB 4/30, 26 January 1922.

63   Hopkinson, 'The Craig-Collins Pacts of 1922', p. 147.

64   *Cork Examiner*, 27 January 1922, p. 5.

65   Lynch, *The Partition of Ireland*, p. 149.

66   Hopkinson, 'The Craig-Collins Pacts of 1922', p. 151.

67   Ibid., p. 152.

68   Bardon, *A History of Ulster*, p. 489.

69   NAI – Department of an Taoiseach – S1095 – Belfast Boycott, 14 March 1922 and UK National Archives – HO 267/13 – Land Registry Transfer of Documents, 16 March 1923.

70   UK National Archives – HO 45/24812 – Miscellaneous matters arising from the Partition of Ireland, 20 June 1922.

71   NAI – Department of an Taoiseach – S6037 – Allocation of Staff Between Provisional Government and Northern Ireland, 1 February 1922.

72   Daly, *The First Department*, p. 111.

73   UK National Archives – HO 267/13 – Land Registry Transfer of Documents, 16 March 1923.

74   Kennedy, *Division and Consensus*, p. 8.

75   McColgan, *British Policy and the Irish Administration*, p. 112.

76   Dolan and Murphy, *Michael Collins*, p. 196.

77   UCD Archives – Ernest Blythe Papers – P24/70 – Policy in Regard to the North-East, 9 August 1922.

78   Bardon, *A History of Ulster*, p. 493.

79   D. Fitzpatrick, 'ERNEST BLYTHE – Orangeman and Fenian', *History Ireland* (Vol. 25, No. 3, May – June 2017), p. 35.

80   McColgan, *British Policy and the Irish Administration*, p. 121.

81   UCD Archives – Ernest Blythe Papers – P24/70 – Policy in Regard to the North-East, 9 August 1922.

82   Ó Beacháin, *From Partition to Brexit*, p. 21.

83   Ferriter, *The Border*, p. 20.

84   M. Laffan, *Judging W.T. Cosgrave* (Dublin: Royal Irish Academy, 2014 [e-reader edition]), loc. 1648.

85   Kennedy, *Division and Consensus*, p. 8.

86   Phoenix, 'Cahir Healy', p. 41.

87   C. Nash, B. Reid and B. Graham, *Partitioned Lives: The Irish Borderlands* (Surrey: Ashgate Publishing Company, 2013), p. 29.

88   Hall, 'Partition and County Louth', p. 262.

89   Ferriter, *The Border*, p. 26.

90   P. Leary, *Unapproved Routes: Histories of the Irish Border, 1922–1972* (Oxford: Oxford University Press, 2016 [e-reader edition]), p. 34.

91   Gibbons, *Drawing the Line*, p. 49.

92   UCD Archives – Ernest Blythe Papers – P24/76 – The Boundary Commission Organisation, 14 October 1922.

93   Ibid.

94   See PRONI – D921/4/5/1 –Newspaper Clippings and Printed Booklets.

95   Ferriter, *The Border*, p. 27.

96   Leary, *Unapproved Routes*, pp. 34–35.

97   Ó Beacháin, *From Partition to Brexit*, p. 23.

98   O. Ozseker, *Forging the Border: Donegal and Derry in Times of Revolution* (Dublin: Irish Academic Press, 2019), p. 197.

99   Leary, *Unapproved Routes*, p. 35.

100 *Report of the Irish Boundary Commission 1925* (Shannon: Irish University Press, 1969), pp. 16–18.

101 D. MacDonald, *Hard Border: Walking Through a Century of Partition* (Dublin, New Island Books, 2018), p. 32.

102 Murray, 'Partition and the Irish Boundary Commission', p. 193.

103 *Report of the Irish Boundary Commission 1925*, p. 85.

104 Ferriter, *The Border*, pp. 33–34.

105 Gibbons, *Drawing the Line*, p. 56.

106 Ozseker, *Forging the Border*, p. 2.

107 Ó Beacháin, *From Partition to Brexit*, p. 26.

108 *Irish Times*, 20 November 1925, p. 7A.

109 J.P. McCarthy, *Kevin O'Higgins: Builder of the Irish State* (Dublin: Irish Academic Press, 2006), p. 217.

110 Ó Beacháin, *From Partition to Brexit*, p. 27.

111 J.H. Whyte, 'Whitehall, Belfast and Dublin: New Light on the Treaty and the Border', *Studies* (Autumn–Winter 1971), p. 241.

112 Gibbons, *Drawing the Line*, p. 57.

113 Lynch, *The Northern IRA and the Early Years of Partition*, p. 3.

114 Fanning, *Fatal Path*, p. 350.

115 Kennedy, *Division and Consensus*, p. 13.

116 Ferriter, *The Border*, p. 35.

117 Bardon, *A History of Ulster*, p. 510.

118 Phoenix, 'Cahir Healy', p. 45.

119 J.M. Curran, 'The Anglo-Irish Agreement of 1925: Hardly a "Damn Good Bargain"', *The Historian* (Vol. 40, No. 1, November 1977), p. 50.

120 Bew, Gibbon and Patterson, *Northern Ireland 1921–1994*, p. 12.

Chapter Seven

1 Bardon, *A History of Ulster*, p. 494.
2 Lynch, *The Northern IRA and the Early Years of Partition*, p. 29.
3 Bardon, *A History of Ulster*, p. 494.
4 Lynch, *The Northern IRA and the Early Years of Partition*, p. 29.
5 Farrell, *Arming the Protestants*, p. 276.
6 Bowman, *Carson's Army*, p. 199.
7 O'Leary, 'Cold House', p. 822.
8 Lynch, *The Northern IRA and the Early Years of Partition*, p. 2.
9 Hezlet, *The 'B' Specials*, p. 51.
10 Bowman, *Carson's Army*, p. 198.
11 Glennon, *From Pogrom to Civil War*, p. 92.
12 Farrell, *Arming the Protestants*, p. 75.
13 Ibid., p. 76.
14 Hezlet, *The 'B' Specials*, p. 54.
15 Glennon, *From Pogrom to Civil War*, p. 92.
16 PRONI – CAB 4/28, 1 December 1921.
17 Bew, Gibbon and Patterson, *Northern Ireland 1921–1994*, p. 35.
18 Glennon, *From Pogrom to Civil War*, pp. 89–90.
19 Lynch, *The Northern IRA and the Early Years of Partition*, p. 81.
20 Ibid.
21 Bowman, *Carson's Army*, p. 195.
22 Glennon, *From Pogrom to Civil War*, p. 38.
23 Lynch, *The Northern IRA and the Early Years of Partition*, pp. 88–89.
24 *Belfast Newsletter*, 23 November 1921, p. 5.
25 Glennon, *From Pogrom to Civil War*, p. 93.
26 Lynch, *The Northern IRA and the Early Years of Partition*, p. 89.
27 *Belfast Newsletter*, 29 November 1921, p. 5.
28 Ibid.
29 PRONI – CAB 4/27, 23 November 1921.
30 PRONI – CAB 4/28, 1 December 1921.
31 Hezlet, *The 'B' Specials*, p. 53.
32 Lynch, *The Northern IRA and the Early Years of Partition*, p. 89.
33 Glennon, *From Pogrom to Civil War*, p. 93.
34 Lynch, *The Northern IRA and the Early Years of Partition*, p. 95.
35 Ibid., p. 96.
36 Glennon, *From Pogrom to Civil War*, p. 94.
37 F. McGarry, *Eoin O'Duffy: A Self-Made Hero* (Oxford: Oxford University Press, 2005), p. 80.
38 Lynch, *The Northern IRA and the Early Years of Partition*, p. 97.
39 Grant, *The Irish Revolution*, p. 122.
40 Ibid.
41 Lawlor, *The Outrages*, p. 195.
42 Grant, *The Irish Revolution*, p. 123.

43   McGarry, *Eoin O'Duffy*, pp. 98–99.

44   Hezlet, *The 'B' Specials*, p. 59.

45   Dooley, *The Irish Revolution*, p. 103.

46   PRONI – CAB 4/33, 16 February 1922.

47   McCluskey, *The Irish Revolution*, pp. 114–15.

48   Lynch, *The Northern IRA and the Early Years of Partition*, p. 100.

49   Ibid.

50   Bardon, *A History of Ulster*, p. 486.

51   Farrell, *Arming the Protestants*, p. 92.

52   Lynch, *The Northern IRA and the Early Years of Partition*, p. 101.

53   Farrell, *Arming the Protestants*, p. 92.

54   PRONI – CAB 4/37, 8 February 1922.

55   House of Commons Debate, 8 February 1922, vol. 150, col 135, available from http://hansard.millbanksystems.com, accessed 28 April 2019.

56   Hezlet, *The 'B' Specials*, p. 59.

57   Ibid., p. 61.

58   G. Ellison and J. Smyth, *The Crowned Harp: Policing Northern Ireland* (London: Pluto Press, 2000), p. 28.

59   Bardon, *A History of Ulster*, p. 489.

60   Lynch, *The Northern IRA and the Early Years of Partition*, p. 111.

61   R. Lynch, 'The Clones Affray, 1922: Massacre or Invasion?' *History Ireland* (Vol. 12, No. 3, Autumn 2004), pp. 34–35.

62   Dooley, *The Irish Revolution*, p. 104.

63   Glennon, *From Pogrom to Civil War*, p. 103.

64   *Freeman's Journal*, 14 February 1922, p. 5.

65   *Freeman's Journal*, 4 March 1922, p. 6.

66   *Belfast Newsletter*, 15 February 1922, p. 5.

67   PRONI – CAB 4/33, 16 February 1922.

68   Farrell, *Arming the Protestants*, p. 93.

69   Ibid.

70   Lynch, *The Northern IRA and the Early Years of Partition*, pp. 115–16.

71   Glennon, *From Pogrom to Civil War*, p. 103.

72   T. Wilson, '"The Most Terrible Assassination That Has Yet Stained the Name of Belfast": the McMahon Murders in Context', *Irish Historical Studies* (Vol. 37, No. 145, May 2010), p. 84.

73   B. Hourican, Dictionary of Irish Biography, available from http://dib.cambridge.org/, accessed 29 April 2019.

74   Glennon, *From Pogrom to Civil War*, p. 103.

75   *Manchester Guardian*, 25 March 1922, p. 8.

76   M. Ward, *Unmanageable Revolutionaries: Women and Irish Nationalism* (London: Pluto Press, 1995), p. 186.

77   Bardon, *A History of Ulster*, pp. 487–88.

78   Farrell, *Arming the Protestants*, p. 100.

79   Bardon, *A History of Ulster*, p. 488.

80 Ibid., p. 489.

81 Lynch, *Revolutionary Ireland*, p. 110.

82 UK National Archives – HO 45/24812 – Royal Ulster Constabulary Establishment and Financial Questions, 22 May 1922.

83 UK National Archives – HO 45/24812 – Miscellaneous matters arising from the Partition of Ireland, 6 May 1922.

84 Farrell, *Arming the Protestants*, p. 111.

85 UK National Archives – HO 45/24812 – Miscellaneous matters arising from the Partition of Ireland, 9 May 1922.

86 Ibid.

87 Ellison and Smyth, *The Crowned Harp*, p. 18.

88 Farrell, *Arming the Protestants*, p. 170.

89 PRONI – HA4/1/114 – Ulster Police Force: Headquarters Staff and Strength of Force, 28 April 1922.

90 PRONI – SO/1/A/1 – Interim Report of the Departmental Committee of Inquiry on Police Reorganisation in Northern Ireland, 28 March 1922.

91 Ellison and Smyth, *The Crowned Harp*, p. 19.

92 PRONI – HA/47/1 – Police Reorganisation Committee: Minutes of Evidence, 28 February 1922.

93 PRONI – SO/1/A/1 – Interim Report of the Departmental Committee of Inquiry on Police Reorganisation in Northern Ireland, 28 March 1922.

94 Farrell, *Arming the Protestants*, p. 143.

95 PRONI – HA/47/1 – Police Reorganisation Committee: Minutes of Evidence, 28 February 1922.

96 Ellison and Smyth, *The Crowned Harp*, p. 19.

97 PRONI – HA/47/1 – Police Reorganisation Committee: Minutes of Evidence, 28 February 1922.

98 UK National Archives – HO 45/24812 – Royal Irish Constabulary Disbandment and other matters, 3 June 1922.

99 PRONI – HA/47/1 – Police Reorganisation Committee: Minutes of Evidence, 1 March 1922.

100 UK National Archives – HO 45/24812 – Royal Irish Constabulary Disbandment and other matters, 3 June 1922.

101 PRONI – HA4/1/114 – Ulster Police Force: Headquarters Staff and Strength of Force, 19 May 1922.

102 Ellison and Smyth, *The Crowned Harp*, p. 19.

103 PRONI – SO/1/A/1 – Interim Report of the Departmental Committee of Inquiry on Police Reorganisation in Northern Ireland, 28 March 1922.

104 Ellison and Smyth, *The Crowned Harp*, p. 20.

105 PRONI – HA/47/1 – Police Reorganisation Committee: Minutes of Evidence, 1 March 1922.

106 Bardon, *A History of Ulster*, p. 499.

107 O'Leary, 'Cold House', p. 822.

108 PRONI – CAB 4/35, 13 March 1922.

109   Ó Beacháin, *From Partition to Brexit*, p. 14.

110   Bardon, *A History of Ulster*, p. 490.

111   *Manchester Guardian*, 25 March 1922, p. 8.

112   Ó Beacháin, *From Partition to Brexit*, p. 15.

113   O'Leary, 'Cold House', p. 822.

114   Farrell, *Arming the Protestants*, p. 99.

115   Dolan and Murphy, *Michael Collins*, p. 195

116   J. Dorney, *The Civil War in Dublin: The Fight for the Irish Capital 1922–1924* (Dublin: Merrion Press, 2017), p. 50.

117   Glennon, *From Pogrom to Civil War*, p. 106.

118   Dorney, *The Civil War in Dublin*, p. 52.

119   See PRONI, CAB 4/68, 15 January 1923 and PRONI – D1098/1/2 – Minute Book of the Ulster Women's Unionist Council Executive Committee, 4 July 1922.

120   Lynch, *The Partition of Ireland*, pp. 167–68.

121   C. McNamara, 'In the Shadow of Altnaveigh: Political Upheaval and Sectarian Violence in County Louth, 1920–1922', in D. Hall and M. Maguire (eds), *County Louth and the Irish Revolution 1912–1923*, (Dublin: Irish Academic Press, 2017) p. 202.

122   Dorney, *The Civil War in Dublin*, pp. 52–53.

123   PRONI – D3788/1/5 – Irish Union of Young Men's Christian Association – Minute Book for Meetings of the Executive Committee of the North of Ireland District – 1901–1922, 4 May 1922.

124   Dorney, *The Civil War in Dublin*, p. 54.

125   Ibid.

126   Lynch, *The Partition of Ireland*, p. 179.

127   NAI – Department of an Taoiseach – S1095 – Belfast Boycott, 21 March 1922.

128   Dorney, *The Civil War in Dublin*, p. 50.

129   NAI – Department of an Taoiseach – S1095 – Belfast Boycott, 2 May 1922.

130   M. Martin, 'The Civil War in Drogheda, January – July 1922', in D. Hall and M. Maguire (eds), *County Louth and the Irish Revolution*, p. 219.

131   Dorney, *The Civil War in Dublin*, pp. 66–67.

132   Glennon, *From Pogrom to Civil War*, p. 288.

133   Dorney, *The Civil War in Dublin*, p. 57.

134   Lynch, *The Partition of Ireland*, p. 153.

135   Glennon, *From Pogrom to Civil War*, p. 150.

136   Ibid., p. 178.

137   Ó Beacháin, *From Partition to Brexit*, p. 17.

138   Lynch, *Revolutionary Ireland*, p. 110.

139   Ozseker, *Forging the Border*, p. 169.

140   Bardon, *A History of Ulster*, p. 491.

141   McNamara, 'In the Shadow of Altnaveigh', p. 208.

142   M. Hopkinson, *Green Against Green: The Irish Civil War* (Dublin: Gill Books, 1998), p. 248.

143   Bardon, *A History of Ulster*, p. 492.

144   Phoenix, 'Cahir Healy', pp. 39–40.

145 Glennon, *From Pogrom to Civil War*, p. 132.

146 Ibid., p. 133.

147 B. Hanley, 'The IRA in Northern Ireland', in J. Crowley, D. Ó Drisceoil and M. Murphy (eds), *Atlas of the Irish Revolution*, p. 831.

Chapter Eight

1 Lord Carswell, 'Founding a Legal System: The Early Judiciary of Northern Ireland', in F.M. Larkin and N.M. Dawson (eds), *Lawyers, the Law and History: Irish Legal History Society Discourses and Other Papers, 2005–2011* (Dublin: Four Courts Press in association with the Irish Legal History Society, 2013), p. 15.

2 V.T.H. Delany, *The Administration of Justice in Ireland* (Dublin: Institute of Public Administration, 1962), p. 23.

3 K.J. Rankin, 'Theoretical Concepts of Partition and the Partitioning of Ireland', *Institute for British-Irish Studies* (Working Paper No. 67, 2006), p. 24.

4 Smith, *Sketch of The Supreme Court of Judicature of Northern Ireland*, p. 4.

5 Delany, *The Administration of Justice in Ireland*, p. 35.

6 A.D. McDonnell, *The Life of Sir Denis Henry: Catholic Unionist* (Belfast: Ulster Historical Foundation, 2000), p. 84.

7 H. Geoghegan, 'The Three Judges of the Supreme Court of the Irish Free State, 1925–36: Their Backgrounds, Personalities and Mindsets', in F.M. Larkin and N.M. Dawson (eds) *Lawyers, the Law and History*, p. 32.

8 *Belfast Telegraph*, 20 February 1920, p. 3.

9 McDonnell, *The Life of Sir Denis Henry*, p. 85.

10 PRONI – CAB 4/12, 4 August 1921.

11 McDonnell, *The Life of Sir Denis Henry*, p. 89.

12 Ibid., pp. 86–87.

13 Phoenix, *Northern Nationalism*, pp. 376–77.

14 O'Leary, 'Cold House', pp. 822–23.

15 E. Phoenix, 'Catholic Unionism: A Case Study: Sir Denis Stanislaus Henry (1864–1925)', in O.P. Rafferty (ed.), *Irish Catholic Identities* (Manchester: Manchester University Press, 2013), p. 292.

16 Lord Carswell, 'Founding a Legal System', p. 18.

17 Phoenix, 'Catholic Unionism', p. 293.

18 Smith, *Sketch of The Supreme Court of Judicature of Northern Ireland*, p. 11.

19 A.D. McDonnell, Dictionary of Irish Biography, available from http://dib.cambridge.org/, accessed 2 May 2019.

20 Ibid.

21 Phoenix, 'Catholic Unionism', p. 300.

22 McDonnell, *The Life of Sir Denis Henry*, p. 88.

23 Lord Carswell, 'Founding a Legal System', pp. 16–17.

24 Ibid., p. 21.

25 McDonnell, *The Life of Sir Denis Henry*, p. 92.

26 Lord Carswell, 'Founding a Legal System', pp. 15 and 20.

27 PRONI – CAB/6/57 – Projected publication of 'Memoranda on the setting up of the Supreme Court of Judicature of Northern Ireland', written by Lord Chief Justice Moore, 4 November 1922..

28 Lord Carswell, 'Founding a Legal System', p. 19.

29 PRONI – CAB/6/57 – Projected publication of 'Memoranda on the setting up of the Supreme Court of Judicature of Northern Ireland', written by Lord Chief Justice Moore, 4 November 1922.

30 Lord Carswell, 'Founding a Legal System', p. 19.

31 PRONI – CAB/6/57 – Projected publication of 'Memoranda on the setting up of the Supreme Court of Judicature of Northern Ireland', written by Lord Chief Justice Moore, 4 November 1922.

32 McDonnell, *The Life of Sir Denis Henry*, pp. 99–100.

33 PRONI – CAB/6/57 – Projected publication of 'Memoranda on the setting up of the Supreme Court of Judicature of Northern Ireland', written by Lord Chief Justice Moore, 4 November 1922.

34 McDonnell, *The Life of Sir Denis Henry*, p. 100.

35 Ibid., p. 101.

36 PRONI – CAB/6/57 – Projected publication of 'Memoranda on the setting up of the Supreme Court of Judicature of Northern Ireland', written by Lord Chief Justice Moore, 4 November 1922.

37 Ibid.

38 McDonnell, *The Life of Sir Denis Henry*, pp. 101–3.

39 PRONI – CAB/6/57 – Projected publication of 'Memoranda on the setting up of the Supreme Court of Judicature of Northern Ireland', written by Lord Chief Justice Moore, 4 November 1922.

40 *Irish Times*, 26 October 1921, p. 6.

41 Smith, *Sketch of The Supreme Court of Judicature of Northern Ireland*, pp. 11–12.

42 Lord Carswell, 'Founding a Legal System', p. 28.

43 McDonnell, *The Life of Sir Denis Henry*, p. 105.

44 Lord Carswell, 'Founding a Legal System, p. 15.

45 McDonnell, *The Life of Sir Denis Henry*, p. 95.

46 PRONI – CAB/6/57 – Projected publication of 'Memoranda on the setting up of the Supreme Court of Judicature of Northern Ireland', written by Lord Chief Justice Moore, 4 November 1922.

47 McDonnell, *The Life of Sir Denis Henry*, p. 106.

48 PRONI – AUS/2/5 – Copies of Reports to Dublin Castle by Departments in response to circula regarding administrative changes necessitated by Government of Ireland Act 1920: Judiciary of Northern Ireland – 1921, 29 April 1921.

49 *Donegal Democrat*, 25 November 1921, p. 3.

50 *Irish Times*, 9 February 1922, p. 3.

51 MacDonald, *Hard Border*, p. 30.

52 Smith, *Sketch of The Supreme Court of Judicature of Northern Ireland*, p. 26.

53 *Freeman's Journal*, 17 Match 1922, p. 5.

54 *Cork Examiner*, 22 March 1922, p. 6.

55 O'Leary, 'Cold House', p. 823.

56 Phoenix, 'Catholic Unionism', pp. 301–302.

57 McDonnell, *The Life of Sir Denis Henry*, p. 113.

58 Smith, *Sketch of The Supreme Court of Judicature of Northern Ireland*, p. 11.

59 *Irish Times*, 27 November 1920, p. 3.

60 Ibid.

61 Ibid.

62 Smith, *Sketch of The Supreme Court of Judicature of Northern Ireland*, p. 18.

63 *Gazette of the Incorporated Law Society of Ireland*, Vol. XVI., No. 2, June,1922, p. 7.

64 Smith, *Sketch of The Supreme Court of Judicature of Northern Ireland*, p. 59.

65 PRONI – CAB/6/57 – Projected publication of 'Memoranda on the setting up of the Supreme Court of Judicature of Northern Ireland', written by Lord Chief Justice Moore, 4 November 1922.

66 Smith, *Sketch of The Supreme Court of Judicature of Northern Ireland*, p. 46.

67 A. Hart, 'The Independent Bar of Northern Ireland – Past and Present', Address to the Wales & Chester Circuit in Cardiff, 22 June 2017.

68 A.R. Hart, Dictionary of Irish Biography, available from http://dib.cambridge.org/, accessed 3 May 2019.

69 W.N. Osborough, 'Landmarks in the History of King's Inns', in K. Ferguson (ed.), *King's Inn Barristers 1868–2004* (Dublin: The Honorable Society of King's Inns, 2005), p. 27.

70 *Cork Examiner*, 2 November 1921, p. 8.

71 Osborough, 'Landmarks in the History of King's Inns', p. 31.

72 A.R. Hart, 'King's Inns and the Foundation of the Inn of Court of Northern Ireland: The Northern Perspective', in F.M. Larkin and N.M. Dawson (eds), *Lawyers, the Law and History*, p. 194.

73 Osborough, 'Landmarks in the History of King's Inns', p. 32.

74 Hart, 'King's Inns and the Foundation of the Inn of Court of Northern Ireland, p. 195.

75 PRONI – CAB/6/57 – Projected publication of 'Memoranda on the setting up of the Supreme Court of Judicature of Northern Ireland', written by Lord Chief Justice Moore, 4 November 1922.

76 Ibid.

77 Ibid.

78 Hart, 'King's Inns and the Foundation of the Inn of Court of Northern Ireland, p. 196.

79 Ibid., pp. 197–98.

80 Ibid., p. 198.

81 PRONI – CAB 4/123, 4 October 1924.

82 Hart, 'King's Inns and the Foundation of the Inn of Court of Northern Ireland, p. 199.

83 Smith, *Sketch of The Supreme Court of Judicature of Northern Ireland*, pp. 54–55.

84 Hart, 'King's Inns and the Foundation of the Inn of Court of Northern Ireland, p. 201.

85 Ibid., p. 200.

86 UK Archives – HO 267/13 – Land Registry Transfer of Documents, 6 November 1922.

87 Smith, *Sketch of The Supreme Court of Judicature of Northern Ireland*, p. 56.

88 *Irish Times*, 9 October 1925, p. 5.

89 Osborough, 'Landmarks in the History of King's Inns', p. 32.

90 Delany, *The Administration of Justice in Ireland*, p. 36.

91 Ibid., p. 39.
92 C. Bell, 'Alternative Justice in Ireland', in N. Dawson, D. Greer and P. Ingram (eds), *One Hundred and Fifty Years of Irish Law* (Belfast: SLS Legal Publication (NI), School of Law, The Queen's University of Belfast, 1996), p. 151.
93 Delany, *The Administration of Justice in Ireland*, p. 38.
94 D. Ferriter, *A Nation and not a Rabble: The Irish Revolution 1913–1923* (Suffolk: Profile Books, 2015), p. 226.
95 M. Kotsonouris, *Retreat from Revolution: The Dáil Courts, 1920–24* (Dublin: Irish Academic Press, 1994), p. 55.
96 McCluskey, *The Irish Revolution*, p. 82.
97 Kotsonouris, *Retreat from Revolution*, p. 55.
98 Grant, *The Irish Revolution*, p. 121.
99 Delany, *The Administration of Justice in Ireland*, p. 39.
100 Geoghegan, 'The Three Judges of the Supreme Court of the Irish Free State, 1925–36: Their Backgrounds, Personalities and Mindsets', p. 30.
101 Ibid., pp. 31–32.
102 M. Kotsonouris, *The Winding-up of the Dáil Courts, 1922–1925: An Obvious Duty* (Dublin: Four Courts Press in association with The Irish Legal History Society, 2004), p. 2.

Chapter Nine

1   Lynch, *The Partition of Ireland*, p. 125.
2   D.S. Johnson, 'The Economic History of Ireland between the Wars', *Irish Economic and Social History* (Vol. 1, 1974), p. 58.
3   C. O'Grada and B.M. Walsh, 'Did (And Does) the Irish Border Matter?', *Institute for British-Irish Studies* (Working Paper No. 60, 2006), p. 1.
4   Hughes, *Defying the IRA?*, p. 87.
5   Ward, *Unmanageable Revolutionaries*, pp. 185–86.
6   PRONI – D1022/2/8 – File entitled, 'Trade Boycott', including memorandum by Clark and a copy of a Sinn Féin decree, 14 November 1921.
7   L.W. White, Dictionary of Irish Biography, available from http://dib.cambridge.org/, accessed 5 May 2019.
8   Lynch, *Revolutionary Ireland*, p. 100.
9   P. Hart, *The I.R.A. and Its Enemies: Violence and Community in Cork, 1916–1923* (Oxford: Oxford University Press, 1998), p. 102.
10 Dooley, *The Irish Revolution*, p. 96.
11 Account of Jimmy Kirke, Blackstaff Given to Rev. Peter Livingstone – I.I.66 – 1986:6H1-2, available from https://monaghan.ie/museum/search-monaghan-war-of-independence-files/, accessed 4 May 2019.
12 Bureau of Military History, 1913–21, Document No. W.S. 183 available from http://www.bureauofmilitaryhistory.ie/, accessed 4 May 2019 and Hall, 'Politics and Revolution in County Louth', p. 13.
13 Lynch, *The Partition of Ireland*, p. 186.

14 Account of Tom Carragher – Donaghmoyne Taken and Edited by Rev. P. Livingstone – 20 December 1965 – 1986:6C1-15, available from https://monaghan.ie/museum/search-monaghan-war-of-independence-files/, accessed 4 May 2019.

15 Bureau of Military History, 1913–21, Document No. W.S. 476 available from http://www.bureauofmilitaryhistory.ie/, accessed 4 May 2019.

16 Ward, *Unmanageable Revolutionaries*, p. 186.

17 PRONI – D1022/2/8 – File entitled, 'Trade Boycott', including memorandum by Clark and a copy of a Sinn Féin decree, 13 August 1920.

18 Lawlor, *The Outrages*, p. 136.

19 Bureau of Military History, 1913–21, Document No. W.S. 183 available from http://www.bureauofmilitaryhistory.ie/, accessed 4 May 2019.

20 Hughes, *Defying the IRA?*, p. 89.

21 Lynch, *The Partition of Ireland*, p. 1181.

22 *Evening Herald*, 10 March 1921, p. 1.

23 *Evening Herald*, 13 April 1921, p. 3.

24 *The Observer*, 26 September 1920, p. 14.

25 *Manchester Guardian*, 12 March 1921, p. 11.

26 PRONI – D1022/2/8 – File entitled, 'Trade Boycott', including memorandum by Clark and a copy of a Sinn Féin decree, 29 October 1920.

27 *Freeman's Journal*, 1 February 1921, p. 3.

28 Johnson, 'The Belfast Boycott', p. 293.

29 Ibid., p. 292.

30 Bureau of Military History, 1913–21, Document No. W.S. 183 available from http://www.bureauofmilitaryhistory.ie/, accessed 4 May 2019.

31 Ibid.

32 Inoue, 'Sinn Féin Propaganda and the "Partition Election"', p. 56.

33 PRONI – D1022/2/8 – File entitled, 'Trade Boycott', including memorandum by Clark and a copy of a Sinn Féin decree, 14 November 1921.

34 PRONI – CAB 4/14, 10 August 1921.

35 PRONI – CAB 4/23, 27 September 1921.

36 PRONI – CAB 4/28, 1 December 1921.

37 NAI – Department of an Taoiseach – S1095 – Belfast Boycott, 23 January 1922.

38 PRONI – CAB 4/30, 26 January 1922.

39 NAI – Department of an Taoiseach – S1095 – Belfast Boycott, 28 February 1922.

40 Maguire, *The Civil Service and the Revolution in Ireland 1912–1938*, p. 136.

41 Ward, *Unmanageable Revolutionaries*, p. 172.

42 C. McCarthy, *Cumann na mBan and the Irish Revolution* (Cork: The Collins Press, 2007), p. 211.

43 NAI – Department of an Taoiseach – S1095 – Belfast Boycott, 6 April 1922.

44 PRONI – COM/62/2/7 – Boycott – Ulster Traders Defence Association, correspondence and notices concerning the boycott of Northern Ireland goods – 1922, May 1922.

45 Johnson, 'The Belfast Boycott', p. 297.

46 PRONI – D1098/1/2 – Minute Book of the Ulster Women's Unionist Council Executive Committee, 4 July 1922.

47 PRONI – D1022/2/8 – File entitled, 'Trade Boycott', including memorandum by Clark and a copy of a Sinn Féin decree, 14 November 1921.
48 Johnson, 'The Belfast Boycott', p. 306.
49 PRONI – CAB 4/68, 15 January 1923.
50 PRONI – D1022/2/8 – File entitled, 'Trade Boycott', including memorandum by Clark and a copy of a Sinn Féin decree, 14 November 1921.
51 Dooley, *The Irish Revolution*, p. 97.
52 PRONI – D1022/2/8 – File entitled, 'Trade Boycott', including memorandum by Clark and a copy of a Sinn Féin decree, 14 November 1921.
53 Johnson, 'The Belfast Boycott', pp. 298 and 299.
54 E. Drea, 'A Gamble Forced Upon Them? A Re-Appraisal of Ulster Bank's Operations in Southern Ireland 1921–32', *Business History* (Vol. 56, No. 7, 2014), p. 1116.
55 Ibid., p. 1116
56 Ibid., p. 1118.
57 UCD Archives – Ernest Blythe Papers – P24/70 – Policy in Regard to the North-East, 9 August 1922.
58 Bureau of Military History, 1913–21, Document No. W.S. 183, available from http://www.bureauofmilitaryhistory.ie/, accessed 5 May 2019.
59 UCD Archives – Ernest Blythe Papers – P24/70 – Policy in Regard to the North-East, 9 August 1922.
60 Bardon, *A History of Ulster*, p. 485.
61 Johnson, 'The Belfast Boycott', p. 307.
62 NAI – Department of an Taoiseach – S1095 – Belfast Boycott, 30 January 1922.
63 Nash, Reid and Graham, *Partitioned Lives*, p. 29.
64 McGee, *Arthur Griffith*, p. 174.
65 PRONI – D921/4/5/1 – Newspaper Clippings and Printed Booklets - IF "ULSTER" CONTRACTS OUT: The Economic Case against Partition, Undated.
66 Ibid.
67 Ferriter, *The Border*, p. 26.
68 PRONI – D921/4/5/1 – Newspaper Clippings and Printed Booklets - IF "ULSTER" CONTRACTS OUT: The Economic Case against Partition, Undated.
69 *Belfast Newsletter*, 1 October 1924, p. 11.
70 *The Times*, 1 January 1923, p. 11.
71 *Irish Times*, 23 February 1923, p. 5.
72 Nash, Reid and Graham, *Partitioned Lives*, p. 29.
73 UK National Archives – HO 267/49 – Customs & Excise, March 1923.
74 *Irish Times*, 23 February 1923, p. 5.
75 UK National Archives – HO 267/49 – Customs & Excise, March 1923.
76 Nash, Reid and Graham, *Partitioned Lives*, p. 30.
77 P. Leary, 'A House Divided: the Murrays of the Border and the Rise and Decline of a Small Irish House', *History Workshop Journal* (Issue 86, July 2018), p. 280.
78 UK National Archives – HO 267/49 – Customs & Excise, March 1923.
79 Ibid.
80 *Irish Times*, 2 March 1923, p. 5.

81 *Irish Times*, 6 March 1923, p. 7.

82 Hall, 'Partition and County Louth', p. 264.

83 *Irish Times*, 8 March 1923, p. 5.

84 Ibid., 28 March 1923, p. 5.

85 Murray, 'Partition and the Irish Boundary Commission', p. 193.

86 *The Times*, 3 March 1923, p. 12.

87 *Irish Times*, 26 February 1923, p. 6.

88 PRONI – D921/4/5/1 – Newspaper Clippings and Printed Booklets - IF "ULSTER" CONTRACTS OUT: The Economic Case against Partition, Undated.

89 Nash, Reid and Graham, *Partitioned Lives*, p. 30.

90 *Irish Times*, 28 March 1923, p. 5.

91 Ibid., 7 April 1923, p. 3.

92 Ibid., 3 April 1923, p. 7.

93 UK National Archives – HO 267/34 – Customs – Applications, 5 March 1923.

94 UK National Archives – HO 267/49 – Customs & Excise, March 1923.

95 *Irish Times*, 2 April 1923, p. 5.

96 *The Times*, 13 September 1923, p. 11.

97 Nash, Reid and Graham, *Partitioned Lives*, p. 32.

98 O Grada and Walsh, 'Did (And Does) the Irish Border Matter?', p. 24.

99 Ibid., p. 22.

100 Nash, Reid and Graham, *Partitioned Lives*, p. 32.

101 O Grada and Walsh, 'Did (And Does) the Irish Border Matter?', p. 24.

102 PRONI – D1506/1/13/3 – Correspondence with Companies Register Office, Dublin, concerning the establishment of Watt and Co. Ltd.

103 *Freeman's Journal*, 26 April 1921, p. 2.

104 Ibid., 21 September 1921, p. 2.

105 Ibid., 17 October 1921, p. 6.

106 *Irish Times*, 13 February 1922, p. 6.

107 *Donegal News*, 11 July 1925, p. 2.

108 Daly, *The First Department*, p. 95.

109 Ibid., p. 110.

110 PRONI – AUS/2/18 – Copies of Reports to Dublin Castle by Departments in response to circula regarding administrative changes necessitated by Government of Ireland Act 1920: Department of Agriculture and Technical Instruction for Ireland – 1921, 20 and 26 January 1921.

111 Ibid., 20 and 26 January 1921.

112 *Irish Times*, 22 January 1926, p. 7.

113 Ibid., 3 June 1921, p. 4.

114 Ibid., 15 May 1921, p. 4.

115 Ibid., 18 May 1921, p. 6.

116 Ibid., 18 May 1923, p. 4.

117 Ibid., 23 May 1925, p. 1.

118 J. Whyte, 'The Permeability of the United Kingdom – Irish Border: A Preliminary Reconnaissance', *Administration* (Vol. 31, No. 3, 1983), pp. 312–13.

119   Ibid., p. 307.
120   *Irish Press*, 15 September 1937, p. 6.
121   *Irish Times*, 29 October 1938, p. 4.
122   Whyte, 'The Permeability of the United Kingdom – Irish Border', p. 308.
123   PRONI – D3788/1/5 – Irish Union of Young Men's Christian Association – Minute Book for Meetings of the Executive Committee of the North of Ireland District – 1901 – 1922, 22 July 1920.
124   Ibid., 4 May 1922.
125   PRONI – D3788/1/6 – Irish Union of Young Men's Christian Association – Minute Book for Meetings of the Executive Committee of the North of Ireland District and Annual General Meetings of the Northern Ireland Council of Y.M.C.A.s – 1922 – 1969, 21 July 1922.
126   Ibid., 30 May 1924.
127   Ibid., 26 September 1939.
128   *Irish Times*, 20 April 1934, p. 4.
129   PRONI – D3875/1/1/1 – Minutes of the Ulster Girl Guides – March 1920 – July 1928, 20 March 1920.
130   *Irish Times*, 15 April 1930, p. 4.
131   Whyte, 'The Permeability of the United Kingdom – Irish Border', p. 308.
132   Ibid., p. 308.
133   *Irish Times*, 13 May 1927, p. 7.
134   *Irish Independent*, 30 October 1923, p. 6.
135   *Freeman's Journal*, 2 November 1923, p. 6.
136   *Irish Times*, 5 November 1923, p. 5.

Chapter Ten

1   Rafferty, 'The Catholic Church and Partition', p. 16.
2   Harris, *The Catholic Church and the Foundation of the Irish State*, p. 6.
3   Whyte, 'The Permeability of the United Kingdom – Irish Border, p. 300.
4   K. Howard, 'Continuity and Change in a Partitioned Civil Society: Whyte Revisited', *Working Papers in British-Irish Studies* (No. 70, 2006), p. 9.
5   Harris, *The Catholic Church and the Foundation of the Irish State*, p. 4.
6   Ibid., p. 12.
7   E. de Bhaldraithe, 'Mixed Marriages and Irish Politics: The Effect of "Ne Temere"', *Studies: An Irish Quarterly Review* (Vol. 77, No. 307, Autumn 1988), p. 289.
8   Ibid., p. 290.
9   O. P. Rafferty, '"Studies" and the Shadow of Modernism', *Studies: An Irish Quarterly Review* (Vol. 100, No. 400, A Century of Studies, Winter 2011), p. 470.
10   Harris, *The Catholic Church and the Foundation of the Irish State*, p. 16.
11   Ibid., p. 47.
12   D. Ferriter, Dictionary of Irish Biography, available from http://dib.cambridge.org/, accessed 6 May 2019.
13   Harris, *The Catholic Church and the Foundation of the Irish State*, p. 47.

14   Ibid., p. 49.

15   P. Maume, Dictionary of Irish Biography, available from http://dib.cambridge.org/, accessed 6 May 2019.

16   M. Harris, 'The Catholic Church, Minority Rights, and the Founding of the Northern Irish State', in D. Keogh and M.H. Haltzel (eds), *Northern Ireland and the Politics of Reconciliation* (Unites States of America: Woodrow Wilson Centre Press and Cambridge University Press, 1993), p. 62.

17   Harris, *The Catholic Church and the Foundation of the Northern Irish State*, p. 52.

18   Ibid., pp. 54–55.

19   Ibid., p. 56.

20   B. Lynn, Dictionary of Irish Biography, available from http://dib.cambridge.org/, accessed 6 May 2019.

21   Bew, Gibbon and Patterson, *Northern Ireland 1921–1994*, p. 43.

22   Harris, *The Catholic Church and the Foundation of the Irish State*, p. 57.

23   Ibid., p. 62.

24   Fanning, *Fatal Path*, p. 169.

25   D. Ferriter, Dictionary of Irish Biography, available from http://dib.cambridge.org/, accessed 6 May 2019.

26   M. Elliott, *The Catholics of Ulster* (London: Penguin Books, 2001), p. 300.

27   Rafferty, 'The Catholic Church and Partition', p. 13.

28   Ibid.

29   Harris, *The Catholic Church and the Foundation of the Irish State*, p. 80.

30   Rafferty, 'The Catholic Church and Partition', p. 14.

31   Ibid.

32   Harris, *The Catholic Church and the Foundation of the Irish State*, p. 86.

33   Ibid., p. 83.

34   *Evening Herald*, 28 December 1920, p. 1.

35   Harris, *The Catholic Church and the Foundation of the Irish State*, p. 86.

36   M. Harris, 'Meeting the Minister', *Fortnight* (No. 196, Supplement: Religion in Ireland, June 1991), p. 4.

37   *Kerryman*, 12 February 1921, p. 6.

38   Rafferty, 'The Catholic Church and Partition', p. 13.

39   Ibid., p. 14.

40   *Anglo-Celt*, 25 June 1921, p. 6.

41   Rafferty, 'The Catholic Church and Partition', p. 13.

42   Harris, *The Catholic Church and the Foundation of the Irish State*, p. 104.

43   Rafferty, 'The Catholic Church and Partition', p. 16.

44   Harris, *The Catholic Church and the Foundation of the Irish State*, pp. 105–106.

45   Ibid., p. 107.

46   Ibid., pp. 110–12.

47   Ibid., p. 94.

48   *Freeman's Journal*, 27 April 1922, p. 5.

49   Harris, *The Catholic Church and the Foundation of the Irish State*, p. 128.

50   Ibid., p. 133.

51 Ibid., p. 136.
52 Ibid., p. 146.
53 Ibid., p. 147.
54 Ibid., p. 150.
55 *Irish Independent*, 13 October 1923, p. 5.
56 *Ulster Herald*, 20 October 1923, p. 3.
57 Harris, *The Catholic Church and the Foundation of the Irish State*, pp. 155–57.
58 Ibid., p. 163.
59 Ibid., p. 167.
60 Ibid., p. 171.
61 *Cork Examiner*, 15 February 1926, p. 7.
62 Harris, *The Catholic Church and the Foundation of the Irish State*, p. 174.
63 A. Acheson, *A History of the Church of Ireland 1691–2001* (Dublin: The Columba Press, 2002), p. 224.
64 *Irish Times*, 27 March 1886, p. 5.
65 D. McCabe, Dictionary of Irish Biography, available from http://dib.cambridge.org/, accessed 10 April 2019 and Acheson, *A History of the Church of Ireland*, p. 225.
66 N.K. Morris, 'Traitors to Their Faith? Protestant Clergy and the Ulster Covenant of 1912', *New Hibernia Review / Iris Éireannach Nua* (Vol. 15, No. 3, Fómhar/Autumn 2011), p. 23.
67 Acheson, *A History of the Church of Ireland*, p. 226.
68 Morris, 'Traitors to Their Faith?', p. 22.
69 Census of Ireland 1911, available from www.census.nationalarchives.ie, accessed 10 April 2019.
70 F. Holmes, *The Presbyterian Church in Ireland: A Popular History* (Dublin: Columba Press, 2000), p. 123.
71 Morris, 'Traitors to Their Faith?', p. 26.
72 B. Hourican, Dictionary of Irish Biography, available from http://dib.cambridge.org/, accessed 10 April 2019.
73 Morris, 'Traitors to Their Faith?', p. 19.
74 Ibid., p. 28.
75 Ibid., p. 29.
76 R.B. McDowell, *The Church of Ireland 1869–1969* (London and Boston: Routledge and Kegan Paul, 1975), p. 103.
77 Acheson, *A History of the Church of Ireland*, p. 226.
78 McDowell, *The Church of Ireland*, p. 104.
79 Ibid.
80 P. Maume, Dictionary of Irish Biography, available from http://dib.cambridge.org/, accessed 11 April 2019.
81 Acheson, *A History of the Church of Ireland*, p. 227.
82 McDowell, *The Church of Ireland*, p. 104.
83 Ibid.
84 Morris, 'Traitors to Their Faith?', p. 19.
85 Ibid., p. 22.
86 Holmes, *The Presbyterian Church in Ireland*, p. 124.

87 Ibid.

88 Morris, 'Traitors to Their Faith?', p. 22.

89 R.L. Cole, *History of Methodism in Ireland* (Belfast: The Irish Methodist Publishing Co. Ltd., 1960), p. 108.

90 Ibid.

91 Morris, 'Traitors to Their Faith?', p. 34.

92 McDowell, *The Church of Ireland*, p. 108.

93 P.J. Dempsey, Dictionary of Irish Biography, available from http://dib.cambridge.org/, accessed 11 April 2019.

94 McDowell, *The Church of Ireland*, p. 108.

95 Acheson, *A History of the Church of Ireland*, p. 228.

96 K. Milne, Dictionary of Irish Biography, available from http://dib.cambridge.org/, accessed 11 April 2019.

97 McDowell, *The Church of Ireland*, p. 109.

98 Morris, 'Traitors to Their Faith?', p. 35.

99 J. McCarthy and L. Lunney, Dictionary of Irish Biography, available from http://dib.cambridge.org/, accessed 11 April 2019.

100 *Irish Times*, 25 October 1919, p. 5.

101 Ibid.

102 Ibid.

103 Ibid., 23 September 1919, p. 4.

104 *Church of Ireland Gazette*, 2 July 1920, p. 422.

105 Ibid.

106 Holmes, *The Presbyterian Church in Ireland*, p. 125.

107 McDowell, *The Church of Ireland*, p. 109.

108 Acheson, *A History of the Church of Ireland*, p. 229.

109 *Irish Times*, 6 May 1922, p. 2.

110 P. Hart, 'The Protestant Experience of Revolution in Southern Ireland', in R. English and G. Walker (eds) *Unionism in Modern Ireland: New Perspectives on Politics and Culture* (London: Macmillan Press Ltd., 1996), pp. 81–90.

111 McDowell, *The Church of Ireland*, p. 109.

112 Ibid.

113 H. Andrews, Dictionary of Irish Biography, available from http://dib.cambridge.org/, accessed 12 April 2019.

114 Holmes, *The Presbyterian Church in Ireland*, p. 126.

115 Cole, *History of Methodism in Ireland*, p. 94.

116 Ibid., p. 95.

117 Ibid., p. 111.

118 McDowell, *The Church of Ireland*, p. 111.

119 Ibid., p. 112.

120 *Irish Times*, 3 November 1928, p. 6.

121 Cole, *History of Methodism in Ireland*, p. 114.

122 Holmes, *The Presbyterian Church in Ireland*, p. 128.

123 Ferriter, *The Border*, p. 23.

124 Acheson, *A History of the Church of Ireland*, p. 229.
125 Central Statistics Office, available from, http://www.cso.ie/en/media/csoie/census/census1926results/volume3/C_5_1926_V3_T1abc.pdf, accessed 15 April 2019.
126 Dooley, *The Irish Revolution*, p. 132.
127 B. Hughes, 'Defining Loyalty: Southern Irish Protestants and the Irish Grants Committee, 1926–30', in I. d'Alton and I. Milne (eds), *Protestant and Irish: The Minority's Search for Place in Independent Ireland* (Cork: Cork University Press, 2019), p. 45.
128 Ferriter, *The Border*, pp. 23–24.
129 Fitzpatrick, *The Two Irelands*, p. viii.
130 C. Morrissey, 'Peace, Protestantism and the Unity of Ireland: The Career of Bolton C. Waller', in d'Alton and Milne, *Protestant and Irish*, p. 52.
131 D. Keogh, *Jews in Twentieth-Century Ireland: Refugees, Anti-Semitism and the Holocaust* (Cork: Cork University Press, 1998), p. 76.
132 D. Ferriter, Dictionary of Irish Biography, available from http://dib.cambridge.org/, accessed 13 April 2019.
133 Keogh, *Jews in Twentieth-Century Ireland*, p. 77.
134 R. Miller, 'The Look of the Irish: Irish Jews and the Zionist Project, 1900–48', *Jewish Historical Studies* (Vol. 43, 2011), p. 206.
135 Ibid., p. 207.
136 Ibid.
137 Keogh, *Jews in Twentieth-Century Ireland*, p. 40.
138 Miller, 'The Look of the Irish', p. 208.
139 Ibid.
140 O. Scharbrodt, T. Sakaranaho, A. Hussain Khan, Y. Shanneik and V. Ibrahim, *Muslims in Ireland: Past and Present* (Edinburgh: Edinburgh University Press, 2015), p.79.

Chapter Eleven

1 *Connaught Telegraph*, 21 December 1831, p. 4.
2 S. Farren, *The Politics of Irish Education 1920–1965* (Belfast: The Queen's University of Belfast Institute of Irish Studies, 1995), p. 5.
3 Ibid., p. 2.
4 D.H. Akenson, *Education and Enmity: The Control of Schooling in Northern Ireland 1920–50* (Belfast: The Queen's University of Belfast Institute of Irish Studies, 1973), p. 12.
5 Farren, *The Politics of Irish Education*, p. 20.
6 Ibid., p. 21.
7 *Freeman's Journal*, 15 April 1921, p. 6.
8 Farren, *The Politics of Irish Education*, p. 3.
9 Harris, *The Catholic Church and the Foundation of the Northern Irish State*, p. 21.
10 Farren, *The Politics of Irish Education*, p. 8.
11 Akenson, *Education and Enmity*, p. 14.
12 Farren, *The Politics of Irish Education*, p. 9.
13 Akenson, *Education and Enmity*, p. 13.
14 Harris, *The Catholic Church and the Foundation of the Northern Irish State*, p. 21.

15 Farren, *The Politics of Irish Education*, p. 12.

16 Ibid., p. 20.

17 D. Kiberd, *Inventing the Nation – The Literature of the Modern Nation* (London: Vintage, 1996), p. 148.

18 Ibid., p. 147.

19 D. Ferriter, Dictionary of Irish Biography, available from http://dib.cambridge.org/, accessed 14 April 2019.

20 Farren, *The Politics of Irish Education*, p. 16.

21 Harris, *The Catholic Church and the Foundation of the Northern Irish State*, p. 31.

22 Farren, *The Politics of Irish Education*, p. 23.

23 Harris, *The Catholic Church and the Foundation of the Northern Irish State*, p. 22.

24 Farren, *The Politics of Irish Education*, p. 24.

25 Ibid., p. 25.

26 Harris, *The Catholic Church and the Foundation of the Northern Irish State*, p. 24.

27 Ibid., p. 25.

28 Farren, *The Politics of Irish Education*, p. 29.

29 Ibid., p. 32.

30 J. Coolahan, *The ASTI and Post-Primary Education in Ireland, 1909–1984* (Dublin: Cumann na Meánmhúinteoií, Éire, 1984), p. 47.

31 Harris, *The Catholic Church and the Foundation of the Northern Irish State*, p. 25.

32 Farren, *The Politics of Irish Education*, p. 29.

33 Ibid., p. 31.

34 Harris, *The Catholic Church and the Foundation of the Northern Irish State*, p. 27.

35 *Ulster Herald*, 13 March 1920, p. 3.

36 R.W. Dudley Edwards, 'Government of Ireland and Education, 1919–1920', *Archivium Hibernicum* (Vol. 37, 1982), p. 26.

37 Harris, *The Catholic Church and the Foundation of the Northern Irish State*, p. 29.

38 *Irish Times*, 15 November 1919, p. 6.

39 Harris, *The Catholic Church and the Foundation of the Northern Irish State*, p. 28.

40 *Freeman's Journal*, 15 April 1921, p. 6.

41 *Freeman's Journal*, 23 April 1921, p. 4.

42 *Irish News*, 19 March 1921, p. 6.

43 Harris, *The Catholic Church and the Foundation of the Northern Irish State*, p. 92.

44 Ibid., p. 92.

45 Farren, *The Politics of Irish Education*, p. 40.

46 Ibid., p. 38.

47 *Freeman's Journal*, 15 April 1921, p. 6.

48 B. Hourican, Dictionary of Irish Biography, available from http://dib.cambridge.org/, accessed 14 April 2019.

49 Akenson, *Education and Enmity*, p. 41.

50 B. Hourican, Dictionary of Irish Biography, available from http://dib.cambridge.org/, accessed 14 April 2019.

51 Akenson, *Education and Enmity*, p. 43.

52 Ibid., p. 51.

53   Farren, *The Politics of Irish Education*, p. 39.

54   Harris, *The Catholic Church and the Foundation of the Northern Irish State*, p. 96.

55   Akenson, *Education and Enmity*, pp. 52–53.

56   Farren, *The Politics of Irish Education*, pp. 39–42, 45, and Harris, *The Catholic Church and the Foundation of the Northern Irish State*, pp. 95–96.

57   N.C. Fleming, 'Lord Londonderry & Education Reform in 1920s Northern Ireland', *History Ireland* (Vol. 9, No. 1, Spring 2001), p. 37.

58   Akenson, *Education and Enmity*, p. 52.

59   B. Hourican, Dictionary of Irish Biography, available from http://dib.cambridge.org/, accessed 14 April 2019.

60   Farren, *The Politics of Irish Education*, p. 46.

61   Ibid., p. 47.

62   Ibid., p. 49.

63   Ibid.

64   Akenson, *Education and Enmity*, p. 46.

65   PRONI – CAB 4/29, 10 January 1922.

66   Ibid.

67   Farren, *The Politics of Irish Education*, p. 43.

68   Harris, *The Catholic Church and the Foundation of the Northern Irish State*, p. 119.

69   Akenson, *Education and Enmity*, p. 44.

70   UK National Archives – HO 45/24812 – Miscellaneous matters arising from the Partition of Ireland, 16 March 1922.

71   Harris, *The Catholic Church and the Foundation of the Northern Irish State*, p. 119.

72   UK National Archives – HO 45/24812 – Miscellaneous matters arising from the Partition of Ireland, 20 June 1922.

73   Akenson, *Education and Enmity*, p. 46.

74   UK National Archives – HO 45/24812 – Miscellaneous matters arising from the Partition of Ireland, 20 June 1922.

75   Farren, *The Politics of Irish Education*, p. 44.

76   Harris, *The Catholic Church and the Foundation of the Northern Irish State*, p. 122.

77   UK National Archives – HO 45/24812 – Miscellaneous matters arising from the Partition of Ireland, 20 June 1922.

78   UCD Archives – Ernest Blythe Papers – P24/70 – Policy in Regard to the North-East, 9 August 1922.

79   Farren, *The Politics of Irish Education*, p. 45.

80   Akenson, *Education and Enmity*, p. 45.

81   PRONI – CAB 4/69, 29 January 1923 and PRONI – CAB 4/70, 9 February 1923.

82   Harris, *The Catholic Church and the Foundation of the Northern Irish State*, p. 124.

83   Farren, *The Politics of Irish Education*, p. 44.

84   Ibid., p. 51.

85   S. Roulston and J. Dallat, 'James Craig, Lord Charlemont and the "Battle of Stranmillis", 1928–33', *Irish Studies Review* (Vol. 9, No. 3, 2001), p. 347.

86   Fleming, 'Lord Londonderry & Education Reform in 1920s Northern Ireland', p. 39.

87   Farren, *The Politics of Irish Education*, p. 52.

88   Harris, *The Catholic Church and the Foundation of the Northern Irish State*, p. 33.

89   Ibid., p. 32.

90   N. Mansergh, *The Government of Northern Ireland: A Study in Devolution* (London: G. Allen & Unwin, 1936), p. 300.

91   Farren, *The Politics of Irish Education*, p. 59.

92   Ibid.

93   Ibid., p. 86.

94   Fleming, 'Lord Londonderry & Education Reform in 1920s Northern Ireland', p. 38.

95   Farren, *The Politics of Irish Education*, p. 66.

96   Fleming, 'Lord Londonderry & Education Reform in 1920s Northern Ireland', p. 39.

97   B. Hourican, Dictionary of Irish Biography, available from http://dib.cambridge.org/, accessed 15 April 2019.

98   Fleming, 'Lord Londonderry & Education Reform in 1920s Northern Ireland', p. 39.

99   Harris, *The Catholic Church and the Foundation of the Northern Irish State*, p. 148.

100 PRONI – BCT/3/1/17 – Details of 1921 re-organisation under DENI, 8 May 1923.

101 S. Ó Buachalla, *Education Policy in Twentieth Century Ireland* (Dublin: Wolfhound Press, 1988), pp. 372–73.

102 Farren, *The Politics of Irish Education*, pp. 106–107.

103 Ó Buachalla, *Education Policy in Twentieth Century Ireland*, p. 254.

104 G. Ó Tuathaigh, 'The Irish State and Language Policy', *Fortnight* (No. 316, Supplement: The Future of Irish, April 1993), p. 4.

105 F.T. Holohan, 'History Teaching in the Irish Free State 1922–35', *History Ireland* (Vol. 2, No. 4, Winter 1994), pp. 53–54.

106 Ibid., p. 55.

107 Farren, *The Politics of Irish Education*, pp. 55–56.

108 McDowell, *The Church of Ireland*, p. 115.

109 Ibid.

110 Ibid., p. 114.

Chapter Twelve

1   Whyte, 'The Permeability of the United Kingdom – Irish Border', p. 310.

2   C. McCarthy, *Trade Unions in Ireland 1894–1960* (Dublin: Institute of Public Administration, 1977), p. 4.

3   E. O'Connor, 'British Labour, Belfast and Home Rule, 1900–14', in L. Marley (ed.), *The British Labour Party and Twentieth-Century Ireland*, p. 58.

4   McCarthy, *Trade Unions in Ireland*, pp. 6–9.

5   Ibid., p. 7.

6   Ibid., p. 8.

7   G. Bell, *Hesitant Comrades: The Irish Revolution and the British Labour Movement* (London: Pluto Press, 2016), pp. 174 and 176.

8   Gibbons, *Drawing the Line*, p. 2.

9   L.W. White, Dictionary of Irish Biography, available from http://dib.cambridge.org/, accessed 17 April 2019.

10   E. O'Connor, 'Taking its Natural Place: Labour and the Third Home Rule Crisis, 1912–14', *Saothar* (Vol. 37, 2012), p. 33.

11   Ibid.

12   Ibid., p. 36.

13   J. Whyte, *Interpreting Northern Ireland* (Oxford: Oxford University Press, 1990), p. 176.

14   Bell, *Hesitant Comrades*, p. 180.

15   Ibid., p. 179.

16   E. O'Connor, *A Labour History of Ireland 1824–2000* (Dublin: University College Dublin Press, 2011), p. 96.

17   Ibid.

18   O'Connor, 'Taking its Natural Place', p. 37.

19   O'Connor, 'British Labour, Belfast and Home Rule', pp. 55–56.

20   C. Reid, 'Protestant Challenges to the "Protestant State": Ulster Unionism and Independent Unionism in Northern Ireland, 1921–1939', *Twentieth Century British History* (Vol. 19, No. 4, 2008), p. 429.

21   O'Connor, 'British Labour, Belfast and Home Rule', p. 64.

22   *Leitrim Observer*, 17 June 1916, p. 5 and *Irish Times*, 7 August 1917, p. 2.

23   *Cork Examiner*, 21 May 1917, p. 4.

24   *Cork Examiner*, 5 August 1916, p. 7.

25   P. Yeates, *A City in Wartime: Dublin 1914–18* (Dublin: Gill & Macmillan, 2011), p. 234.

26   Ferriter, *A Nation and not a Rabble*, p. 179.

27   P. Yeates, *A City in Turmoil – Dublin 1919–21* (Dublin: Gill & Macmillan, 2012), p. 5.

28   G. Walker, 'The Northern Ireland Labour Party in the 1920s', *Saothar* (Vol. 10, 1984), p. 19.

29   O'Connor, *A Labour History of Ireland*, p. 109.

30   Ibid., p. 117.

31   Ibid., p. 118.

32   McCarthy, *Trade Unions in Ireland*, p. 46.

33   Ibid., p. 60.

34   O'Connor, *A Labour History of Ireland*, p. 118.

35   Parkinson, *Belfast's Unholy War*, p. 30.

36   O'Connor, *A Labour History of Ireland*, p. 118.

37   Ibid., p. 118.

38   Bell, *Hesitant Comrades*, p. 189.

39   A. Morgan, *Labour and Partition: The Belfast Working Class 1905–23* (London: Pluto Press, 1991), p. 321.

40   Bell, *Hesitant Comrades*, p. 184.

41   *Irish Times*, 14 July 1920, p. 5.

42   Gibbons, *Drawing the Line*, p. 4.

43   Ibid., p. 39.

44   Gibbons, 'Labour and Irish Revolution: From Investigation to Deportation', p. 74.

45   Ibid., p. 75.

46   O'Connor, *A Labour History of Ireland*, p. 118.

47   F. Devine and E. O'Connor, 'Fifty Years Of The Northern Ireland Committee', *Saothar* (Vol. 20, 1995), p. 3.

48   O'Connor, *A Labour History of Ireland*, p. 192.

49   *Irish Times*, 2 August 1921, p. 3.

50   *Belfast Newsletter*, 4 August 1921, p. 5.

51   Ibid., p. 6.

52   McCarthy, *Trade Unions in Ireland*, p. 54.

53   M. Maguire, 'Labour in County Louth, 1912–1923', in Hall and Maguire (eds), *County Louth and the Irish Revolution 1912–1923*, p. 81.

54   O'Connor, *A Labour History of Ireland*, p. 109.

55   Ibid., p. 188.

56   Walker, 'The Northern Ireland Labour Party in the 1920s', p. 19.

57   Ibid.

58   Morgan, *Labour and Partition*, p. xv.

59   O'Connor, *A Labour History of Ireland*, p. 193.

60   A. Edwards, *A History of the Northern Ireland Labour Party: Democratic Socialism and Sectarianism* (Manchester: Manchester University Press, 2009), p. 9.

61   Walker, 'The Northern Ireland Labour Party in the 1920s', p. 19.

62   Morgan, *Labour and Partition*, p. 321.

63   P. Hadden, *'Divide and Rule': Labour and the Partition of Ireland* (Dublin: MIM Publications, August 1980), p. 1.

64   Pakenham (Lord Longford), *Peace by Ordeal*, p. 130.

65   McCarthy, *Trade Unions in Ireland*, p. 2.

66   O'Connor, *A Labour History of Ireland*, p. 188.

67   Edwards, *A History of the Northern Ireland Labour Party*, p. 11.

68   Walker, 'The Northern Ireland Labour Party in the 1920s', p. 20.

69   Morgan, *Labour and Partition*, p. 323.

70   Walker, 'The Northern Ireland Labour Party in the 1920s, p. 21.

71   Ibid.

72   O'Connor, *A Labour History of Ireland*, p. 196.

73   Morgan, *Labour and Partition*, p. 323.

74   Buckland, *The Factory of Grievances*, p. 29.

75   O'Leary, 'Cold House', p. 824.

76   O'Connor, *A Labour History of Ireland*, p. 197.

77   McCarthy, *Trade Unions in Ireland*, p. 316.

78   Devine and O'Connor, 'Fifty Years of the Northern Ireland Committee', p. 3.

79   O'Connor, *A Labour History of Ireland*, p. 193.

80   *Fermanagh Herald*, 8 August 1925, p. 3.

81   *Irish Times*, 8 January 1926, p. 5.

82   O'Connor, *A Labour History of Ireland*, p. 199.

83   Walker, 'The Northern Ireland Labour Party in the 1920s', pp. 22–23.

84   Morgan, *Labour and Partition*, p. 323.

85   *Belfast Newsletter*, 10 March 1934, p. 6.

86   Buckland, *The Factory of Grievances*, p. 30.

87   Edwards, *A History of the Northern Ireland Labour Party*, p. 20.

88   McCarthy, *Trade Unions in Ireland*, p. 314.

89   Ibid., pp. 316–21.
90   Devine and O'Connor, 'Fifty Years of the Northern Ireland Committee', p. 4.
91   Ó Buachalla, *Education Policy in Twentieth Century Ireland*, p. 85.
92   T.J. O'Connell, *History of the Irish National Teachers' Organisation, 1868–1968* (Dublin: Irish National Teachers' Organisation, 1970), pp. 24–25.
93   Ibid., p. 60.
94   Ibid., p. 28.
95   Ibid., p. 29.
96   Ibid.
97   Ibid.
98   *Irish Times*, 30 March 1920, p. 4.
99   O'Connell, *History of the Irish National Teachers' Organisation*, p. 23.
100 Coolahan, *The ASTI and Post-Primary Education in Ireland*, p. 38.
101 Ibid., p. 48.
102 Ibid., p. 56.

Chapter Thirteen

1   *Irish Times*, 9 August 1922, p. 5.
2   M.H.C. Baker, *Irish Railways since 1916* (London, Ian Allan, 1972), p. 35.
3   Ibid., p. 43.
4   UK National Archives – HO 267/26 – Legislative Powers with regards to Irish Railways, 28 July 1923.
5   PRONI – CAB 4/107, 26 March 1924.
6   Press clipping of *Northern Whig* article in UK National Archives – HO 267/16 – Imperial Secretary's Department Northern Ireland – Railways, Northern Ireland – Rail Merger Plan Between Great Britain, Northern Ireland and the Irish Free State, 21 December 1922.
7   Y. Kharchenko, 'Optimism and Promise: The Dundalk, Newry and Greenore Railway and the Greenore Community, 1873–1951', *Journal of the County Louth Archaeological and Historical Society* (Vol. 27, No. 4, 2012), p. 643.
8   *Irish Independent*, 25 January 1923, p. 6.
9   UK National Archives – HO 267/16 – Imperial Secretary's Department Northern Ireland – Railways, Northern Ireland – Rail Merger Plan Between Great Britain, Northern Ireland and the Irish Free State, 1 February 1923.
10   Ibid.
11   UK National Archives – HO 267/16 – Imperial Secretary's Department Northern Ireland – Railways, Northern Ireland – Rail Merger Plan Between Great Britain, Northern Ireland and the Irish Free State, 1 August 1923 and *Ulster Herald*, 12 January 1924, p. 5.
12   Baker, *Irish Railways since 1916*, pp. 44 and 46.
13   *Irish Independent*, 17 May 1923, p. 6.
14   *Irish Times*, 10 January 1951, p. 1.
15   A. Carpenter, R. Loeber, H. Campbell, L. Hurley, J. Montague and E. Rowley (eds), *Art and Architecture of Ireland Volume IV: Architecture 1600–2000* (Dublin: Royal Irish Academy, 2015), p. 143.

16 *Irish Times*, 14 March 1928, p. 5.

17 Northern Ireland House of Common Debates, Vol. 1 (1921), 26 September, p. 206; available from www. http://stormontpapers.ahds.ac.uk, accessed 17 April 2019.

18 *Irish Times*, 27 September 1923, p. 3.

19 Ibid., p. 4.

20 Carpenter, Loeber, Campbell, Hurley, Montague and Rowley (eds), *Art and Architecture of Ireland*, p. 143.

21 *Irish Times*, 23 March 1923, p. 4.

22 Ibid., 27 May 1923, p. 6.

23 Ibid., 26 March 1929, p. 5.

24 *Irish Independent*, 14 September 1923, p. 6.

25 *Belfast Newsletter*, 29 February 1924, p. 8.

26 Ibid., 16 February 1926, p. 7.

27 *Donegal News*, 24 November 1928, p. 9.

28 Ibid., 25 February 1928, p. 6.

29 K.J. Rankin, 'The Creation and Consolidation of the Irish Border', *Institute for British-Irish Studies* (Working Paper No. 48, 2005), p. 25.

30 Leary, *Unapproved Routes*, p. 68.

31 UCD Archives – Ernest Blythe Papers – P24/95 – Meeting of Executive Council, 23 May 1925.

32 PRONI – CAB 4/67, 11 January 1923.

33 *Scotsman*, 14 September 1923, p. 7.

34 *Anglo-Celt*, 22 September 1923, p. 1.

35 *Ulster Herald*, 29 September 1929, p. 7.

36 Press clipping of *Irish News* article in PRONI – COM 62/1/38, Boundaries of Northern Ireland – Seaward, 17 September 1923.

37 Leary, *Unapproved Routes*, p. 69.

38 Ibid., p. 67.

39 Ibid.

40 UCD Archives – Ernest Blythe Papers – P24/95 – Meeting of Executive Council, 23 May 1925.

41 Leary, *Unapproved Routes*, p. 70.

42 Ibid., p. 71.

43 *Irish Times*, 25 July 1929, p. 5.

44 Leary, *Unapproved Routes*, p. 71.

45 Ibid., p. 72.

46 *Sligo Champion*, 10 August 1929, p. 4.

47 *Donegal News*, 27 July 1929, p. 4.

48 Leary, *Unapproved Routes*, p. 75.

49 Ibid., pp. 75–76.

50 Ibid., p. 78.

51 Ibid., p. 79.

52 *Irish Times*, 10 July 1950, p. 1.

53 Leary, *Unapproved Routes*, p. 93.

54 UCD Archives – Ernest Blythe Papers – P24/150 – Belfast Waterworks, 9 July 1925.

55 Kennedy, *Division and Consensus*, p. 29.

56 *Belfast Telegraph*, 26 February 1920, p. 3.

57 McColgan, *British Policy and the Irish Administration*, pp. 114–15.

58 PRONI – CAB 4/68, 15 January 1923.

59 PRONI – CAB 4/32, 14 February 1922.

60 PRONI – CAB 4/72, 28 February 1923.

61 *Irish Independent*, 8 June 1928, p. 8.

62 *Belfast Newsletter*, 9 April 1929, p. 9.

63 M. Manning and M. McDowell, *Electricity Supply in Ireland: The History of the ESB* (Dublin: Gill and MacMillan, 1984), p. 1.

64 Ibid., p. 13.

65 Ibid., p. 163.

66 M. Kennedy, 'The Realms of Practical Politics: North-South Co-operation on the Erne Hydro-Electric Scheme, 1942–57', *Institute for British-Irish Studies* (Working Paper 25, 2006), p. 1.

67 Manning and McDowell, *Electricity Supply in Ireland*, p. 163.

68 Ibid.

69 Kennedy, 'The Realms of Practical Politics'.

70 *Irish Times*, 6 March 1940, p. 2 and 3 February 1945, p. 4.

71 Kennedy, 'The Realms of Practical Politics', p. 3.

72 Ibid., p. 2.

73 Manning and McDowell, *Electricity Supply in Ireland*, p. 165.

74 Kennedy, 'The Realms of Practical Politics', p. 3.

75 *Irish Times*, 21 June 1950, p. 3.

76 *Irish Independent*, 21 January 1922, p. 6.

77 Ibid.

78 PRONI – COM/21/28 – Partition: Request from the Inspector General of the RUC that Mail Directed to the Ulster Special Constabulary stationed at Urney, Co. Tyrone Should not be Delivered via Clady Railway Station in the Irish Free State – 1923–1924, 28 December 1923.

79 Ibid., 28 December 1923.

80 Ibid., 2 May 1924.

81 PRONI – COM/21/33 – Partition: Complaints from Residents in Northern Ireland border areas who are within the authority of Irish Free State postal districts – 1924–1926, 6 August 1925.

82 PRONI – CAB 4/38, 1 April 1922.

83 PRONI – COM/21/21 – Partition: Representations Calling for the Establishment of a new Post Office on the Northern Ireland side of the Border at Belcoo, Co. Femanagh – 1922–1924, 22 November 1922.

84 Ibid., 25 April 1923.

85 *Anglo-Celt*, 23 December 1922, p. 1

86 Press clipping of *Northern Whig* article in UK National Archives – HO 267/239 – Free State Troops in Uniform over Northern Border, 30 January 1923.

87 PRONI – COM/21/21 – Partition: Representations Calling for the Establishment of a new Post Office on the Northern Ireland side of the Border at Belcoo, Co. Femanagh – 1922–1924, 24 May 1923.

88 Ibid., 28 August 1923.

89 Ibid., 6 March 1924.

90 Ibid., 28 April 1924 and 7 May 1924.

91 PRONI – COM/21/33 – Partition: Complaints from Residents in Northern Ireland border areas who are within the authority of Irish Free State postal districts – 1924–1926, 31 December 1925.

92 Fitzpatrick, 'Partition, Postal Services and Ulster Unionist Politics 1921–27', p. 10.

93 PRONI - CAB 4/5, 24 June 1921.

94 Fitzpatrick, 'Partition, Postal Services and Ulster Unionist Politics 1921–27', p. 14.

95 Ibid., p. 22.

96 Ibid., p. 24.

97 PRONI – CAB 4/187, 1 March 1927.

98 *Irish Times*, 20 January 1928, p. 5 and 21 September 1928, p. 4.

99 Fitzpatrick, 'Partition, Postal Services and Ulster Unionist Politics 1921–27', p. 39.

Chapter Fourteen

1 Gaelic Athletic Association (hereafter referred to as GAA) Central Council Meeting Minutes/GAA/CC/01/02, 8 September 1917 and 22 December 1922.

2 P. Duffy and G. Ó Tuathaigh, 'Croke Park', in G. Ó Tuathaigh (ed.), *The GAA & Revolution in Ireland 1913–1923* (Cork: The Collins Press, 2015), p. 47.

3 P. Rouse, *Sport & Ireland: A History* (Oxford: Oxford University Press, 2015), p. 273.

4 D. McAnallen, 'The GAA, Unionism and Partition, 1913–23', in G Ó Tuathaigh (ed.), *The GAA & Revolution in Ireland*, p. 106.

5 *Irish Independent*, 24 July 1923, p. 10.

6 McAnallen, 'The GAA, Unionism and Partition', p. 119.

7 D. Hassan, 'The GAA in Ulster', in M. Cronin, W. Murphy, and P. Rouse (eds), *The Gaelic Athletic Association 1884–2009* (Dublin: Irish Academic Press, 2009), pp. 83–84.

8 See D. McAnallen (2011): *'Playing on the Fourth Green Field' – The Gaelic Athletic Association and the Northern Ireland State, 1921–1968*, PhD Thesis, NUI, Galway for details on attacks on the GAA by Northern Ireland security forces, including killings, arrests and club hall burnings.

9 Ibid., p. 51.

10 McAnallen, 'The GAA, Unionism and Partition, 1913–23', p. 121.

11 E. Phoenix, 'G.A.A.'s Era of Turmoil in Northern Ireland', *Fortnight* (No. 211, 17 December 1984 – 20 January 1985), p. 8.

12 McAnallen, 'The GAA, Unionism and Partition, 1913–23', p. 122.

13 Ibid.

14 Ibid., pp. 122–23.

15 Ibid., p. 124.

16 M. Cronin, M. Duncan, P. Rouse, *The GAA: County by County* (Cork: The Collins Press, 2011), p. 28.

17 McAnallen, 'The GAA, Unionism and Partition', pp. 124–25.

18 Cronin, Duncan, Rouse, *The GAA: County by County*, p. 54.

19 McAnallen, 'The GAA, Unionism and Partition', p. 128.

20 McAnallen, 'Playing on the Fourth Green Field', p. 43.

21 M. de Burca, *The GAA: A History* (Dublin: Gill & Macmillan Ltd., 2000), p. 145.

22 *Gaelic Athlete*, 21 March 1925, p. 2.

23 For details on the formation of the IRFU, see L. O'Callaghan, *Rugby in Munster: A Social and Cultural History* (Cork: Cork University Press, 2011) and E. van Esbeck, *The Story of Irish Rugby* (London: Hutchinson, 1986).

24 Minute Book of the Northern Branch of the Irish Rugby Football Union (hereafter called IRFU) 1922–25, D3867/A/6, 28 April 1925.

25 Rouse, *Sport & Ireland*, p. 269.

26 See Records of the IRFU (Ulster Branch), D3867.

27 Minute Book of the Northern Branch of the IRFU 1925–28, D3867/A/7, 6 July 1926.

28 Minute Book of the Northern Branch of the IRFU 1922–25, D3867/A/6, 28 September 1923.

29 Minute Book of the Northern Branch of the IRFU 1925–28, D3867/A/7, 6 July 1926.

30 Minute Book of the Northern Branch of the IRFU 1922–25, D3867/A/6, 8 November 1922.

31 L. O'Callaghan, 'Rugby Football and Identity Politics in Free State Ireland', *Éire-Ireland* (Volume 48, Issue 1 & 2, Spring / Summer 2013), pp. 158–59.

32 Minute Book of the Northern Branch of the IRFU 1925–28, D3867/A/7, IRFU AGM 26 October 1926.

33 O'Callaghan, 'Rugby Football and Identity Politics in Free State Ireland', p. 159.

34 Ibid., p. 161.

35 Ibid., p. 162.

36 Ibid.

37 *Belfast Newsletter*, 24 April 1928, p. 6.

38 Ibid.

39 Minute Book of the Belfast Bowling Club – 1915–1925, D4337/1/6.

40 *Irish Independent*, 18 October 1922, p. 6.

41 *Belfast Newsletter*, 3 June 1929, p. 7.

42 Examples include James Wilton, Irish Football Association (IFA) chairman and Ulster Unionist representative on Derry Corporation, and Thomas Moles, Ulster Unionist Westminster MP and on the governing body of the IFA and IBA.

43 *Irish Times*, 31 July 1961, p. 5.

44 *Belfast Newsletter*, 7 March 1929, p. 2.

45 *Irish Times*, 18 March 1932, p. 11.

46 *Belfast Newsletter*, 21 April 1926, p. 10.

47 *Sunday Independent*, 27 March 1927, p. 14.

48 *Belfast Newsletter*, 18 October 1929, p. 2.

49 *Irish Times*, 10 July 1930, p. 8.

50 *Evening Herald*, 9 July 1930, p. 1.

51 *Belfast Newsletter*, 27 May 1938, p. 2.

52 *Belfast Newsletter*, 6 January 1941, p. 2.

53 For military and security links in Irish boxing, see J. Sugden, *Boxing and Society: An International Analysis* (Manchester: Manchester University Press, 1996) and D. Fitzpatrick, '"Unofficial Emissaries": British Army Boxers in the Irish Free State, 1926', *Irish Historical Studies* (Vol. 30, No. 118, November 1996).

54 *Belfast Newsletter*, 31 March 1913, p. 4.

55 *Evening Herald*, 19 May 1928, p. 2.

56 B. Flynn, *The Little Book of Irish Boxing* (Dublin: The History Press Ireland, 2015), p. 21.

57 *Irish Times*, 14 December 1926, p. 10.

58 Ibid.

59 *Irish Times*, 4 December 1929, p. 4.

60 *Belfast Newsletter*, 29 April 1932, p. 13.

61 S. Reid, 'Identity and Cricket in Ireland in the Mid-Nineteenth Century' *Sport in Society: Cultures, Commerce, Media, Politics* (Vol. 15, No. 2, 2012), pp. 147–49.

62 Ibid., p. 147.

63 Minute Book of the Northern Cricket Union – 1908–1919, D4213/A/15, 23 February 1910.

64 J.C. Hiles, *A History of Senior Cricket in Ulster* (Down: Hilltop Publications, 2003), p. 94.

65 Minute Book of the Northern Cricket Union – 1919–1928, D4213/A/1, 2 July 1920.

66 B. Keane, 'Murder Stops Play – Eventually! "Gentlemen of Ireland Versus the Military of Ireland"', 3 June 1921, *History Ireland* (Vol. 21, No. 5, September/October 2013), pp. 38–40.

67 Minute Book of the Northern Cricket Union – 1919–1928, D4213/A/1, 22 June 1921.

68 Ibid., 3 July 1922.

69 Ibid., 6 February 1923 and 28 May 1923.

70 Ibid., 25 February 1924.

71 Ibid., 24 April 1925.

72 Hiles, *A History of Senior Cricket in Ulster*, p. 94.

73 Rouse, *Sport & Ireland*, p. 273.

74 *Irish Times*, 5 November 1937, p. 13.

75 A. Holland, *The Little Book of Show Jumping* (Dublin: The History Press Ireland, 2015), pp. 23–24.

76 *Freeman's Journal*, 8 February 1923, p. 7 and www.tennisireland.ie, accessed 23 April 2019.

77 *Freeman's Journal*, 8 February 1923, p. 7.

78 *Irish Independent*, 18 April 1923, p. 10.

79 *Irish Independent*, 25 May 1926, p.2.

80 *Belfast Newsletter*, 27 May 1928, p. 10 and 15 May 1930, p. 3.

81 *Irish Times*, 19 January 1927, p. 10.

82 T. Wynne (Compiled) and C. Glennon (ed.), *Ninety Years of the Irish Hockey Union* (Kildare: Leinster Leader, 1985), pp. 66 and 70.

83 J. Sugden and A. Bairner, *Sport, Sectarianism and Society in a Divided Ireland* (Leicester: Leicester University Press, 1993) p. 63.

84 See Irish Hockey Association, DCSA/13/1/2, Irish Hockey Union Minute Book, Volume II, September 1898 to February 1922.

85 Ibid.

86 Sugden and Bairner, *Sport, Sectarianism and Society in a Divided Ireland*, p. 63.

87 Ulster Ladies' Hockey Union Minute Book – 1919–1921, D3982/A/2/1, 20 September 1920.

88 *Belfast Newsletter*, 27 April 1925, p. 10.

89 Ibid.

90 Ibid.

91 R. Higgins, "'The Hallmark of Pluperfect Respectability": The Early Development of Golf in Irish Society', *Éire-Ireland* (Volume 48, Issue 1 & 2, Spring / Summer 2013), p. 16.

92 Ibid., p. 20.

93 W.A. Menton, *The Golfing Union of Ireland 1891–1991* (Dublin: Gill and Macmillan, 1991), p. 54.

94 Higgins, "'The Hallmark of Pluperfect Respectability"', p. 23.

95 D. Mulhall, "'A Gift from Scotland": Golf's Early Days in Ireland', *History Ireland* (Vol. 14, No. 5, September – October 2006), p. 36.

96 F. D'Arcy, *Horses, Lords and Racing Men – The Turf Club 1790–1990* (Kildare: The Turf Club, 1991), p. 257.

97 Ibid.

98 D'Arcy, *Horses, Lords and Racing Men*, p. 255 and Rouse, *Sport & Ireland*, pp. 256–57.

99 D'Arcy, *Horses, Lords and Racing Men*, p. 258.

100 Ibid.

101 Rouse, *Sport & Ireland*, p. 258.

102 D'Arcy, *Horses, Lords and Racing Men*, p. 243.

103 M. Cronin and R. Higgins, *Places we Play: Ireland's Sporting Heritage* (Cork: The Collins Press, 2011), p. 179.

104 Rouse, *Sport & Ireland*, p. 286.

105 D. Toms, 'The Electric Hare – Greyhound Racing's Development in Ireland, 1927–58', *Irish Economic and Social History* (Volume 40, 2013), p. 70.

106 Ibid., p. 84.

107 J. Magee, 'The Legacy of Master McGrath: Coursing and Sporting Heroes in Ireland', *Sport in History* (Vol. 25, No. 1, 2005), p. 94.

108 Ibid.

109 Ibid., p. 95.

110 Minute Book of the Motor Cycle Union of Ireland, Ulster Centre – 1912–1921, D3133/1.

111 B. Lynch, *Green Dust – Ireland's Unique Motor Racing History 1900–1939* (Dublin: Portobello Publishing, 1988), p. 54.

112 Ibid., p. 51.

113 Ibid.

114 Ibid., p. 52.

115 Lynch, *Green Dust*, p. 52 and W.A. McMaster, *A History of Motorsport in Ireland 1903–1969* (Belfast: Century Newspapers Ltd., 1970), p. 21.

116 McMaster, *A History of Motorsport in Ireland*, p. 67.

117   T. Hunt, *The Little Book of Irish Athletics* (Dublin: The History Press Ireland, 2017), p. 27.

118   *Ireland's Saturday Night*, 27 May 1922, p. 4.

119   P. Griffin, *The Politics of Irish Athletics 1850–1990* (Leitrim: Marathon Publications, 1990), p. 68.

120   Ibid., p. 72.

121   P. Reynolds, "'A FIRST-CLASS SPLIT'": Political Conflict in Irish Athletes, 1924–1940', *History Ireland* (Vol. 20, No. 4, 2012), p. 31.

122   Hunt, *The Little Book of Irish Athletics*, p. 28.

123   Ibid.

124   *Football Sports Weekly*, 29 August 1925, p. 2.

125   Reynolds, "'A FIRST-CLASS SPLIT'", pp. 31–32.

126   Ibid., p. 32.

127   T Hunt, "'In our Case, it Seems Obvious the British Organising Committee Piped the Tune": The Campaign for Recognition of "Ireland" in the Olympic Movement, 1935–1956', *Sport in Society: Cultures, Commerce, Media, Politics* (2 January 2015), p. 2.

128   *Partition in Irish Athletics Booklet* (Dublin: Gaedeal-Cumann Lutcleas agus Rotuideacta na h-Eireann, 1946), p. 3.

129   See C. Moore, *The Irish Soccer Split* (Cork: Cork University Press, 2015).

130   Ibid., p. 232.

131   Ibid.

132   Ibid., p. 234.

133   *Ireland's Saturday Night*, 9 June 1923, p. 3.

134   *Ireland's Saturday Night*, 24 March 1923, p. 3.

135   See Moore, *The Irish Soccer Split*.

136   Ibid., p. 234.

SOURCES AND BIBLIOGRAPHY

Primary

Public Record Office of Northern Ireland (PRONI), 2 Titanic Boulevard, Titanic Quarter, Belfast, County Antrim, BT3 9HQ, United Kingdom

AUS/2/18 – Copies of Reports to Dublin Castle by Departments in response to circula regarding administrative changes necessitated by Government of Ireland Act 1920: Department of Agriculture and Technical Instruction for Ireland – 1921

AUS/2/5 – Copies of Reports to Dublin Castle by Departments in response to circula regarding administrative changes necessitated by Government of Ireland Act 1920: Judiciary of Northern Ireland – 1921

BCT/3/1/17 – Details of 1921 re-organisation under DENI

CAB/4 – Cabinet Papers of the Stormont Administration

CAB/6/57 – Projected publication of 'Memoranda on the setting up of the Supreme Court of Judicature of Northern Ireland', written by Lord Chief Justice Moore

COM/21/21 – Partition: Representations Calling for the Establishment of a new Post Office on the Northern Ireland side of the Border at Belcoo, Co. Femanagh – 1922–1924

COM/21/28 – Partition: Request from the Inspector General of the RUC that Mail Directed to the Ulster Special Constabulary stationed at Urney, Co. Tyrone Should not be Delivered via Clady Railway Station in the Irish Free State – 1923–1924

COM/21/33 – Partition: Complaints from Residents in Northern Ireland border areas who are within the authority of Irish Free State postal districts – 1924–1926

COM 62/1/38, Boundaries of Northern Ireland – Seaward

COM/62/2/7 – Boycott – Ulster Traders Defence Association, correspondence and notices concerning the boycott of Northern Ireland goods – 1922

D1022/2/14 – Copy Correspondence of Clark Concerning Procedural Matters in Connection with Setting up of the Northern Ireland Parliament – April 1921–June 1921

D1022/2/17 – Files of Correspondence, mainly between Clark and Sir James Craig, Dealing with Various Aspects of the Setting Up of the Northern Ireland Ministries and Departments – 1921–1922

D1022/2/2 – Files Entitled, 'N. Ireland consecutive draft', including accounts of Clark's first impressions of Dublin and Northern Ireland

D1022/2/3 – File entitled, 'Fermanagh Vigilance Force'

D1022/2/4 – Files containing copies of papers relating to two conferences between the Chief Secretary of Ireland, Sir Hamar Greenwood, the Standing Committee of the Ulster Unionist Council, and representatives of trade unions and labour organisations

D1022/2/8 – File entitled, 'Trade Boycott', including memorandum by Clark and a copy of a Sinn Féin decree

D1022/2/9 – File entitled, 'Special Constabulary: table of progress, S.C. scheme'

D1098/1/2 – Minute Book of the Ulster Women's Unionist Council Executive Committee

D1506/1/13/3 – Correspondence with Companies Register Office, Dublin, concerning the establishment of Watt and Co. Ltd

D3133/1 – Minute Book of the Motor Cycle Union of Ireland, Ulster Centre – 1912–1921

D3788/1/5 – Irish Union of Young Men's Christian Association – Minute Book for Meetings of the Executive Committee of the North of Ireland District – 1901–1922

D3788/1/6 – Irish Union of Young Men's Christian Association – Minute Book for Meetings of the Executive Committee of the North of Ireland District and Annual General Meetings of the Northern Ireland Council of Y.M.C.A.s – 1922–1969

D3867 – Irish Rugby Football Union (Ulster Branch)

D3867/A/6 – Minute Book of the Northern Branch of the IRFU 1922–25

D3867/A/7 – Minute Book of the Northern Branch of the IRFU 1925–28

D3875/1/1/1 – Minutes of the Ulster Girl Guides – March 1920–July 1928

D3982/A/2/1 – Ulster Ladies' Hockey Union Minute Book – 1919–1921

D4213 – Minute Book of the Northern Cricket Union

D4213/A/15 – Minute Book of the Northern Cricket Union – 1908–1919
D4213/A/1 – Minute Book of the Northern Cricket Union – 1919–1928
D4337/1/6 – Minute Book of the Belfast Bowling Club – 1915–1925
D921/2/1 – Correspondence, Telegrams and Accounts Concerning the South Down Election – 1921
D921/4/5/1 – Newspaper Clippings and Printed Booklets
HA4/1/114 – Ulster Police Force: Headquarters Staff and Strength of Force
HA/47/1 – Police Reorganisation Committee: Minutes of Evidence
SO/1/A/1 – Interim Report of the Departmental Committee of Inquiry on Police Reorganisation in Northern Ireland

UK National Archives, Kew, Richmond, Surrey, TW9 4DU

CO 904/185 – The British in Ireland: Dublin Castle Records – Irish Government. Judicial Proceedings, Enquiries and Miscellaneous Record, 1872–1926, 1920
HO 267/13 – Land Registry Transfer of Documents
HO 267/16 – Imperial Secretary's Department Northern Ireland – Railways, Northern Ireland – Rail Merger Plan Between Great Britain, Northern Ireland and the Irish Free State
HO 267/239 – Free State Troops in Uniform over Northern Border
HO 267/26 – Legislative Powers with regards to Irish Railways
HO 267/34 – Customs – Applications
HO 267/49 – Customs & Excise
HO 45/24812 – Miscellaneous matters arising from the Partition of Ireland
PRO 30/67/40 – Papers and Correspondence Relating to the Disruption of the Irish Unionist Alliance and the Formation of the Unionist Anti-Partition League, undated.

The Gaelic Athletic Association Archive, Cusack Stand, St Joseph's Avenue, Croke Park, Dublin 3

Central Council Meeting Minutes/GAA/CC/01/02

The National Archives of Ireland, Bishop Street, Dublin 8

Department of the Taoiseach
    S1095 – *Belfast Boycott*

S6037 – Allocation of Staff Between Provisional Government and Northern Ireland

NEBB/1/1/3 – *North Eastern Boundary Bureau*

University College Dublin (UCD) Archives, School of History and Archives, University College Dublin, Belfield, Dublin 4

Ernest Blythe Papers

P24/22 – Office Correspondence Relating to the Peace Negotiations, June–September 1921

P24/70 – Policy in Regard to the North-East

P24/76 – The Boundary Commission Organisation

P24/95 – Meeting of Executive Council

P24/150 – Belfast Waterworks

Dublin City Library and Archive, 144 Pearse Street, Dublin 2

Dublin City Archives – Minutes of the Municipal Council of the City of Dublin, 13 September 1920

Irish Hockey Association, DCSA/13/1/2, Irish Hockey Union Minute Book, Volume II – September 1898 to February 1922

Newspapers and Magazines

Anglo-Celt
Belfast Newsletter
Belfast Telegraph
Chicago Daily Tribune
Church of Ireland Gazette
Connaught Telegraph
Cork Examiner
Donegal Democrat
Donegal News
Evening Herald
Fermanagh Herald

Football Sports Weekly
Freeman's Journal
Gaelic Athlete
Gazette of the Incorporated Law Society of Ireland
Ireland's Saturday Night
Irish Independent
Irish News
Irish Press
Irish Times
Kerryman
Leitrim Observer
Manchester Guardian
Punch
Scotsman
Sligo Champion
Strabane Chronicle
Sunday Independent
The Observer
The Times
Ulster Herald
Westmeath Independent

Books

Acheson, A., *A History of the Church of Ireland 1691–2001* (Dublin: The Columba Press, 2002).

Akenson, D.H., *Education and Enmity: The Control of Schooling in Northern Ireland 1920–50* (Belfast: The Queen's University of Belfast Institute of Irish Studies, 1973).

Baker, M.H.C., *Irish Railways since 1916* (London, Ian Allan, 1972).

Bardon, J., *A History of Ulster* (Belfast: The Blackstaff Press, 2001).

Barritt, D.P. and Carter, C.F., *The Northern Ireland Problem: A Study in Group Relations* (Oxford: Oxford University Press, 1972).

Bell, G., *Hesitant Comrades: The Irish Revolution and the British Labour Movement* (London: Pluto Press, 2016).

Bew, P., Gibbon, P. and Patterson, H., *Northern Ireland 1921–1994: Political Forces and Social Classes* (London: Serif, 1995).

Bowman, J., *De Valera and the Ulster Question 1917–1973* (Oxford: Oxford University Press, 1989).

Bowman, T., *Carson's Army: The Ulster Volunteer Force, 1910–22* (Manchester: Manchester University Press, 2007).

Buckland, P., *Irish Unionism: Two: Ulster Unionism and the Origins of Northern Ireland 1886–1922* (Dublin: Gill and Macmillan, 1973).

Buckland, P., *The Factory of Grievances: Devolved Government in Northern Ireland 1921–39* (Dublin: Gill and Macmillan, 1979).

Carpenter, A., Loeber, R., Campbell, H., Hurley, L., Montague, J. and Rowley, E. (eds), *Art and Architecture of Ireland Volume IV: Architecture 1600–2000* (Dublin: Royal Irish Academy, 2015).

Cole, R.L., *History of Methodism in Ireland* (Belfast: The Irish Methodist Publishing Co. Ltd., 1960).

Coolahan, J., *The ASTI and Post-Primary Education in Ireland, 1909–1984* (Dublin: Cumann na Meánmhúinteoií, Éire, 1984).

Cronin, M. and Higgins, R., *Places we Play: Ireland's Sporting Heritage* (Cork: The Collins Press, 2011).

Cronin, M., Duncan, M. and Rouse, P., *The GAA: County by County* (Cork: The Collins Press, 2011).

Curran, J.M., *The Birth of the Irish Free State 1921–1923* (Alabama: The University of Alabama Press, 1980).

D'Arcy, F.A., *Horses, Lords and Racing Men – The Turf Club 1790–1990* (Kildare: The Turf Club, 1991).

de Burca, M., *The GAA: A History* (Dublin: Gill & Macmillan Ltd., 2000).

Daly, M.E., *The First Department: A History of the Department of Agriculture* (Dublin: Institute of Public Administration, 2002).

Delany, V.T.H, *The Administration of Justice in Ireland* (Dublin: Institute of Public Administration, 1962).

Dolan, A. and Murphy, W., *Michael Collins: The Man and the Revolution* (Cork: The Collins Press, 2018).

Dooley, T., *The Irish Revolution, 1912–23: Monaghan* (Dublin: Four Courts Press, 2017).

Dorney, J., *The Civil War in Dublin: The Fight for the Irish Capital 1922–1924* (Dublin: Merrion Press, 2017).

Edwards, A., *A History of the Northern Ireland Labour Party: Democratic Socialism and Sectarianism* (Manchester: Manchester University Press, 2009).

Elliott, M., *The Catholics of Ulster* (London: Penguin Books, 2001).

Ellison, G. and Smyth, J., *The Crowned Harp: Policing Northern Ireland* (London: Pluto Press, 2000).

Fanning, R., *Fatal Path: British Government and Irish Revolution 1910–1922* (London: Faber & Faber, 2013).

Fanning, R., *The Irish Department of Finance 1922–58* (Dublin: Institute of Public Administration, 1978).

Farrell, M., *Arming the Protestants: The Formation of the Ulster Special Constabulary and the Royal Ulster Constabulary, 1920–7* (London: Pluto Press, 1983).

Farrell, M., *Northern Ireland: The Orange State* (London: Pluto Press, 1980).

Farren, S., *The Politics of Irish Education 1920–1965* (Belfast: The Queen's University of Belfast Institute of Irish Studies, 1995).

Ferriter, D., *Judging Dev: A Reassessment of the Life and Legacy of Eamon de Valera* (Dublin: Royal Irish Academy, 2007).

Ferriter, D., *A Nation and not a Rabble: The Irish Revolution 1913–1923* (Suffolk: Profile Books, 2015).

Ferriter, D., *The Border: The Legacy of a Century of Anglo-Irish Politics* (London: Profile Books, 2019).

Fitzpatrick, D., *The Two Irelands 1912–1939* (Oxford: Oxford University Press, 1998).

Flynn, B., *The Little Book of Irish Boxing* (Dublin: The History Press Ireland, 2015).

Follis, B.A., *A State Under Siege: The Establishment of Northern Ireland, 1920–1925* (Oxford, Clarendon Press, 1995).

Gibbons, I., *Drawing the Line: The Irish Border in British Politics* (London: Haus Publishing, 2018).

Glennon, K., *From Pogrom to Civil War: Tom Glennon and the Belfast IRA* (Cork: Mercier Press, 2013).

Grant, A., *The Irish Revolution 1912–23: Derry* (Dublin: Four Courts Press, 2018).

Griffin, P., *The Politics of Irish Athletics 1850–1990* (Leitrim: Marathon Publications, 1990).

Gwynn, D., *The History of Partition (1912–1925)* (Dublin, The Richview Press, 1950).

Hadden, P., *'Divide and Rule': Labour and the Partition of Ireland* (Dublin: MIM Publications, August 1980).

Harris, M., *The Catholic Church and the Foundation of the Northern Irish State* (Cork: Cork University Press, 1993).

Hart, P., *The I.R.A. and its Enemies: Violence and Community in Cork, 1916–1923* (Oxford: Oxford University Press, 1998).

Hennessey, T., *A History of Northern Ireland 1920–1996* (Dublin: Gill and Macmillan, 1997).

Hennessey, T., *Dividing Ireland: World War One and Partition* (London: Routledge, 1998).

Hezlet, A., *The 'B' Specials: A History of The Ulster Special Constabulary* (London: Tom Stacey Ltd., 1972).

Hiles, J.C., *A History of Senior Cricket in Ulster* (Down: Hilltop Publications, 2003).

Holland, A., *The Little Book of Show Jumping* (Dublin: The History Press Ireland, 2015).

Holmes, F., *The Presbyterian Church in Ireland: A Popular History* (Dublin: Columba Press, 2000).

Hopkinson, M., *Green Against Green: The Irish Civil War* (Dublin: Gill Books, 1998).

Hughes, B., *Defying the IRA? Intimidation, Coercion, and Communities During the Irish Revolution* (Liverpool: Liverpool University Press, 2016).

Hunt, T., *The Little Book of Irish Athletics* (Dublin: The History Press Ireland, 2017).

Jackson, A., *Home Rule: An Irish History 1800–2000* (London: Weidenfeld & Nicolson, 2003).

Jackson, A., *Judging Redmond and Carson* (Dublin: Royal Irish Academy, 2018).

Kendle, J., *Walter Long, Ireland and the Union, 1905–1920* (Canada: Glendale Publishing Ltd., 1992).

Kennedy, D., *The Widening Gulf: Northern Attitudes to the Independent Irish State 1919–49* (Belfast: The Blackstaff Press, 1988).

Kennedy, M., *Division and Consensus: The Politics of Cross-Border Relations in Ireland, 1925–1969* (Dublin: Institute of Public Administration, 2000).

Keogh, D., *Jews in Twentieth-Century Ireland: Refugees, Anti-Semitism and the Holocaust* (Cork: Cork University Press, 1998).

Kiberd, D., *Inventing the Nation – The Literature of the Modern Nation* (London: Vintage, 1996).

Kotsonouris, M., *Retreat from Revolution: The Dáil Courts, 1920–24* (Dublin: Irish Academic Press, 1994).

Kotsonouris, M., *The Winding-up of the Dáil Courts, 1922–1925: An Obvious Duty* (Dublin: Four Courts Press in association with the Irish Legal History Society, 2004).

Laffan, M., *Judging W.T. Cosgrave* (Dublin: Royal Irish Academy, 2014 [e-reader edition]).

Laffan, M., *The Partition of Ireland 1911–1925* (Dundalk, Dundalgan Press, 2004).

Lawlor, P., *The Outrages 1920–1922: The IRA and the Ulster Special Constabulary in the Border Campaign* (Cork: Mercier Press, 2011).

Leary, P., *Unapproved Routes: Histories of the Irish Border, 1922–1972* (Oxford: Oxford University Press, 2016 [e-reader edition]).

Lustick, I.S., *Unsettled States, Disputed Lands: Britain and Ireland, France and Algeria, Israel and the West Bank-Gaza* (Ithaca: Cornell University Press, 1993).

Lynch, B., *Green Dust – Ireland's Unique Motor Racing History 1900–1939* (Dublin: Portobello Publishing, 1988).

Lynch, R., *Revolutionary Ireland, 1912–25* (London: Bloomsbury Publishing PLC, 2015).

Lynch, R., *The Northern IRA and the Early Years of Partition, 1920–1922* (Dublin: Irish Academic Press, 2006).

Lynch, R., *The Partition of Ireland 1918–1925* (Cambridge: Cambridge University Press, 2019).

Lyons, F.S.L., *Ireland Since the Famine* (London: Fontana Press, 1985).

MacDonald, D., *Hard Border: Walking Through a Century of Partition* (Dublin, New Island Books, 2018).

Maguire, M., *The Civil Service and the Revolution in Ireland 1912–1938: 'Shaking the Blood-Stained Hand of Mr Collins'* (Manchester: Manchester University Press, 2009).

Mansergh, N., *The Government of Northern Ireland: A Study in Devolution* (London: G. Allen & Unwin, 1936).

Mansergh, N., *The Unresolved Question: The Anglo-Irish Settlement and Its Undoing 1912-72* (Yale: Yale University Press, 1991).

Manning, M. and McDowell, M., *Electricity Supply in Ireland: The History of the ESB* (Dublin: Gill and MacMillan, 1984).

McCarthy, C., *Trade Unions in Ireland 1894-1960* (Dublin: Institute of Public Administration, 1977).

McCarthy, C., *Cumann na mBan and the Irish Revolution* (Cork: The Collins Press, 2007).

McCarthy, J.P., *Kevin O'Higgins: Builder of the Irish State* (Dublin: Irish Academic Press, 2006).

McCluskey, F., *The Irish Revolution, 1912-23: Tyrone* (Dublin: Four Courts Press, 2014).

McColgan, J., *British Policy and the Irish Administration 1920-22* (London: George Allen & Unwin, 1983).

McDermott, J., *Northern Divisions: The Old IRA and the Belfast Pogroms 1920-22* (Belfast: Beyond the Pale Publications Ltd, 2001).

McCullagh, D., *De Valera: Rise 1882-1932* (Dublin: Gill Books, 2017).

McDonnell, A.D., *The Life of Sir Denis Henry: Catholic Unionist* (Belfast: Ulster Historical Foundation, 2000).

McDowell, R.B, *The Irish Convention 1917-18* (London: Routledge and Kegan Paul Ltd, 1970).

McDowell, R.B., *The Church of Ireland 1869-1969* (London and Boston: Routledge and Kegan Paul, 1975).

McGarry, F., *Eoin O'Duffy: A Self-Made Hero* (Oxford: Oxford University Press, 2005).

McGee, O., *Arthur Griffith* (Dublin: Merrion Press, 2015).

McMaster, W.A., *A History of Motorsport in Ireland 1903-1969* (Belfast: Century Newspapers Ltd., 1970).

Menton, W.A., *The Golfing Union of Ireland 1891-1991* (Dublin: Gill and Macmillan, 1991).

Milligan, S., *Puckoon* (London: Penguin Books, 1963).

Moore, C., *The Irish Soccer Split* (Cork: Cork University Press, 2015).

Morgan, A., *Labour and Partition: The Belfast Working Class 1905-23* (London: Pluto Press, 1991).

Nash, C., Reid, B. and Graham, B., *Partitioned Lives: The Irish Borderlands* (Surrey: Ashgate Publishing Company, 2013).

Ó Beacháin, D., *From Partition to Brexit: The Irish Government and Northern Ireland* (Manchester: Manchester University Press, 2019).

O'Brien, J., *Discrimination in Northern Ireland, 1920–1939: Myth or Reality?* (Newcastle upon Tyne: Cambridge Scholars Publishing, 2010).

Ó Buachalla, S., *Education Policy in Twentieth Century Ireland* (Dublin: Wolfhound Press, 1988).

O'Callaghan, L., *Rugby in Munster: A Social and Cultural History* (Cork: Cork University Press, 2011).

O'Connell, T.J., *History of the Irish National Teachers' Organisation, 1868–1968* (Dublin: Irish National Teachers' Organisation, 1970).

O'Connor, E., *A Labour History of Ireland 1824–2000* (Dublin: University College Dublin Press, 2011).

O'Day, A., *Irish Home Rule 1867–1921* (Manchester: Manchester University Press, 1998).

O'Donoghue, B., *Activities Wise and Otherwise: The Career of Sir Henry Augustus Robinson 1898–1922* (Dublin: Irish Academic Press, 2015).

Other, A.N., *Report of the Irish Boundary Commission 1925* (Shannon: Irish University Press, 1969).

Ozseker, O., *Forging the Border: Donegal and Derry in Times of Revolution* (Dublin: Irish Academic Press, 2019).

Pakenham, F. (Lord Longford), *Peace by Ordeal* (London: Sidgwick & Jackson, 1972).

Parkinson, A.F., *Belfast's Unholy War: The Troubles of the 1920s* (Dublin: Four Courts Press, 2004).

Phoenix, E., *Northern Nationalism: Nationalist Politics, Partition and the Catholic Minority in Northern Ireland 1890–1940* (Belfast: Ulster Historical Foundation, 1994).

Rouse, P., *Sport & Ireland: A History* (Oxford: Oxford University Press, 2015).

Scharbrodt, O., Sakaranaho, T., Hussain Khan, A., Shanneik, Y. and Ibrahim, V., *Muslims in Ireland: Past and Present* (Edinburgh: Edinburgh University Press, 2015).

Smith, G.H., *Sketch of the Supreme Court of Judicature of Northern Ireland: From its Establishment Under the Imperial Act of 1920 Down to the Present Time* (Belfast: Northern Whig, 1926).

Sugden, J., *Boxing and Society: An International Analysis* (Manchester: Manchester University Press, 1996).

Sugden, J. and Bairner, A., *Sport, Sectarianism and Society in a Divided Ireland* (Leicester: Leicester University Press, 1993).

Townshend, C., *The Republic: The Fight for Irish Independence* (London: Penguin Books, 2013).

van Esbeck, E., *The Story of Irish Rugby* (London: Hutchinson, 1986).

Ward, M., *Unmanageable Revolutionaries: Women and Irish Nationalism* (London: Pluto Press, 1995).

Whyte, J., *Interpreting Northern Ireland* (Oxford: Oxford University Press, 1990).

Wynne, T. (Complied) and Glennon, C. (ed.), *Ninety Years of the Irish Hockey Union* (Kildare: *Leinster Leader*, 1985).

Yeates, P., *A City in Wartime: Dublin 1914–18* (Dublin: Gill & Macmillan, 2011).

Yeates, P., *A City in Turmoil – Dublin 1919–21* (Dublin: Gill & Macmillan, 2012).

Book Chapters

Bell, C., 'Alternative Justice in Ireland', in N. Dawson, D. Greer and P. Ingram (eds), *One Hundred and Fifty Years of Irish Law* (Belfast: SLS Legal Publication [NI], School of Law, The Queen's University of Belfast, 1996).

Lord Carswell, 'Founding a Legal System: The Early Judiciary of Northern Ireland', in F.M. Larkin and N.M. Dawson (eds), *Lawyers, the Law and History: Irish Legal History Society Discourses and Other Papers, 2005–2011* (Dublin: Four Courts Press in association with the Irish Legal History Society, 2013).

Duffy, P., and Ó Tuathaigh, G., 'Croke Park', in G. Ó Tuathaigh (ed.) *The GAA & Revolution in Ireland 1913-1923* (Cork: The Collins Press, 2015).

Geoghegan, H., 'The Three Judges of the Supreme Court of the Irish Free State, 1925–36: Their Backgrounds, Personalities and Mindsets', in F.M. Larkin and N.M. Dawson (eds), *Lawyers, the Law and History: Irish Legal History Society Discourses and Other Papers, 2005–2011* (Dublin: Four Courts Press in association with The Irish Legal History Society, 2013).

Gibbons, I., 'Labour and Irish Revolution: From Investigation to Deportation', in L. Markey (ed.), *The British Labour Party and Twentieth-Century Ireland: The Cause of Ireland, the Cause of Labour* (Manchester: Manchester University Press, 2016).

Hall, D., 'Politics and Revolution in County Louth, 1912–1923', in D. Hall and M. Maguire (eds), *County Louth and the Irish Revolution 1912–1923* (Dublin: Irish Academic Press, 2017).

Hanley, B., 'The IRA in Northern Ireland', in J. Crowley, D. Ó Drisceoil and M. Murphy (eds), *Atlas of the Irish Revolution* (Cork: Cork University Press, 2017).

Harris, M., 'The Catholic Church, Minority Rights, and the Founding of the Northern Irish State', in D. Keogh and M.H. Haltzel (eds), *Northern Ireland and the Politics of Reconciliation* (Unites States of America: Woodrow Wilson Centre Press and Cambridge University Press, 1993).

Hart, A.R., 'King's Inns and the Foundation of the Inn of Court of Northern Ireland: The Northern Perspective', in F.M. Larkin and N.M. Dawson (eds), *Lawyers, the Law and History: Irish Legal History Society Discourses and Other Papers, 2005–2011* (Dublin: Four Courts Press in association with The Irish Legal History Society, 2013).

Hart, P., 'The Protestant Experience of Revolution in Southern Ireland', in R. English and G. Walker (eds) *Unionism in Modern Ireland: New Perspectives on Politics and Culture* (London: Macmillan Press Ltd., 1996).

Hassan, D., 'The GAA in Ulster', in M. Cronin, W. Murphy and P. Rouse (eds), *The Gaelic Athletic Association 1884–2009* (Dublin: Irish Academic Press, 2009).

Hill, M., 'Women in Northern Ireland, 1922–39' in J. Crowley, D. Ó Drisceoil and M. Murphy (eds), *Atlas of the Irish Revolution* (Cork: Cork University Press, 2017).

Hughes, B., 'Defining Loyalty: Southern Irish Protestants and the Irish Grants Committee, 1926–30', in I. d'Alton and I. Milne (eds), *Protestant and Irish: The Minority's Search for Place in Independent Ireland* (Cork: Cork University Press, 2019).

Johnson, D.S., 'The Belfast Boycott, 1920–1922', in J.M. Goldstrom and L.A. Clarkson (eds), *Irish Population, Economy, and Society: Essays in Honour of the late K.H. Connell* (Oxford: Clarendon Press, 1981).

Lynch, R., 'The Boundary Commission', in J. Crowley, D. Ó Drisceoil and M. Murphy (eds), *Atlas of the Irish Revolution* (Cork: Cork University Press, 2017).

Maguire, M., 'Labour in County Louth, 1912–1923', in D. Hall and M. Maguire (eds), *County Louth and the Irish Revolution 1912–1923* (Dublin: Irish Academic Press, 2017).

Martin, M., 'The Civil War in Drogheda, January–July 1922', in D. Hall and M. Maguire (eds), *County Louth and the Irish Revolution 1912–1923* (Dublin: Irish Academic Press, 2017).

McAnallen, D., 'The GAA, Unionism and Partition, 1913–23', in G. Ó Tuathaigh (ed.) *The GAA & Revolution in Ireland 1913–1923* (Cork: The Collins Press, 2015).

McNamara, C., 'In the Shadow of Altnaveigh: Political Upheaval and Sectarian Violence in County Louth, 1920–1922', in D. Hall and M. Maguire (eds), *County Louth and the Irish Revolution 1912–1923* (Dublin: Irish Academic Press, 2017).

Morrissey, C., 'Peace, Protestantism and the Unity of Ireland: The Career of Bolton C. Waller', in I. d'Alton and I. Milne (eds), *Protestant and Irish: The Minority's Search for Place in Independent Ireland* (Cork: Cork University Press).

O'Connor, E., 'British Labour, Belfast and Home Rule, 1900–14', in L. Marley (ed.), *The British Labour Party and Twentieth-Century Ireland: The Cause of Ireland, the Cause of Labour* (Manchester: Manchester University Press, 2016).

O'Leary, B., '"Cold House": The Unionist Counter-Revolution and the Invention of Northern Ireland', in J. Crowley, D. Ó Drisceoil and M. Murphy (eds), *Atlas of the Irish Revolution* (Cork: Cork University Press, 2017).

Osborough, W.N., 'Landmarks in the History of King's Inns', in K. Ferguson (ed.), *King's Inn Barristers 1868–2004* (Dublin: The Honorable Society of King's Inns, 2005).

Phoenix, E., 'Catholic Unionism: A Case Study: Sir Denis Stanislaus Henry (1864–1925)', in O.P. Rafferty (ed.), *Irish Catholic Identities* (Manchester: Manchester University Press, 2013).

Whyte, J., 'How Much Discrimination Was There Under the Unionist Regime, 1921–1968?', in T. Gallagher and J. O'Connell (eds),

Contemporary Irish Studies (Manchester: Manchester University Press, 1983).

Journals and Periodicals

Boyce, D.G., 'British Conservative Opinion, the Ulster Question, and the Partition of Ireland, 1912–21', *Irish Historical Studies*, 17, 65 (March 1970).

Coakley, J. and O'Dowd, L., 'The Irish Border and North-South Cooperation', *Institute for British-Irish Studies*, Working Paper No. 47 (2005).

Curran, J.M., 'The Anglo-Irish Agreement of 1925: Hardly a "Damn Good Bargain"', *The Historian*, 40, 1 (November 1977).

de Bhaldraithe, E., 'Mixed Marriages and Irish Politics: The Effect of "Ne Temere"', *Studies: An Irish Quarterly Review*, 77, 307 (Autumn 1988).

Deignan, P., 'PR & the Sligo Borough Election of January 1919', *History Ireland*, 17, 3 (May–June 2009).

Devine, F. and O'Connor, E., 'Fifty Years of the Northern Ireland Committee', *Saothar*, 20 (1995).

Dooley, T.A.M., 'From the Belfast Boycott to the Boundary Commission: Fears and Hopes in County Monaghan, 1920–26', *Clogher Record*, 15, 1 (1994).

Drea, E., 'A Gamble Forced Upon Them? A Re-Appraisal of Ulster Bank's Operations in Southern Ireland 1921–32', *Business History*, 56, 7 (2014).

Dudley Edwards, R.W., 'Government of Ireland and Education, 1919–1920', *Archivium Hibernicum*, 37 (1982).

Fitzpatrick, C., 'Partition, Postal Services and Ulster Unionist Politics 1921–27', *International Journal of Regional and Local History* (1 June 2016).

Fitzpatrick, D., 'ERNEST BLYTHE – Orangeman and Fenian', *History Ireland*, 25, 3 (May–June 2017).

Fitzpatrick, D., '"Unofficial Emissaries": British Army Boxers in the Irish Free State, 1926', *Irish Historical Studies*, 30, 118 (November 1996).

Fleming, N.C., 'Lord Londonderry & Education Reform in 1920s Northern Ireland', *History Ireland*, 9, 1 (Spring 2001).

Greer, A., 'Sir James Craig and the Construction of Parliament Buildings at Stormont', *Irish Historical Studies*, 31, 123 (May 1999).

Hall, D., 'Partition and County Louth', *Journal of the County Louth Archaeological and Historical Society*, 27, 2 (2010).

Harris, M., 'Meeting the Minister', *Fortnight*, 196 (Supplement: Religion in Ireland, June 1991).

Higgins, R., '"The Hallmark of Pluperfect Respectability": The Early Development of Golf in Irish Society', *Éire-Ireland*, 48, 1 & 2 (Spring / Summer 2013).

Holohan, F.T., 'History Teaching in the Irish Free State 1922–35', *History Ireland*, 2, 4 (Winter 1994).

Hopkinson, M., 'The Craig-Collins Pacts of 1922: Two Attempted Reforms of the Northern Ireland Government', *Irish Historical Studies*, 27, 106 (November 1990).

Howard, K., 'Continuity and Change in a Partitioned Civil Society: Whyte Revisited', *Working Papers in British-Irish Studies*, 70 (2006).

Hunt, T., '"In Our Case, it Seems Obvious the British Organising Committee Piped the Tune": The Campaign for Recognition of "Ireland" in the Olympic Movement, 1935–1956', *Sport in Society: Cultures, Commerce, Media, Politics* (2 January 2015).

Inoue, K., 'Sinn Féin Propaganda and the "Partition Election", 1921', *Studia Hibernica*, 30 (1998/1999).

Johnson, D.S., 'The Economic History of Ireland Between the Wars', *Irish Economic and Social History*, 1 (1974).

Keane, B., 'Murder Stops Play – Eventually! "Gentlemen of Ireland Versus the Military of Ireland", 3 June 1921', *History Ireland*, 21, 5 (September / October 2013).

Kennedy, M., 'The Realms of Practical Politics: North-South Co-operation on the Erne Hydro-Electric Scheme, 1942–57', *Institute for British-Irish Studies*, Working Paper 25 (2006).

Kharchenko, Y., 'Optimism and Promise: The Dundalk, Newry and Greenore Railway and the Greenore Community, 1873–1951', *Journal of the County Louth Archaeological and Historical Society*, 27, 4 (2012).

Leary, P., 'A House Divided: the Murrays of the Border and the Rise and Decline of a Small Irish House', *History Workshop Journal*, 86 (July 2018).

Loughlin, J., 'Creating "A Social and Geographical Fact": Regional Identity and the Ulster Question 1880s–1920s', *Past & Present*, 195 (May 2007).

Lynch, R., 'The Clones Affray, 1922: Massacre or Invasion?' *History Ireland*, 12, 3 (Autumn 2004).

Magee, J., 'The Legacy of Master McGrath: Coursing and Sporting Heroes in Ireland', *Sport in History*, 25, 1 (2005).

Miller, R., 'The Look of the Irish: Irish Jews and the Zionist Project, 1900–48', *Jewish Historical Studies*, 43 (2011).

Morris, N.K., 'Traitors to Their Faith? Protestant Clergy and the Ulster Covenant of 1912', *New Hibernia Review / Iris Éireannach Nua*, 15, 3 (Fómhar/Autumn 2011).

Mulhall, D., '"A Gift from Scotland": Golf's Early Days in Ireland', *History Ireland*, 14, 5 (September – October 2006).

Murphy, R., 'Walter Long and the Making of the Government of Ireland Act, 1919–20', *Irish Historical Studies*, 25, 97 (May 1986).

Murray, P., 'Partition and the Irish Boundary Commission: A Northern Nationalist Perspective', *Clogher Record*, 18, 2 (2004).

O'Callaghan, L., 'Rugby Football and Identity Politics in Free State Ireland', *Éire-Ireland*, 48, 1 & 2 (Spring / Summer 2013).

O'Connor, E., 'Taking its Natural Place: Labour and the Third Home Rule Crisis, 1912–14', *Saothar*, 37 (2012).

Ó Grada, C. and Walsh, B.M., 'Did (and Does) the Irish Border Matter?', *Institute for British-Irish Studies*, Working Paper No. 60 (2006).

Ó Tuathaigh, G., 'The Irish State and Language Policy', *Fortnight*, 316 (Supplement: The Future of Irish, April 1993).

Phoenix, E., 'Cahir Healy (1877–1970): Northern Nationalist Leader', *Clogher Record*, 18, 1 (2003).

Phoenix, E., 'G.A.A.'s Era of Turmoil in Northern Ireland', *Fortnight*, 211 (17 December 1984 – 20 January 1985).

Rafferty, O., 'The Catholic Church and Partition, 1918–22', *Irish Studies Review*, 5, 2 (Autumn 2007).

Rafferty, O.P., '"Studies" and the Shadow of Modernism', *Studies: An Irish Quarterly Review*, 100, 400 (A Century of Studies, Winter 2011).

Rankin, K.J., 'The Creation and Consolidation of the Irish Border', *Institute for British-Irish Studies*, Working Paper No. 48 (2005).

Rankin, K.J., 'Theoretical Concepts of Partition and the Partitioning of Ireland', *Institute for British-Irish Studies*, Working Paper No. 67 (2006).

Reid, C., 'Protestant Challenges to the "Protestant State": Ulster Unionism and Independent Unionism in Northern Ireland, 1921–1939', *Twentieth Century British History*, 19, 4 (2008).

Reid, S., 'Identity and Cricket in Ireland in the Mid-Nineteenth Century' *Sport in Society: Cultures, Commerce, Media, Politics*, 15, 2 (2012).

Reynolds, P., '"A FIRST-CLASS SPLIT": Political Conflict in Irish Athletes, 1924–1940', *History Ireland*, 20, 4 (2012).

Roulston, S. and Dallat, J., 'James Craig, Lord Charlemont and the "Battle of Stranmillis", 1928–33', *Irish Studies Review*, 9, 3 (2001).

Toms, D., 'The Electric Hare – Greyhound Racing's Development in Ireland, 1927–58', *Irish Economic and Social History*, 40 (2013).

Walker, G., 'The Northern Ireland Labour Party in the 1920s', *Saothar*, 10 (1984).

Wilson, T., '"The Most Terrible Assassination That Has Yet Stained the Name of Belfast": the McMahon Murders in Context', *Irish Historical Studies*, 37, 145 (May 2010).

Whyte, J., 'The Permeability of the United Kingdom – Irish Border: A Preliminary Reconnaissance', *Administration*, 31, 3 (1983).

Whyte, J.H., 'Whitehall, Belfast and Dublin: New Light on the Treaty and the Border, *Studies* (Autumn – Winter 1971).

Electronic Sources

Australian Dictionary of Biography, available from http://adb.anu.edu.au

Bureau of Military History, 1913–21, available from http://www.bureauofmilitaryhistory.ie/

Census of Ireland 1911, available from www.census.nationalarchives.ie

Central Statistics Office, available from http://www.cso.ie/en/media/csoie/census/census1926results/volume3/C_5_1926_V3_T1abc.pdf

Dáil Éireann Debates, available from www.oireachtas-debates.gov.ie

Dictionary of Irish Biography, available from http://dib.cambridge.org/

House of Commons Debates, available from http://hansard.millbanksystems.com

Monaghan County Council – War of Independence Files, available from https://monaghan.ie/museum/monaghan-war-of-independence-files/

Northern Ireland House of Common Debates, available from http://stormontpapers.ahds.ac.uk

Tennis Ireland, available from www.tennisireland.ie

Other

Hart, A. (2017), 'The Independent Bar of Northern Ireland – Past and Present', Address to the Wales & Chester Circuit in Cardiff.

McAnallen, D. (2011), 'Playing on the Fourth Green Field' – The Gaelic Athletic Association and the Northern Ireland State, 1921–1968, PhD Thesis, NUI, Galway.

Partition in Irish Athletics Booklet (Dublin: Gaedeal-Cumann Lutcleas agus Rotuideacta na h-Eireann, 1946).

INDEX